The Gig Bag Book of SCALES for all Keyboards

Compiled by Len Vogler

Over 220 scales, in all twelve keys, for all keyboardists presented in standard notation and easy-to-read diagrams.

Amsco Publications
New York/London/Sydney

Cover photograph by Randall Wallace
Project editor: Ed Lozano
Interior design and layout by Len Vogler

Order No. AM 946924
US International Standard Book Number: 0.8256.1661.1
UK International Standard Book Number: 0.7119.6882.9

Exclusive Distributors:
Music Sales Corporation
257 Park Avenue South, New York, NY 10010 USA
Music Sales Limited
8/9 Frith Street, London W1V 5TZ England
Music Sales Pty. Limited
120 Rothschild Street, Rosebery, Sydney, NSW 2018, Australia

Printed in the United States of America by
Vicks Lithograph and Printing Corporation

Contents

Basic Scale Theory Scale Construction 8
- Major Scales 10
- Key Signatures 10
- Circle of Fifths 12
- Minor Scales 13
- A natural minor *(Aeolian)* 13
- A harmonic minor 14
- A melodic minor ascending 14
- A melodic minor descending 14
- Jazz Melodic Minor Scales 15

The Modal Scales 16
- Dorian 16
- Phrygian 16
- Lydian 17
- Lydian Flat-Seven 17
- Mixolydian 18
- Locrian 18

Other Scale Forms 19
- Pentatonic Major Scales 19
- Pentatonic Minor Scales 19
- Blues Scales 20
- Whole Tone Scales 20

How to Use This Book 21

Major Scales
- C major 23
- G major 24
- D major 25
- A major 26
- E major 27
- B major 28
- F♯ major 29
- C♯ major 30
- F major 31
- B♭ major 32
- E♭ major 33
- A♭ major 34
- D♭ major 35
- G♭ major 36
- C♭ major 37

Natural Minor Scales *(Aeolian)*
- A natural minor *(Aeolian)* 38
- E natural minor *(Aeolian)* 39
- B natural minor *(Aeolian)* 40
- F♯ natural minor *(Aeolian)* 41
- C♯ natural minor *(Aeolian)* 42
- G♯ natural minor *(Aeolian)* 43
- D♯ natural minor *(Aeolian)* 44
- A♯ natural minor *(Aeolian)* 45
- D natural minor *(Aeolian)* 46
- G natural minor *(Aeolian)* 47
- C natural minor *(Aeolian)* 48
- F natural minor *(Aeolian)* 49
- B♭ natural minor *(Aeolian)* 50
- E♭ natural minor *(Aeolian)* 51
- A♭ natural minor *(Aeolian)* 52

Harmonic Minor Scales

A harmonic minor 53
E harmonic minor 54
B harmonic minor 55
F♯ harmonic minor 56
C♯ harmonic minor 57
G♯ harmonic minor 58
D♯ harmonic minor 59
A♯ harmonic minor 60
D harmonic minor 61
G harmonic minor 62
C harmonic minor 63
F harmonic minor 64
B♭ harmonic minor 65
E♭ harmonic minor 66
A♭ harmonic minor 67

Melodic Minor Scales

A melodic minor *(ascending)* 68
A melodic minor *(descending)* 69
E melodic minor *(ascending)* 70
E melodic minor *(descending)* 71
B melodic minor *(ascending)* 72
B melodic minor *(descending)* 73
F♯ melodic minor *(ascending)* 74
F♯ melodic minor *(descending)* 75
C♯ melodic minor *(ascending)* 76
C♯ melodic minor *(descending)* 77
G♯ melodic minor *(ascending)* 78
G♯ melodic minor *(descending)* 79
D♯ melodic minor *(ascending)* 80
D♯ melodic minor *(descending)* 81
A♯ melodic minor *(ascending)* 82
A♯ melodic minor *(descending)* 83
D melodic minor *(ascending)* 84
D melodic minor *(descending)* 85
G melodic minor *(ascending)* 86
G melodic minor *(descending)* 87
C melodic minor *(ascending)* 88
C melodic minor *(descending)* 89
F melodic minor *(ascending)* 90
F melodic minor *(descending)* 91
B♭ melodic minor *(ascending)* 92
B♭ melodic minor *(descending)* 93
E♭ melodic minor *(ascending)* 94
E♭ melodic minor *(descending)* 95
A♭ melodic minor *(ascending)* 96
A♭ melodic minor *(descending)* 97

Jazz Melodic Minor

A jazz melodic minor 98
E jazz melodic minor 99
B jazz melodic minor 100
F♯ jazz melodic minor 101
C♯ jazz melodic minor 102
G♯ jazz melodic minor 103
D♯ jazz melodic minor 104
A♯ jazz melodic minor 105
D jazz melodic minor 106
G jazz melodic minor 107

C jazz melodic minor 108
F jazz melodic minor 109
B♭ jazz melodic minor 110
E♭ jazz melodic minor 111
A♭ jazz melodic minor 112

Dorian Scales

D Dorian 113
A Dorian 114
E Dorian 115
B Dorian 116
F♯ Dorian 117
C♯ Dorian 118
G♯ Dorian 119
D♯ Dorian 120
G Dorian 121
C Dorian 122
F Dorian 123
B♭ Dorian 124
E♭ Dorian 125
A♭ Dorian 126
D♭ Dorian 127

Phrygian Scales

E Phrygian 128
B Phrygian 129
F♯ Phrygian 130
C♯ Phrygian 131
G♯ Phrygian 132
D♯ Phrygian 133
A♯ Phrygian 134
E♯ Phrygian 135
A Phrygian 136
D Phrygian 137
G Phrygian 138
C Phrygian 139
F Phrygian 140
B♭ Phrygian 141
E♭ Phrygian 142

Lydian Scales

F Lydian 143
C Lydian 144
G Lydian 145
D Lydian 146
A Lydian 147
E Lydian 148
B Lydian 149
F♯ Lydian 150
B♭ Lydian 151
E♭ Lydian 152
A♭ Lydian 153
D♭ Lydian 154
G♭ Lydian 155
C♭ Lydian 156
F♭ Lydian 157

Lydian Flat-Seven Scales

F Lydian flat-seven 158
C Lydian flat-seven 159

G Lydian flat-seven 160
D Lydian flat-seven 161
A Lydian flat-seven 162
E Lydian flat-seven 163
B Lydian flat-seven 164
F♯ Lydian flat-seven 165
B♭ Lydian flat-seven 166
E♭ Lydian flat-seven 167
A♭ Lydian flat-seven 168
D♭ Lydian flat-seven 169
G♭ Lydian flat-seven 170
C♭ Lydian flat-seven 171
F♭ Lydian flat-seven 172

Mixolydian Scales

G Mixolydian 173
D Mixolydian 174
A Mixolydian 175
E Mixolydian 176
B Mixolydian 177
F♯ Mixolydian 178
C♯ Mixolydian 179
G♯ Mixolydian 180
C Mixolydian 181
F Mixolydian 182
B♭ Mixolydian 183
E♭ Mixolydian 184
A♭ Mixolydian 185
D♭ Mixolydian 186
G♭ Mixolydian 187

Locrian Scales

B Locrian 188
F♯ Locrian 189
C♯ Locrian 190
G♯ Locrian 191
D♯ Locrian 192
A♯ Locrian 193
E♯ Locrian 194
B♯ Locrian 195
E Locrian 196
A Locrian 197
D Locrian 198
G Locrian 199
C Locrian 200
F Locrian 201
B♭ Locrian 202

Pentatonic Major Scales

C pentatonic 203
G pentatonic 204
D pentatonic 205
A pentatonic 206
E pentatonic 207
B pentatonic 208
F♯ pentatonic 209
C♯ pentatonic 210
F pentatonic 211
B♭ pentatonic 212
E♭ pentatonic 213
A♭ pentatonic 214

D♭ pentatonic 215
G♭ pentatonic 216
C♭ pentatonic 217

Pentatonic Minor Scales

A pentatonic minor 218
E pentatonic minor 219
B pentatonic minor 220
F♯ pentatonic minor 221
C♯ pentatonic minor 222
G♯ pentatonic minor 223
D♯ pentatonic minor 224
A♯ pentatonic minor 225
D pentatonic minor 226
G pentatonic minor 227
C pentatonic minor 228
F pentatonic minor 229
B♭ pentatonic minor 230
E♭ pentatonic minor 231
A♭ pentatonic minor 232

Blues Scales

C blues 233
G blues 234
D blues 235
A blues 236
E blues 237
B blues 238
F♯ blues 239
C♯ blues 240
F blues 241
B♭ blues 242
E♭ blues 243
A♭ blues 244
D♭ blues 245
G♭ blues 246
C♭ blues 247

Whole Tone Scales

C whole tone 248
G whole tone 249
D whole tone 250
A whole tone 251
E whole tone 252
B whole tone 253
F♯ whole tone 254
C♯ whole tone 255
F whole tone 256
B♭ whole tone 257
E♭ whole tone 258
A♭ whole tone 259
D♭ whole tone 260
G♭ whole tone 261
C♭ whole tone 262

Basic Scale Theory Scale Construction

Scales are the foundation on which most music is based. A scale is made up of a series of tones arranged in a specific interval pattern. An *interval* is the distance between two tones, the smallest of which is called a *half step*. A half step corresponds to the closest distance between two piano keys.

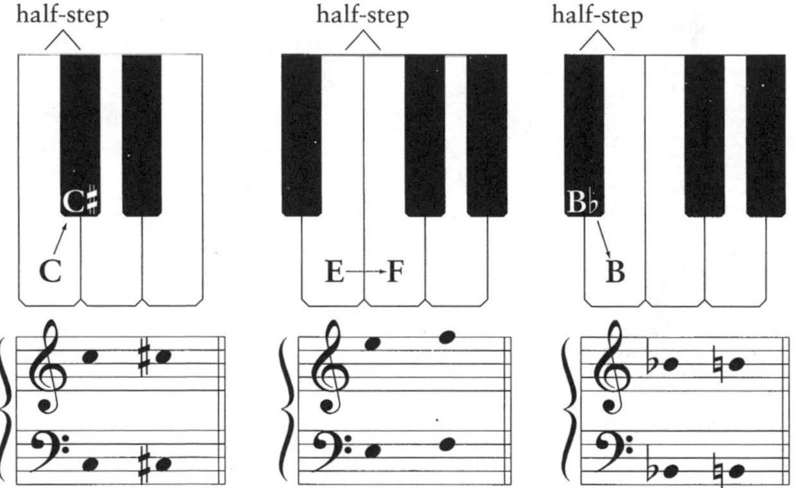

A *whole step* is equal to the distance of two half-steps. On the piano a whole step covers the distanc of three keys.

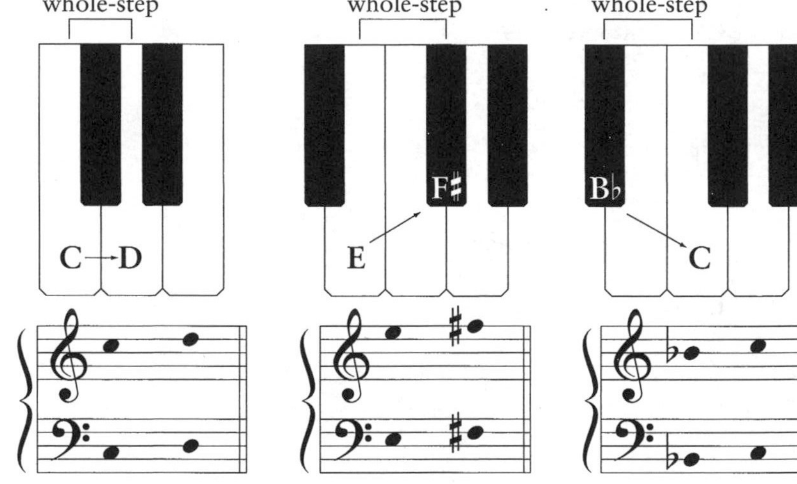

Half steps and whole steps are two basic types of *intervals* used when discussing the distance between neighboring notes in a scale. Other intervals are needed when talking about scale steps, or *degrees* as they relate to each other or to the first tone. or *tonic,* of a scale. These intervals are named as follows.

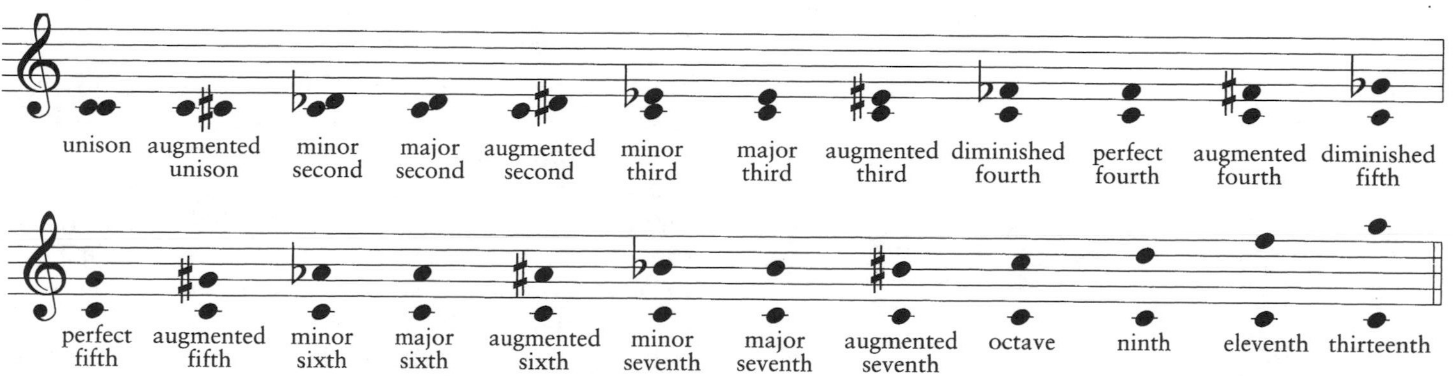

Notice the minor second is the same as a half step and the major second is equal to a whole step.

Major Scales

The quality of a scale—whether it is major, minor, etc.—is determined by the arrangement of half steps and whole steps. The major scale has a half step between the third and fourth degrees and another between the seventh and eighth degrees. All other scale steps are separated from their neighbors by a whole step. This arrangement of half steps and whole steps is the same for all major scales.

C major scale

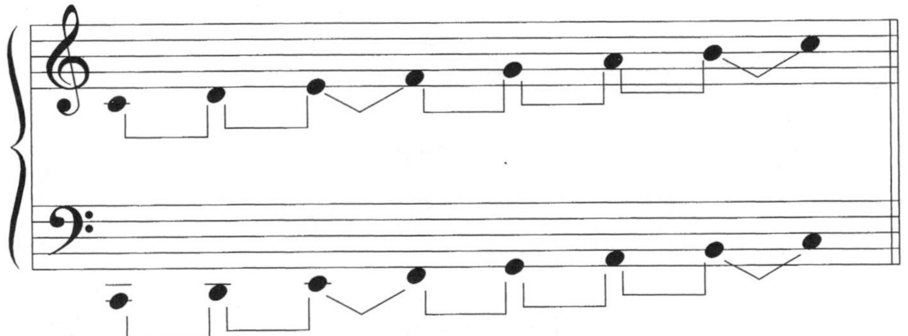

It is common to refer to scale steps by Roman numerals. Notice the relationship of these numbers to the naming of intervals.

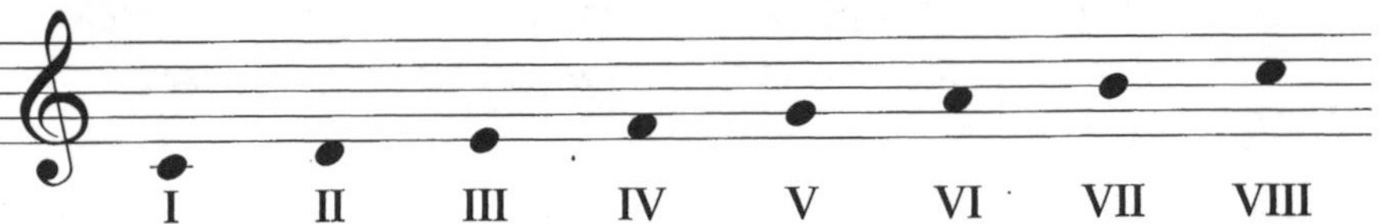

Key Signatures

Now that you know how a C major scale is constructed, let's look at how this relates to other major scales. If you divide the C major scale in half, you will notice that the first half and second half each use the same configuration of half steps and whole steps—and that the two halves are separated by a whole step. Since the half-step/whole-step formula is the same for both halves of the scale, and since all major scales use the same formula, you can construct a new scale that begins with the second half of the C major scale. The example below shows that the resulting scale will be a G major scale. Unlike the C major scale, which has no sharps or flats, the G major scale must always have an F♯ to make it conform to the major-scale formula of half steps and whole steps. Since the key of G major always contains an F♯, this F♯ appears in the *key signature* of G major.

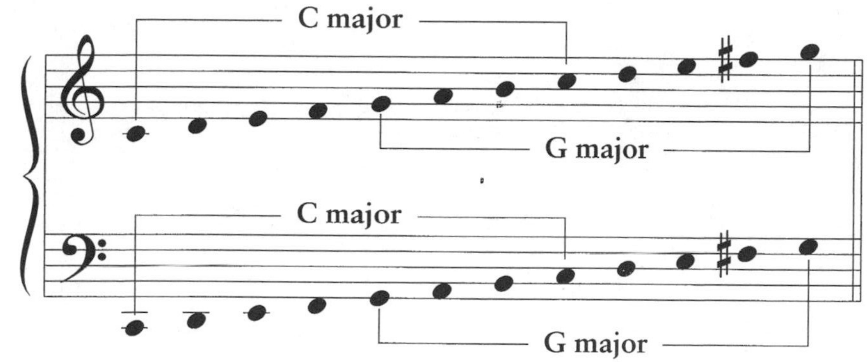

Key signature of G major

Now, do the same thing with a G major scale that we did above with the C scale. The new scale starts on D and has two sharps: F♯ and C♯. As a result, the key signature for D major contains two sharps. Notice that with each new scale the seventh degree is sharped and this sharp is added to the right of the previous sharps in the key signature.

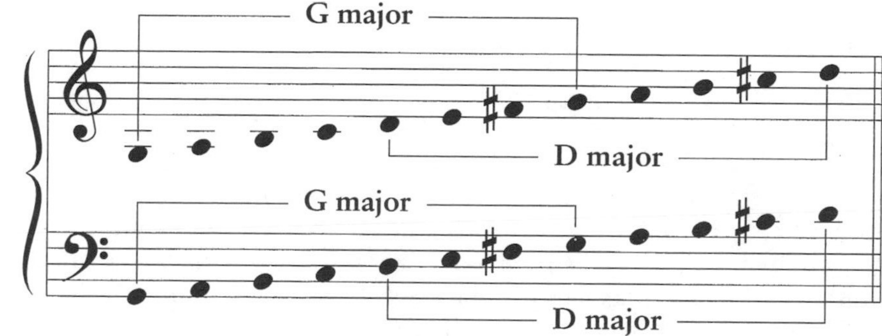

Key signature of D major

Circle of Fifths

By now you have probably noticed a pattern developing; we take the fifth degree of a scale to start a new scale, and with each new scale we add a sharp. The chart below is referred to as the *circle of fifths*—it starts with C major and progresses around the circle by fifths through all the keys, ending back at C major. By using this chart you will be able to play and write in all twelve major scales.

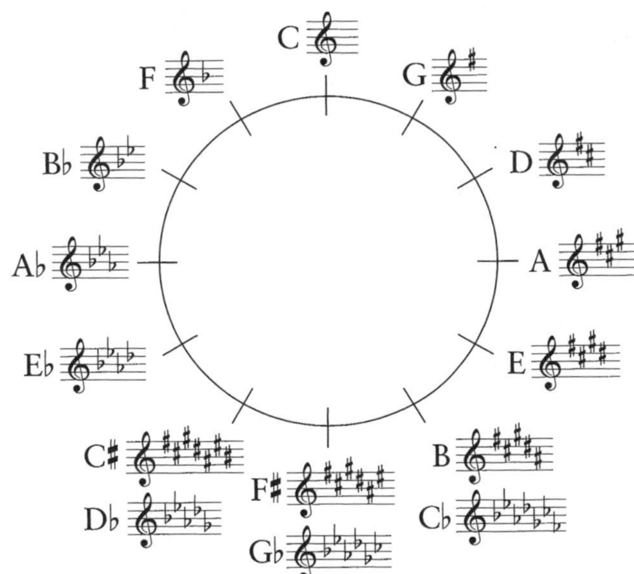

Minor Scales

There are three different types of minor scales: *natural (Aeolian), harmonic,* and *melodic.* All major scales have a corresponding *relative minor* scale. The scale can be found by starting on the sixth step of any major scale. For example, start on the sixth step of a C scale and by using the same formula for the major scale an A minor scale will created. Therefore, A minor is the relative minor of C major. This scale is said to be *natural,* or *pure,* because it follows the major-scale formula without altering the key signature.

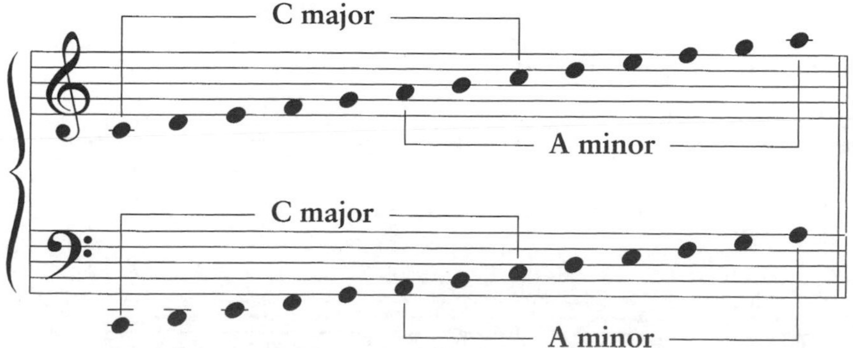

A natural minor *(Aeolian)*

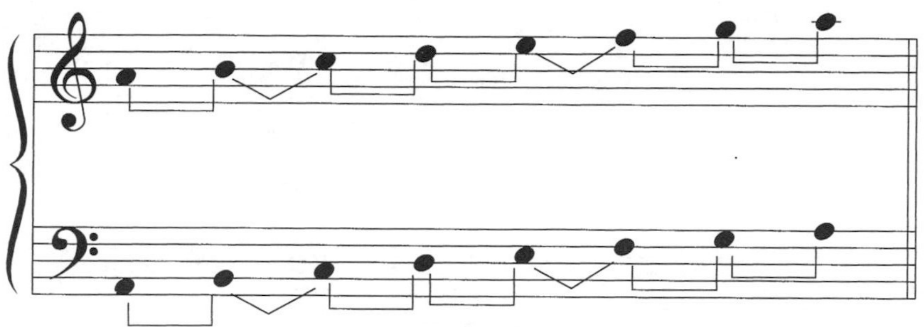

The harmonic minor scale has half steps between scale steps two and three, five and six. and seven and eight. Notice the distance between scale steps six and seven is a minor third.

A harmonic minor

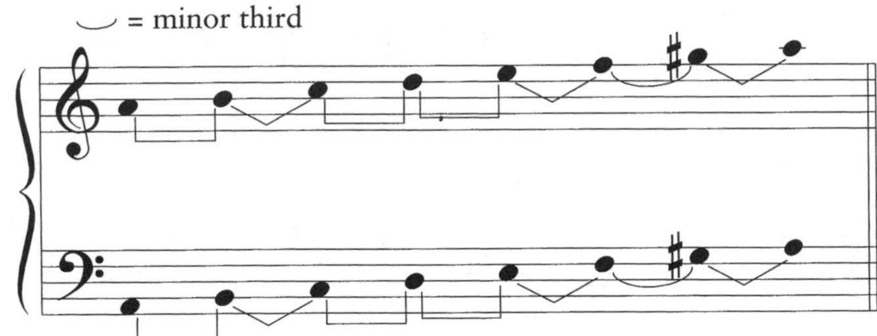

The melodic minor scale's ascending order finds half steps between two and three and between seven and eight. Unlike any of the other scales that have been discussed so far, melodic minor scales have a different descending order. The descending order has half steps between degrees six and five and between three and two—with a whole step between steps eight and seven.

A melodic minor ascending

A melodic minor descending

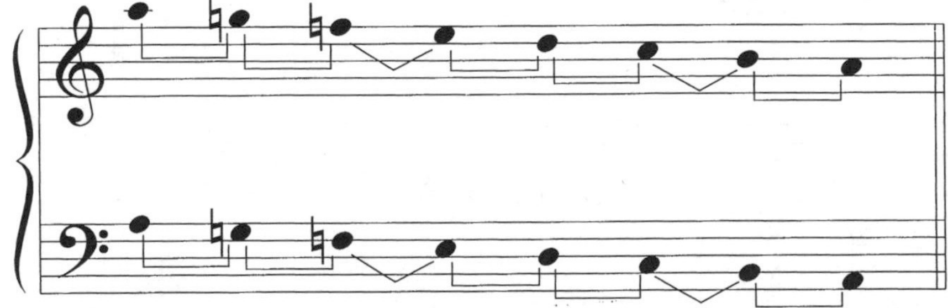

Jazz Melodic Minor Scales

The jazz melodic minor scale is the same as the melodic minor scale except it's descending pattern is the same as it's ascending pattern. The formula is whole-step, half-step, whole-step, whole-step, whole-step, whole-step, and half-step.

C jazz melodic minor scale

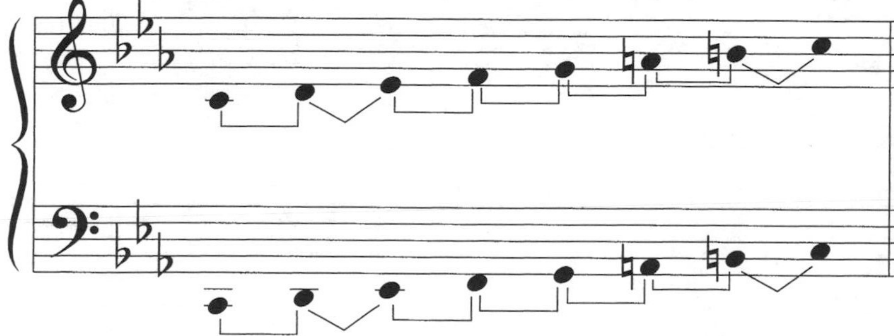

The Modal Scales

Dorian

The Dorian scale begins on the second degree of the major scale. The formula for the Dorian scale is whole-step, half-step, whole-step, whole-step, whole-step, half-step, and a whole-step. The Dorian scale resembles the natural minor scale with a sharped sixth.

D Dorian scale

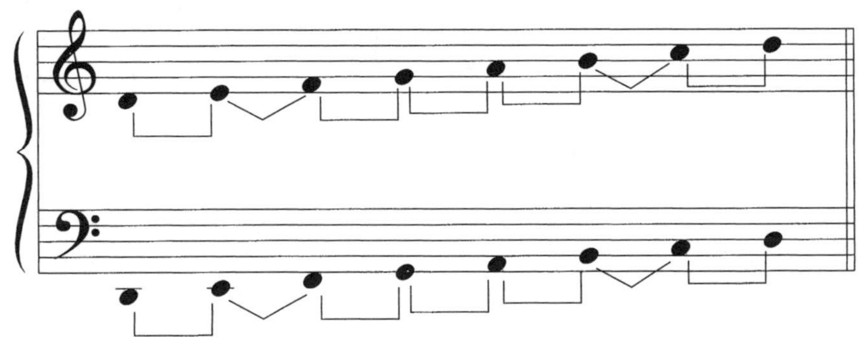

Phrygian

The Phrygian scale begins on the third degree of the major scale. The Phrygian scale formula is half-step, whole-step, whole-step, whole-step, half-step, whole-step, and a whole-step.

E Phrygian scale

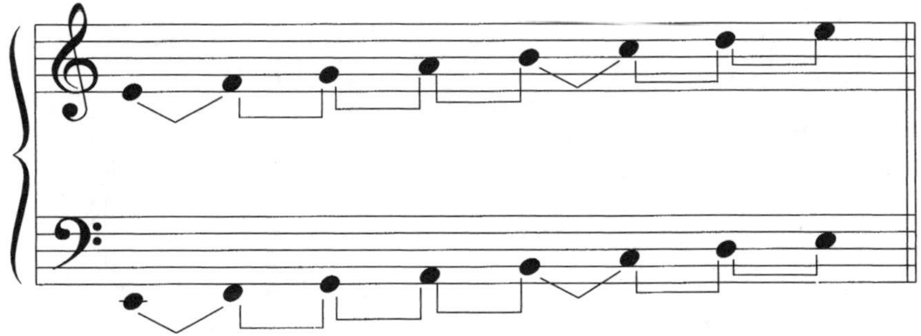

Lydian

The Lydian scale begins on the fourth degree of the major scale. The formula for this scale is whole-step, whole-step, whole-step, half-step, whole-step, whole-step, and a half-step.

F Lydian scale

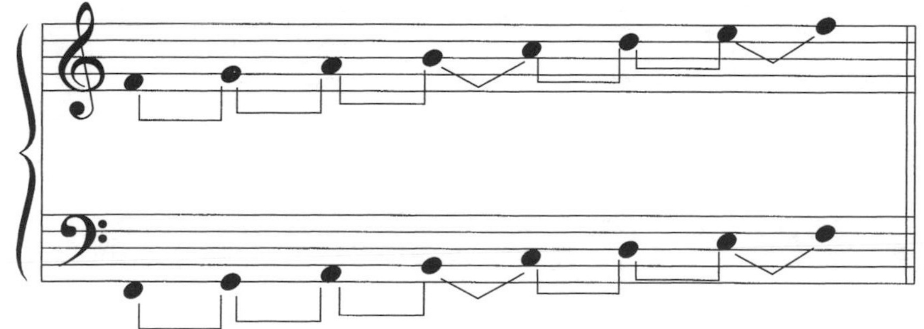

Lydian Flat-Seven

The Lydian flat-seven is just like the Lydian scale except the seventh degree of the scale is flatted. The formula for this scale is whole-step, whole-step, whole-step, half-step, whole-step, half-step, and whole-step.

F Lydian flat-seven scale

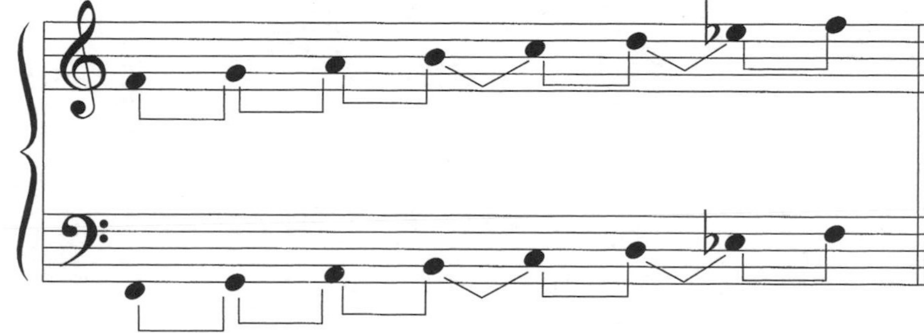

Mixolydian

The Mixolydian scale begins on the fifth degree of the major scale. The formula for this scale is whole-step, whole-step, half-step, whole-step, whole-step, half-step, and a whole-step.

G Mixolydian scale

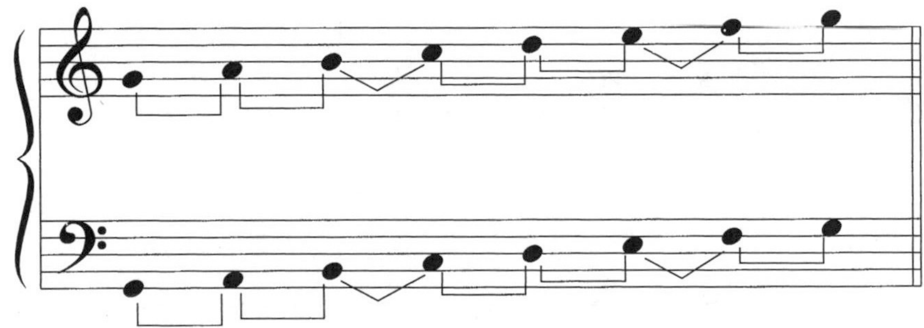

Locrian

The last mode is Locrian, which begins on the seventh degree of the major scale. The Locrian formula is half-step, whole-step, whole-step, half-step, whole-step, whole-step, and a whole-step.

B Locrian scale

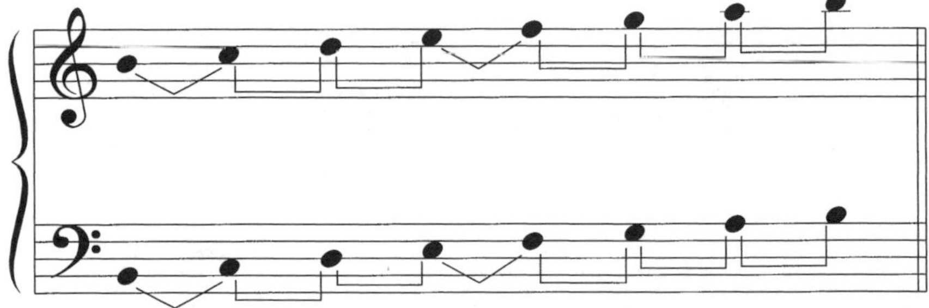

Other Scale Forms

Pentatonic Major Scales

The pentatonic scales are five-note scales. These scales can be heard in the solos of many rock and blues guitar players. The formula for the pentatonic major scale is whole-step, whole-step, minor third, whole-step, and a minor third.

C pentatonic scale

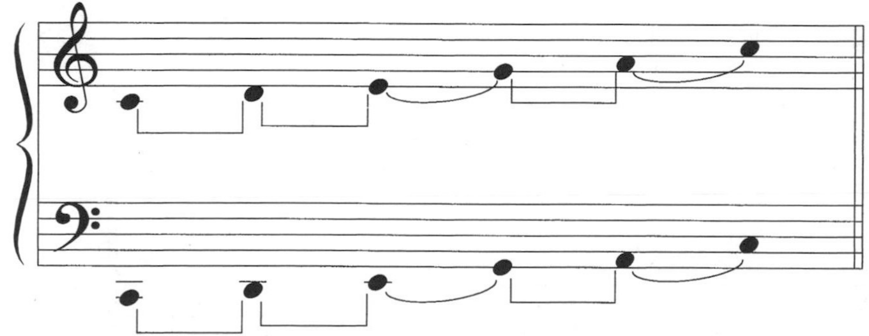

Pentatonic Minor Scales

The pentatonic minor is also a five-note scale. The formula for these scales is minor third, whole-step, whole-step, minor third, and a whole-step.

C pentatonic minor scale

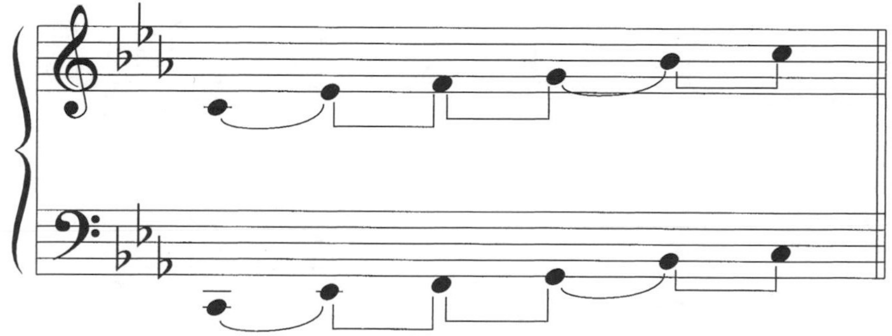

Blues Scales

The blues scales can be found in a variety of blues, rock and jazz styles. The formula for these scales is minor third, half-step, half-step, half-step, half-step, minor third, and a whole-step.

C blues scale

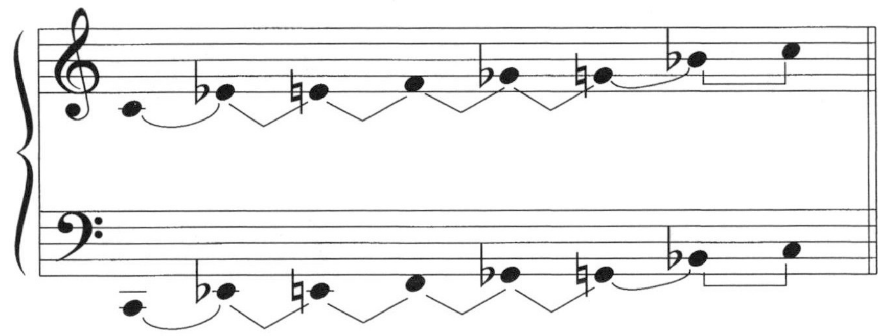

Whole Tone Scales

The whole tone scale has the simplest formula—it consists of all whole-steps. Unlike traditional scales, the whole tone scales do not contain basic intervals like the perfect fourth, perfect fifth and the leading tone.

Impressionistic composers of the early 20th century incorporated the use of whole tone scales into their musical style.

C whole tone scale

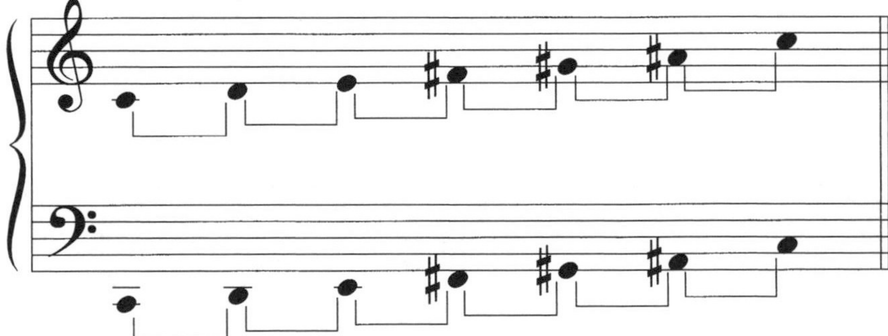

How to Use This Book

The subsequent pages are a graphic and musical representation of the major, natural minor *(Aeolian),* harmonic minor, and melodic minor pentatonic major, pentatonic minor, jazz melodic minor, whole tone scales, and the Dorian, Phrygian, Lydian, Lydian flat-seven, Mixolydian, and Locrian modes.

Each scale is displayed as a diagram and in music notation. The scales in each section start with no sharps and no flats and continue in order through the "circle of fifths" (see page 12) until all twelve scales are demonstrated.

The keyboard diagram consists of two elements, the notes to be played in the scale and the fingering to be used. The gray keys on the keyboard diagram show which notes are to be played.

The white circles with numbers inside them represent the right-hand fingering and the black circles are for the left-hand fingering. The numbers inside the circles correspond to the fingers of each hand with ① being the thumb, ② the index finger, ③ the forefinger, ④ the ring finger, and ⑤ the pinky finger.

Below the keyboard diagram is the scale written in music notation. To the right of the clefs in the treble and bass are the key signatures (see page 10), to the right of them are notes of the scale. The small numbers that appear over some of the notes are fingering numbers. Notice that only certain notes are numbered, the first and last notes and the pivot points. Pivot points are where the fingers cross over the thumb or the thumb crosses under the fingers.

The keyboard diagram and music display the fingering and notation for two octaves of the scale. It is good practice to play and learn both octaves, this will improve your reading skills and dexterity.

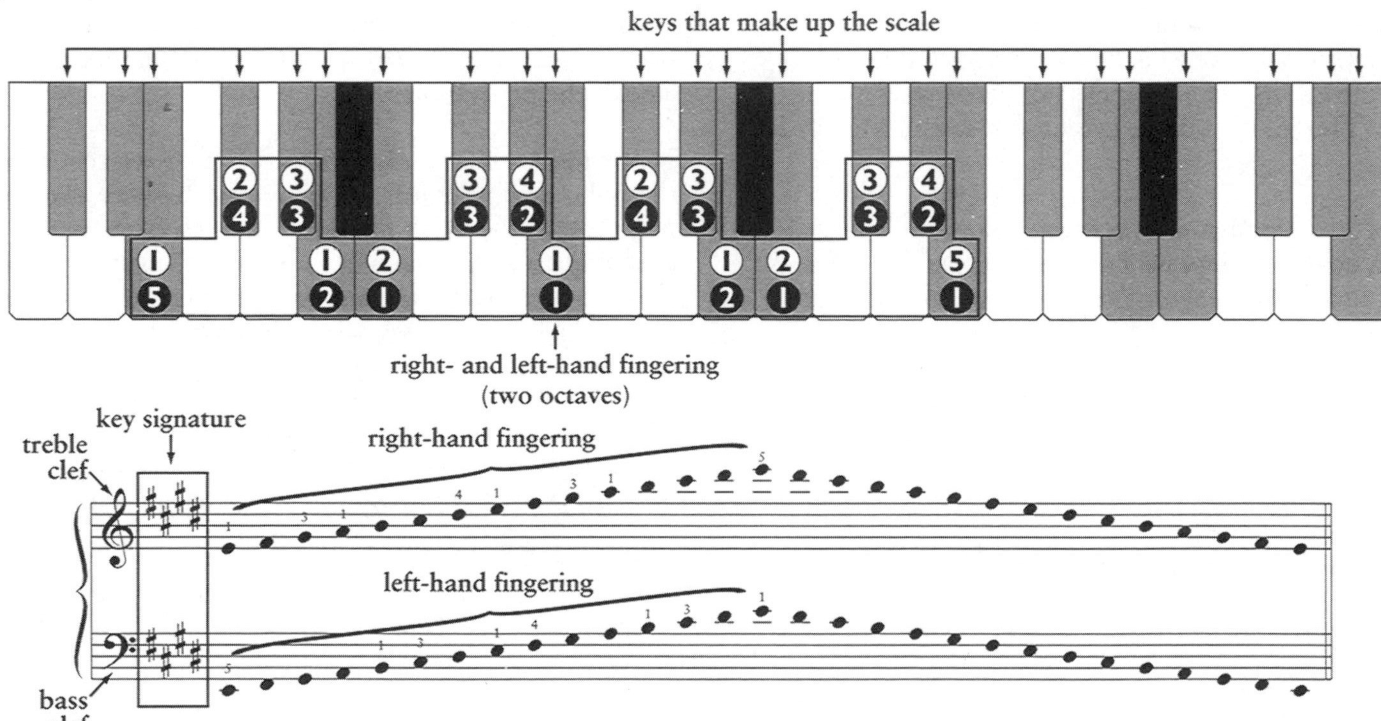
keys that make up the scale
right- and left-hand fingering
(two octaves)
key signature
treble clef
right-hand fingering
left-hand fingering
bass clef

C major

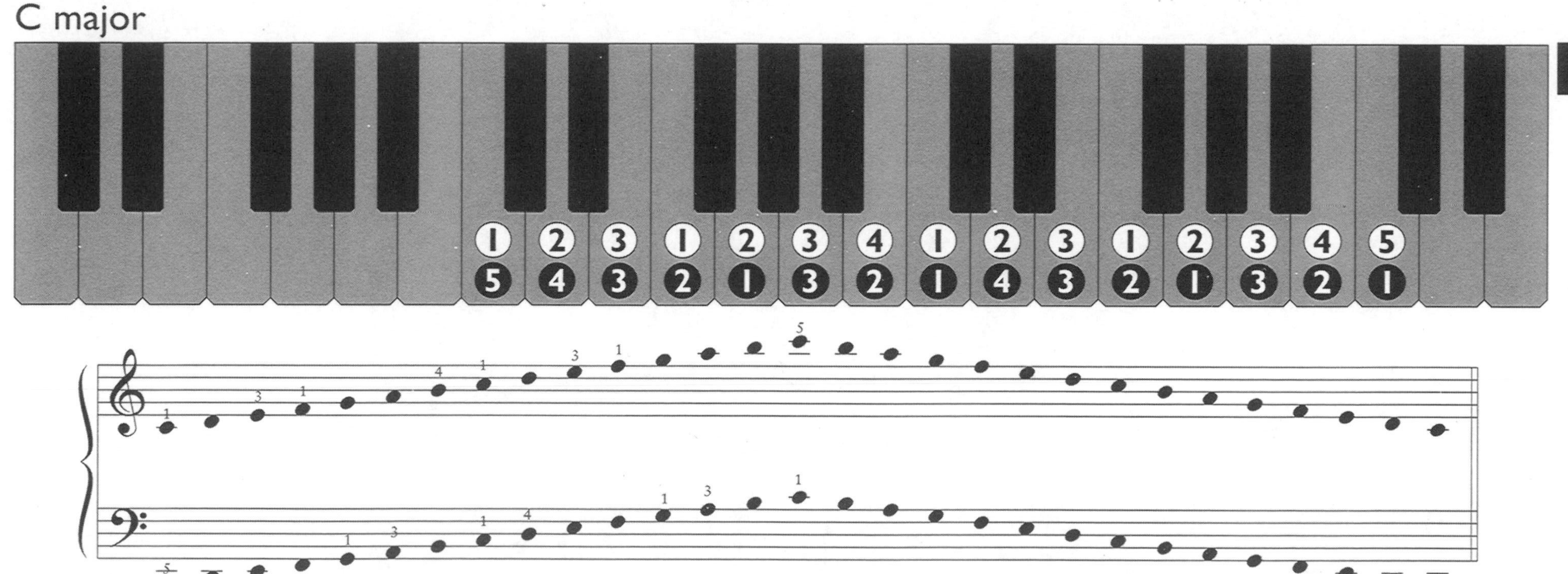

G major

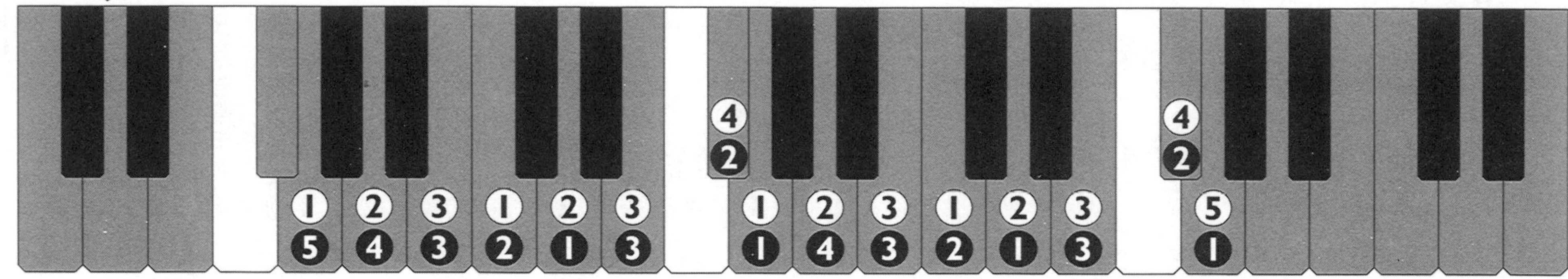

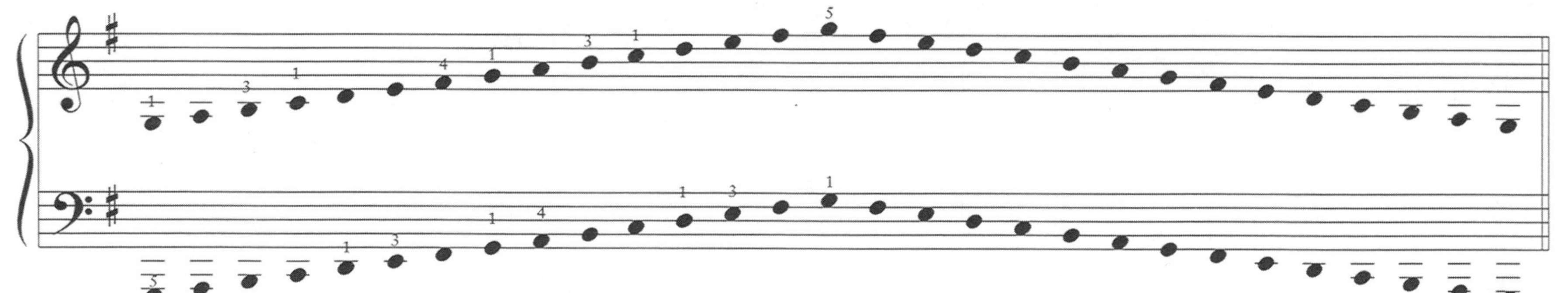

D major

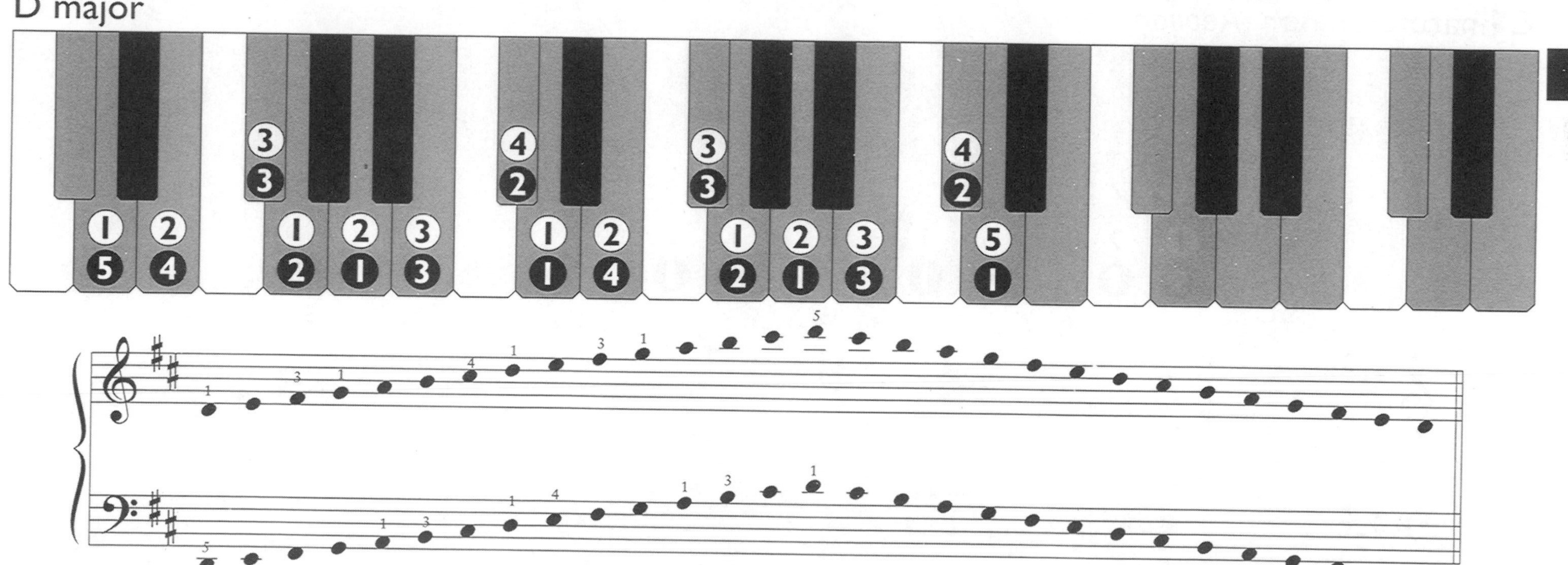

A major

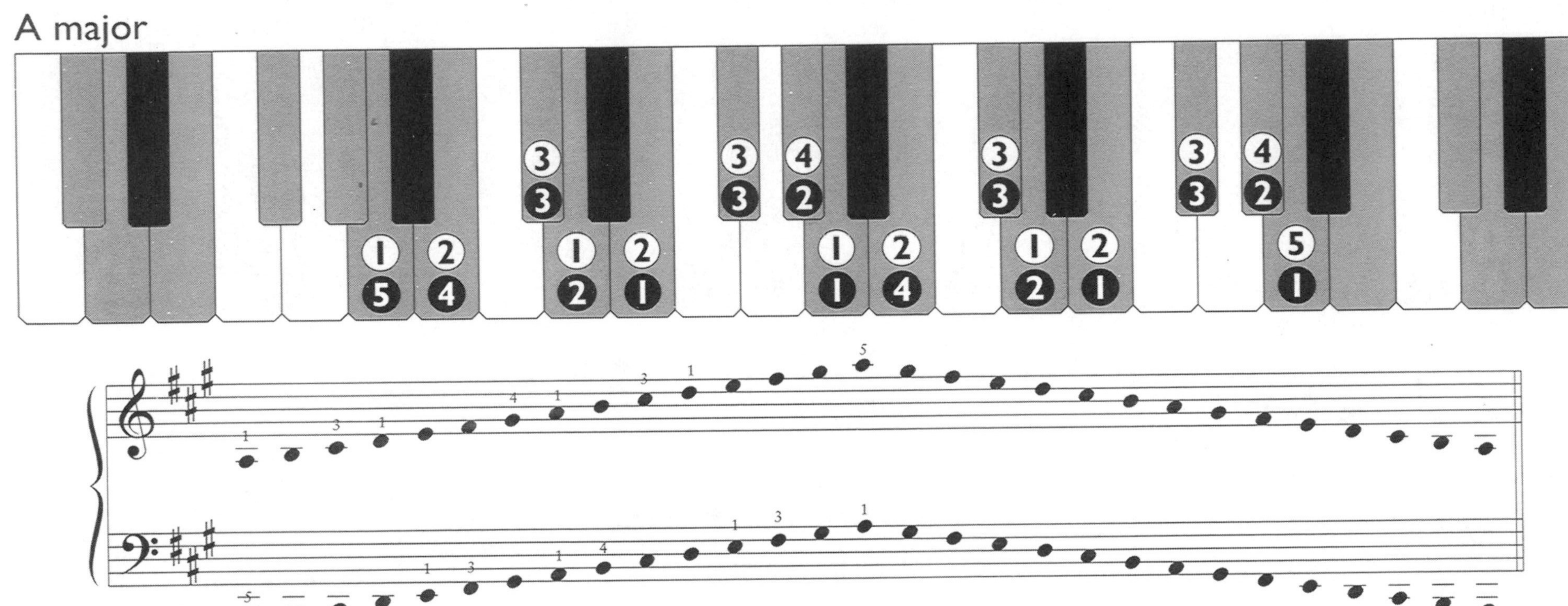

E major

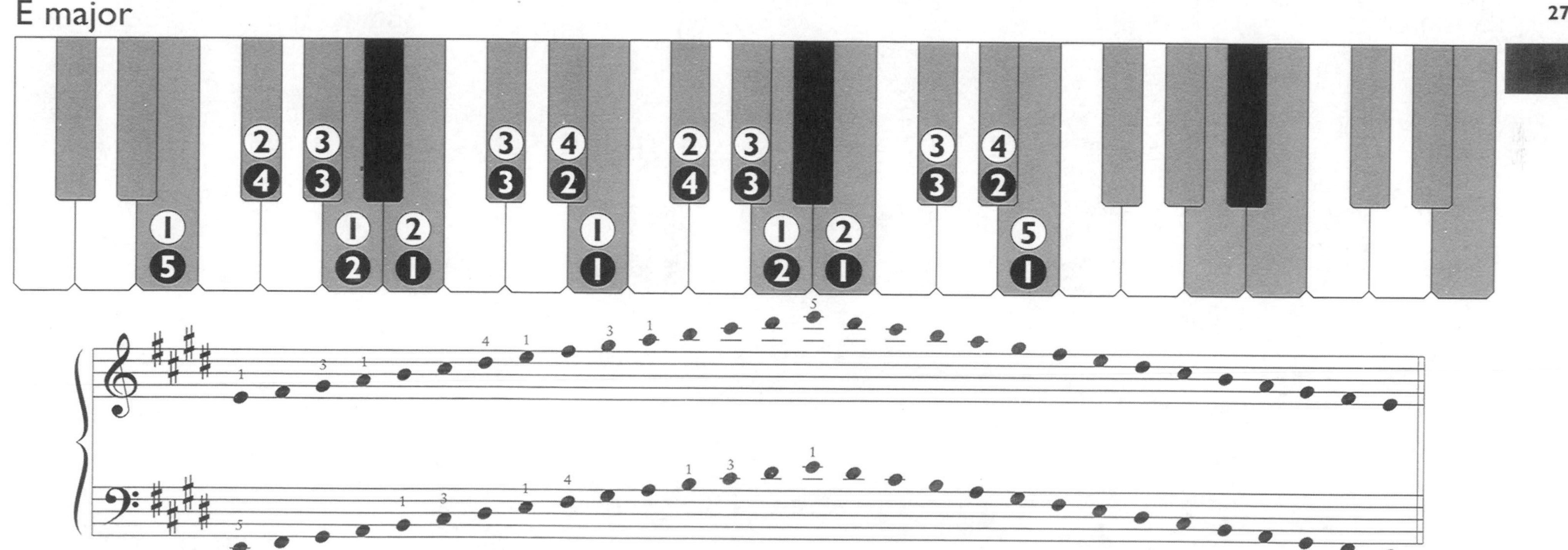

B major

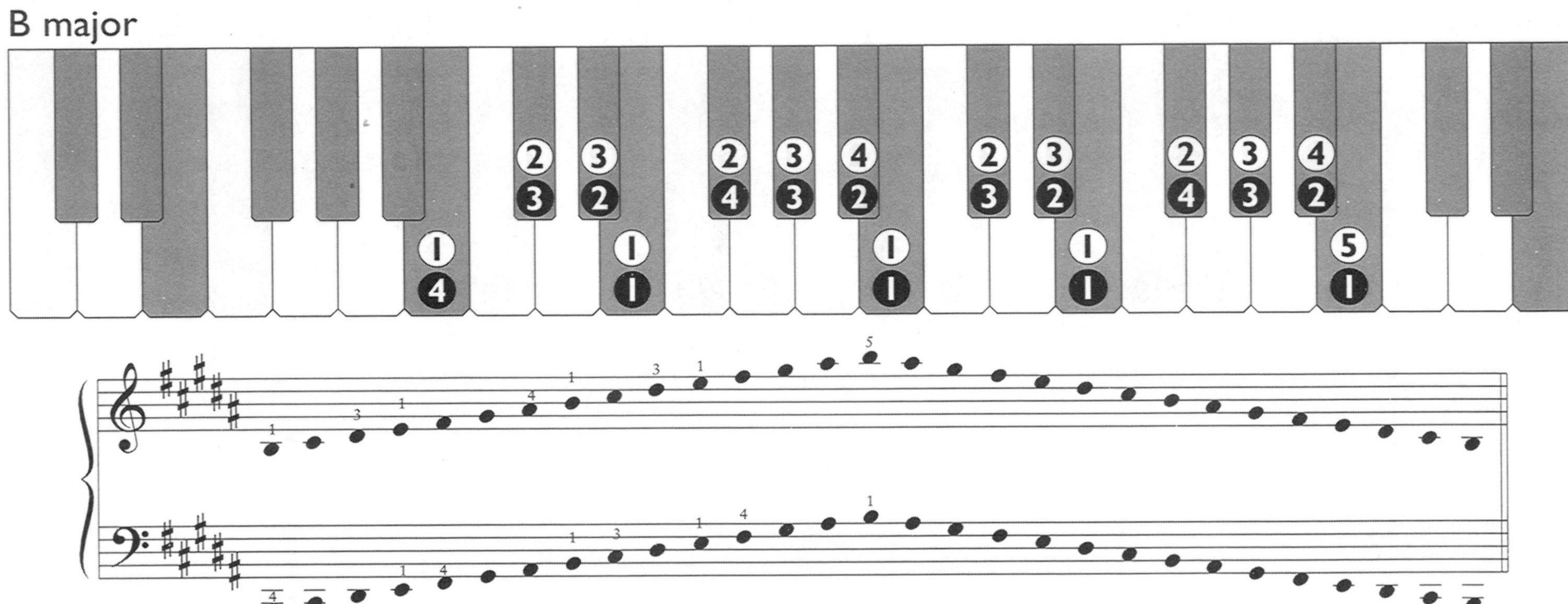

F♯ major

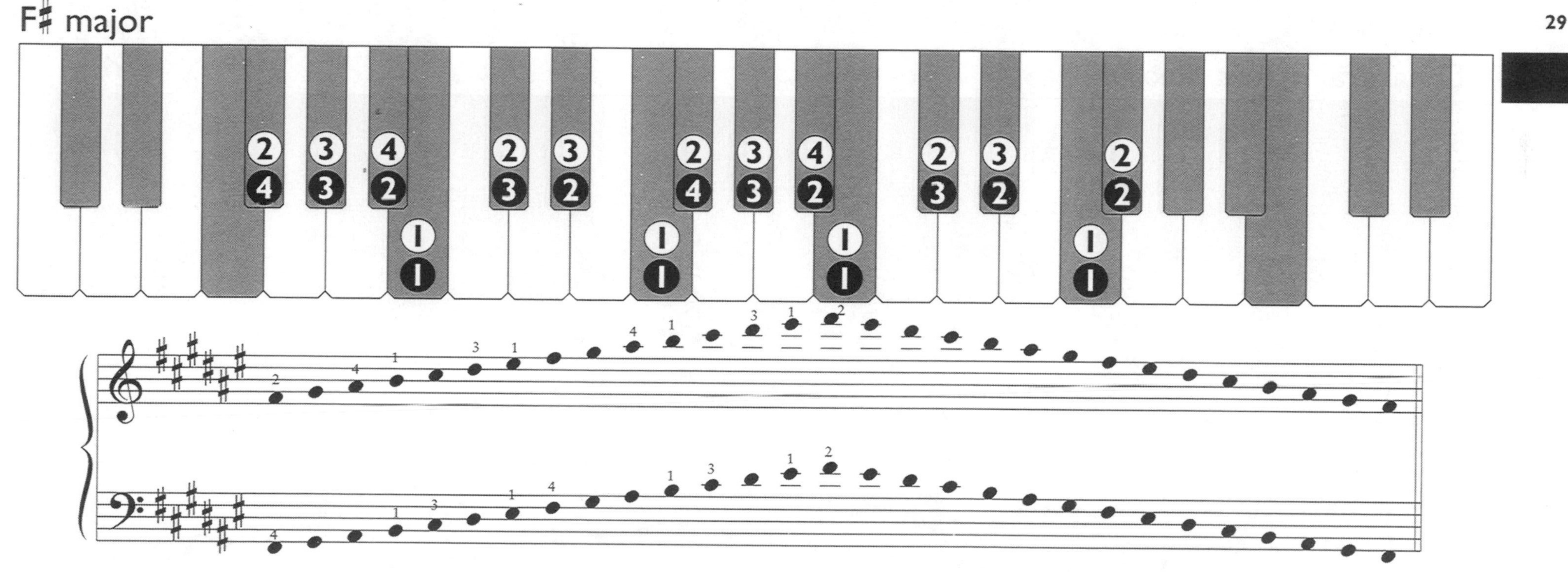

C♯ major

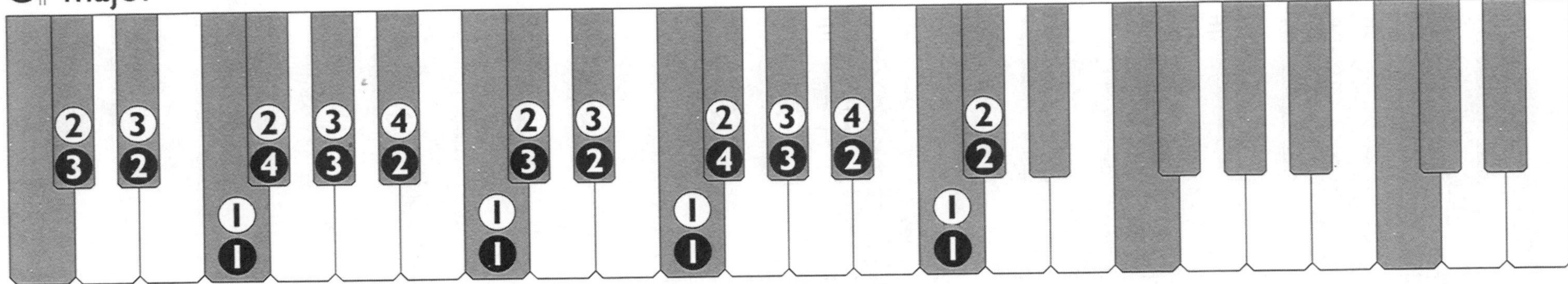

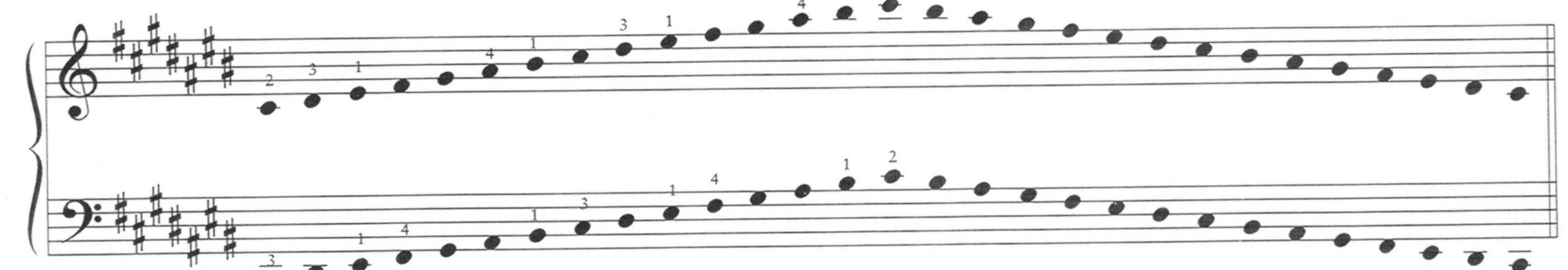

F major

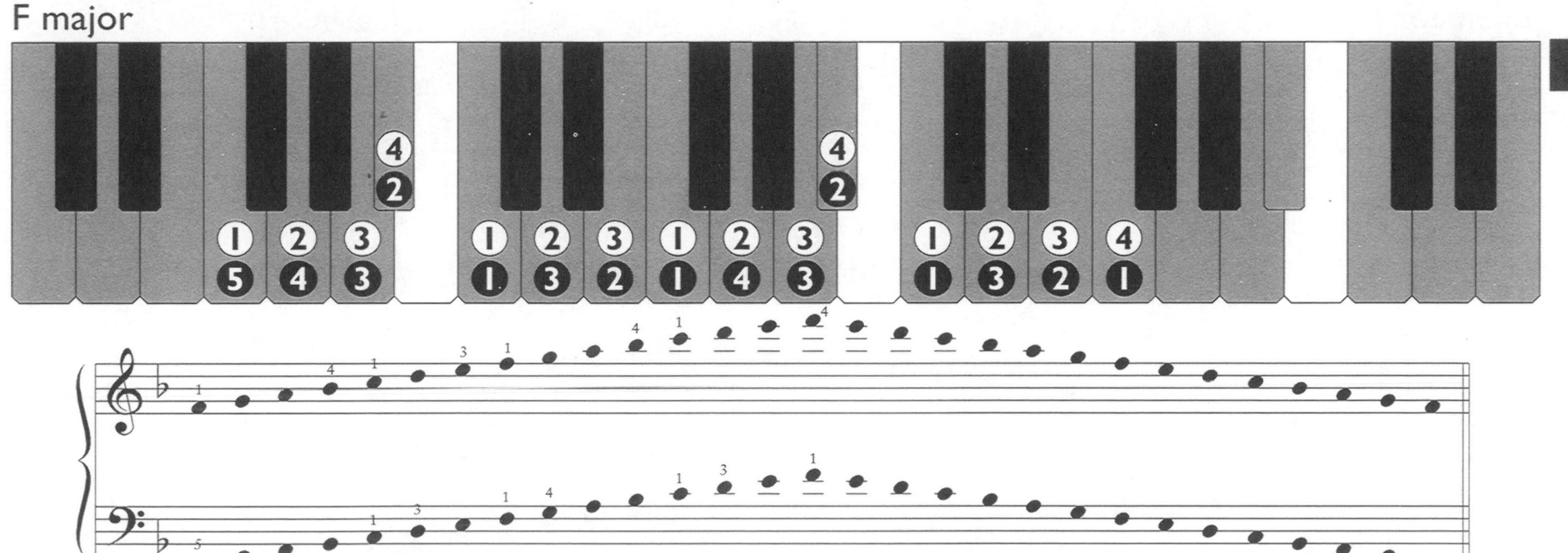

B♭ major

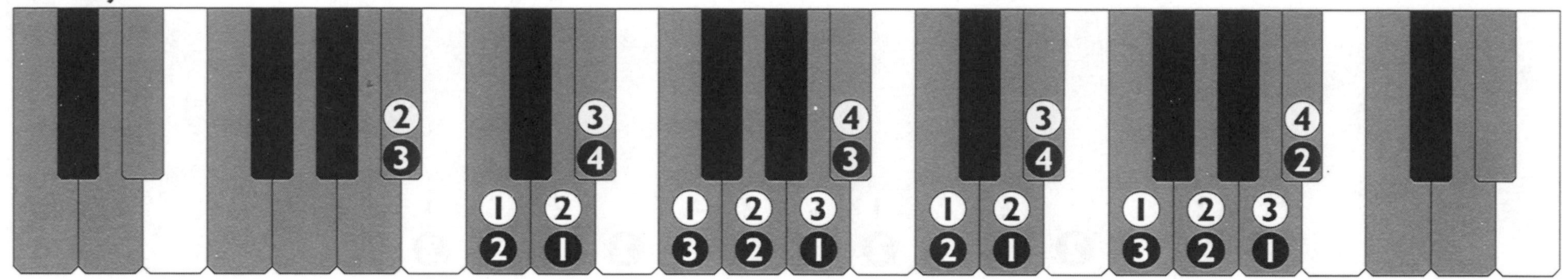

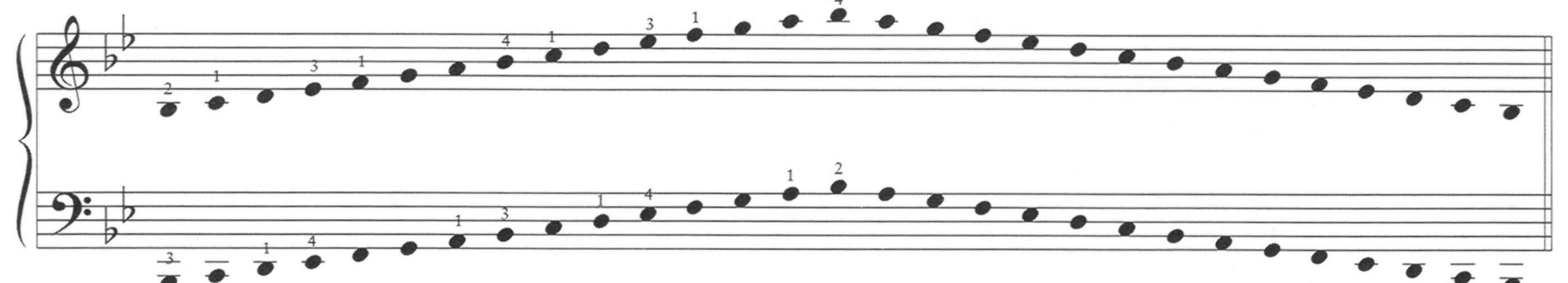

E♭ major

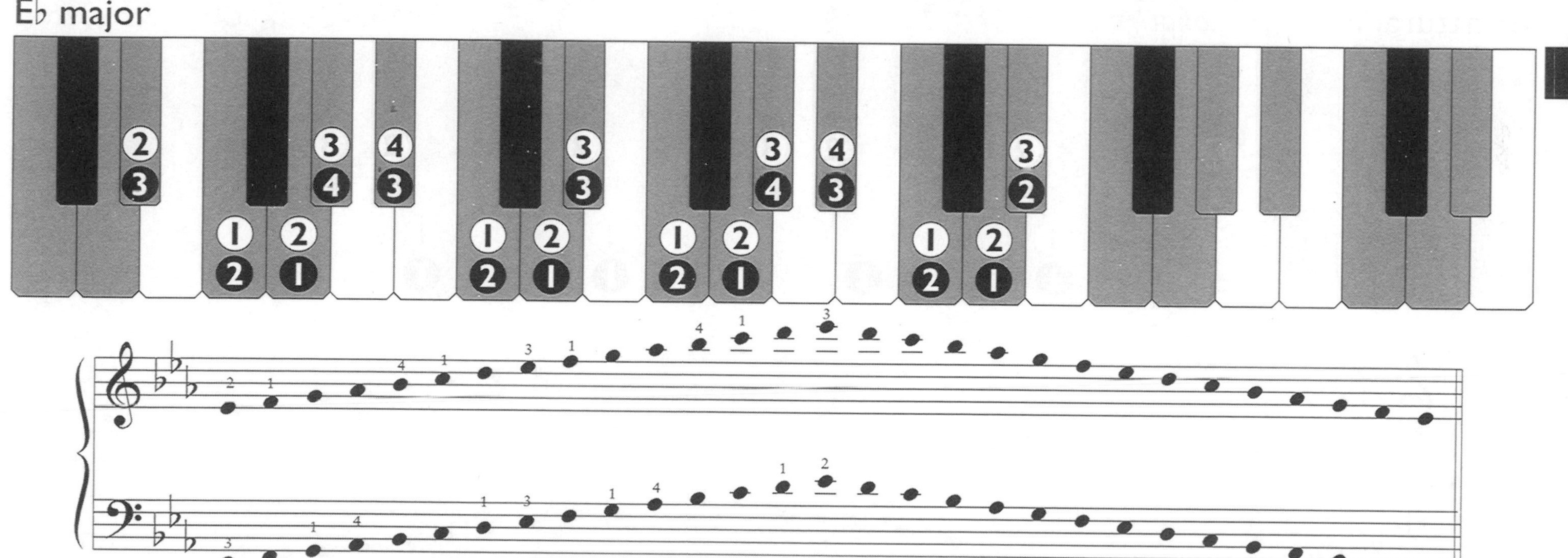

A♭ major

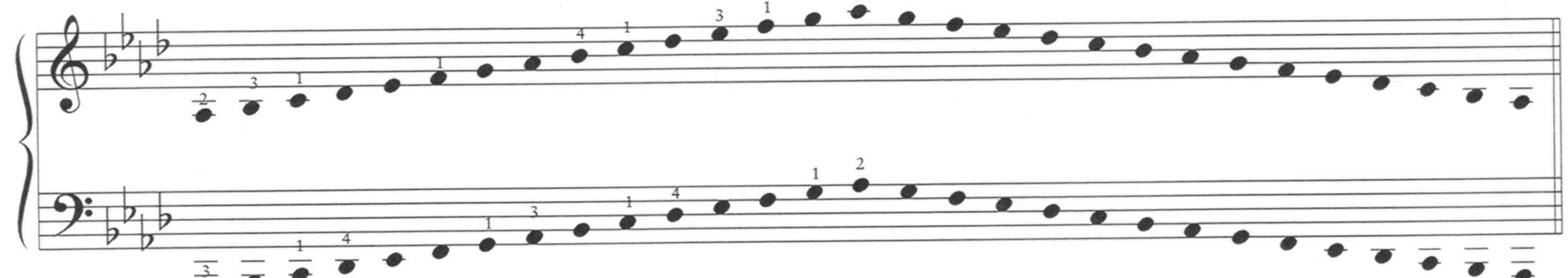

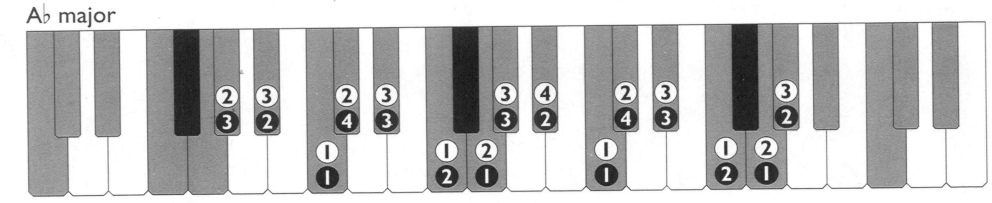

D♭ major

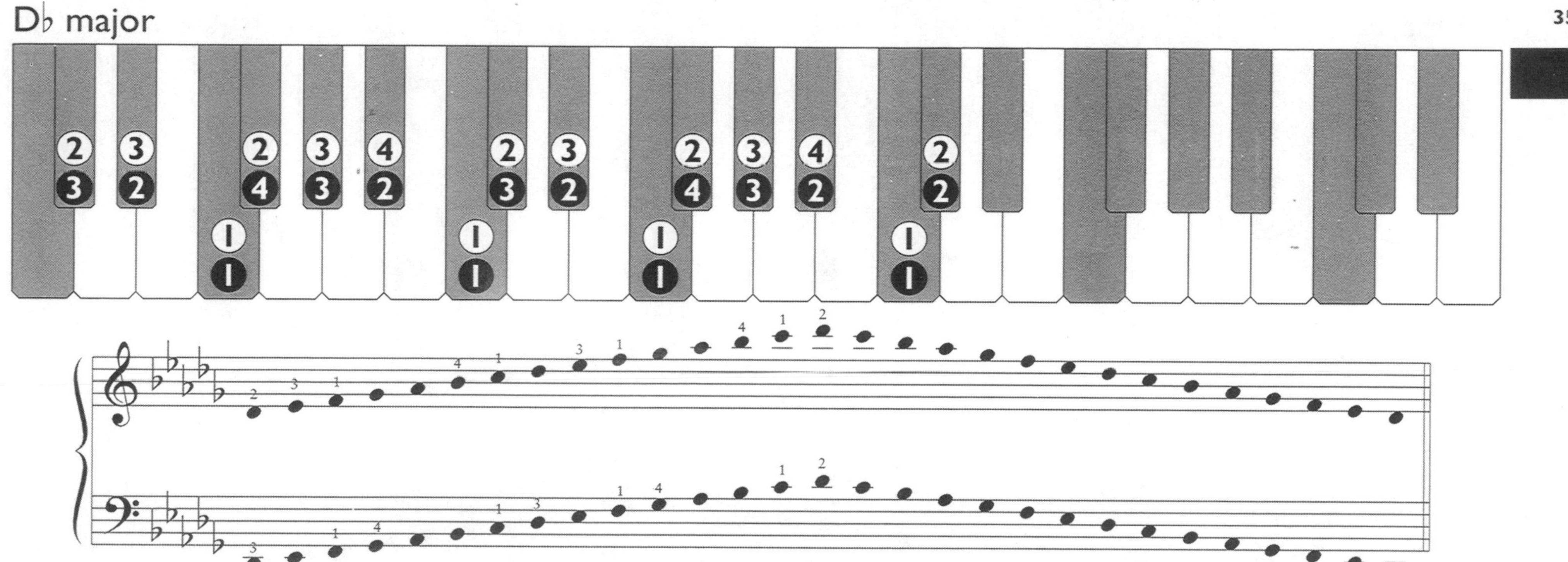

G♭ major

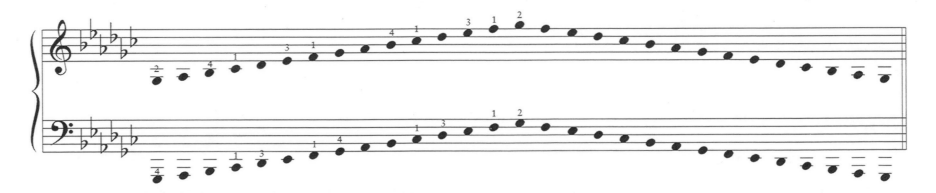

C♭ major

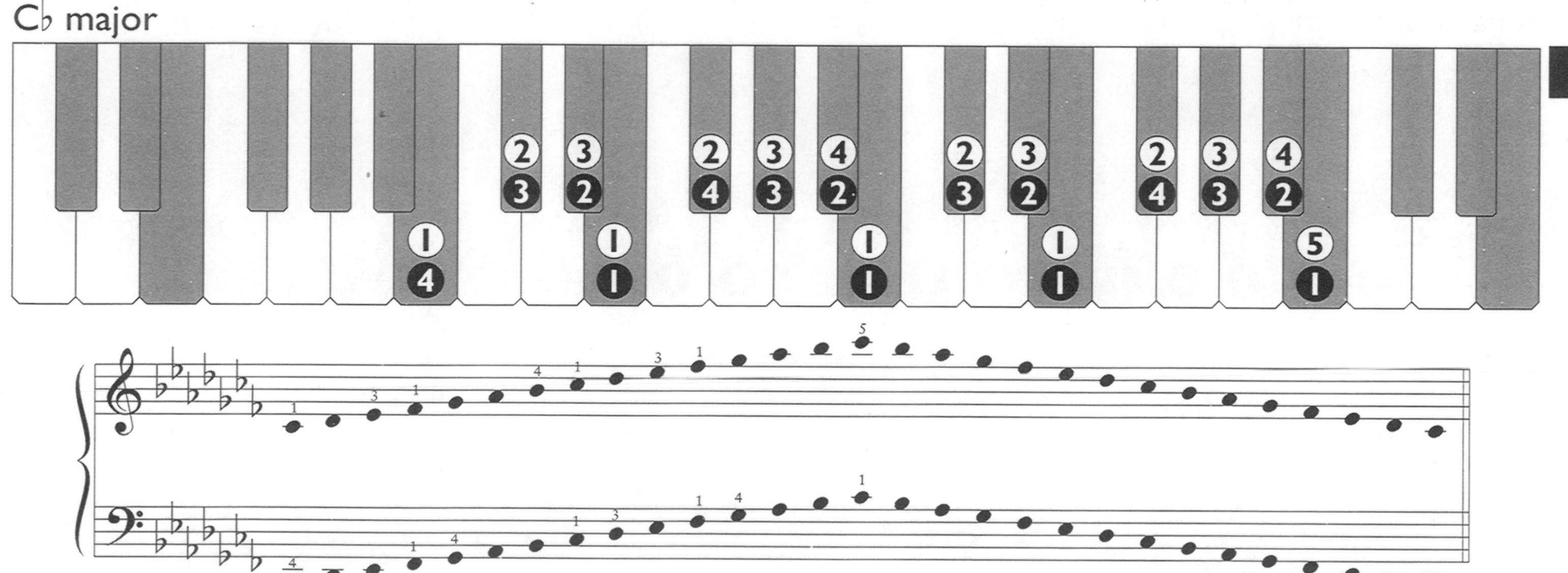

A natural minor *(Aeolian)*

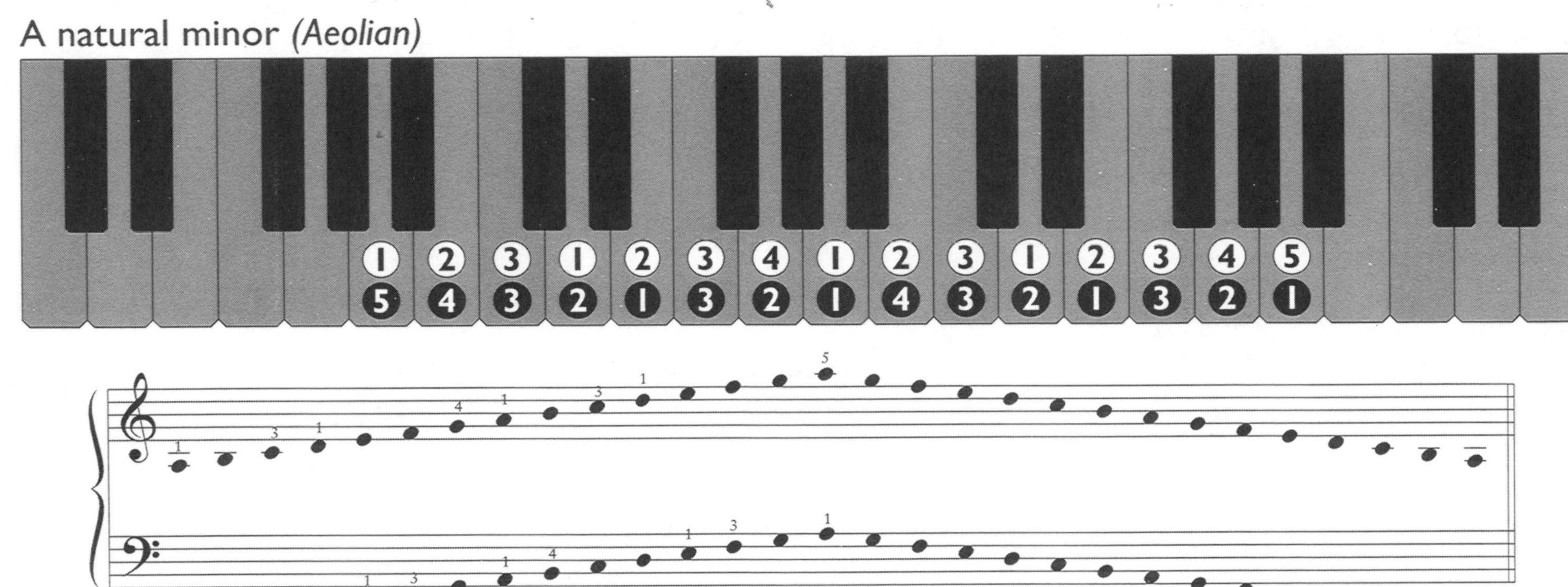

E natural minor *(Aeolian)*

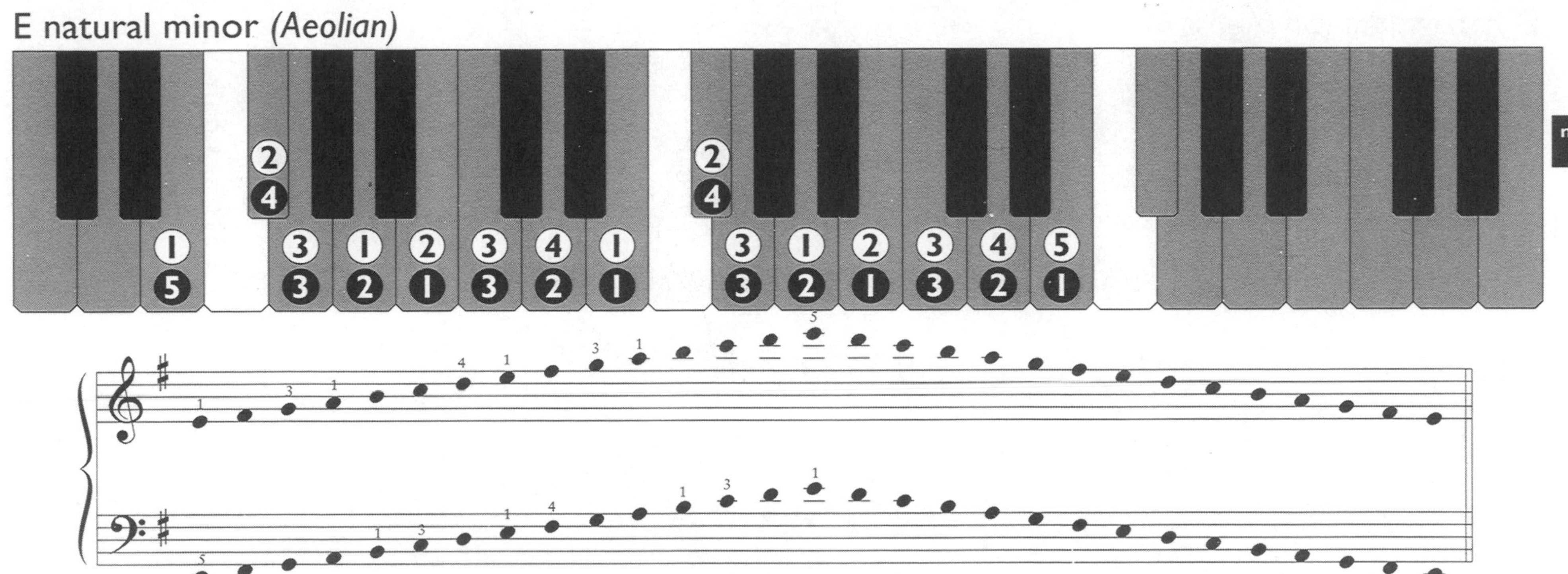

B natural minor *(Aeolian)*

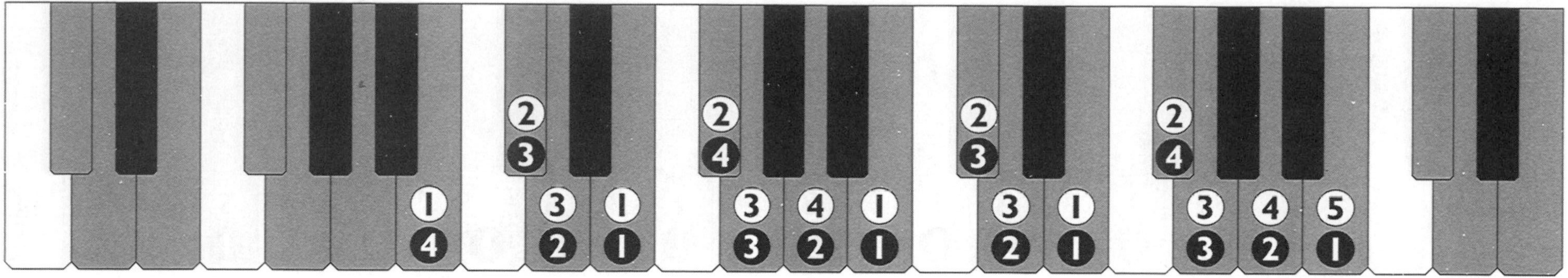

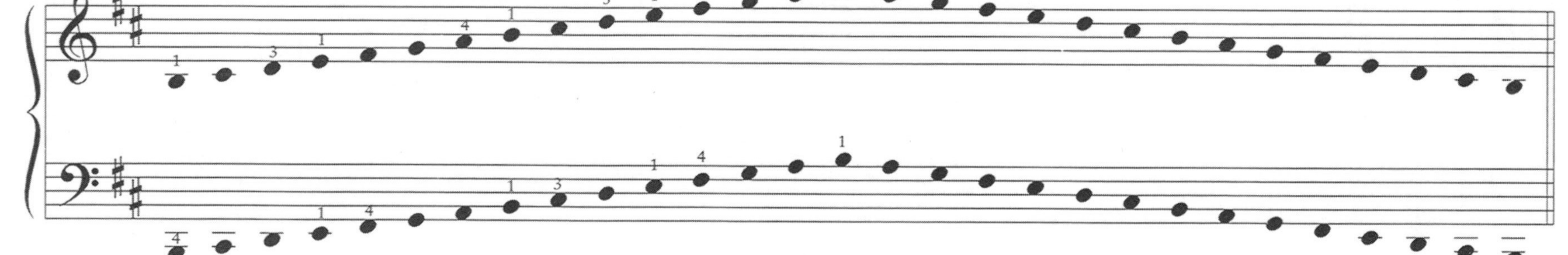

F♯ natural minor *(Aeolian)*

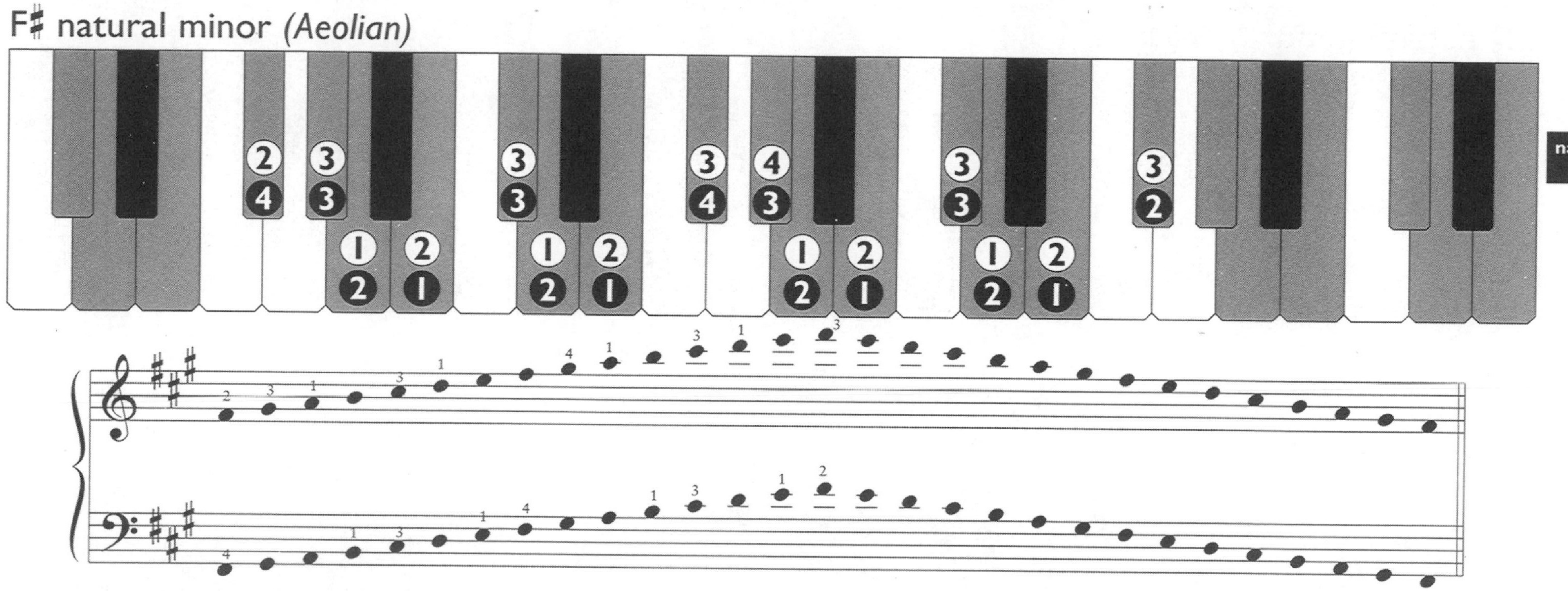

C♯ natural minor *(Aeolian)*

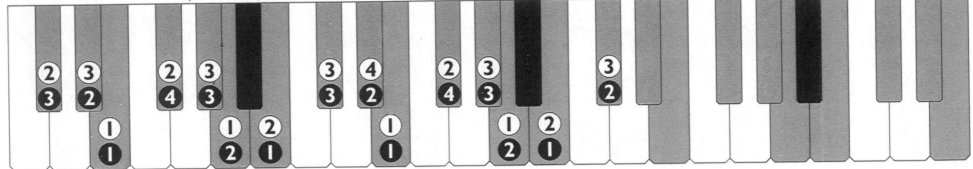

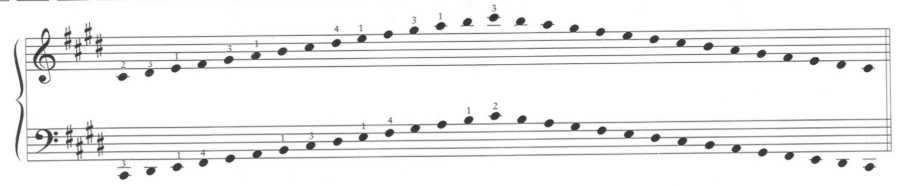

G♯ natural minor *(Aeolian)*

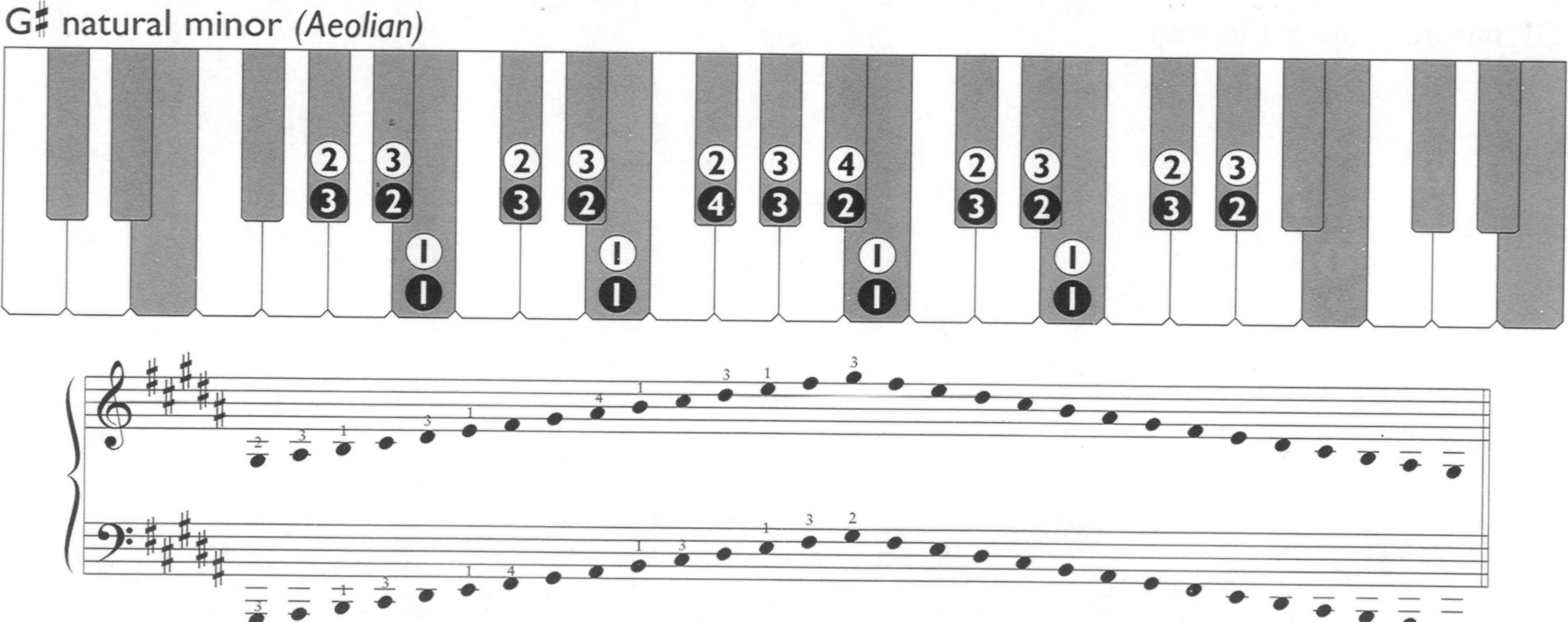

D♯ natural minor *(Aeolian)*

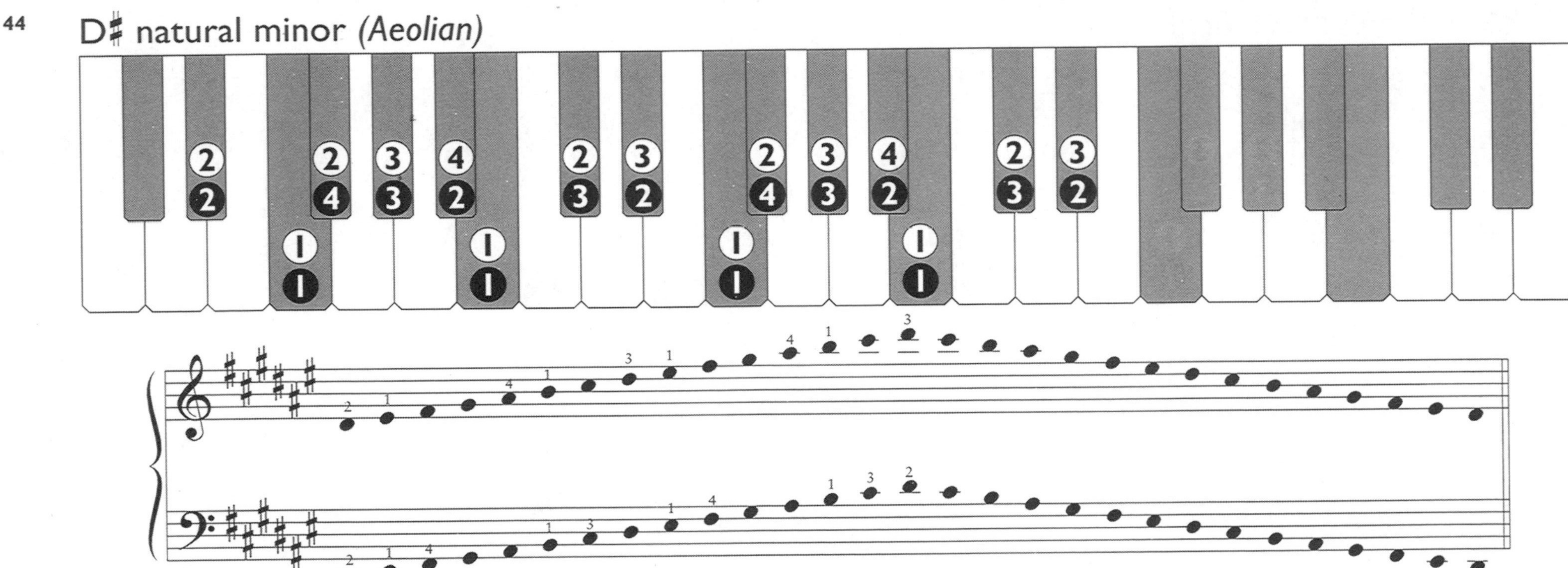

A♯ natural minor *(Aeolian)*

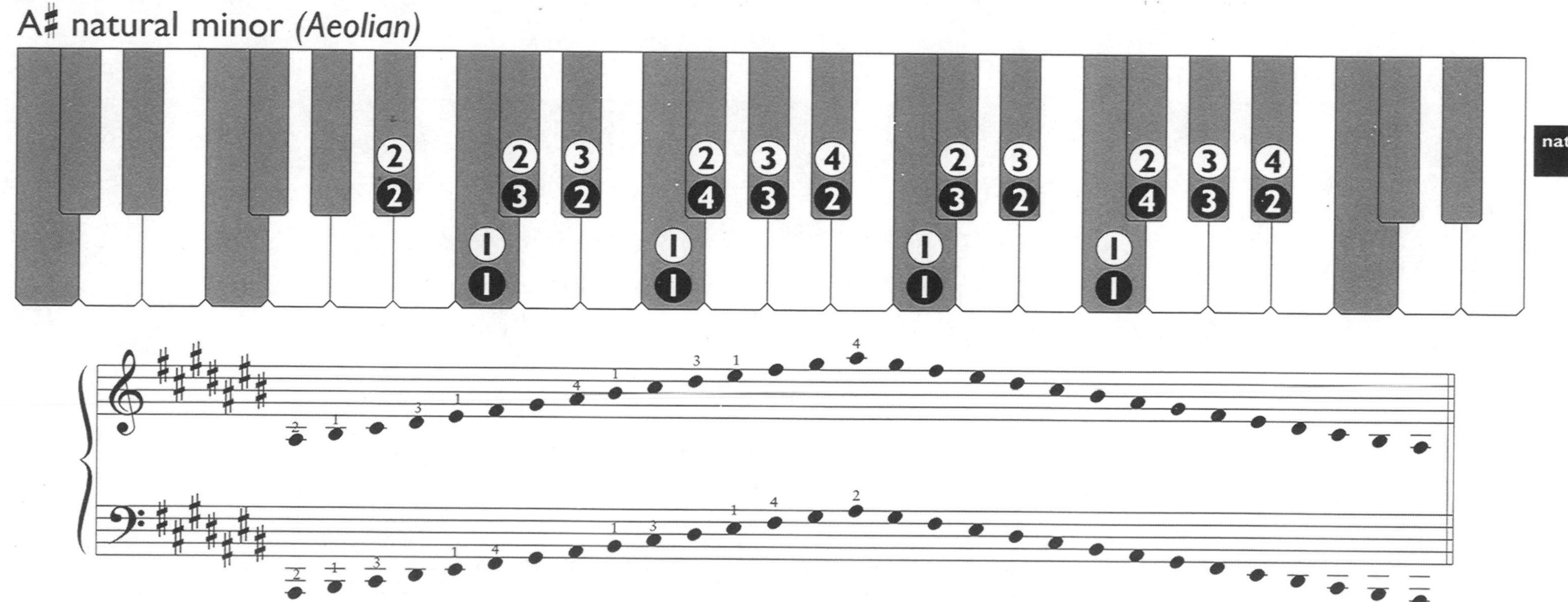

D natural minor *(Aeolian)*

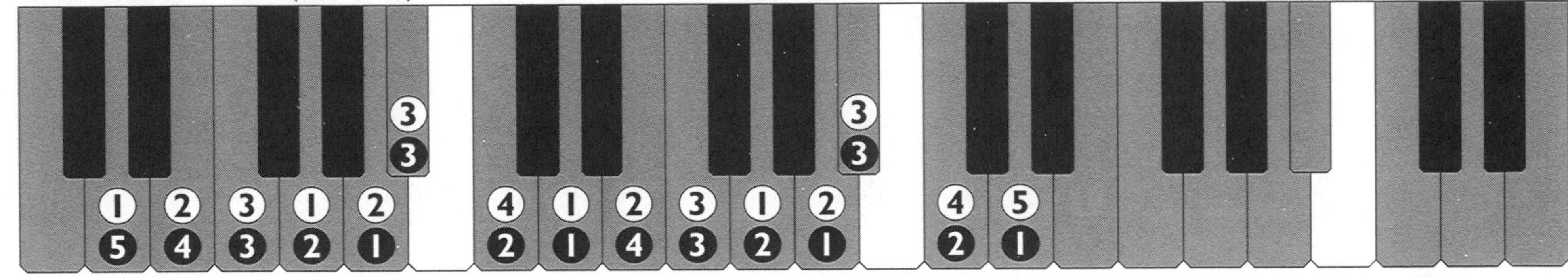

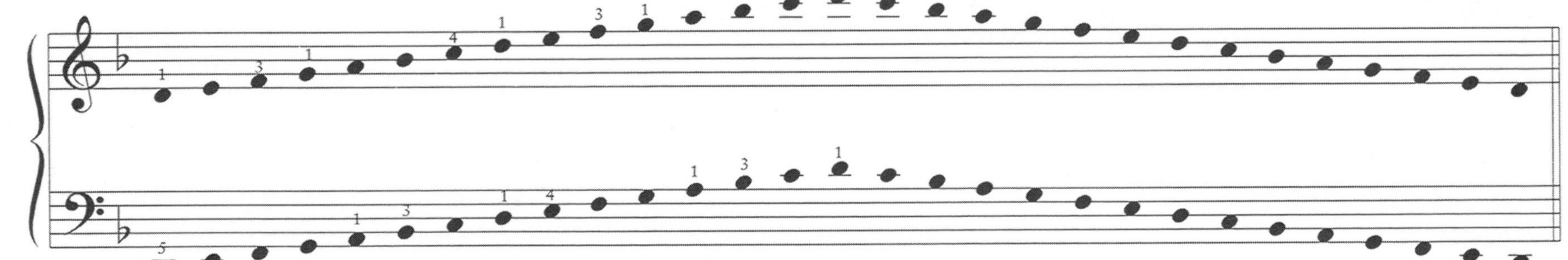

G natural minor *(Aeolian)*

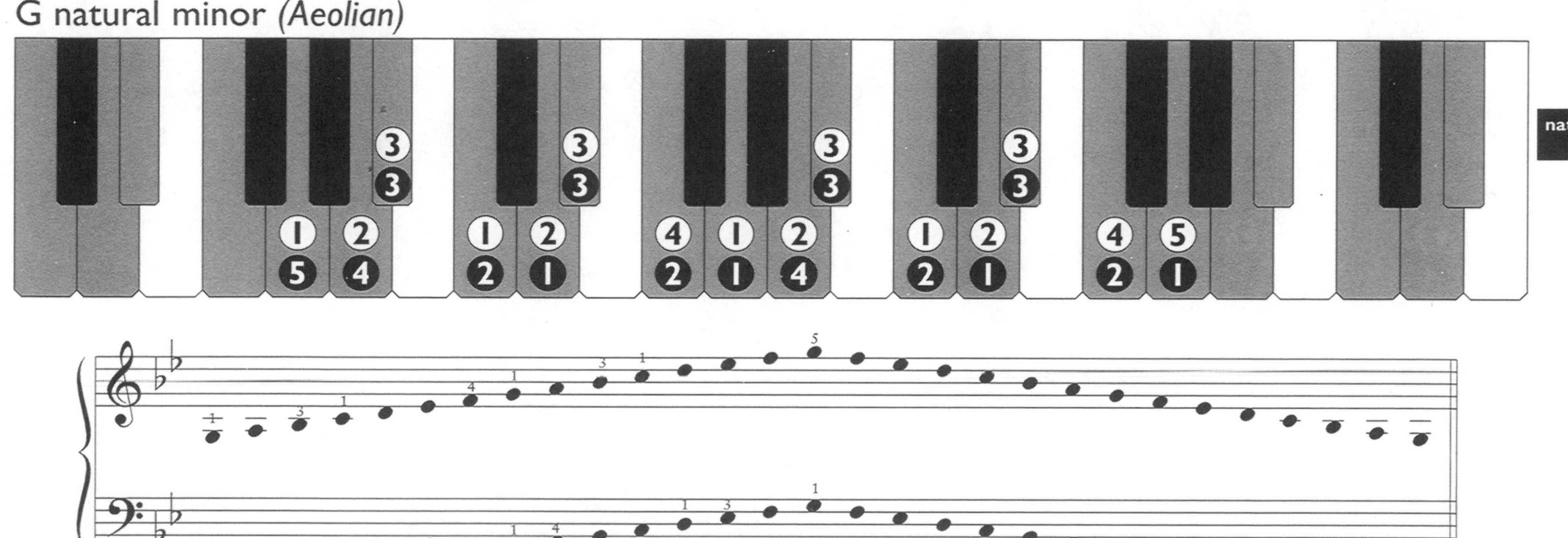

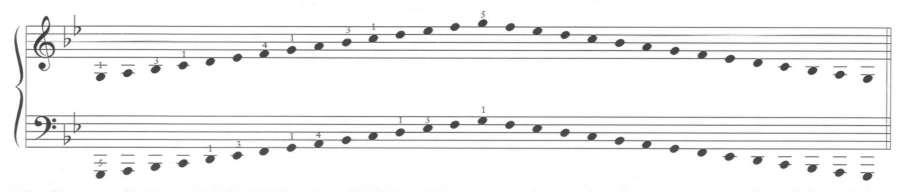

C natural minor *(Aeolian)*

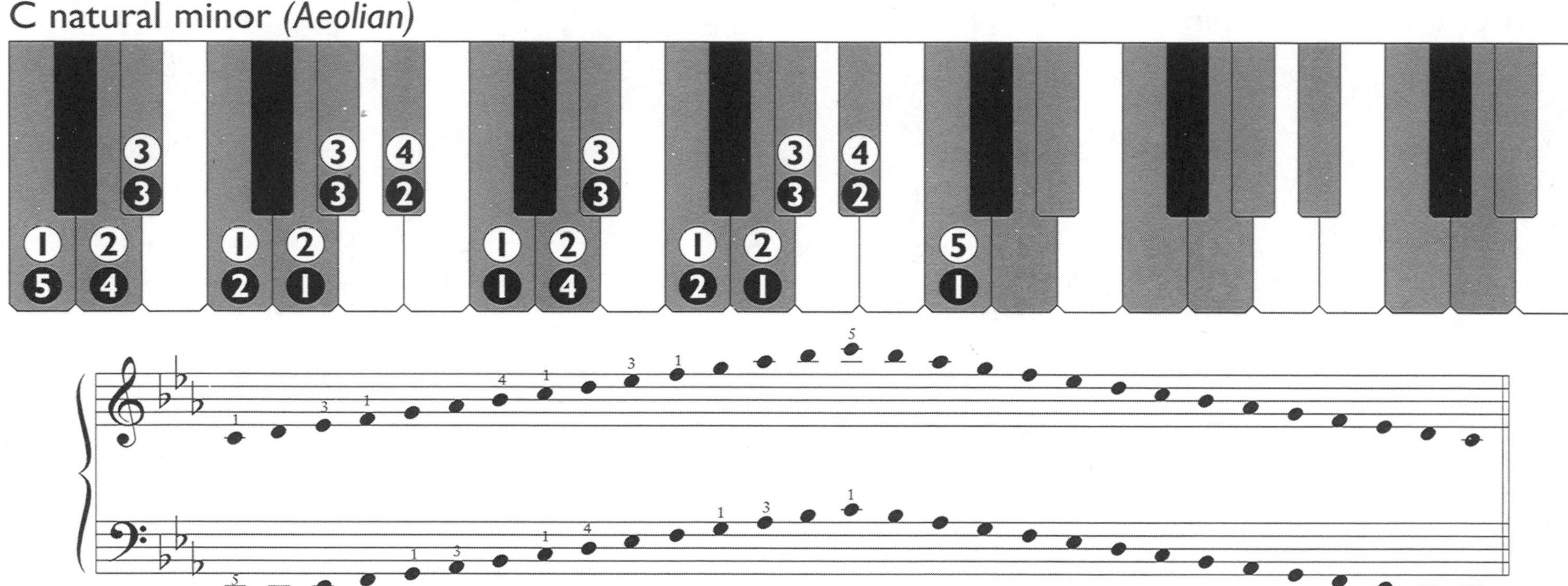

F natural minor *(Aeolian)*

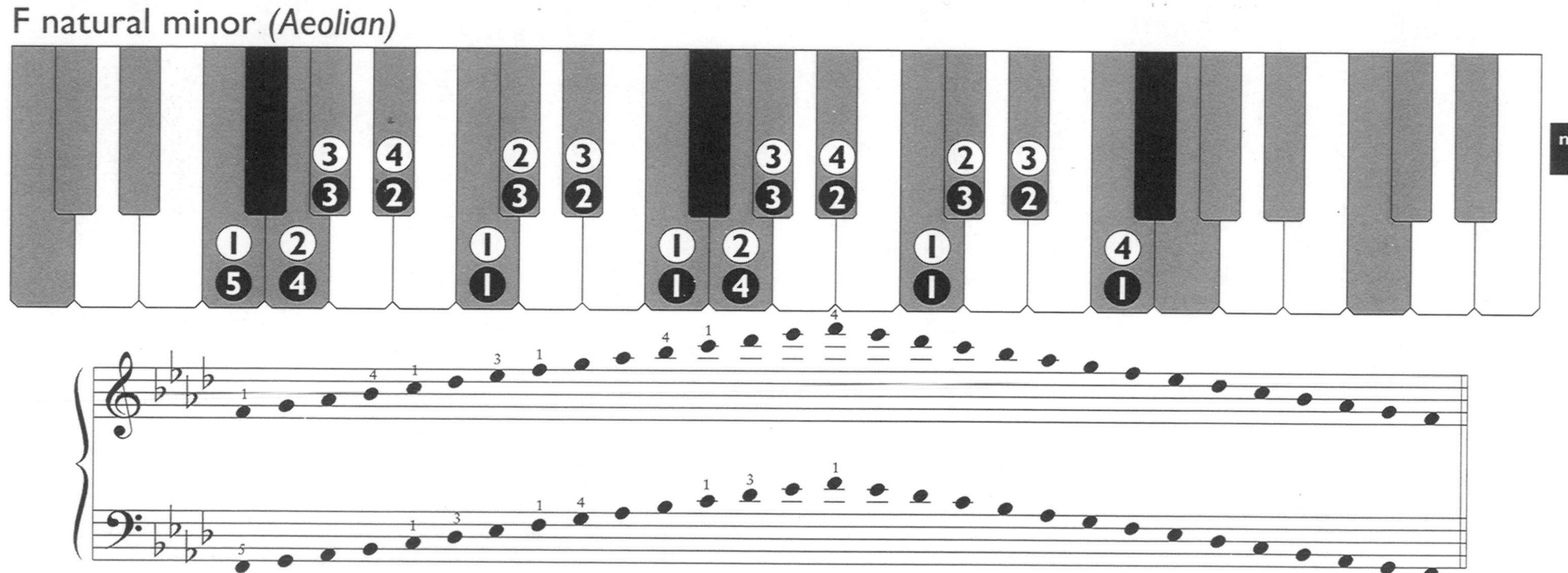

B♭ natural minor *(Aeolian)*

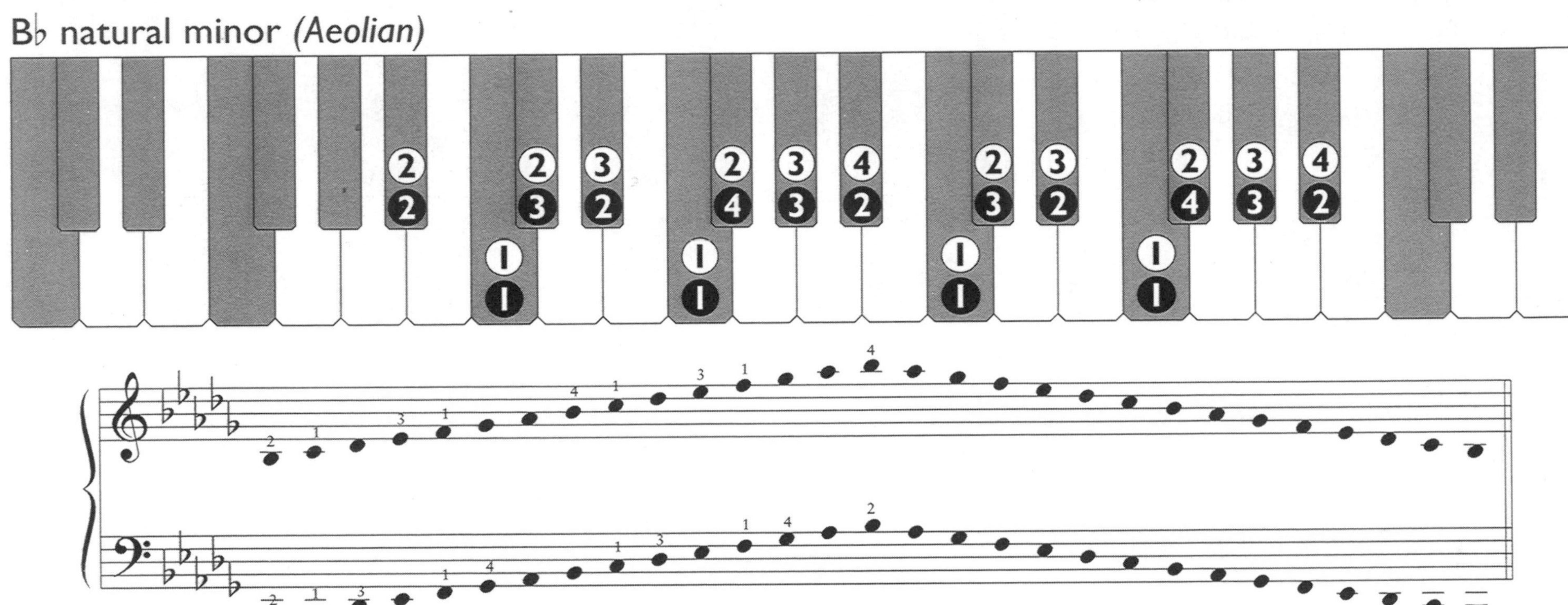

E♭ natural minor *(Aeolian)*

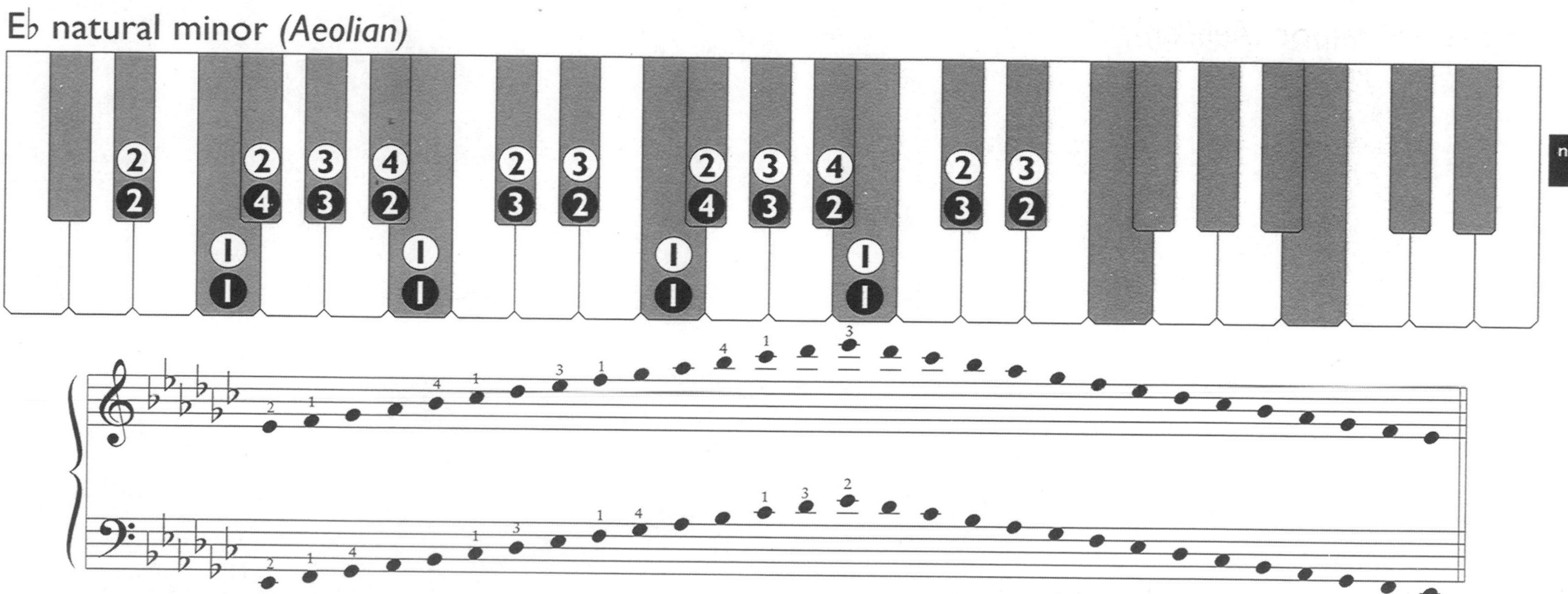

A♭ natural minor *(Aeolian)*

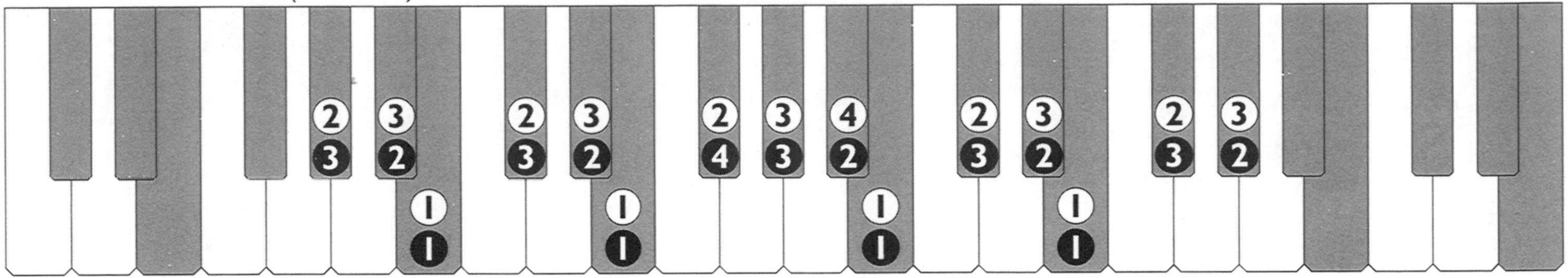

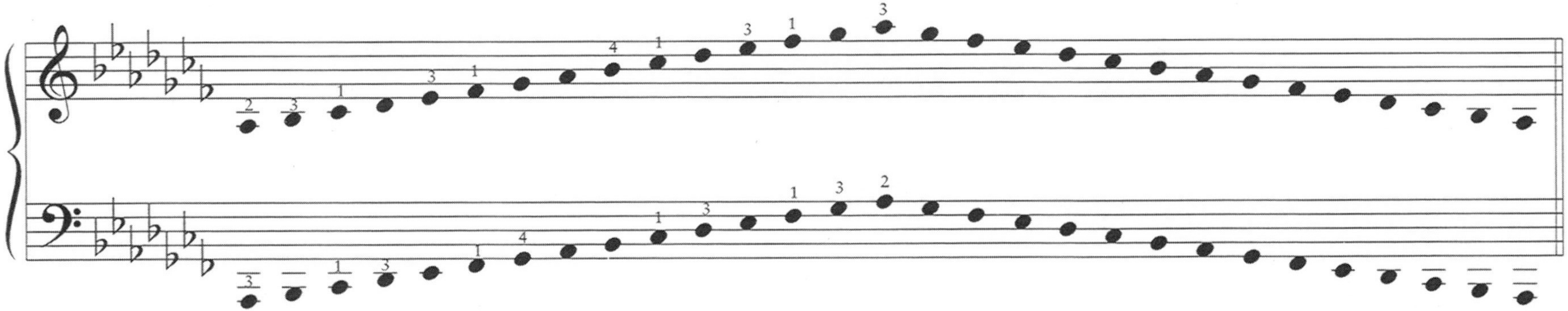

A harmonic minor

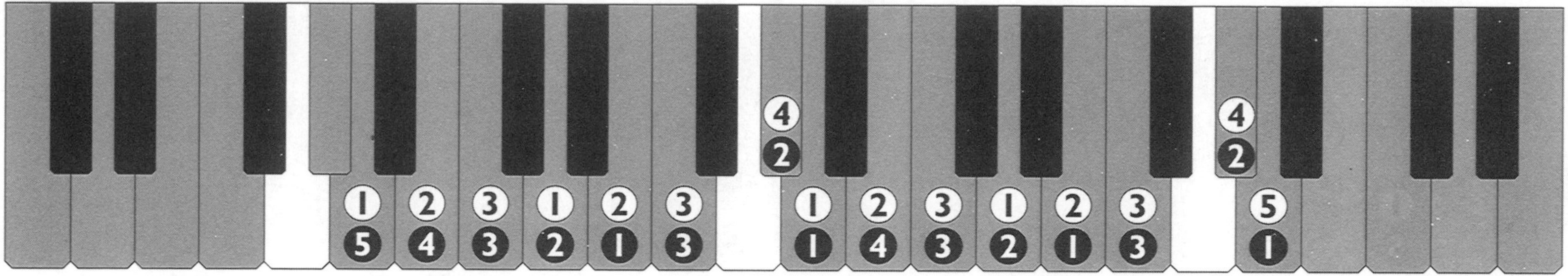

E harmonic minor

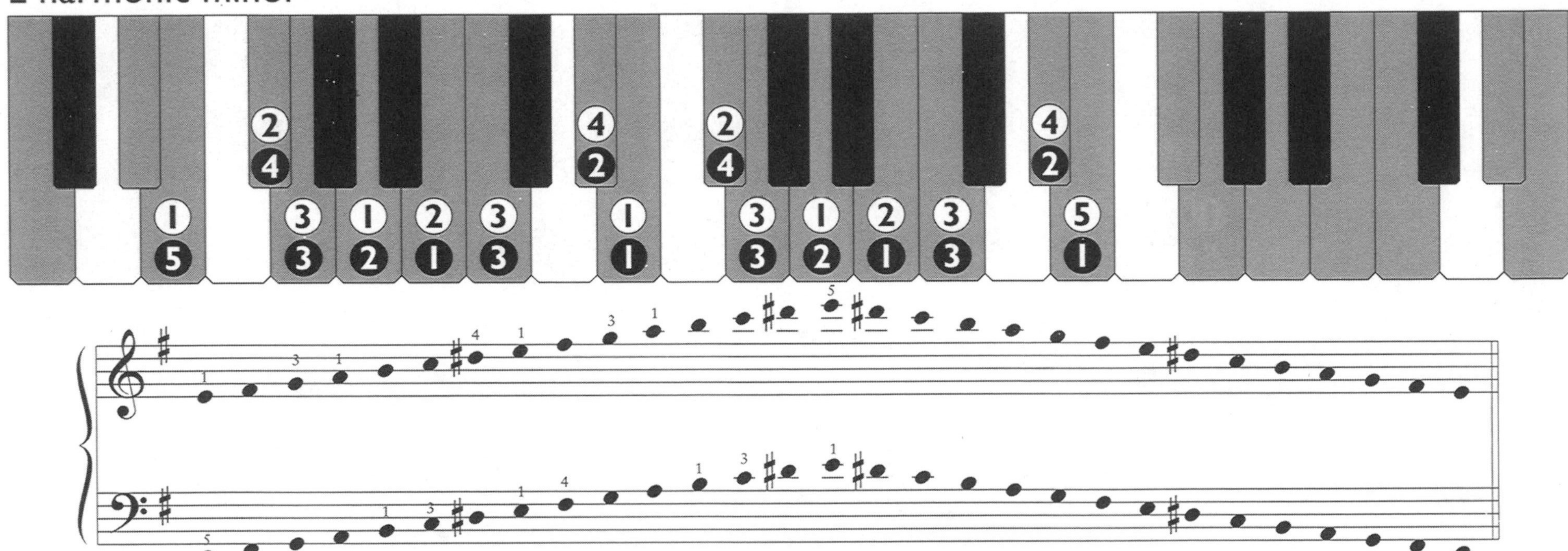

B harmonic minor

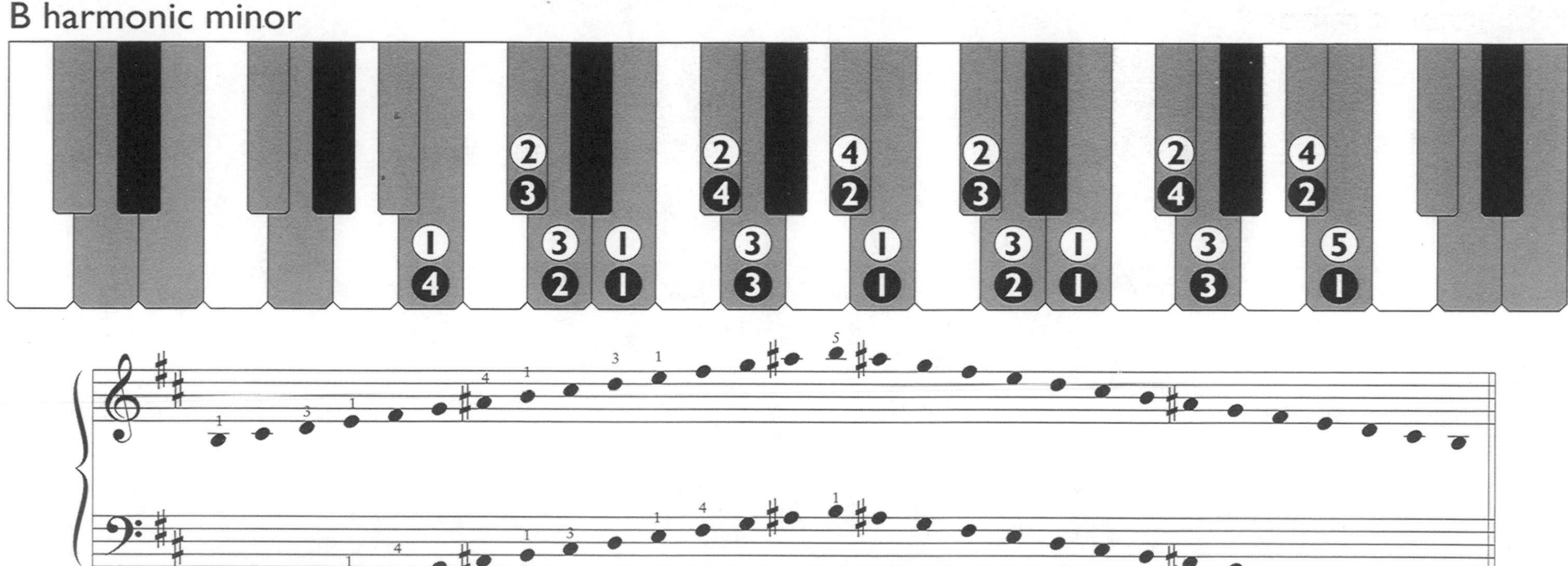

F♯ harmonic minor

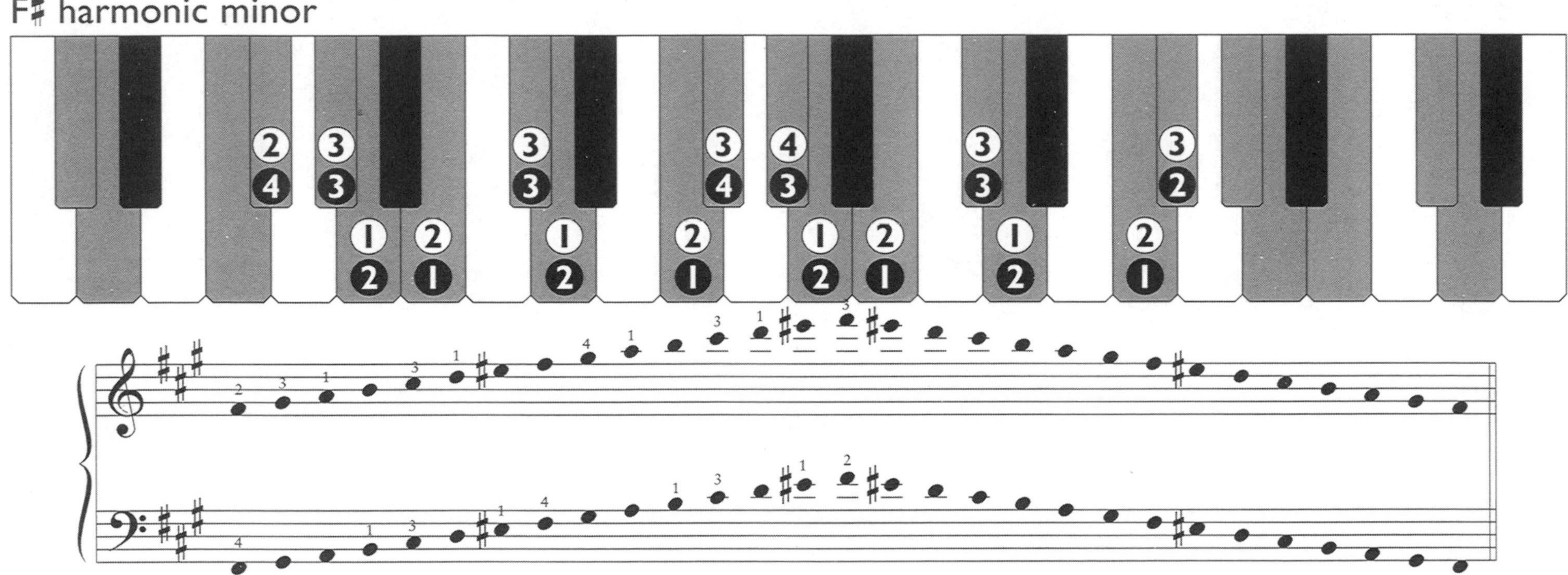

C♯ harmonic minor

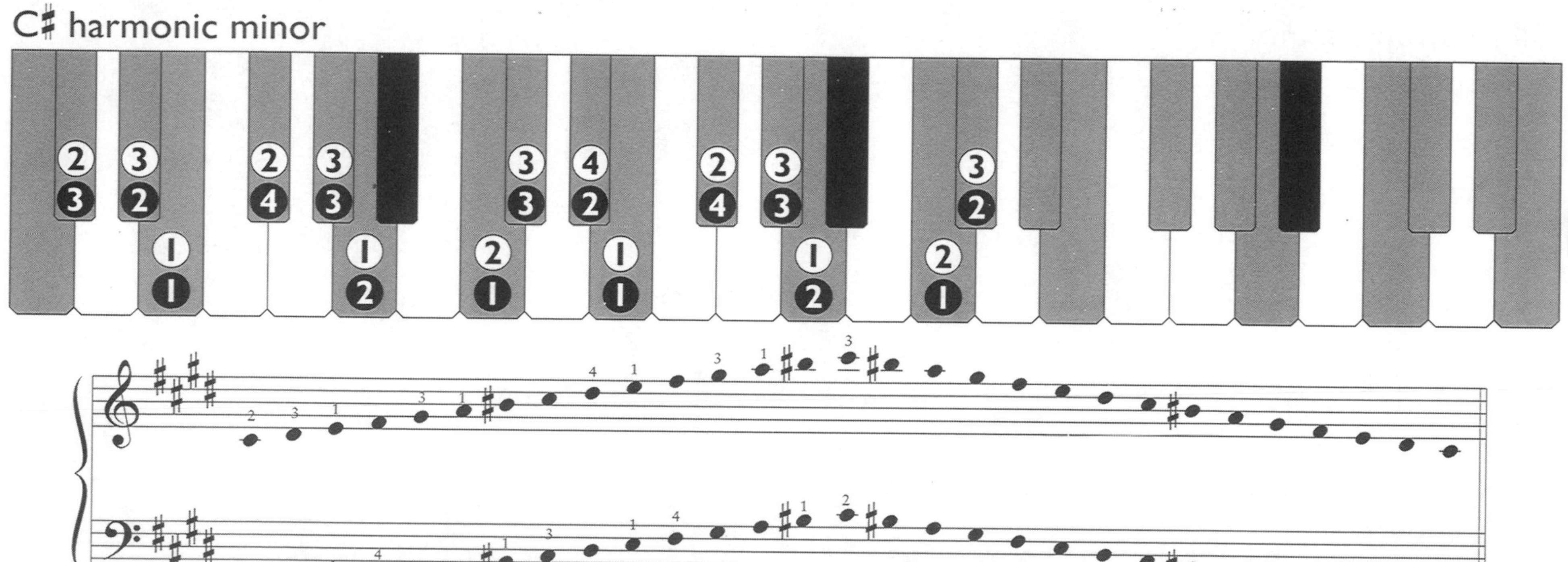

G♯ harmonic minor

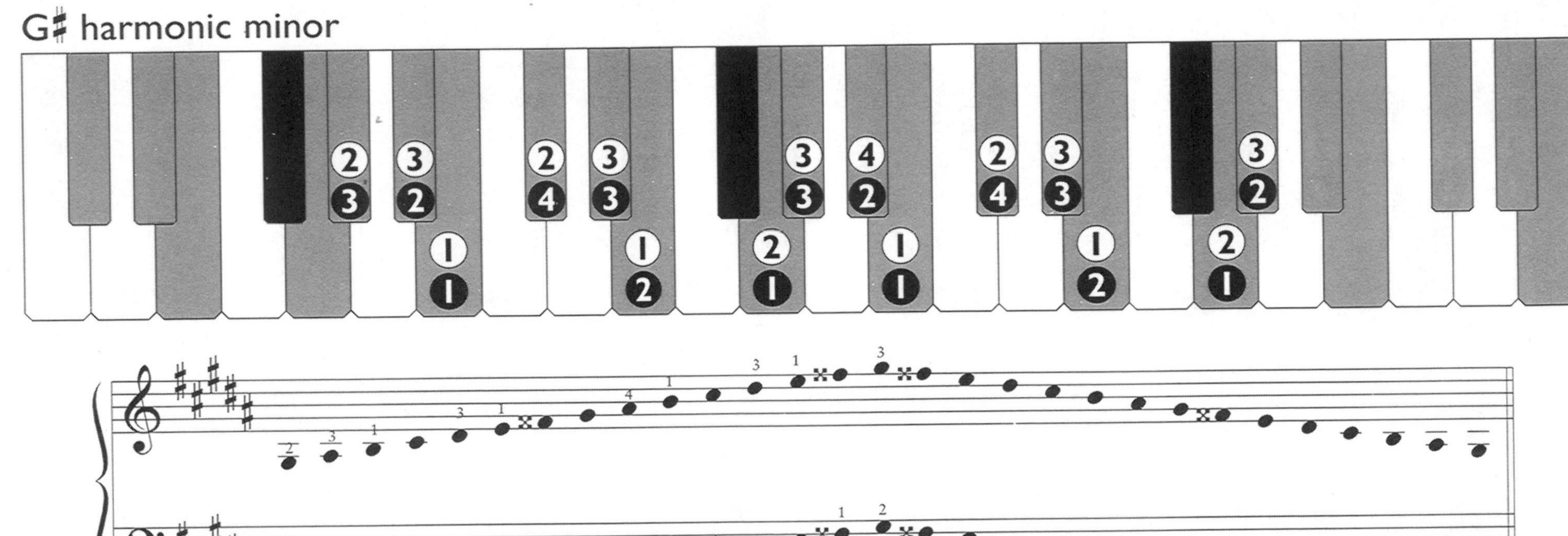

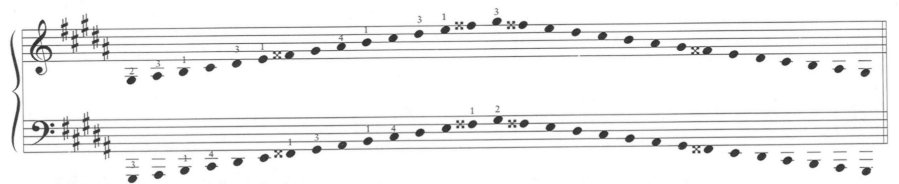

D♯ harmonic minor

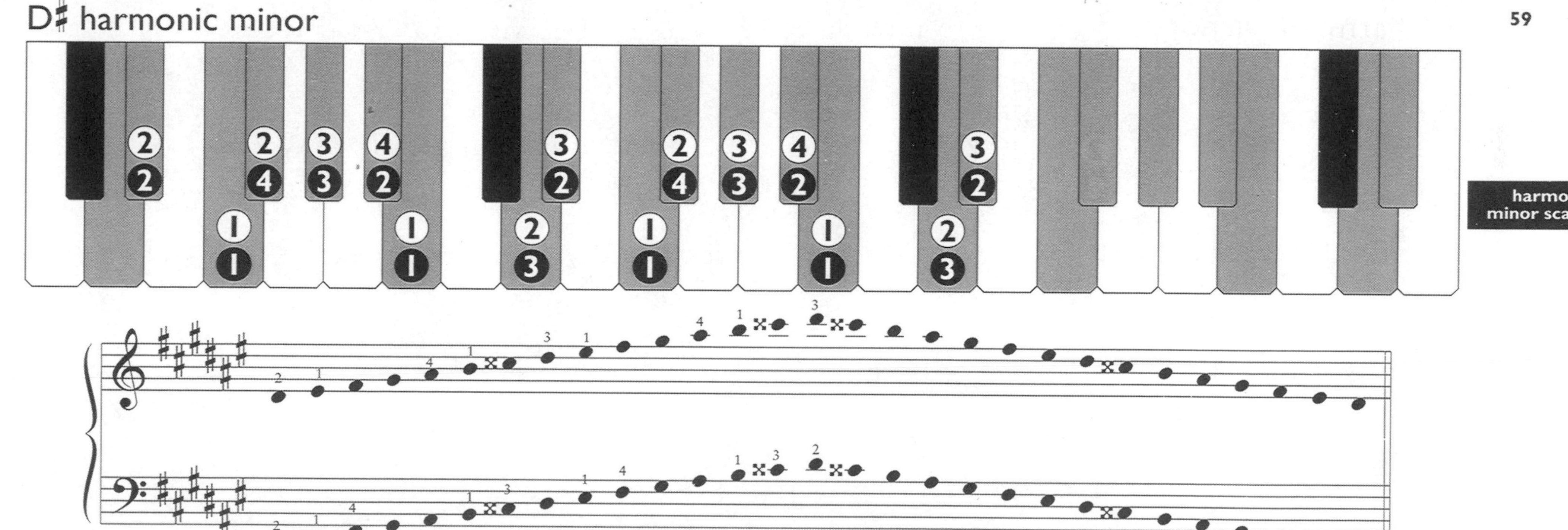

A♯ harmonic minor

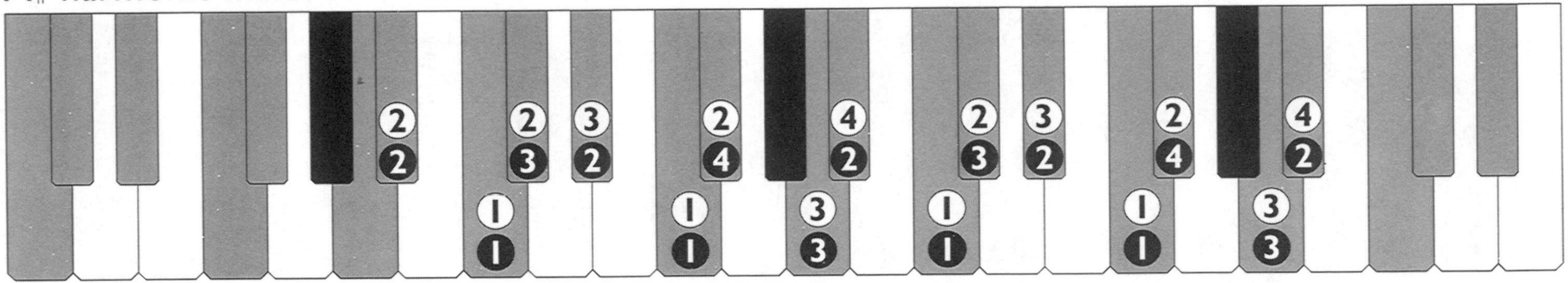

D harmonic minor

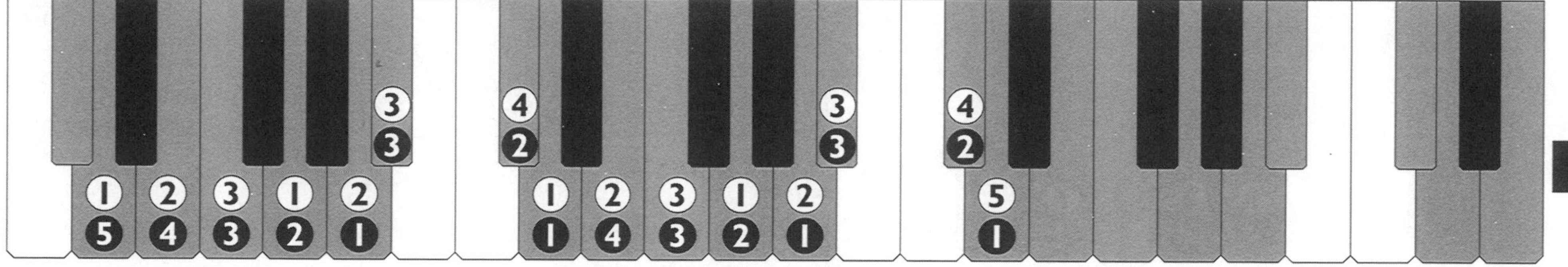

G harmonic minor

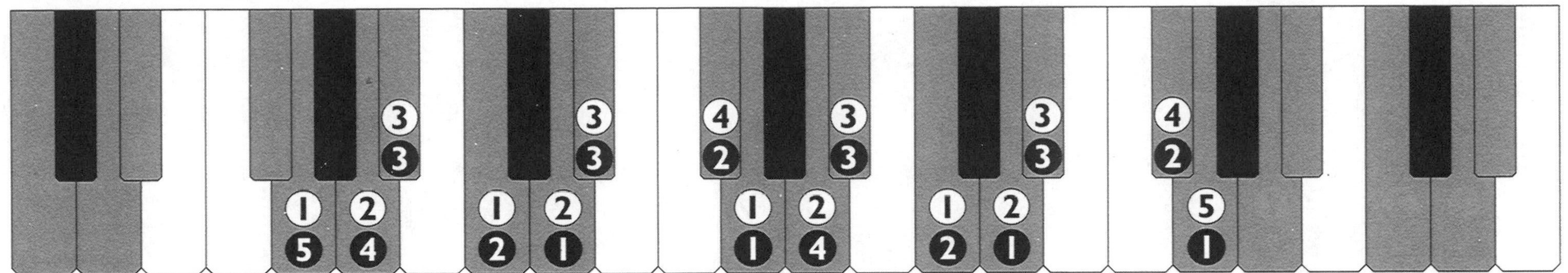

C harmonic minor

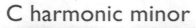

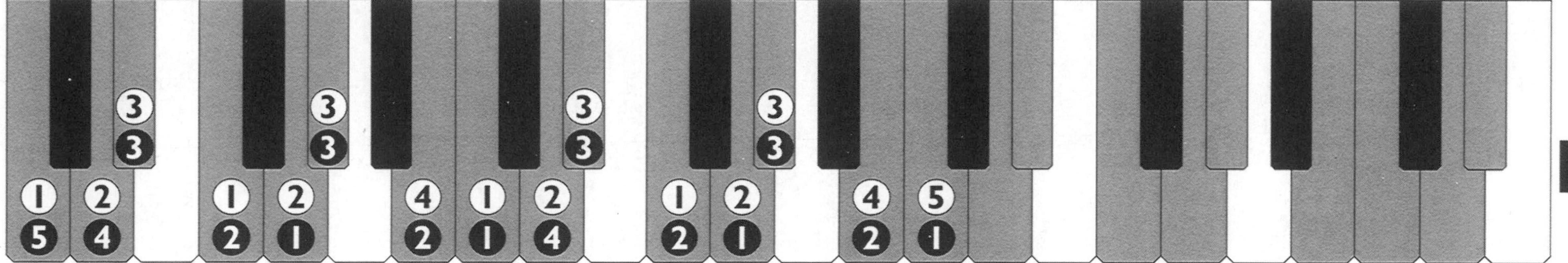

F harmonic minor

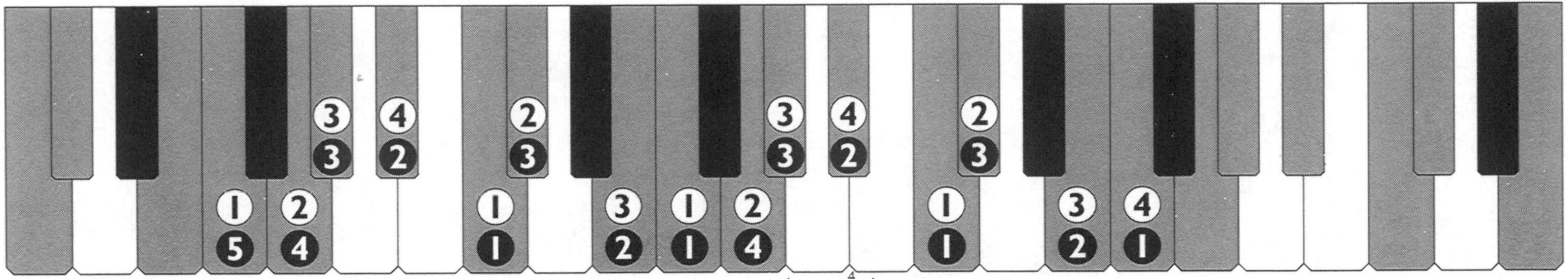

B♭ harmonic minor

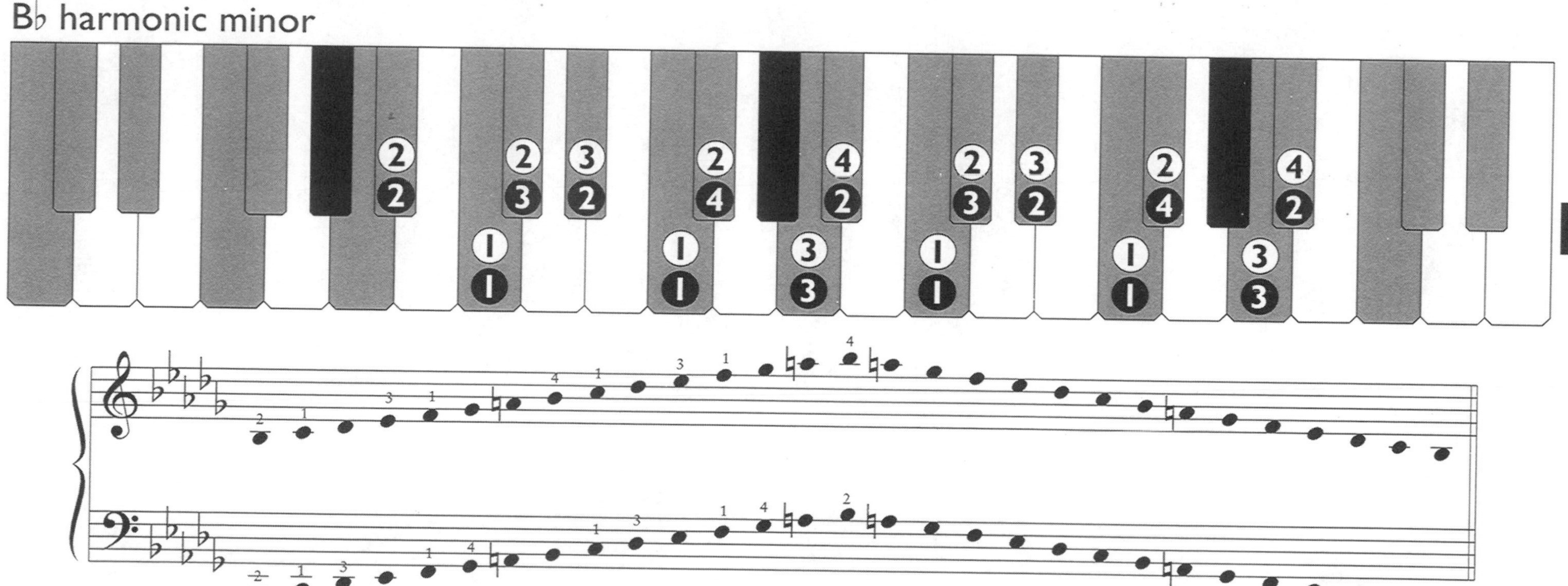

E♭ harmonic minor

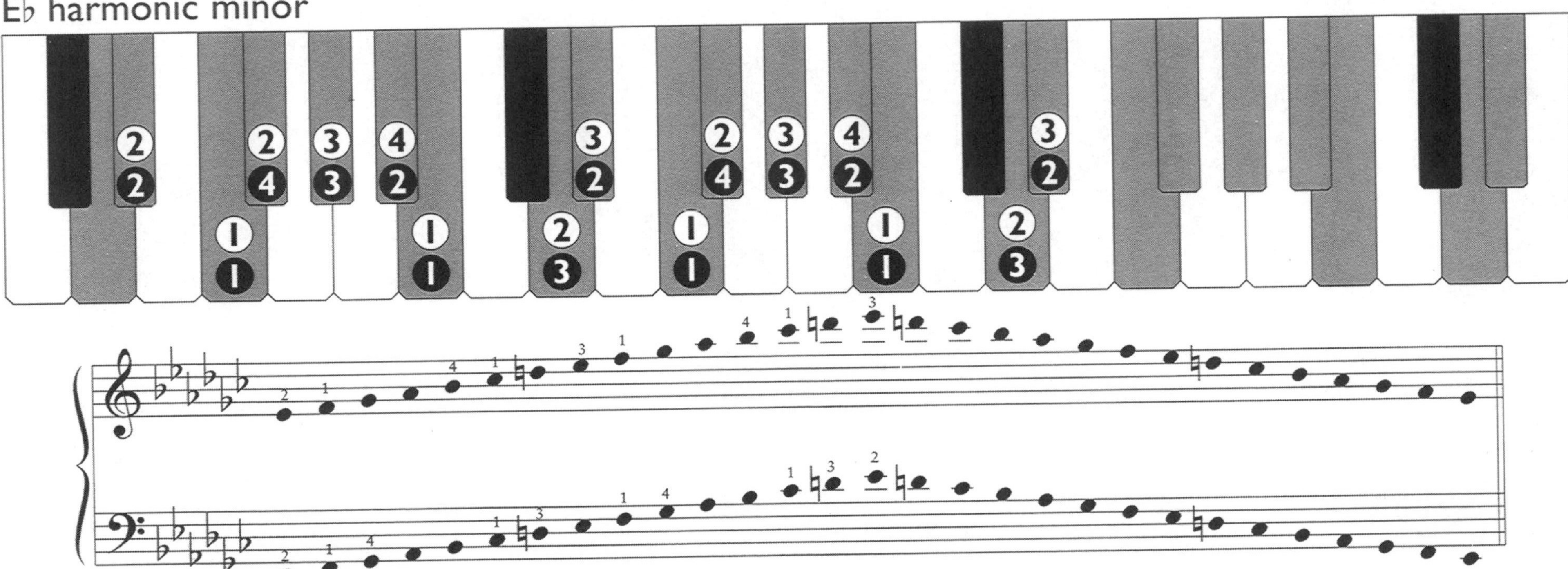

A♭ harmonic minor

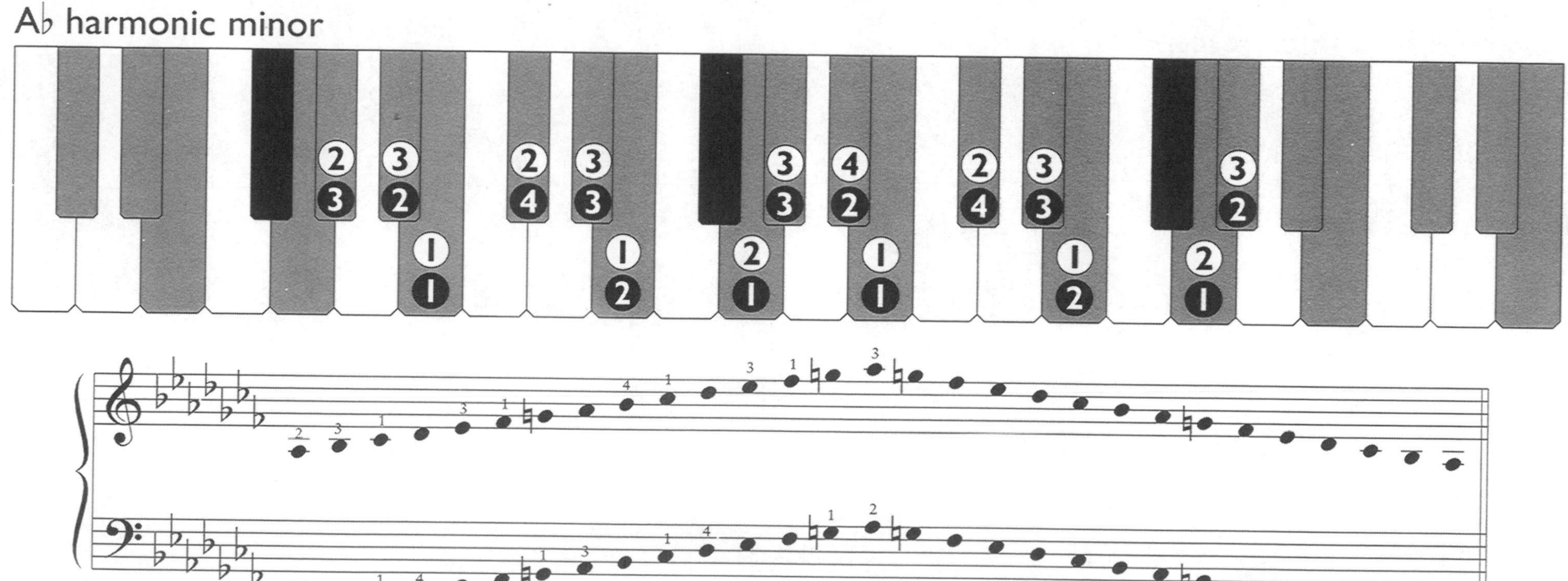

A melodic minor *(ascending)*

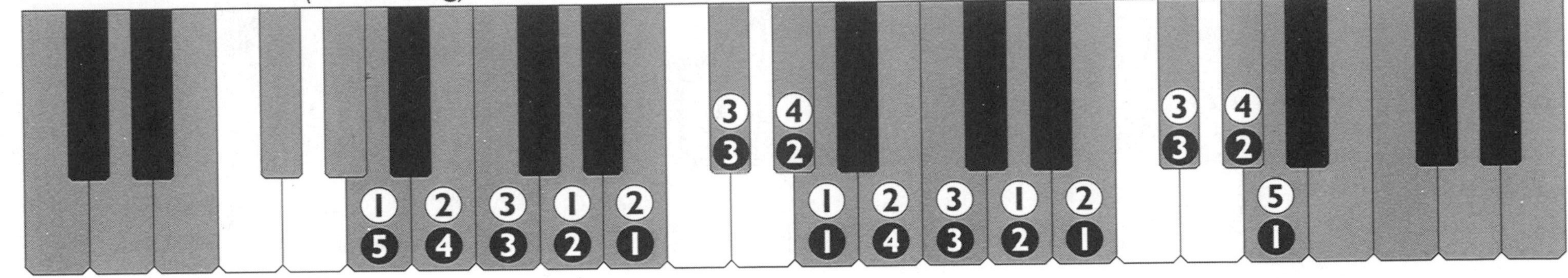

A melodic minor *(descending)*

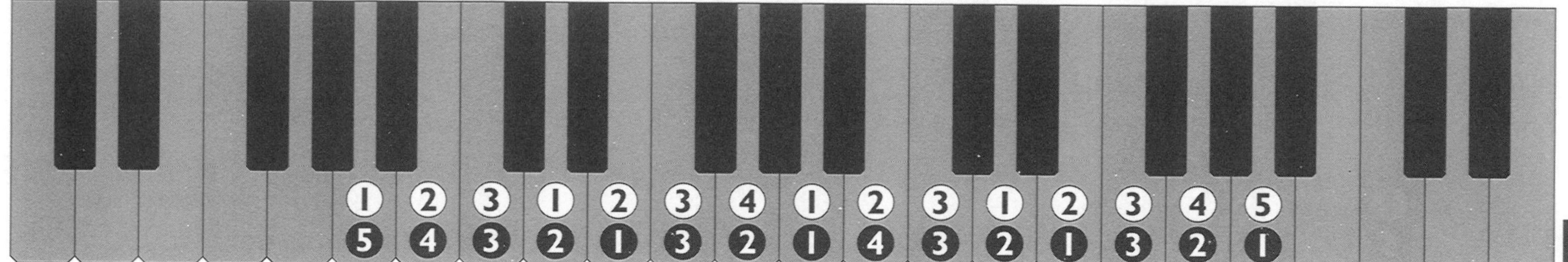

E melodic minor *(ascending)*

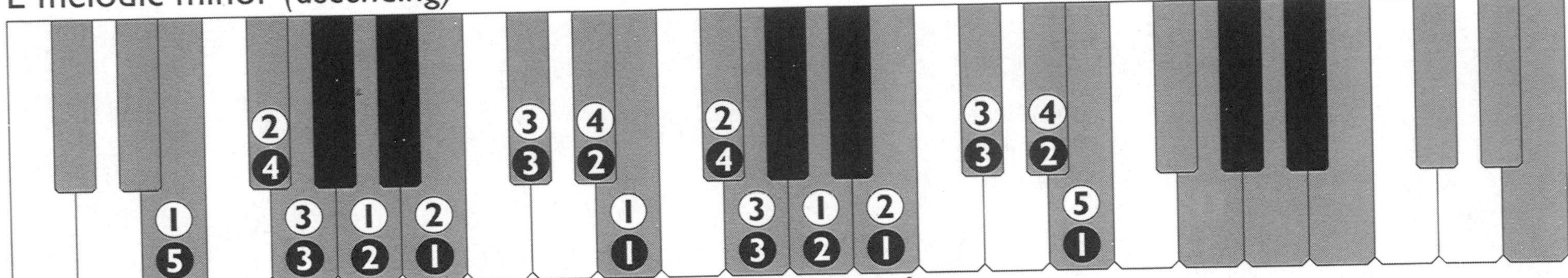

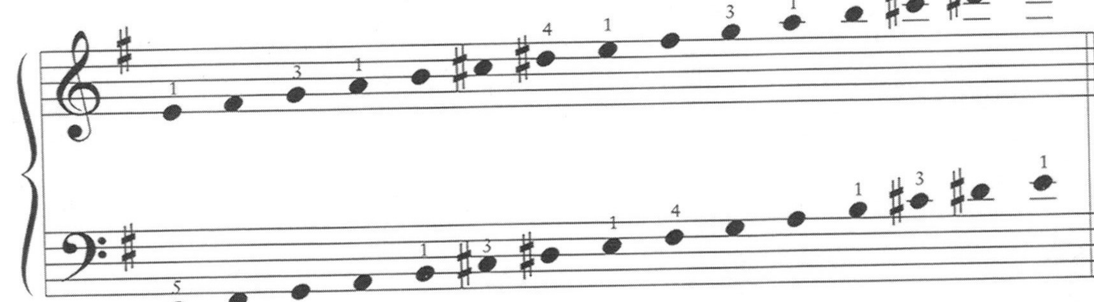

E melodic minor *(descending)*

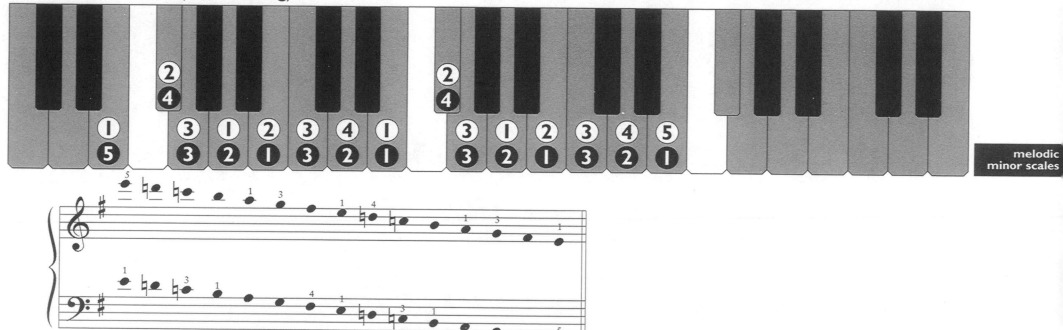

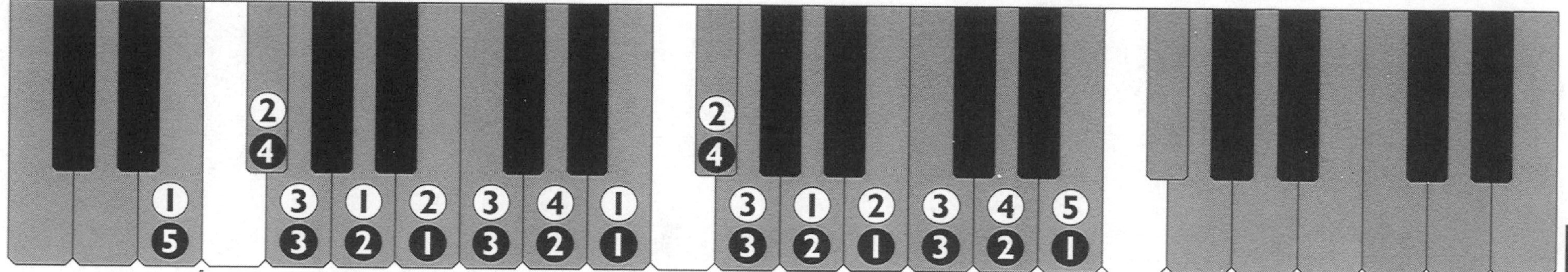

B melodic minor *(ascending)*

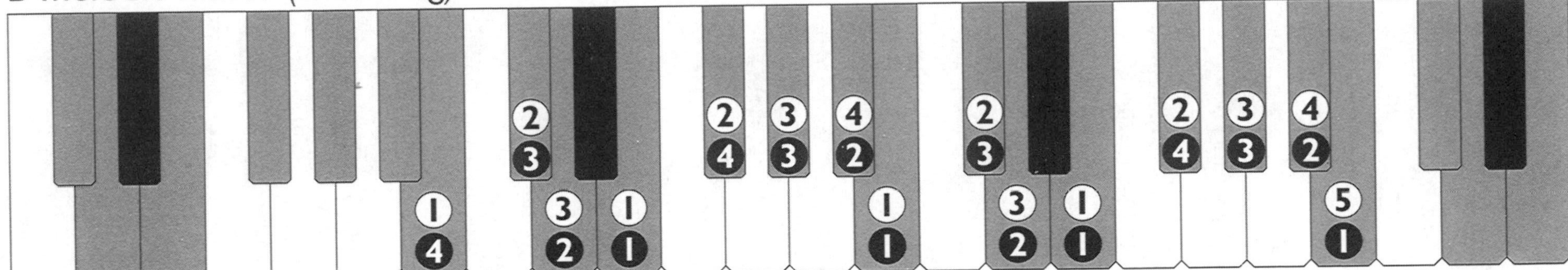

B melodic minor *(descending)*

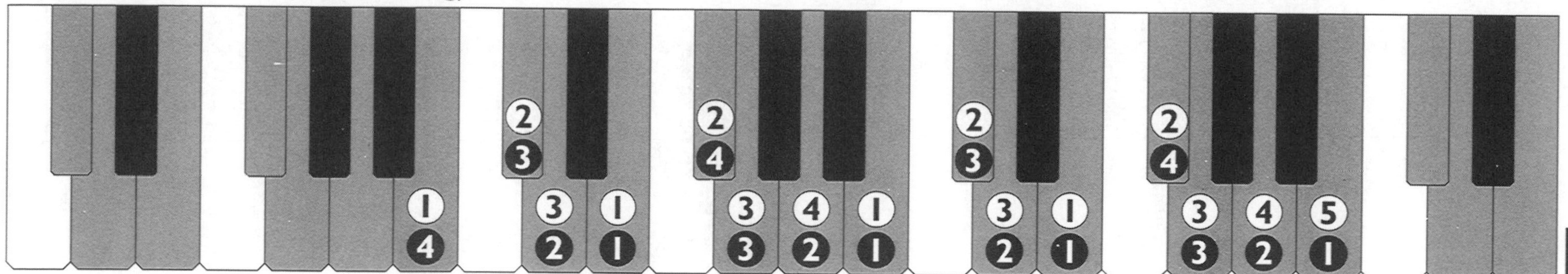

F♯ melodic minor *(ascending)*

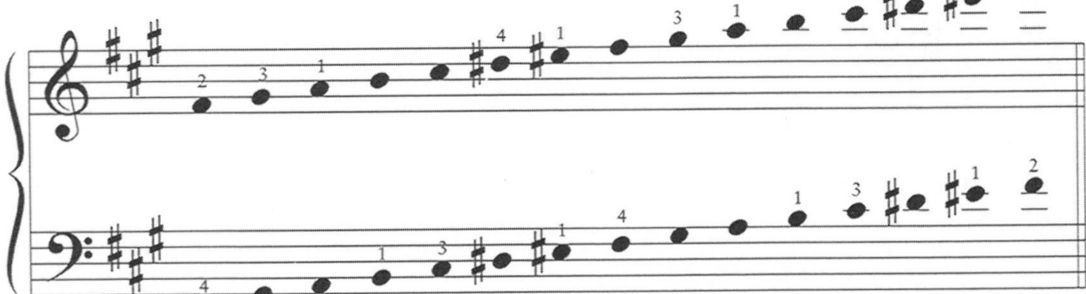

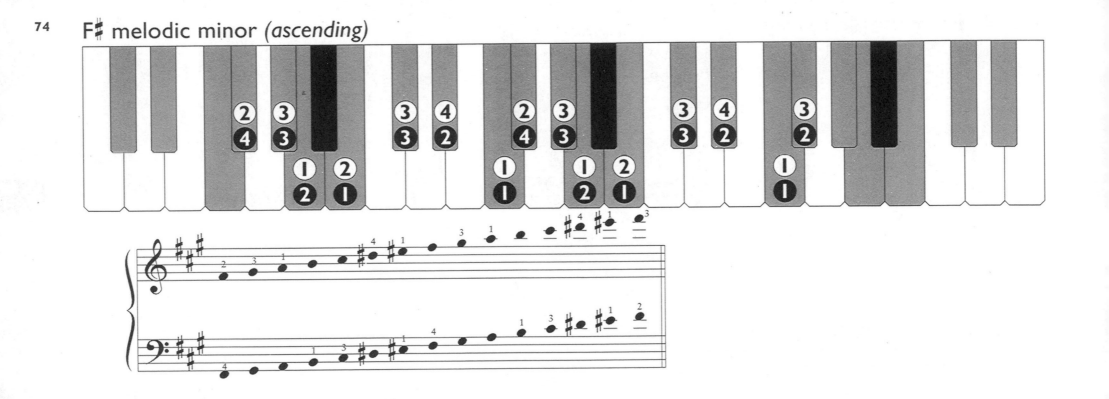

F♯ melodic minor *(descending)*

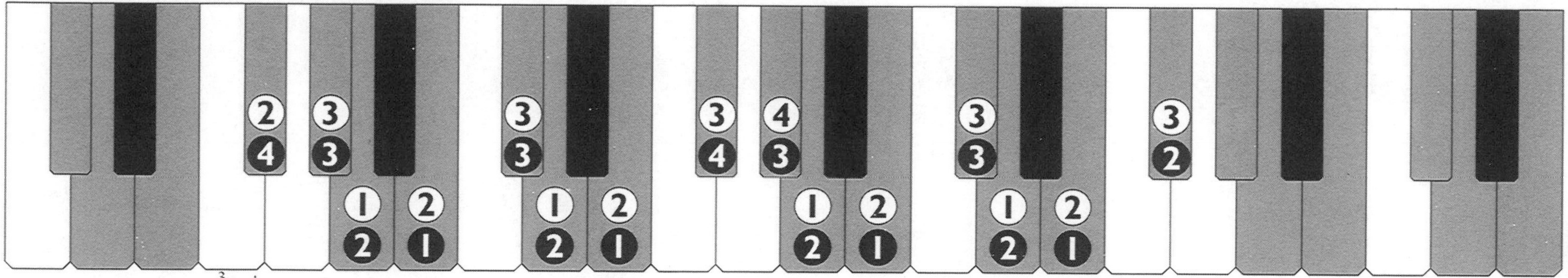

C♯ melodic minor *(ascending)*

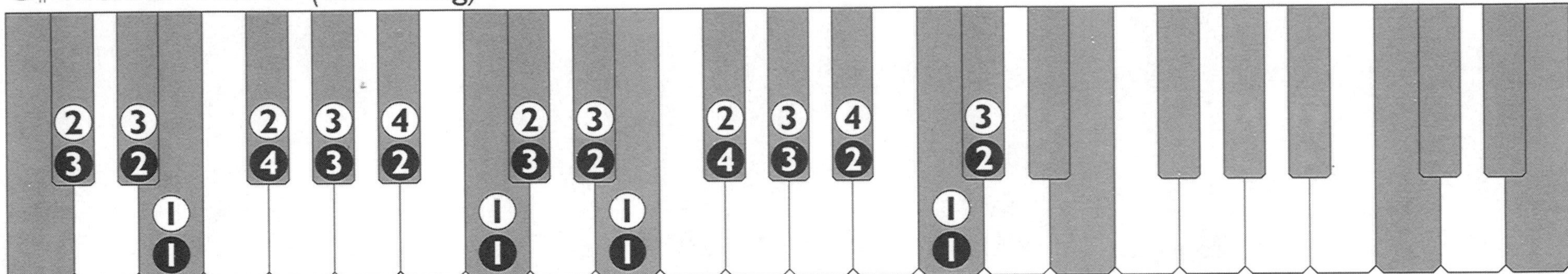

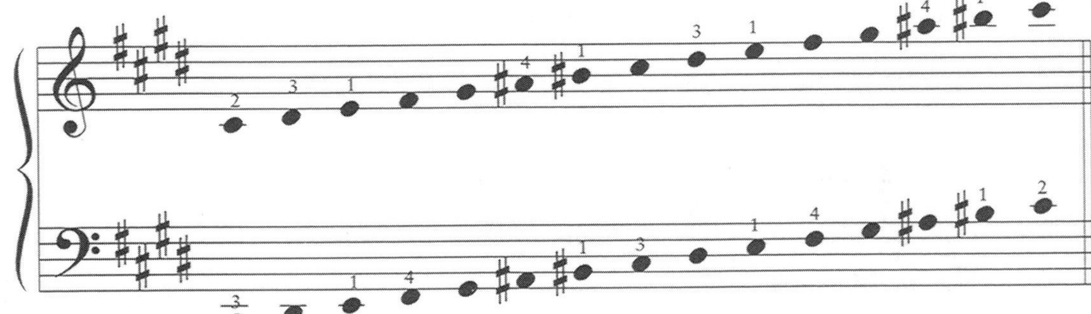

C♯ melodic minor *(descending)*

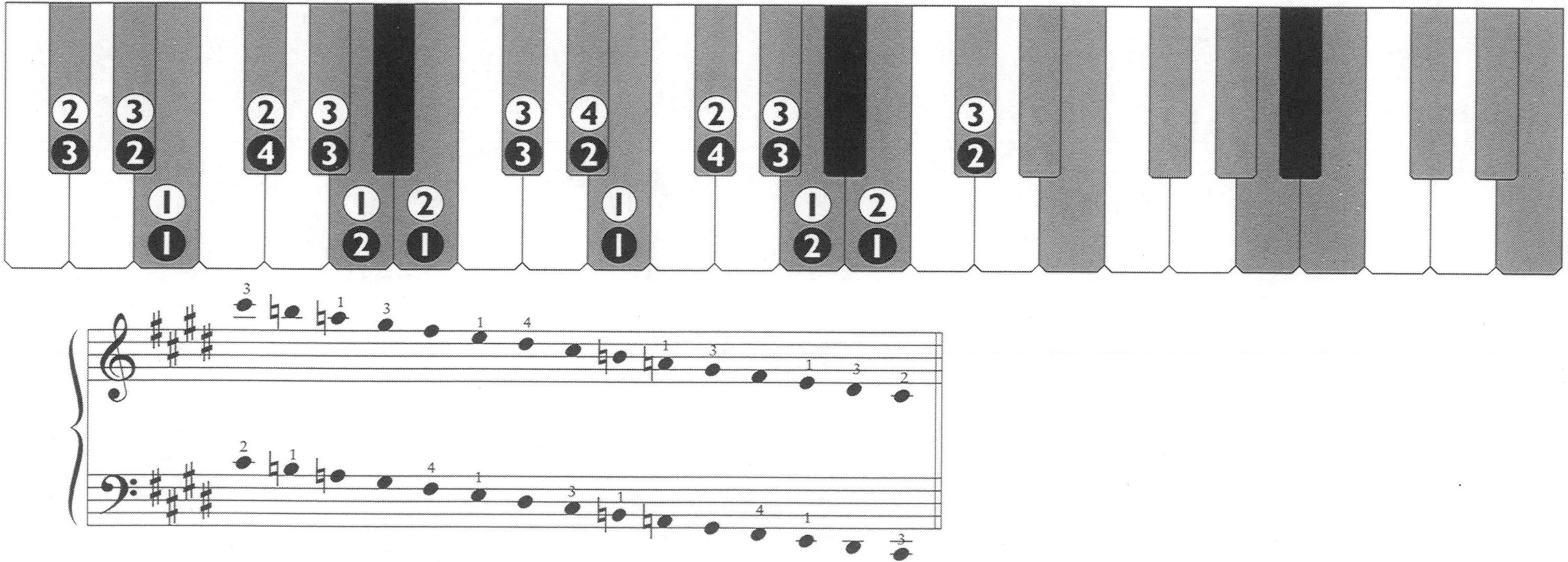

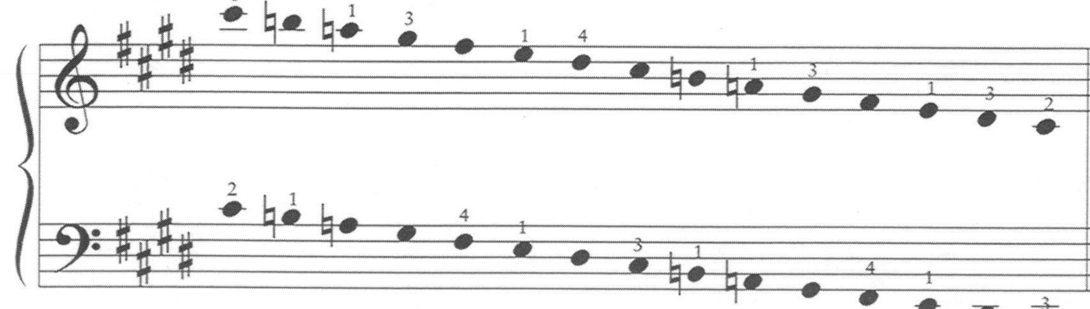

G♯ melodic minor *(ascending)*

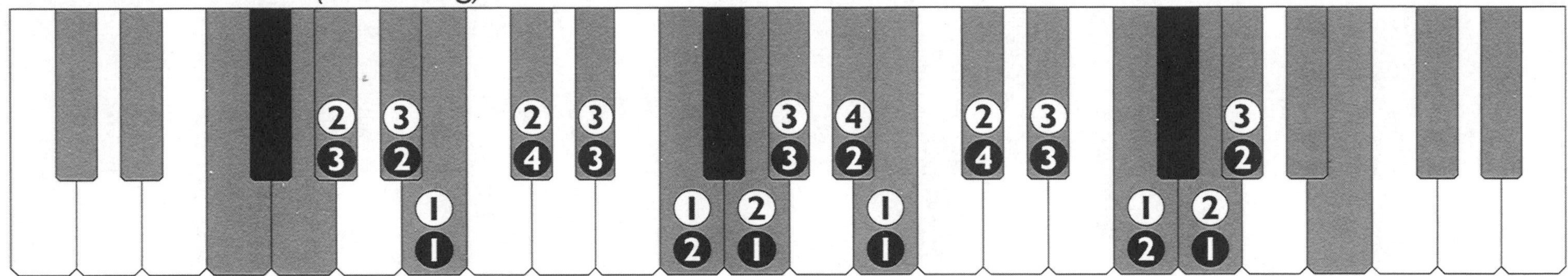

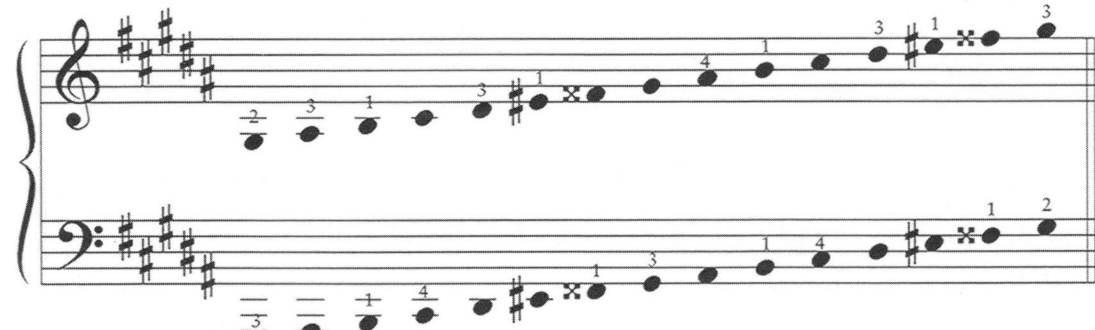

G♯ melodic minor *(descending)*

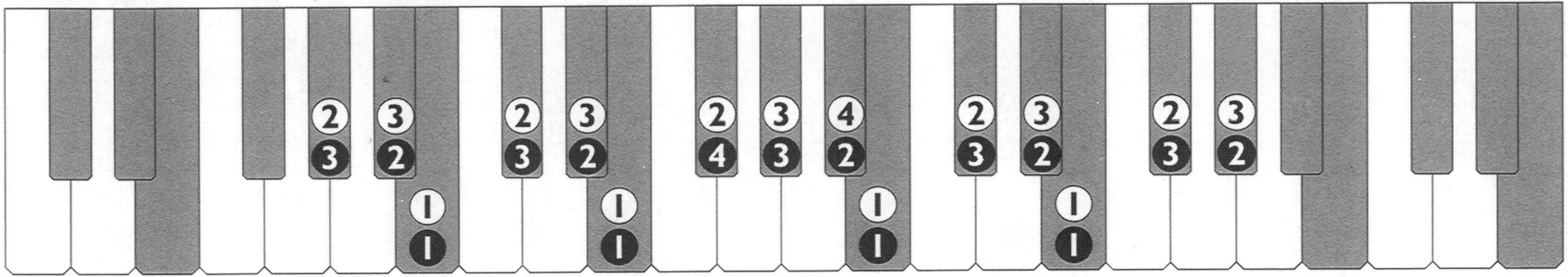

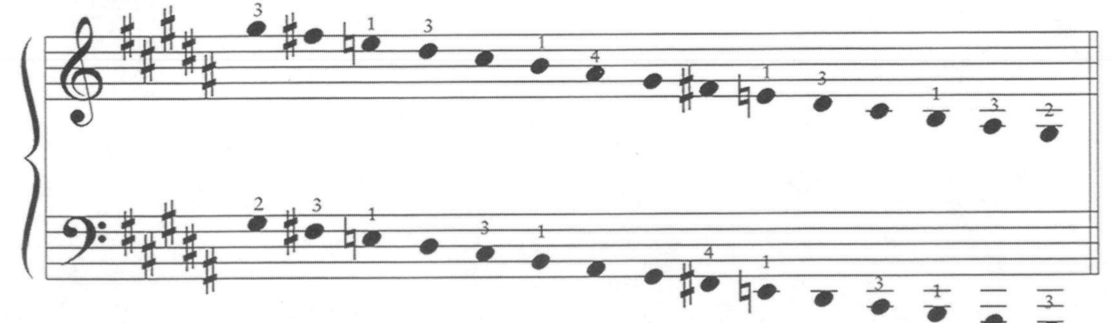

D♯ melodic minor *(ascending)*

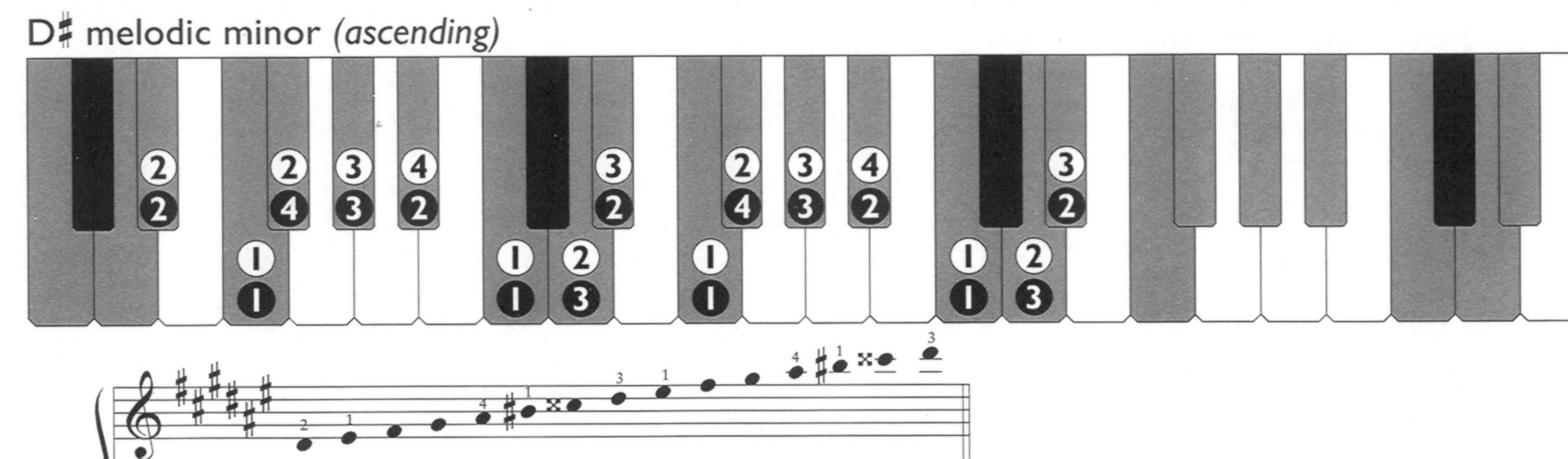

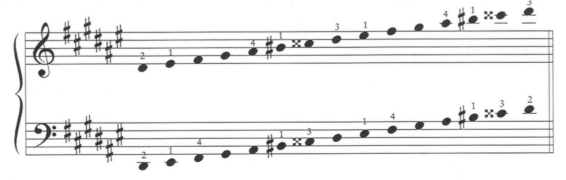

D♯ melodic minor *(descending)*

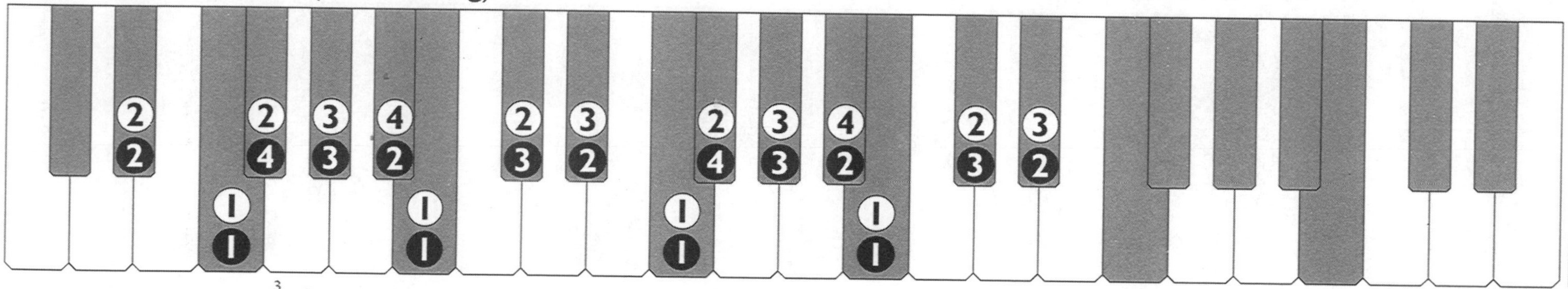

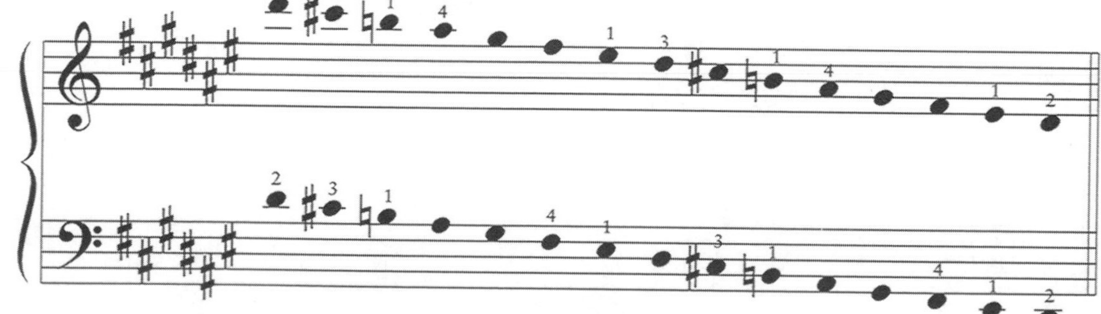

A♯ melodic minor *(ascending)*

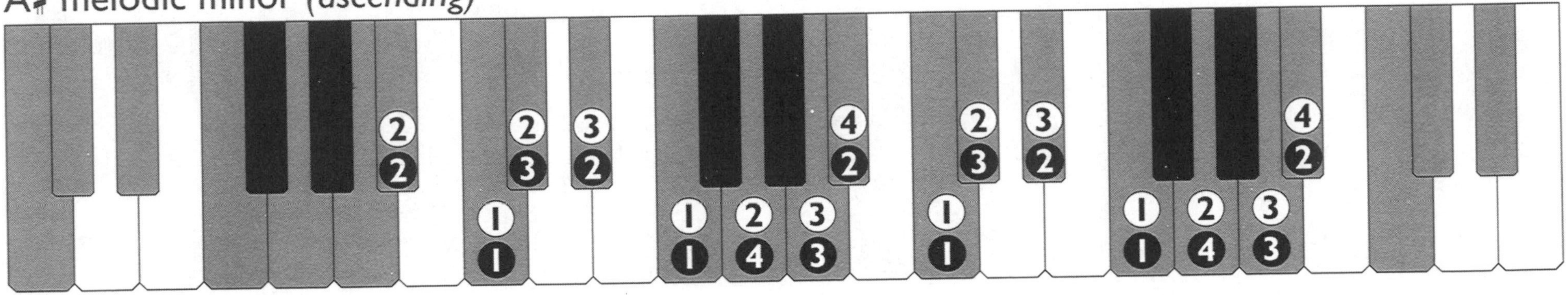

A♯ melodic minor *(descending)*

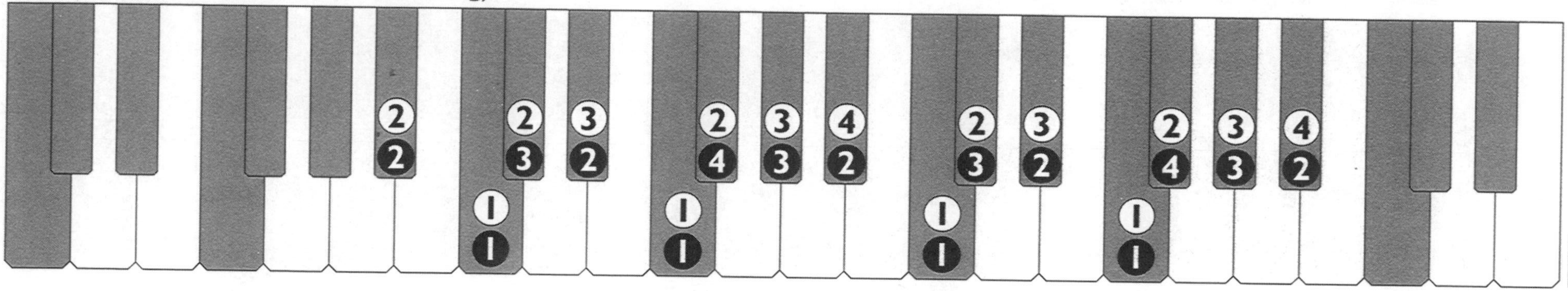

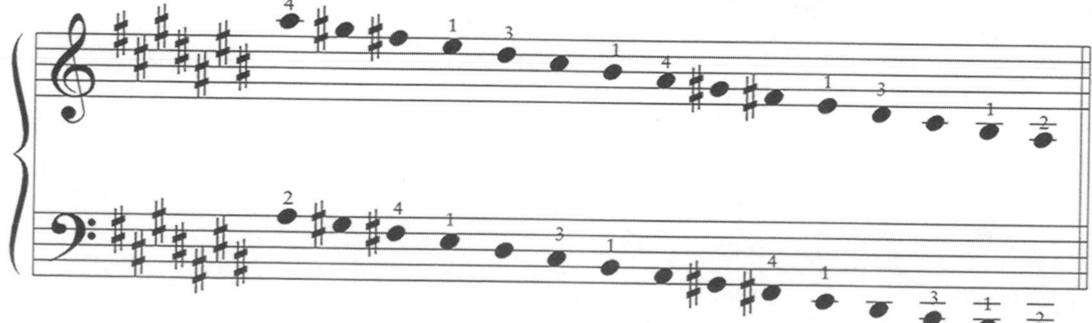

D melodic minor *(ascending)*

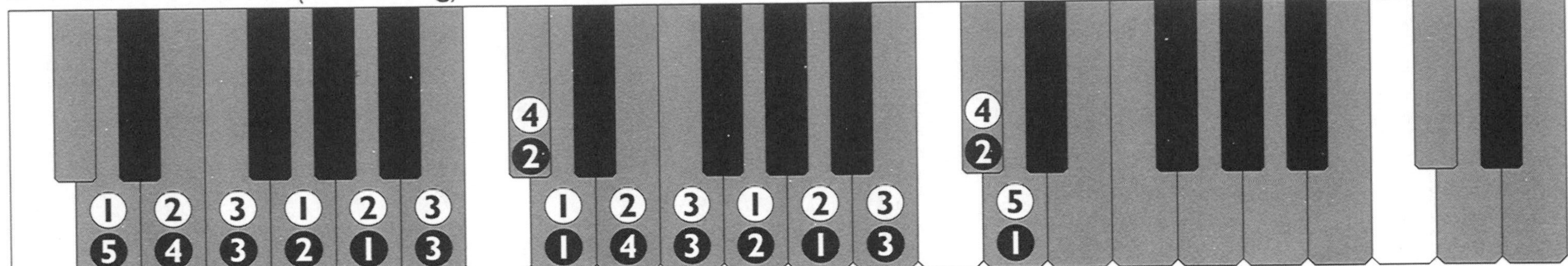

D melodic minor *(descending)*

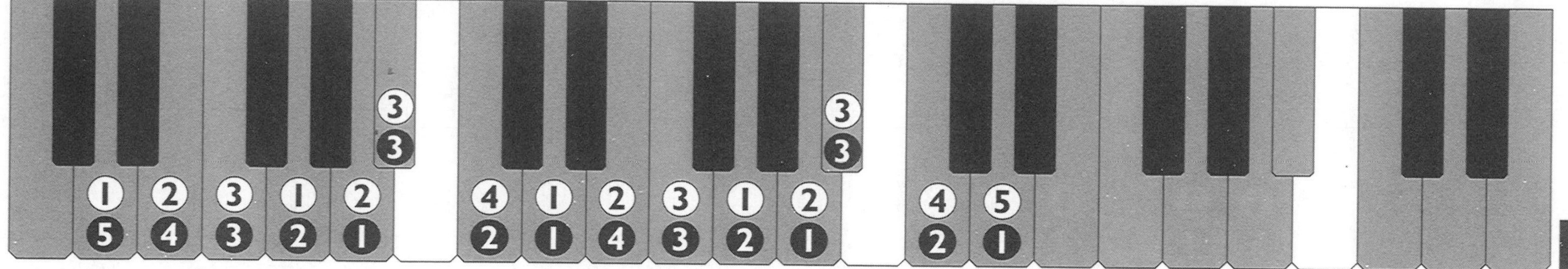

G melodic minor *(ascending)*

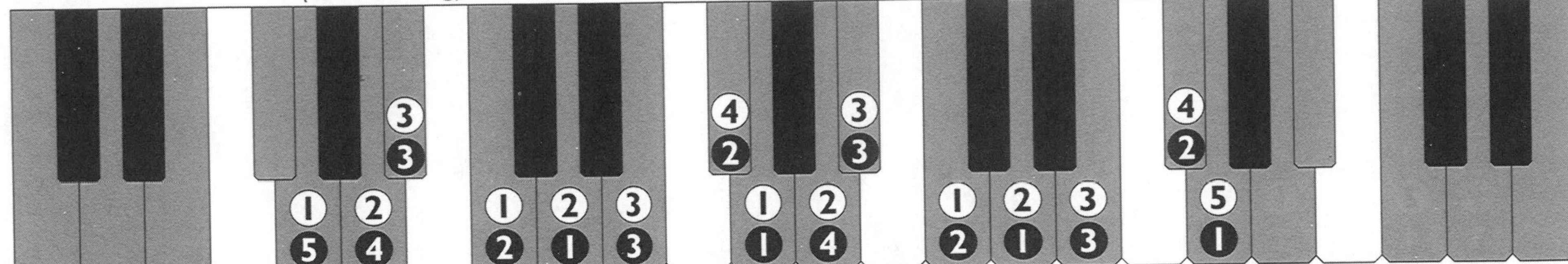

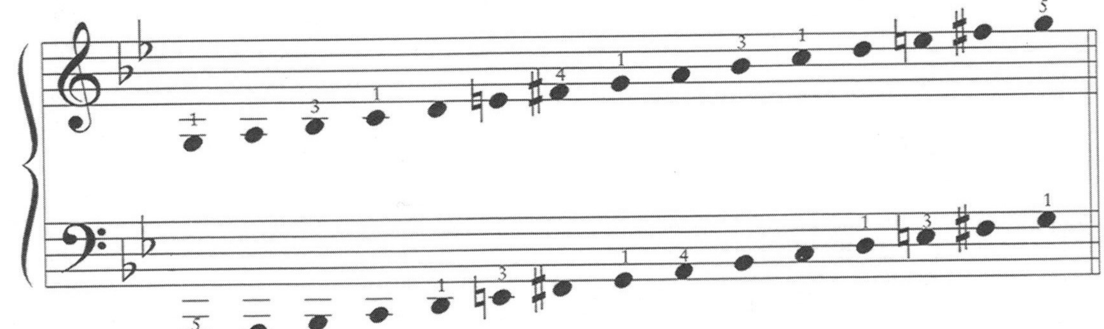

G melodic minor *(descending)*

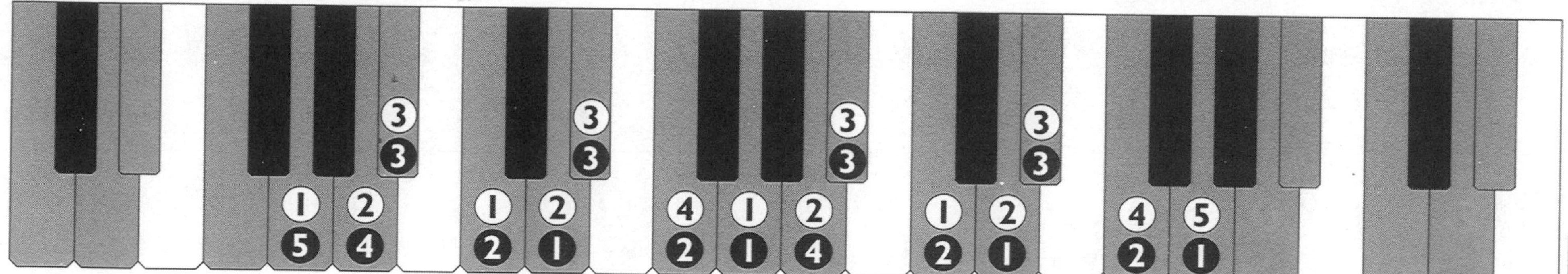

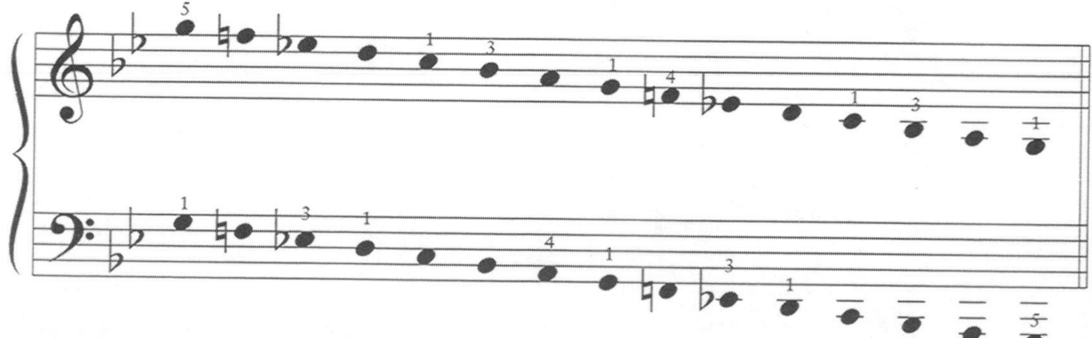

C melodic minor *(ascending)*

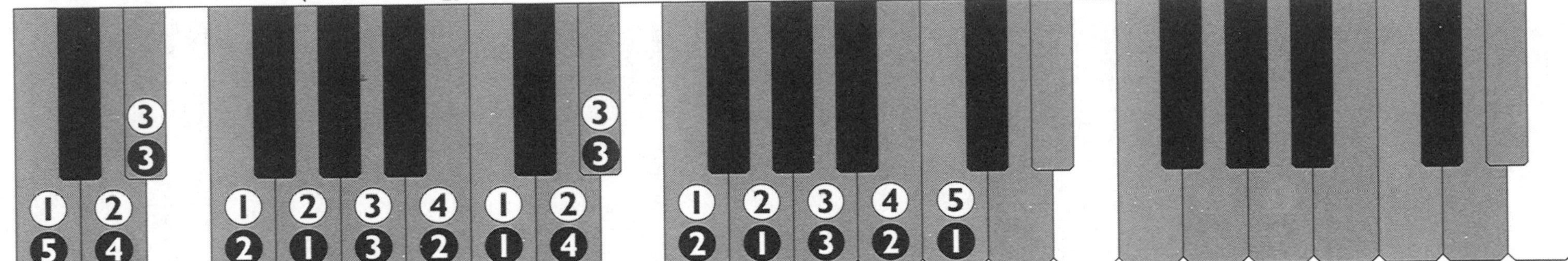

C melodic minor *(descending)*

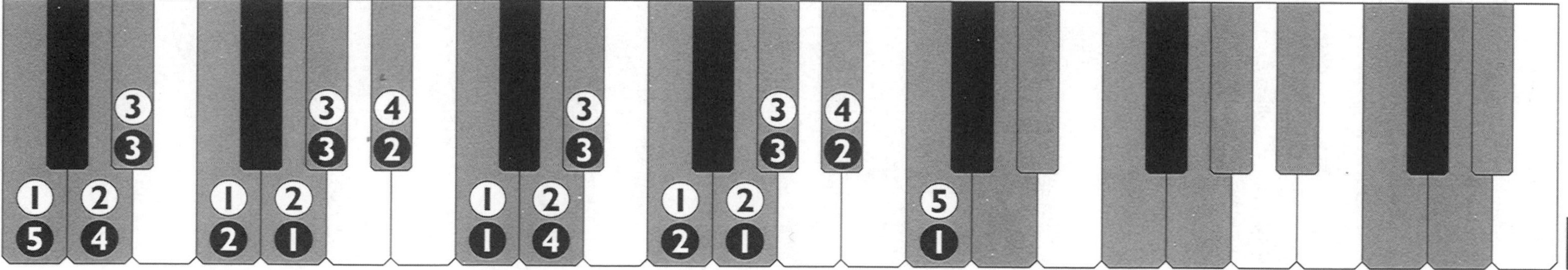

F melodic minor *(ascending)*

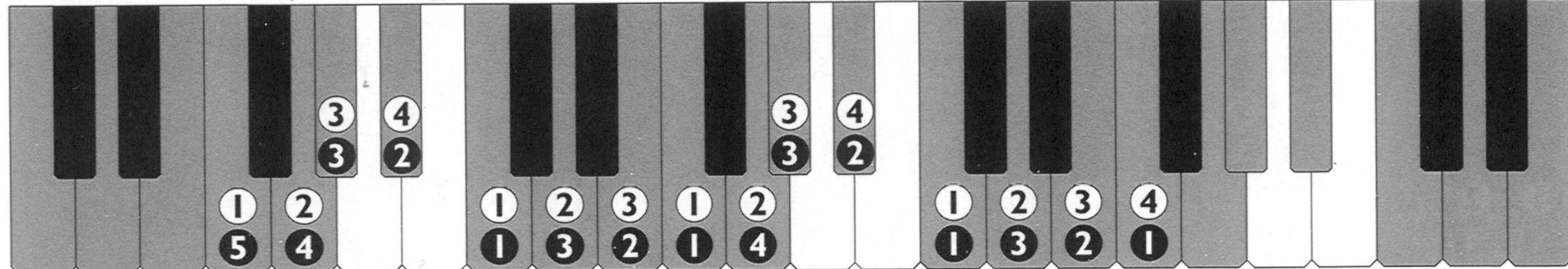

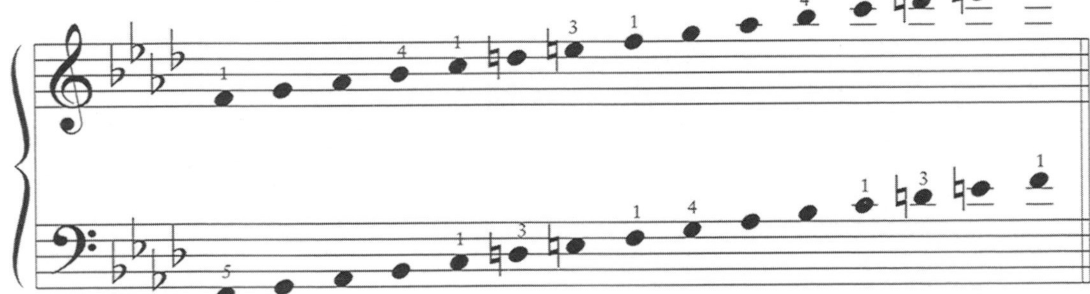

F melodic minor *(descending)*

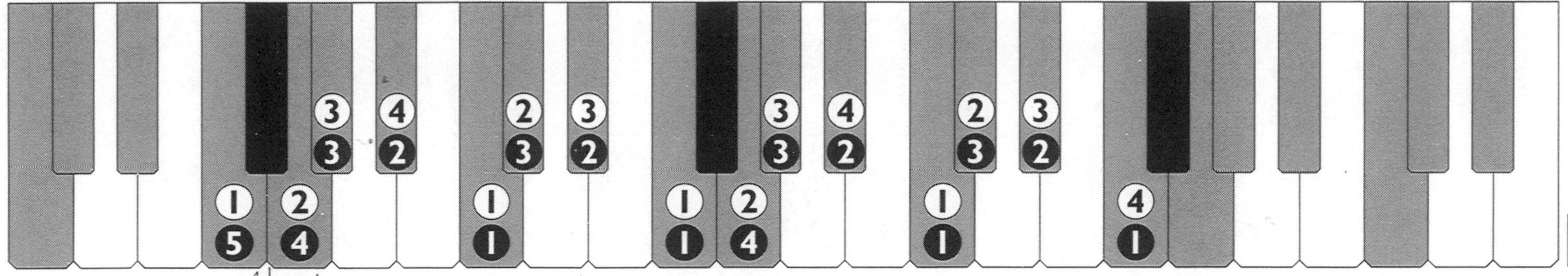

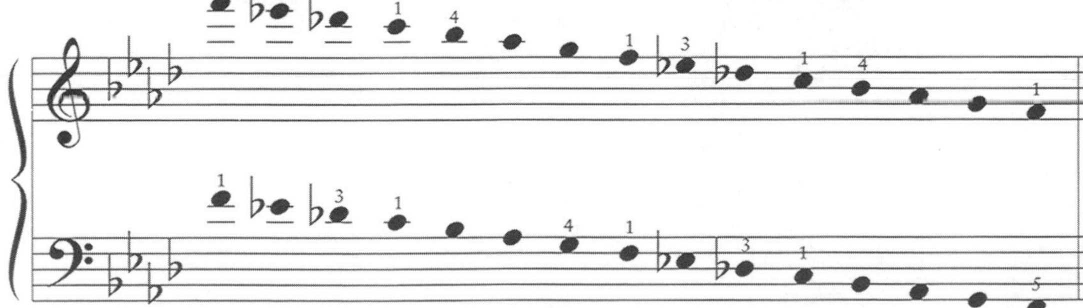

B♭ melodic minor *(ascending)*

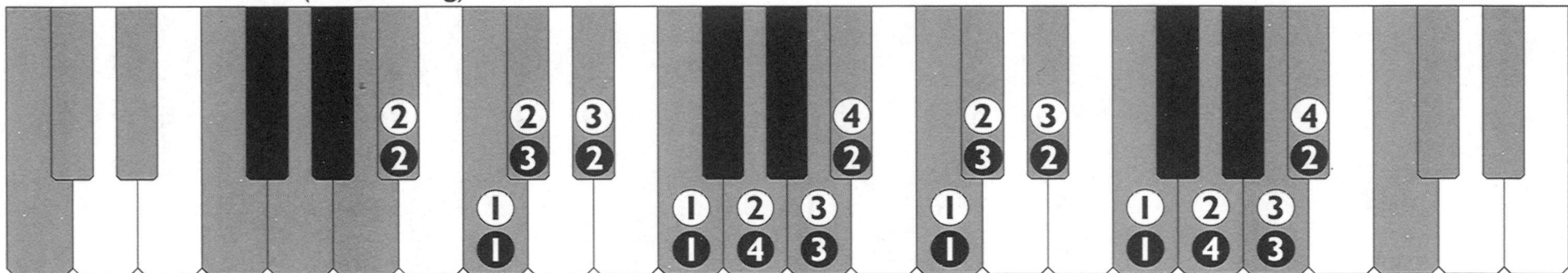

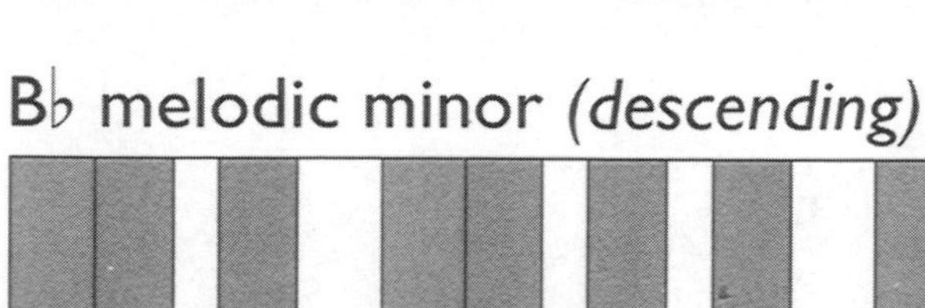

B♭ melodic minor *(descending)*

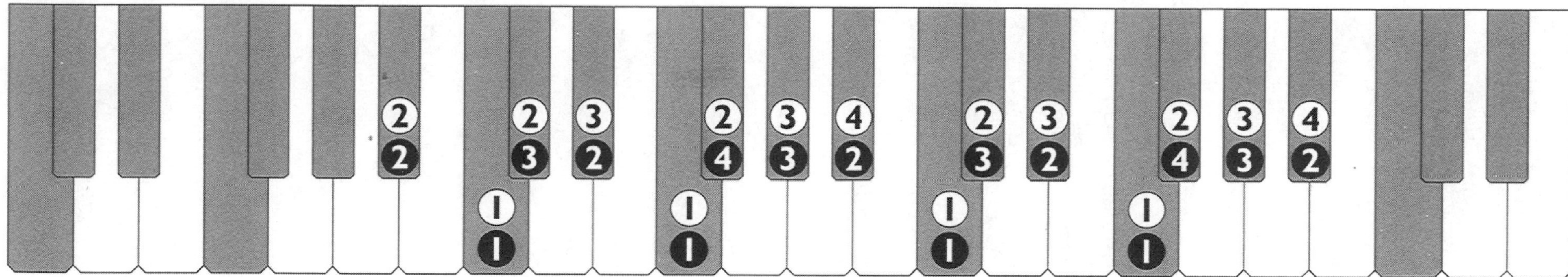

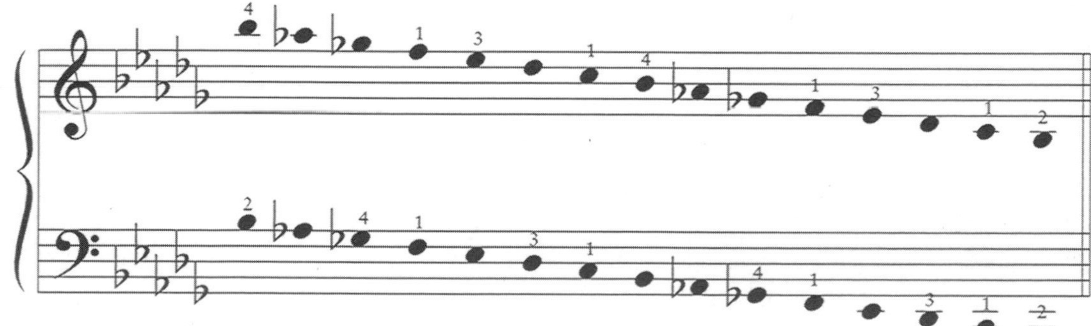

E♭ melodic minor *(ascending)*

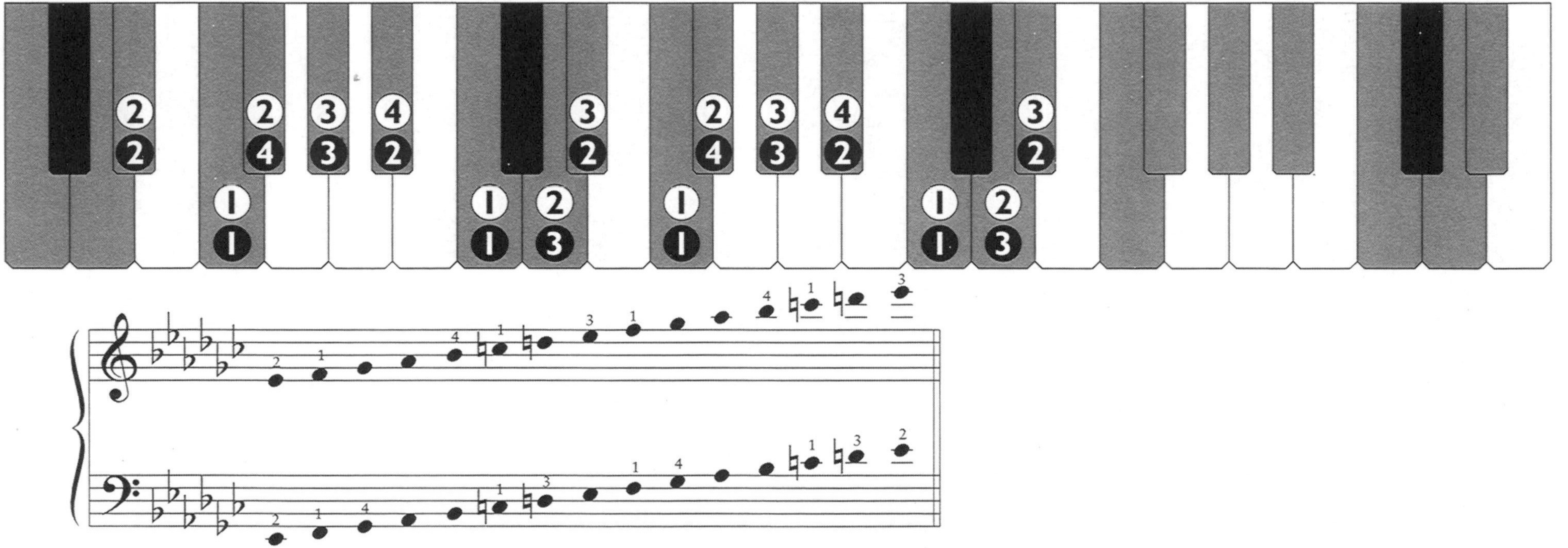

E♭ melodic minor *(descending)*

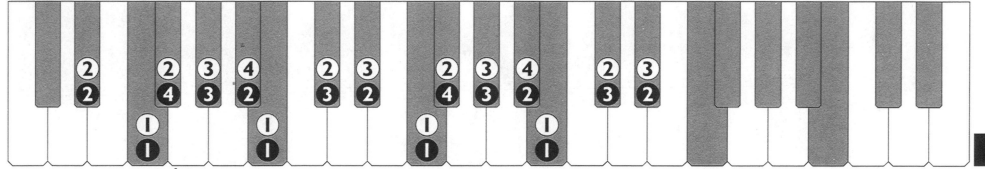

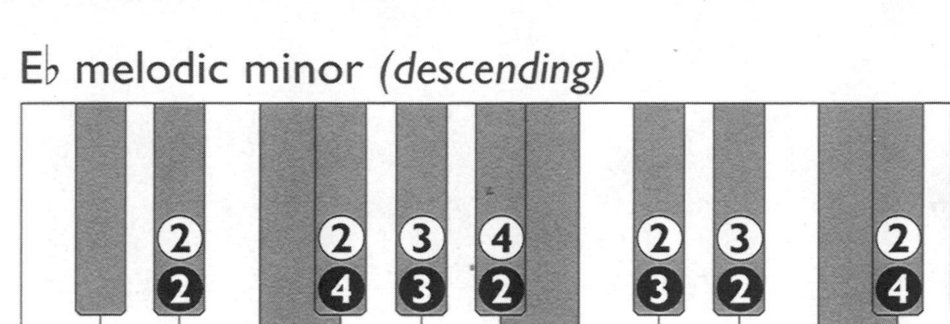

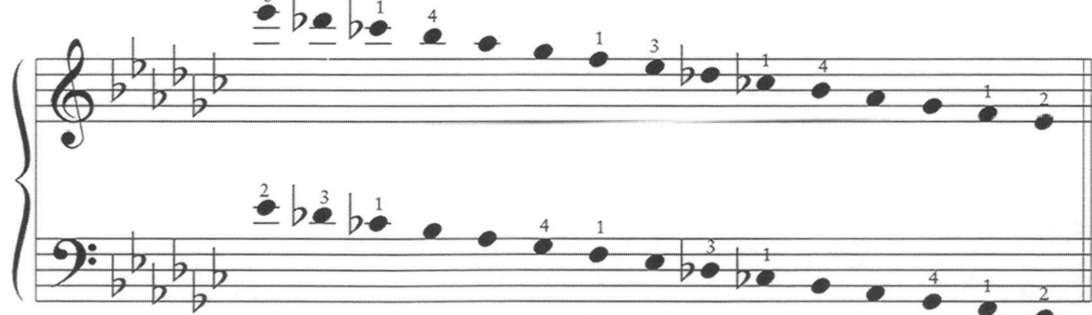

A♭ melodic minor *(ascending)*

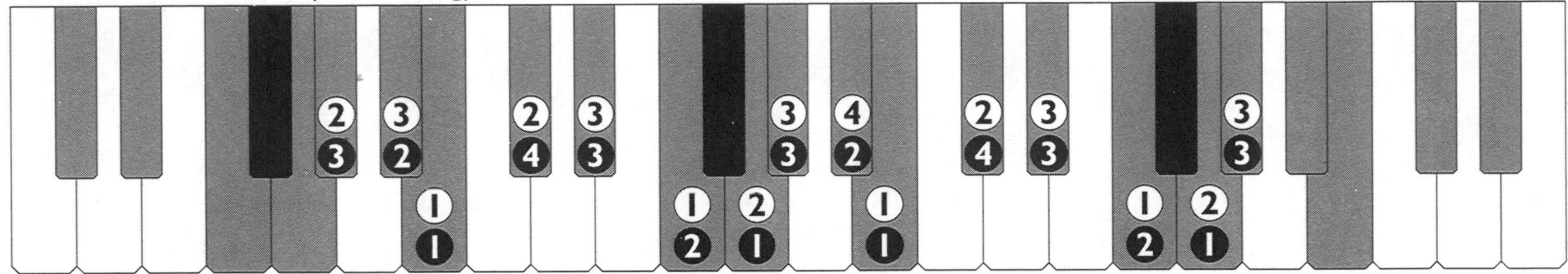

A♭ melodic minor *(descending)*

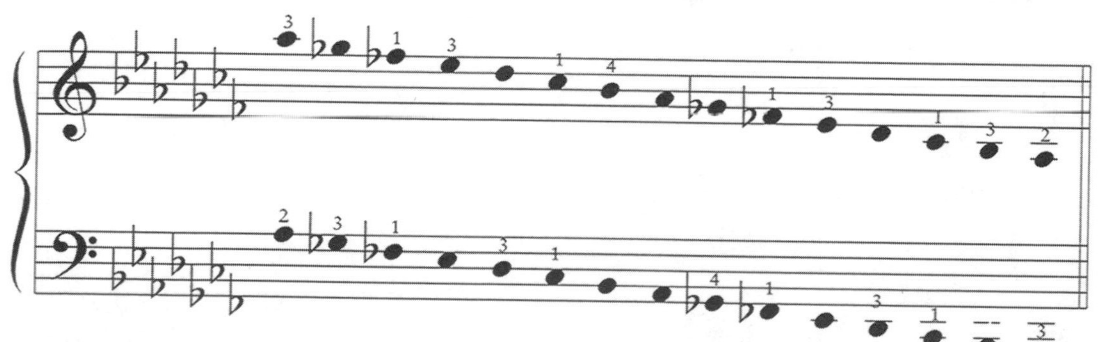

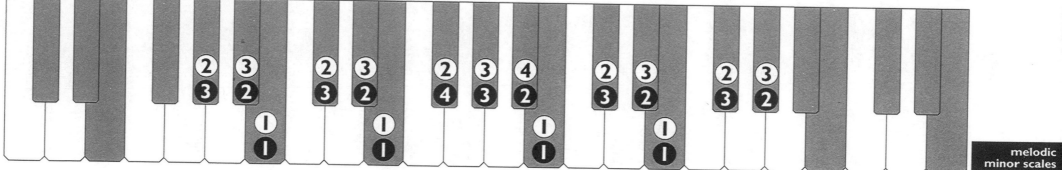

A jazz melodic minor

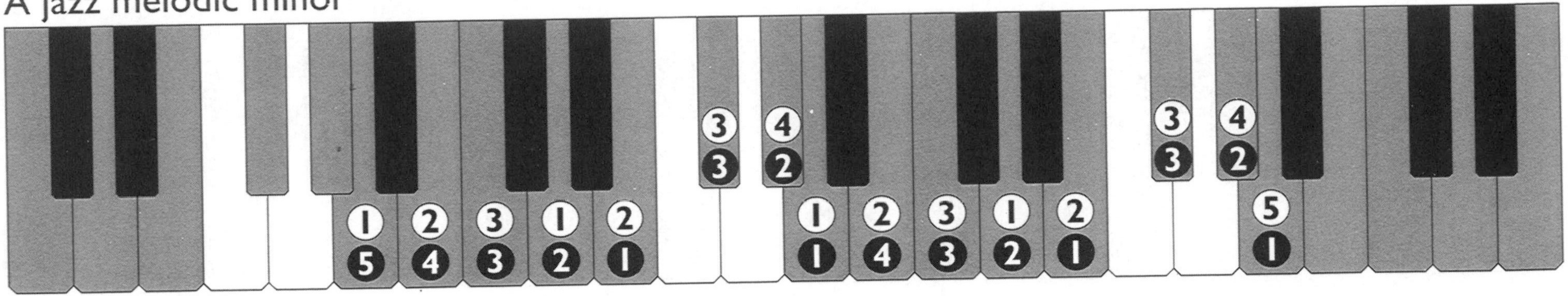

E jazz melodic minor

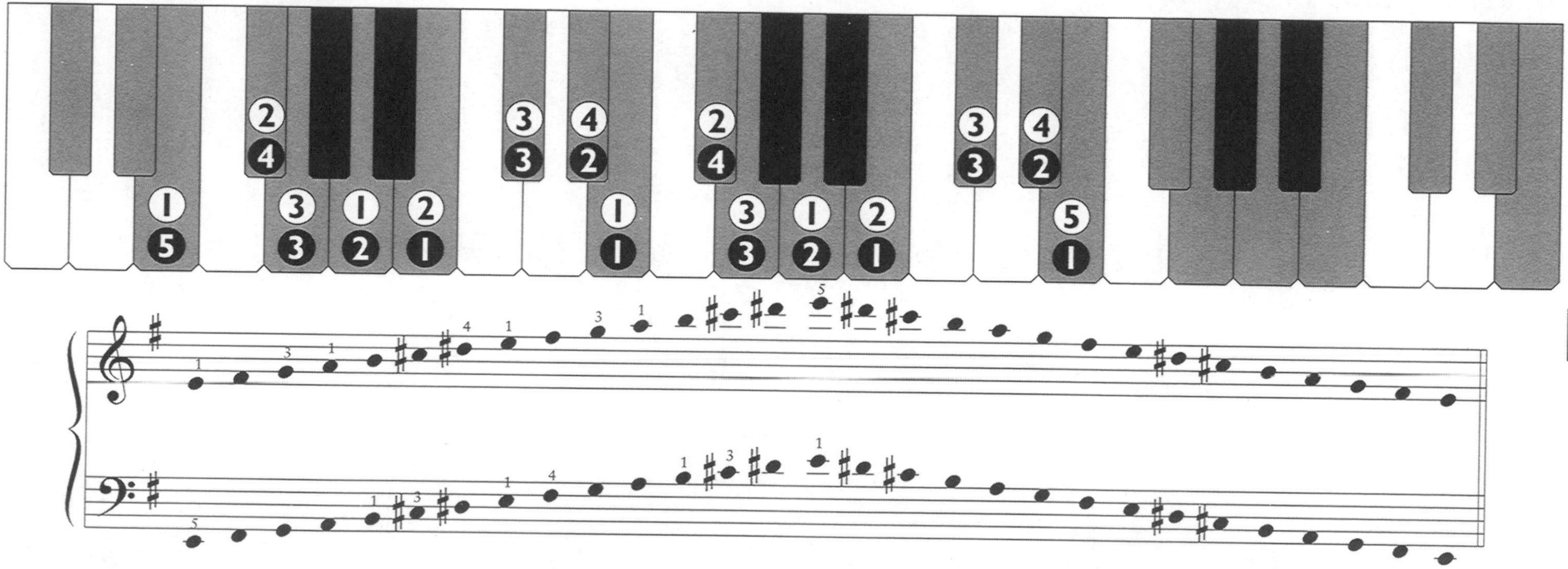

B jazz melodic minor

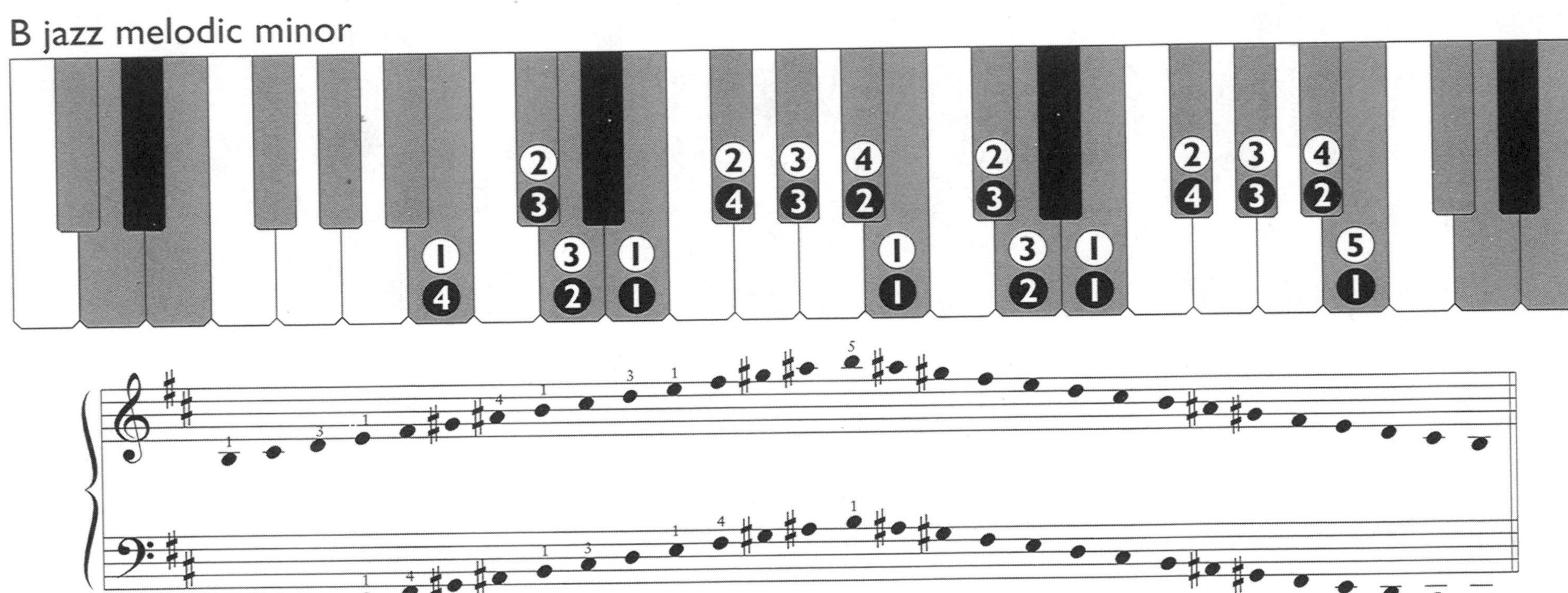

F♯ jazz melodic minor

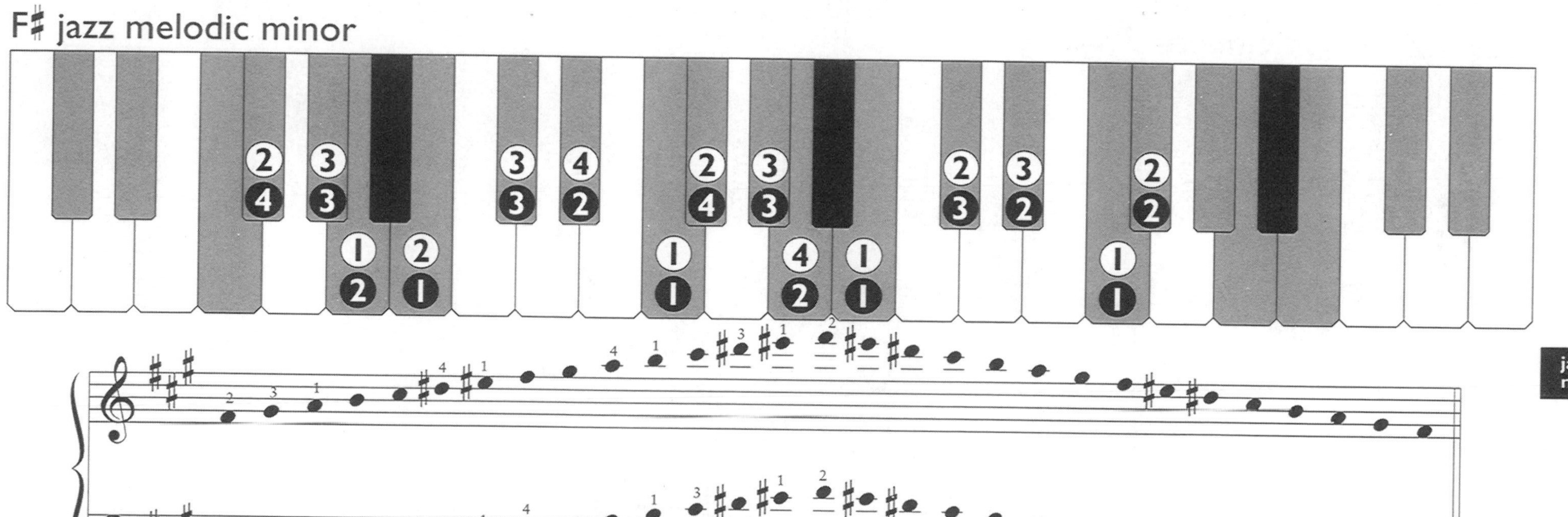

C♯ jazz melodic minor

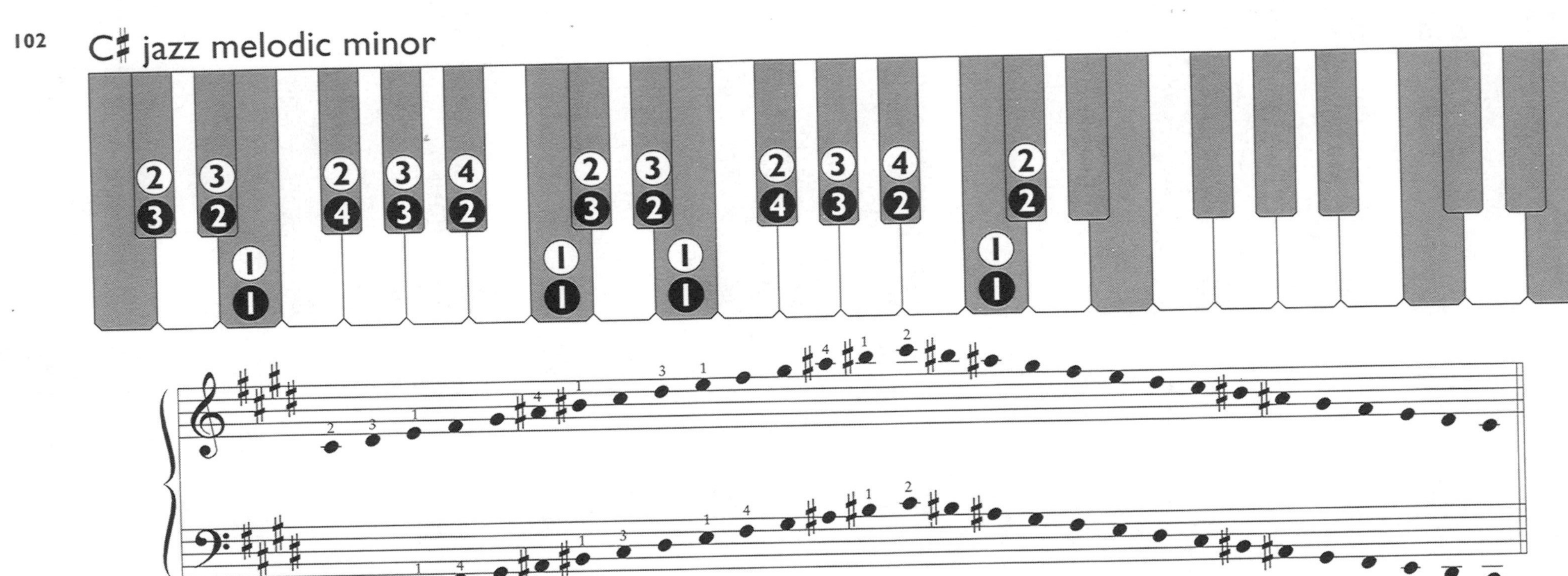

G♯ jazz melodic minor

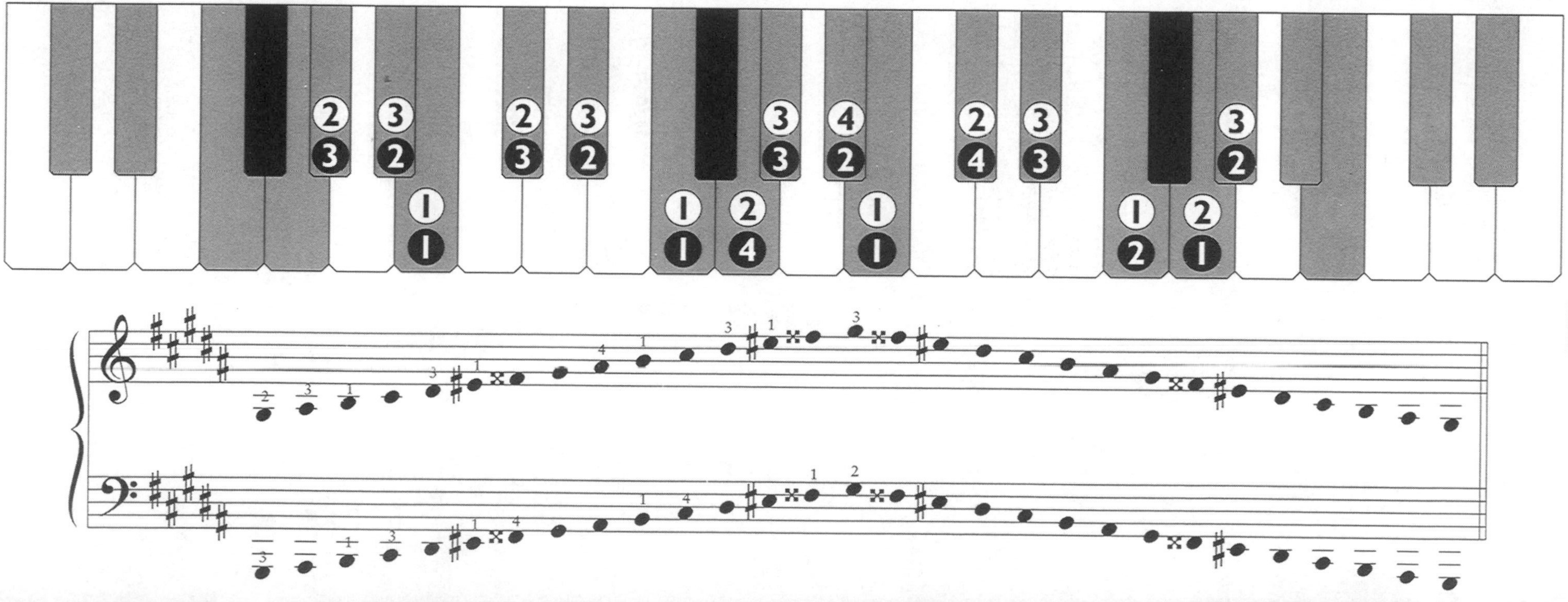

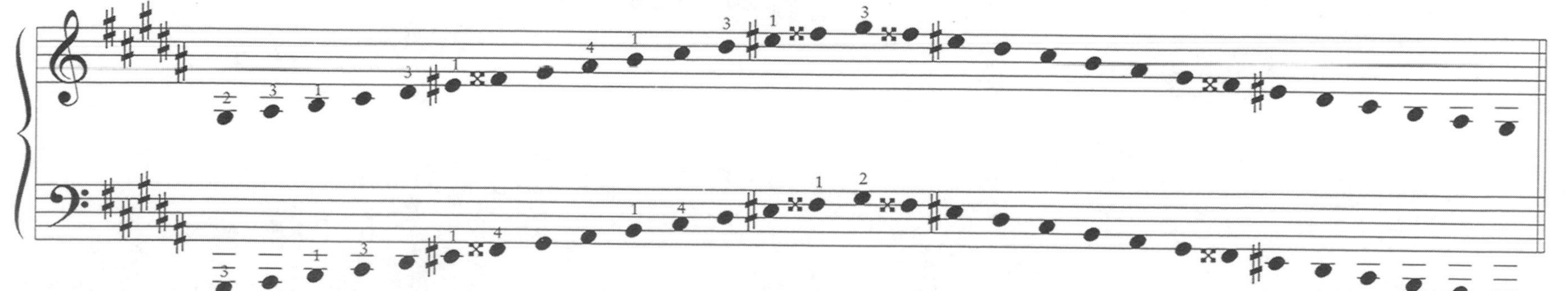

D♯ jazz melodic minor

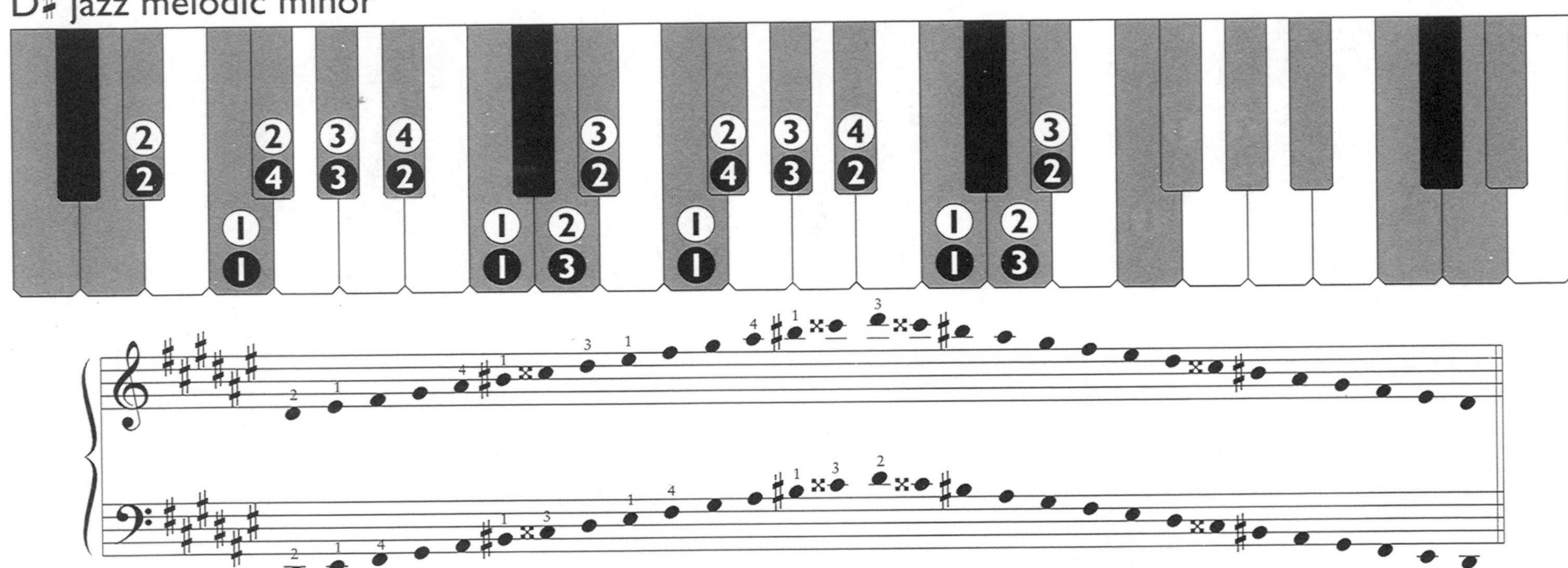

A♯ jazz melodic minor

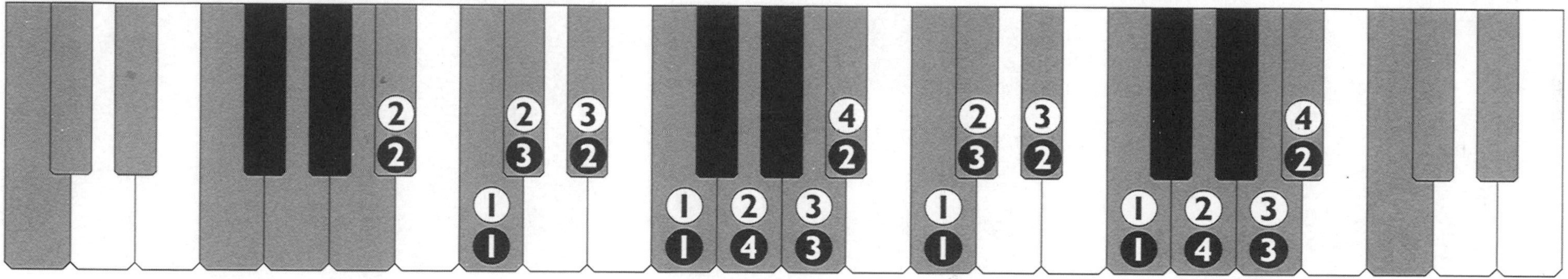

D jazz melodic minor

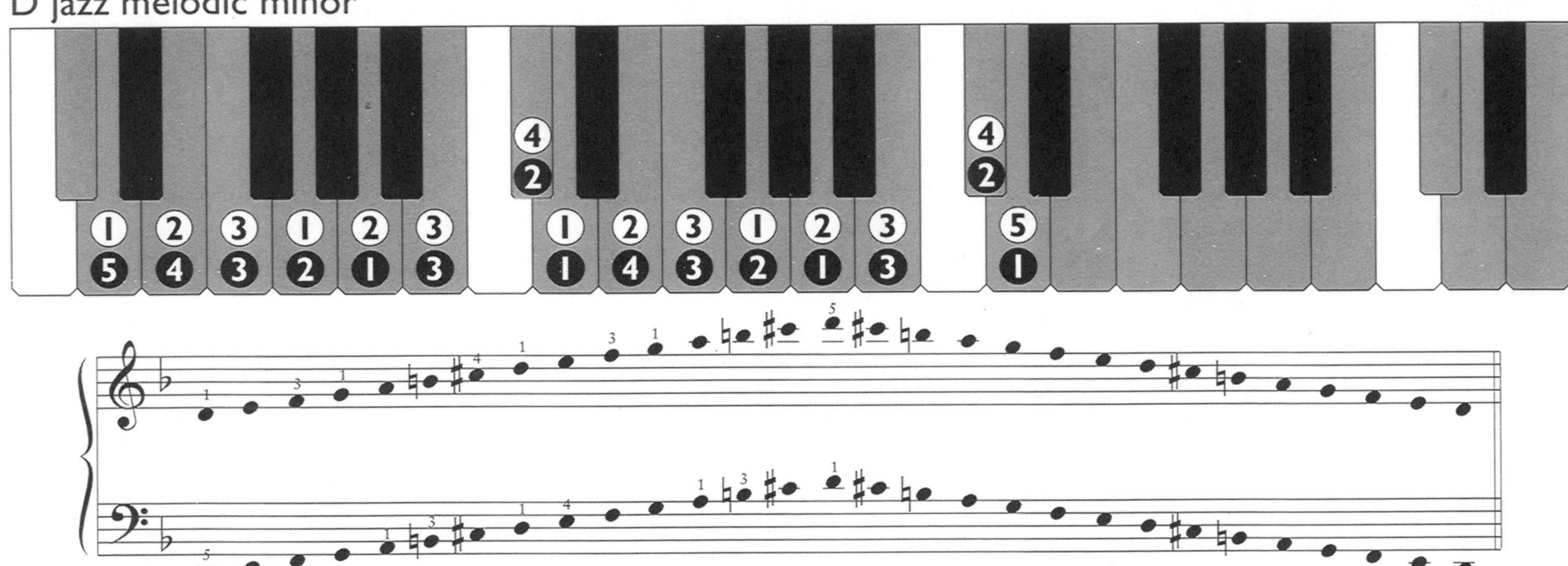

G jazz melodic minor

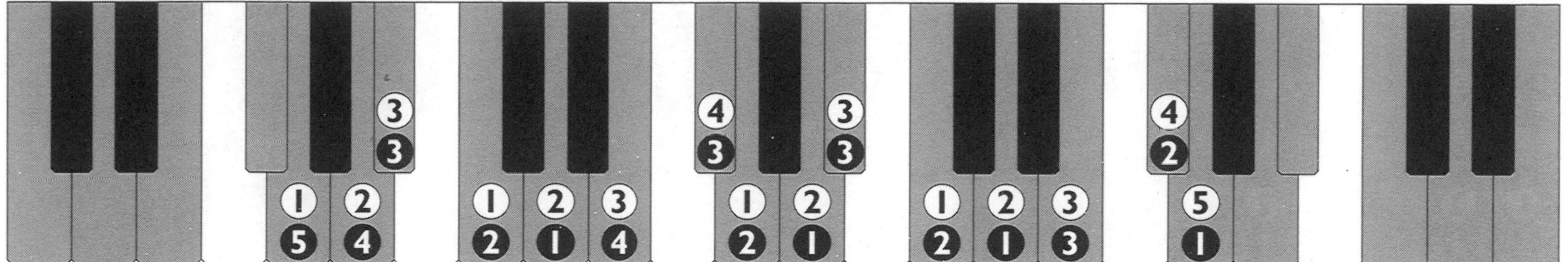

C jazz melodic minor

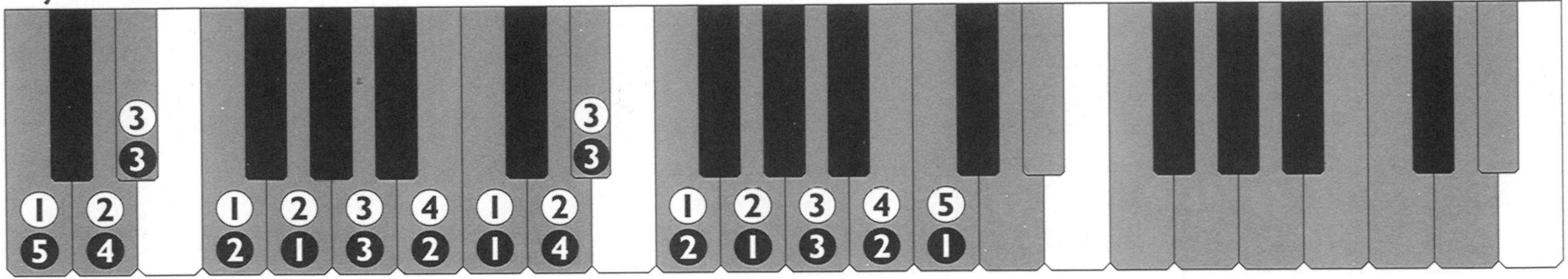

F jazz melodic minor

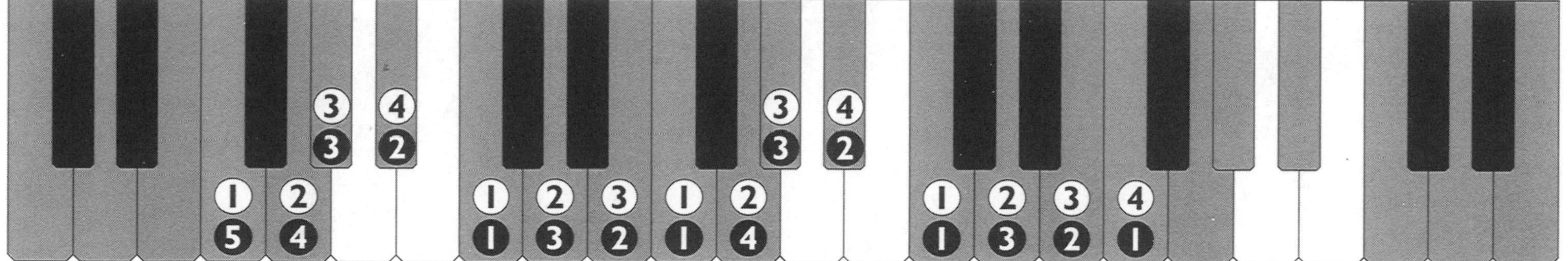

B♭ jazz melodic minor

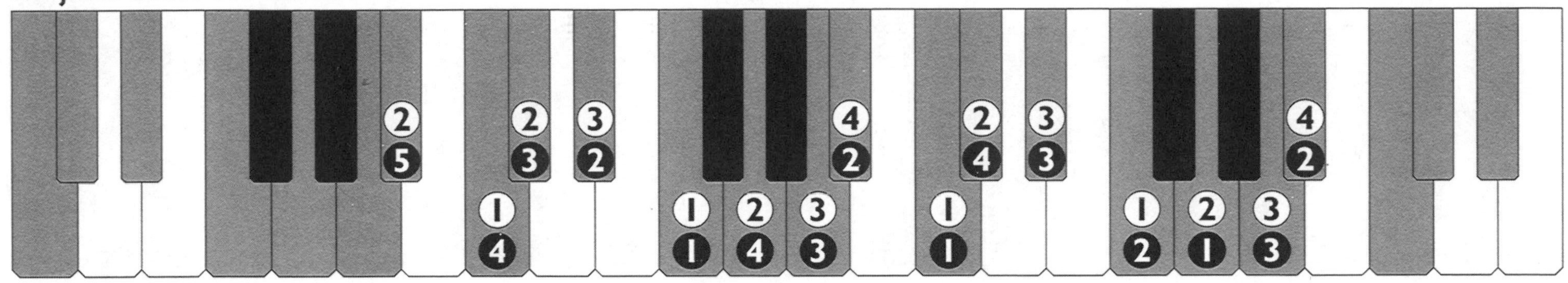

E♭ jazz melodic minor

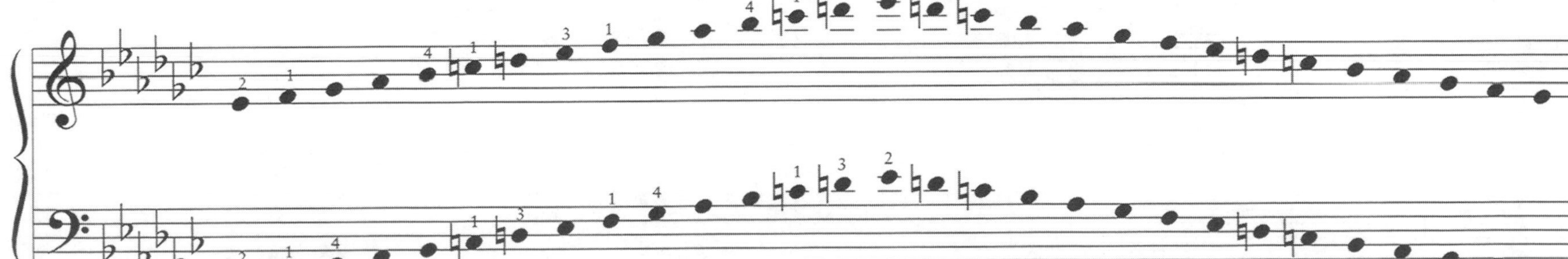

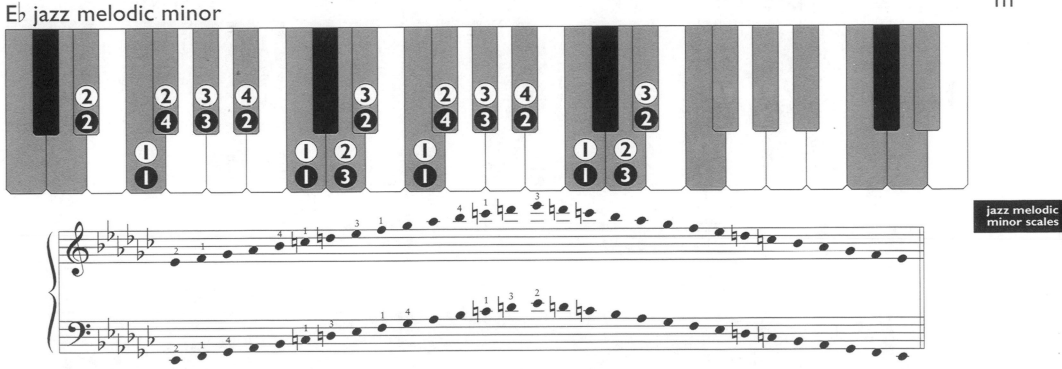

A♭ jazz melodic minor

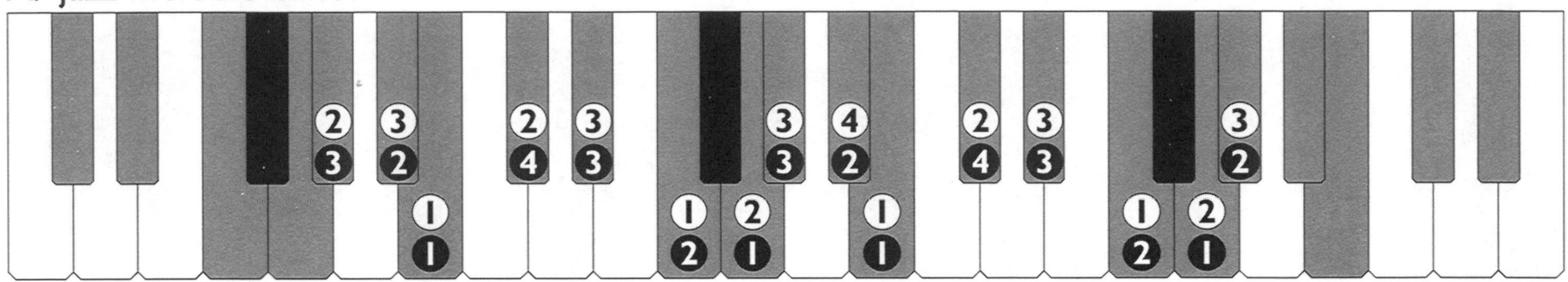

D Dorian

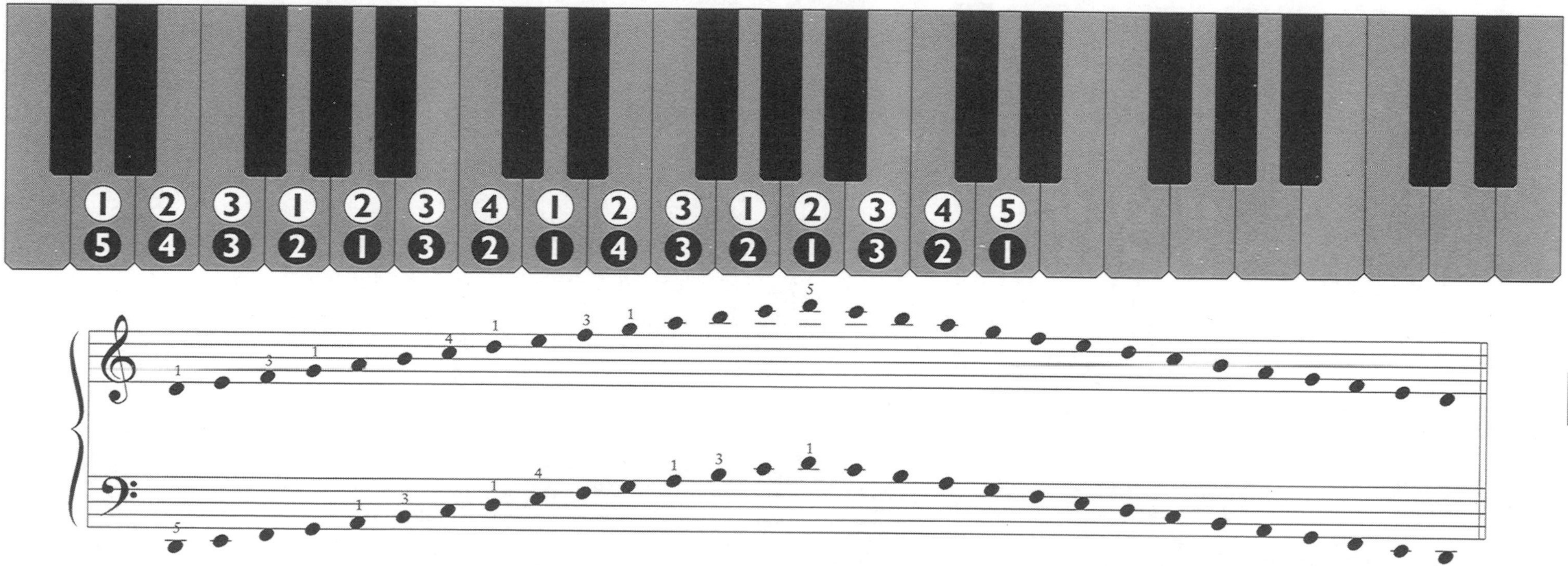

1 2 3 1 2 3 4 1 2 3 1 2 3 4 5

5 4 3 2 1 3 2 1 4 3 2 1 3 2 1

A Dorian

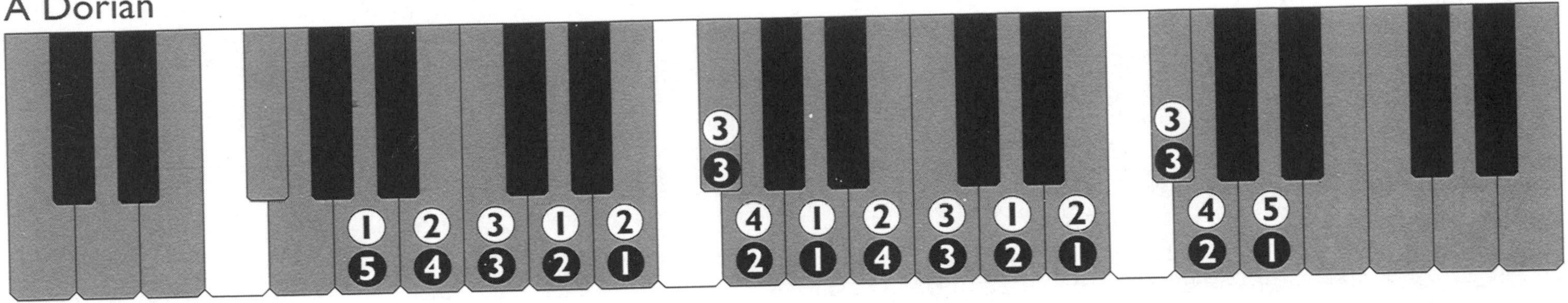

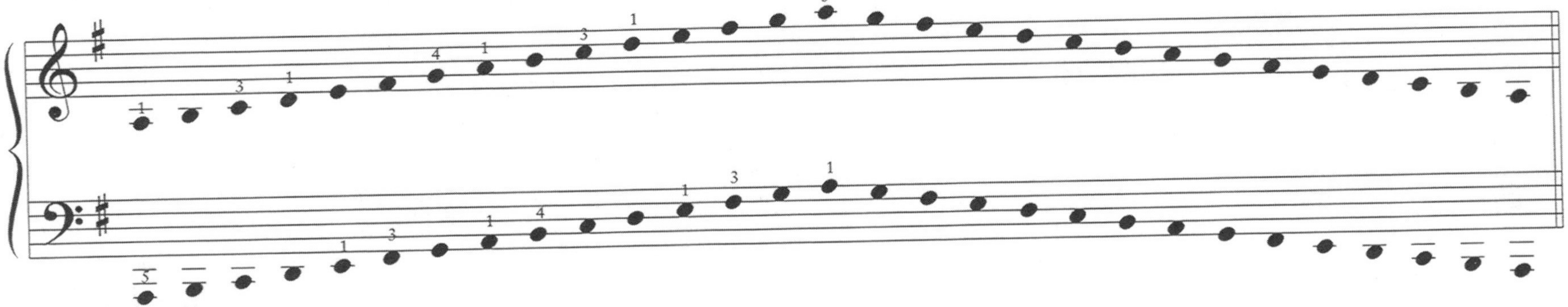

E Dorian

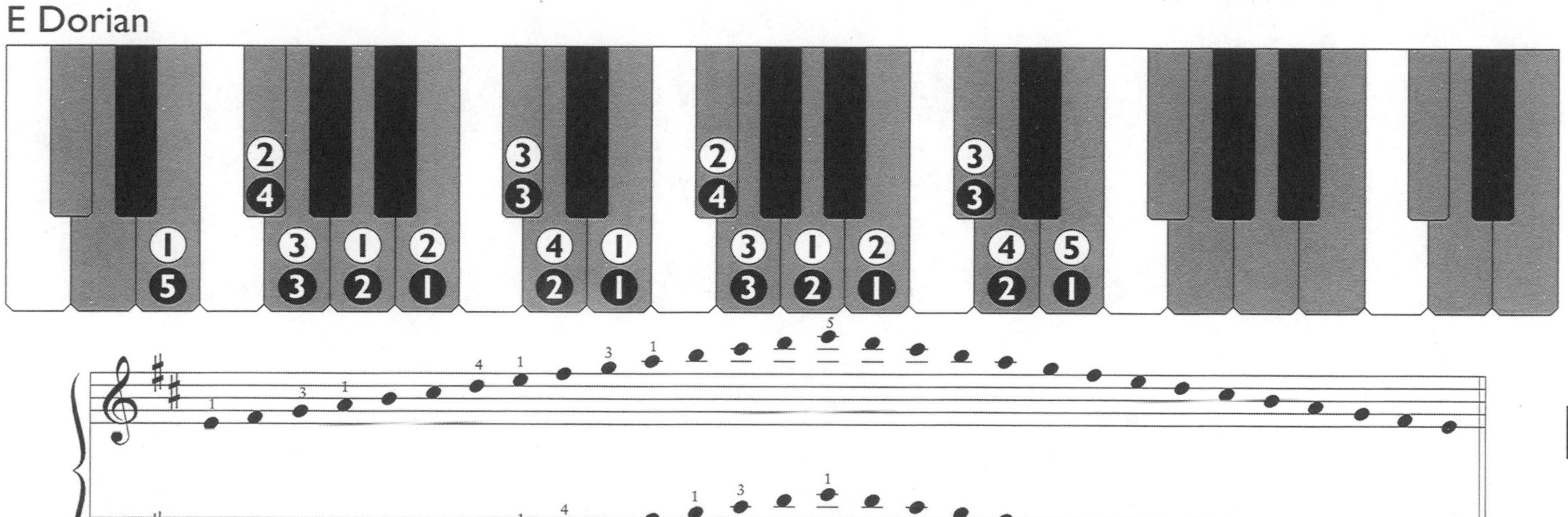

B Dorian

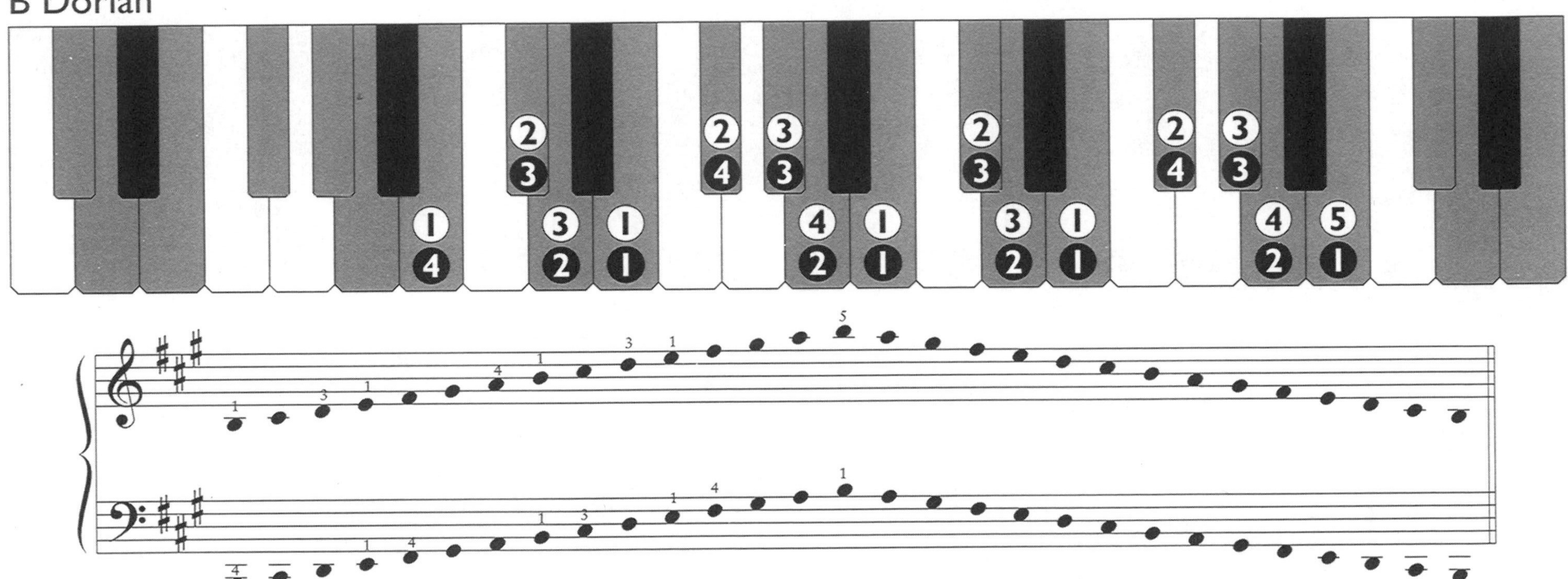

F♯ Dorian

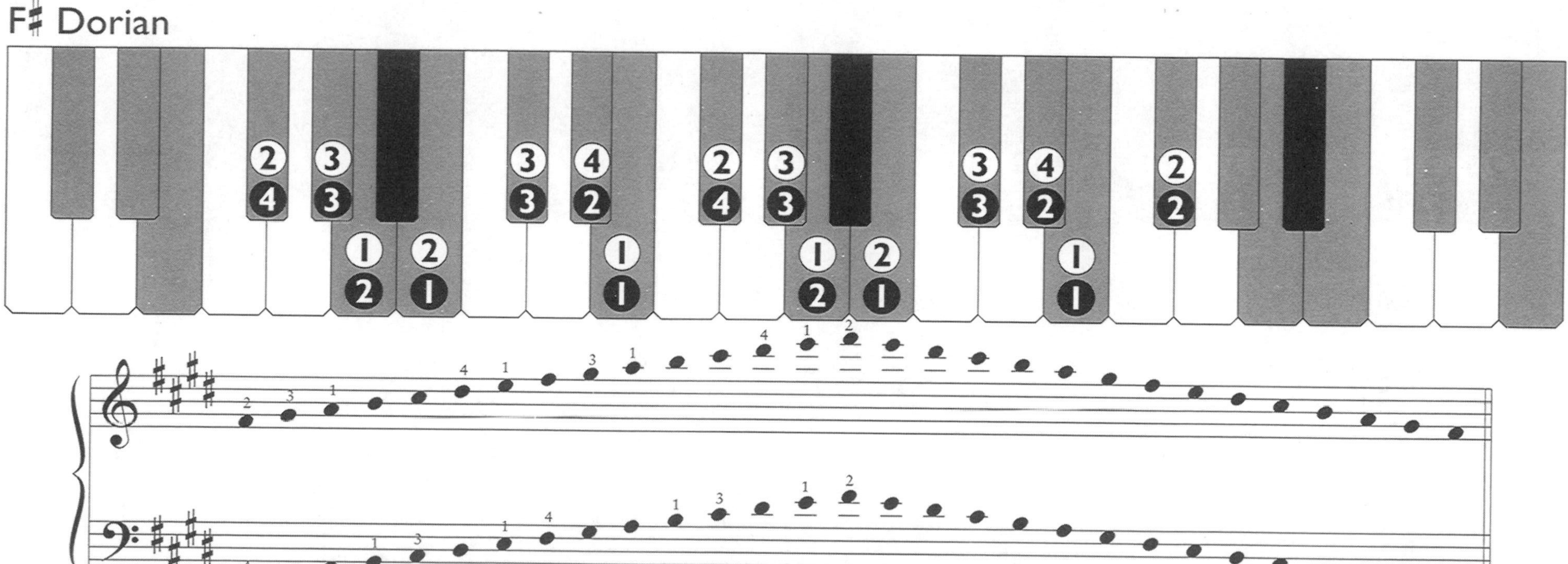

C♯ Dorian

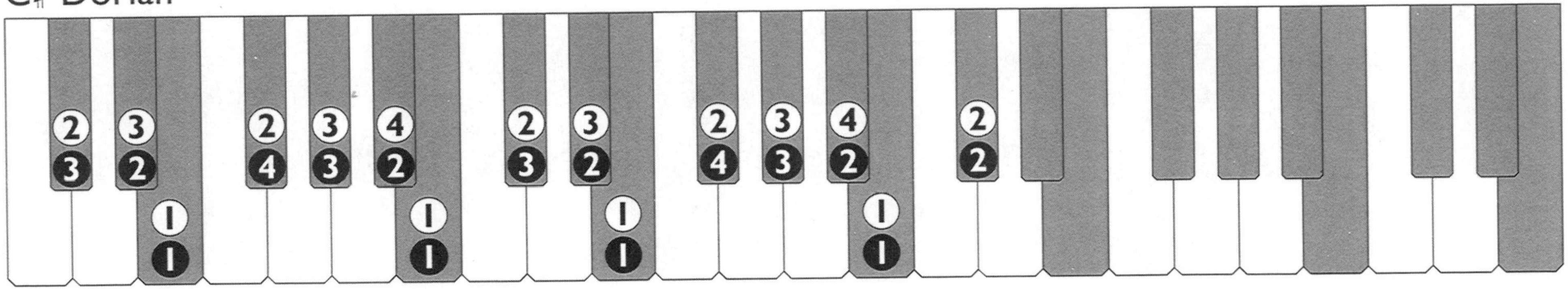

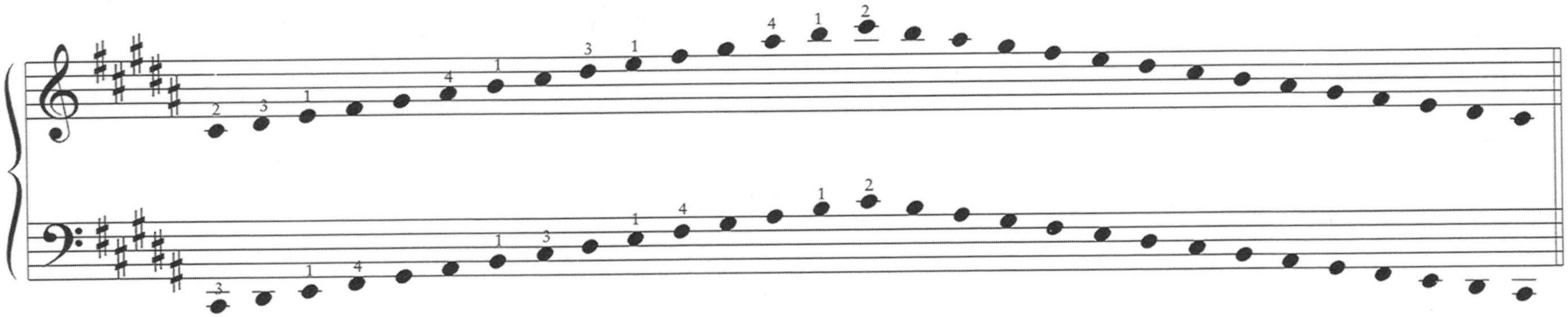

G♯ Dorian

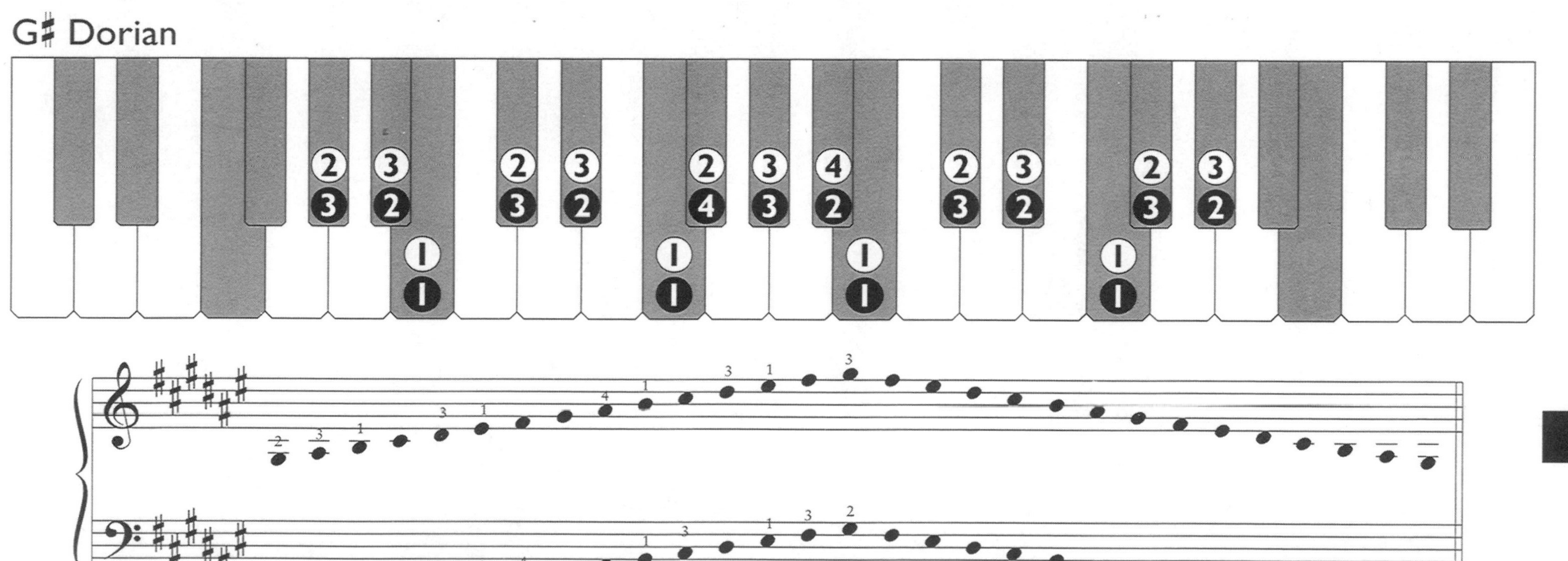

D♯ Dorian

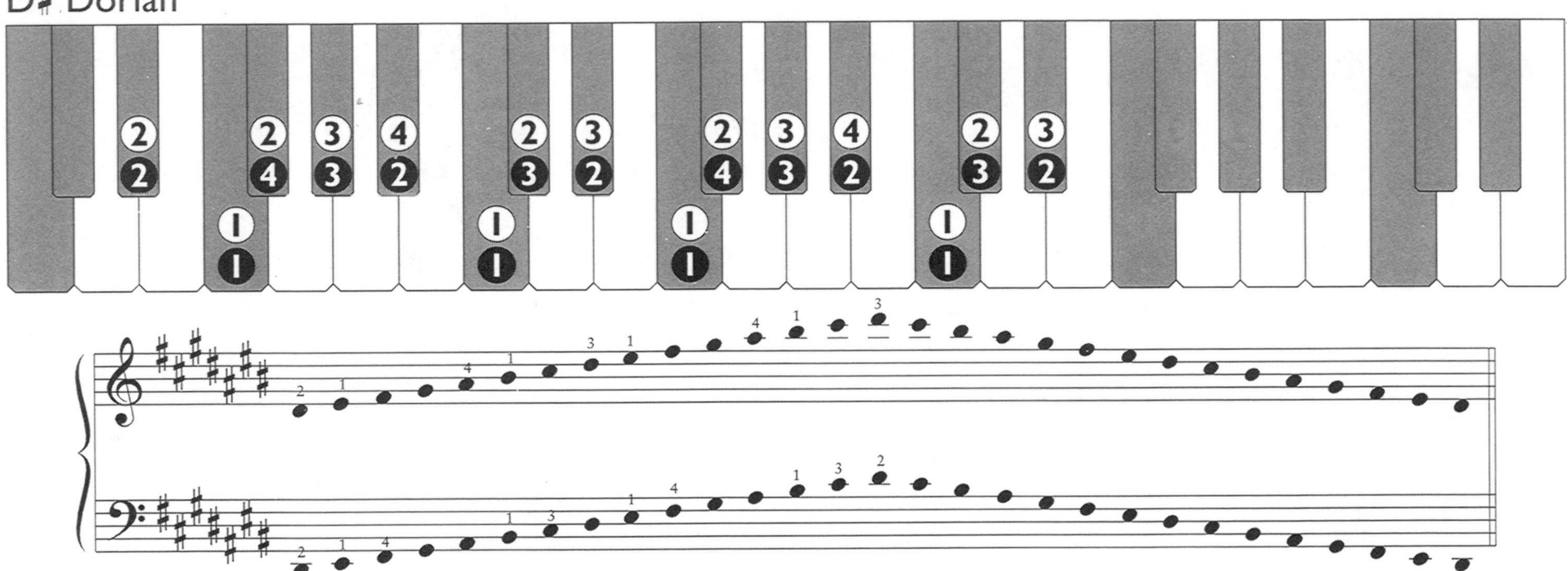

G Dorian

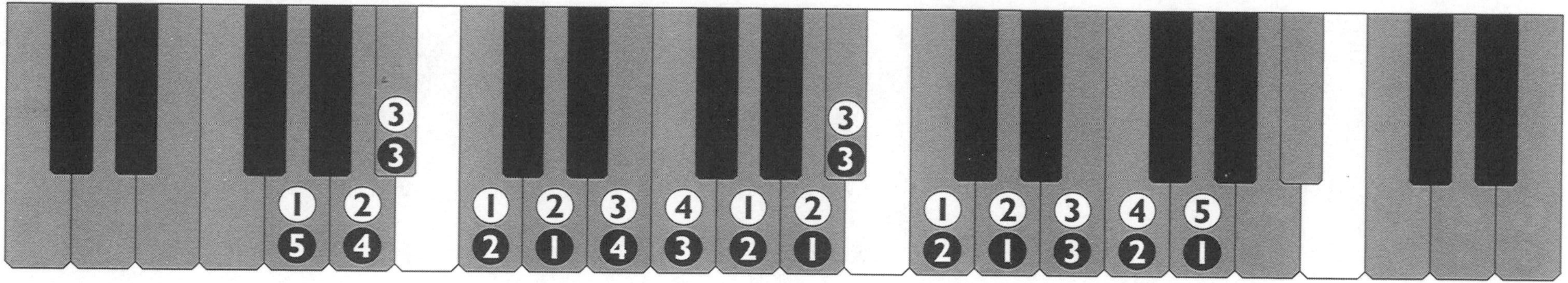

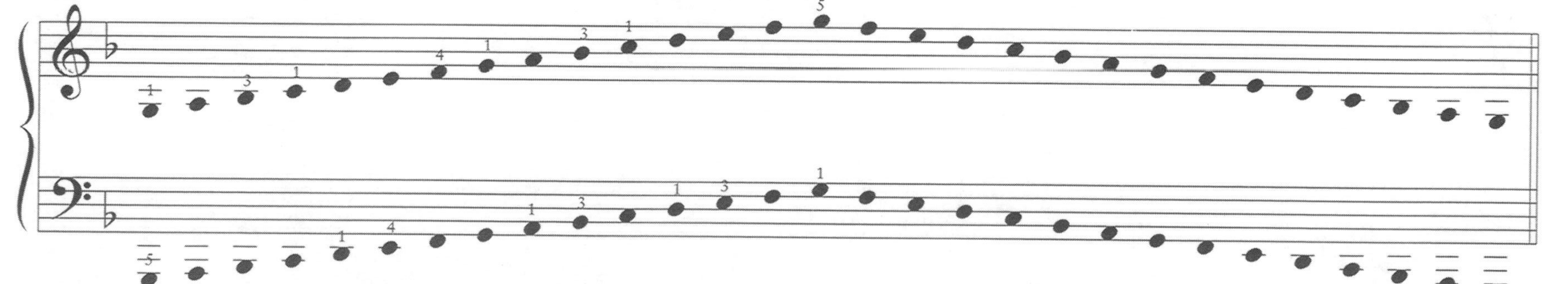

C Dorian

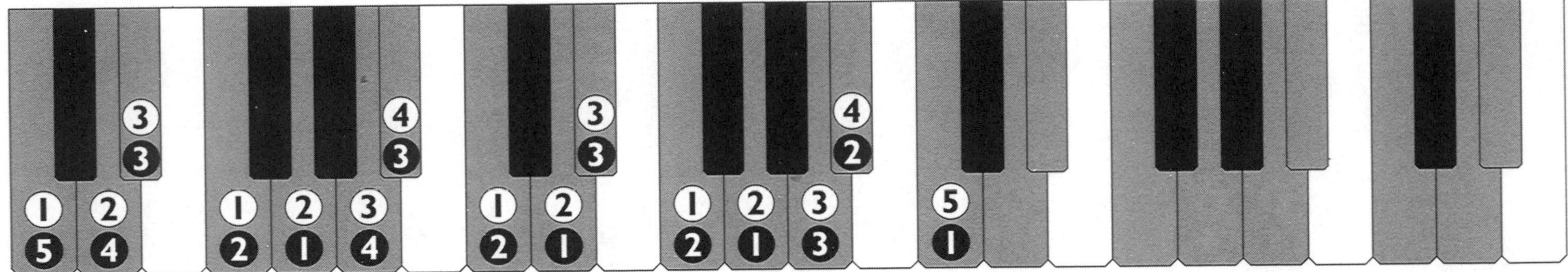

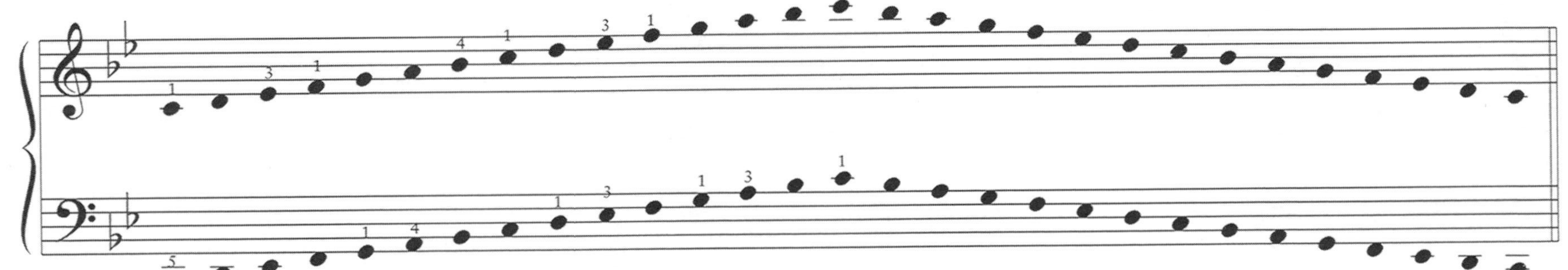

F Dorian

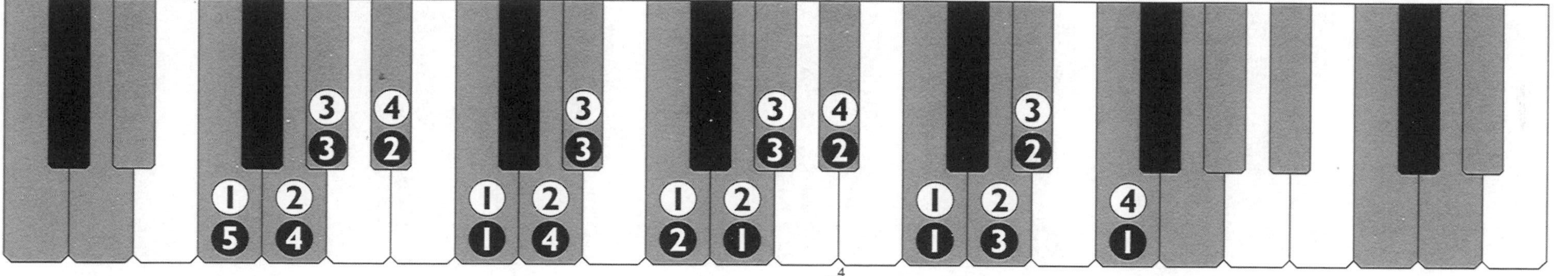

B♭ Dorian

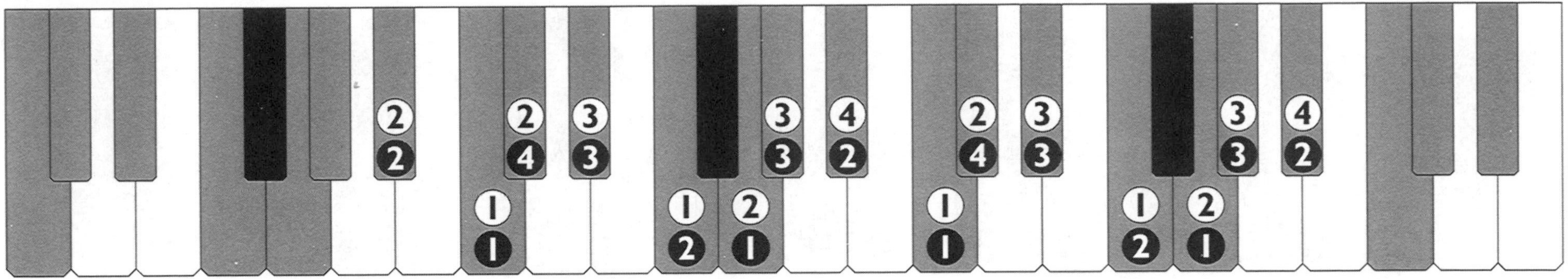

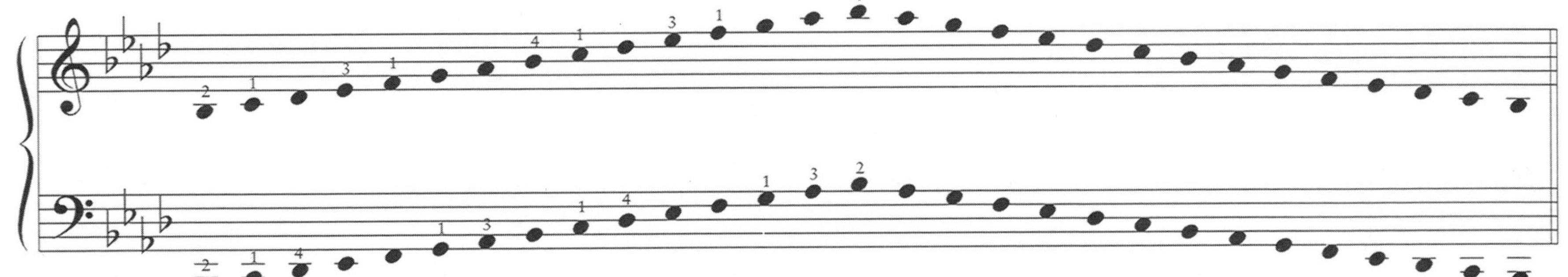

E♭ Dorian

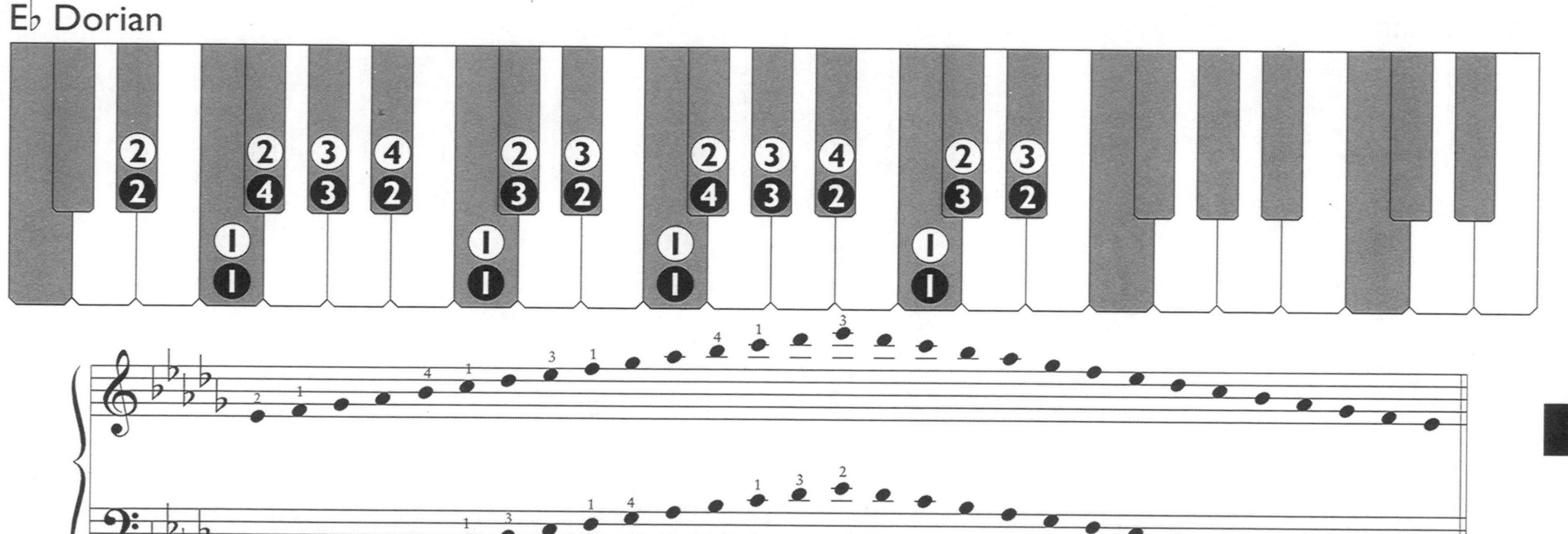

A♭ Dorian

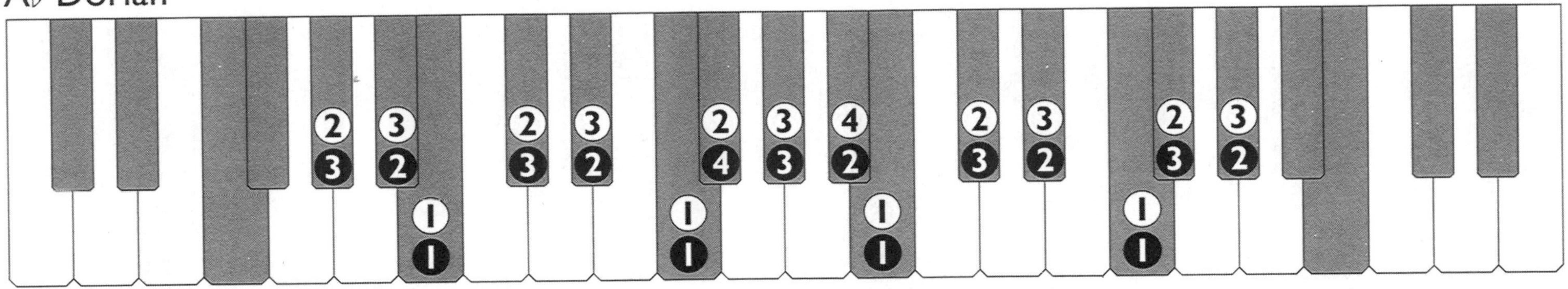

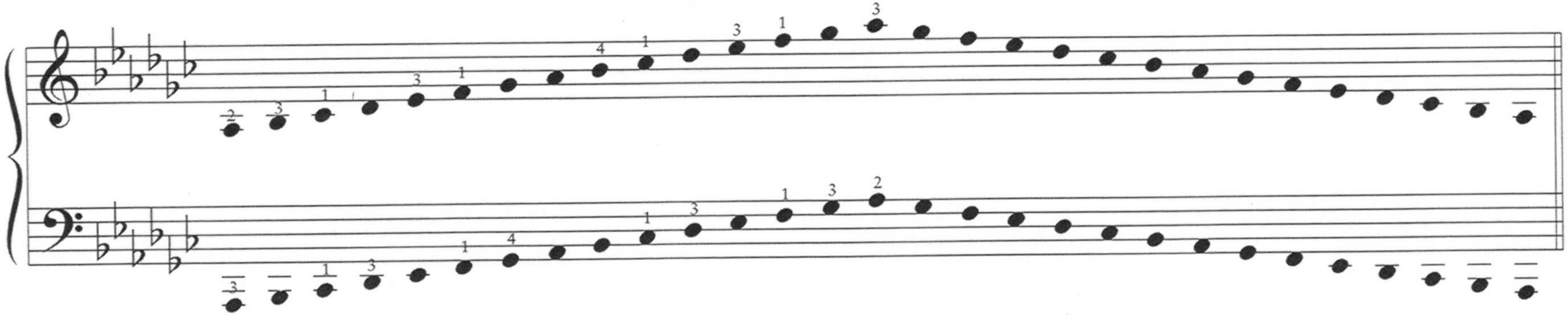

D♭ Dorian

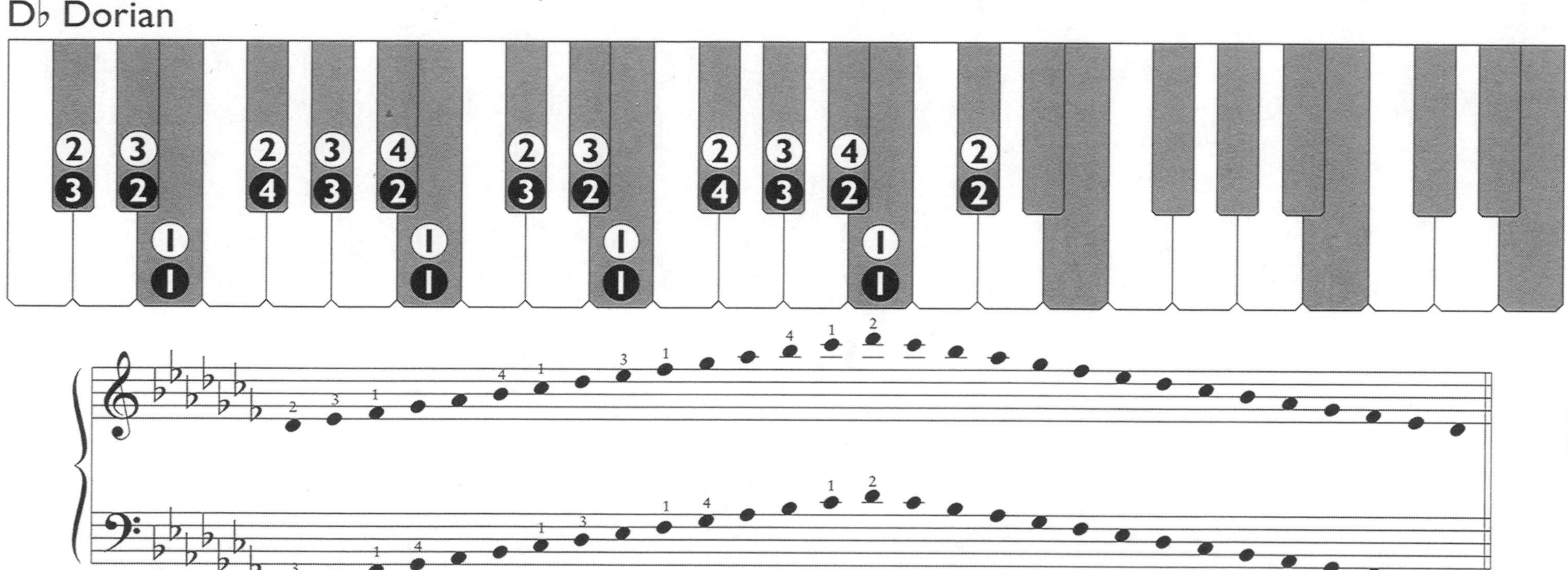

E Phrygian

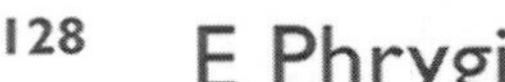

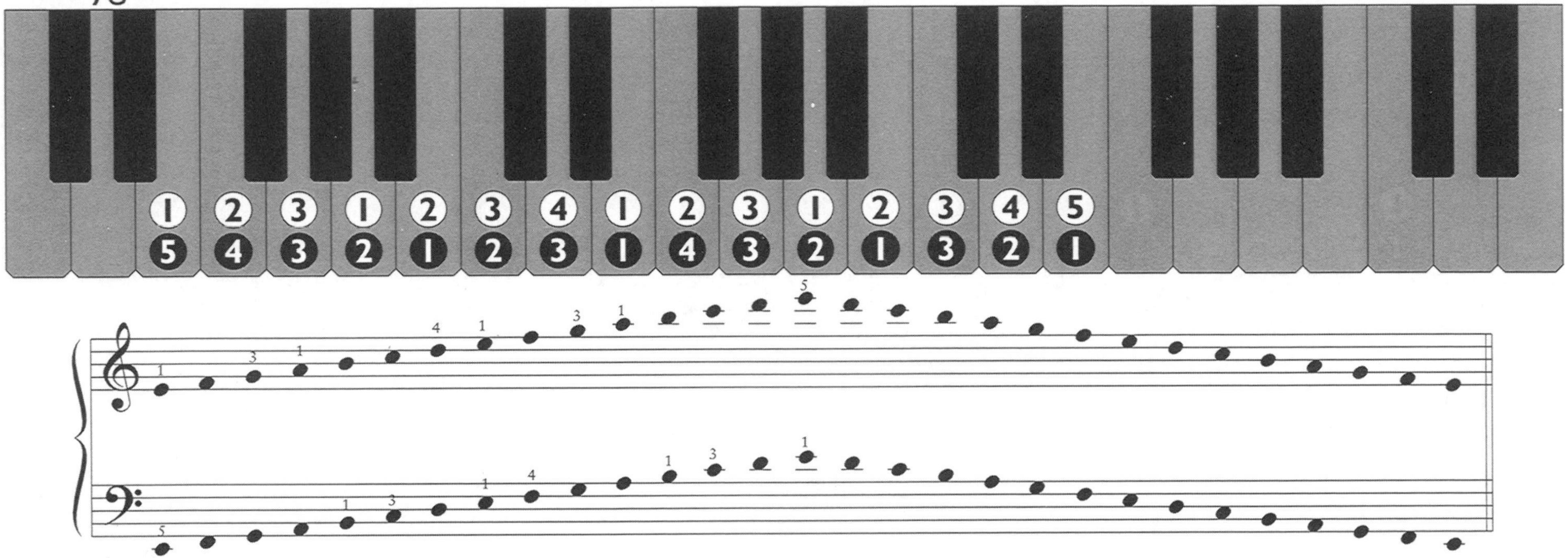

B Phrygian

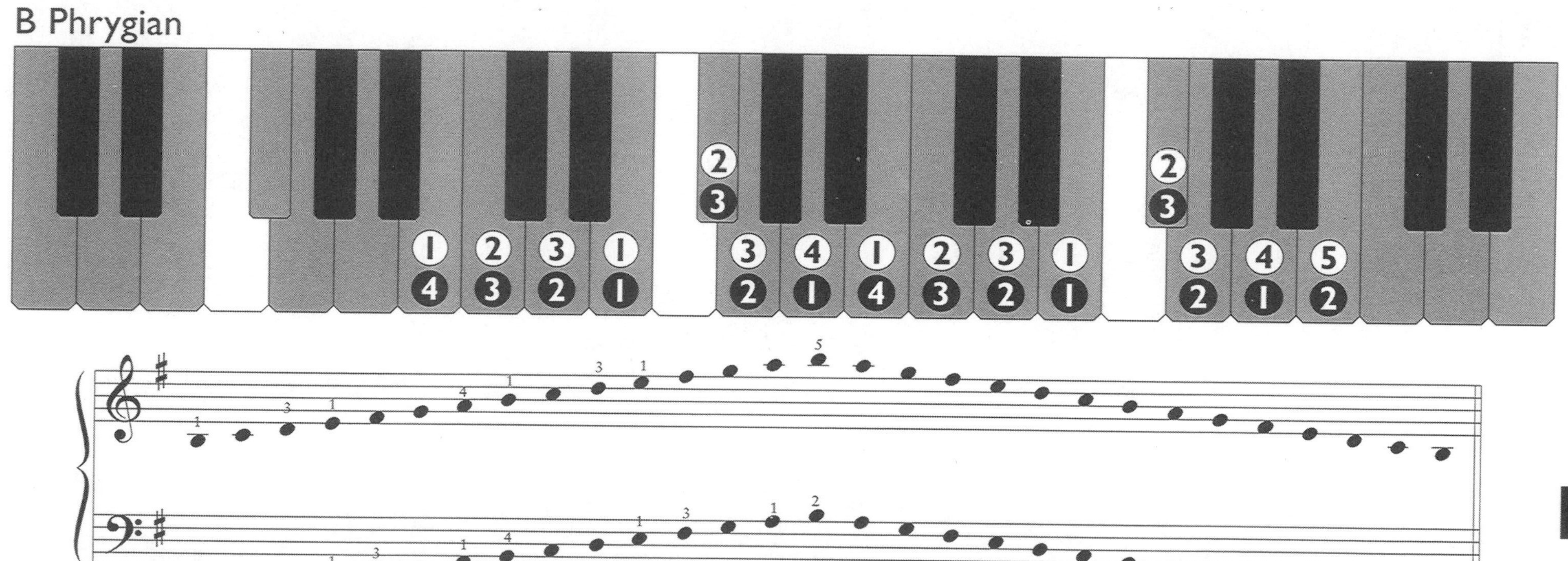

F♯ Phrygian

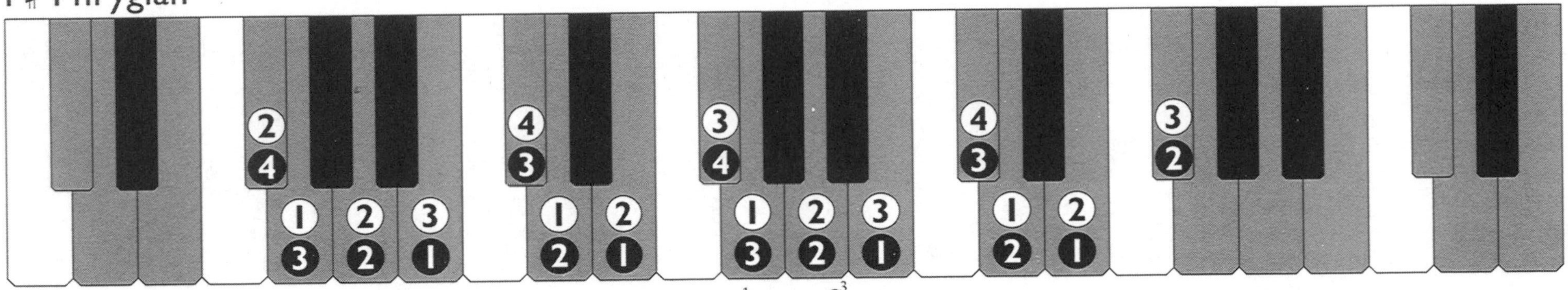

C♯ Phrygian

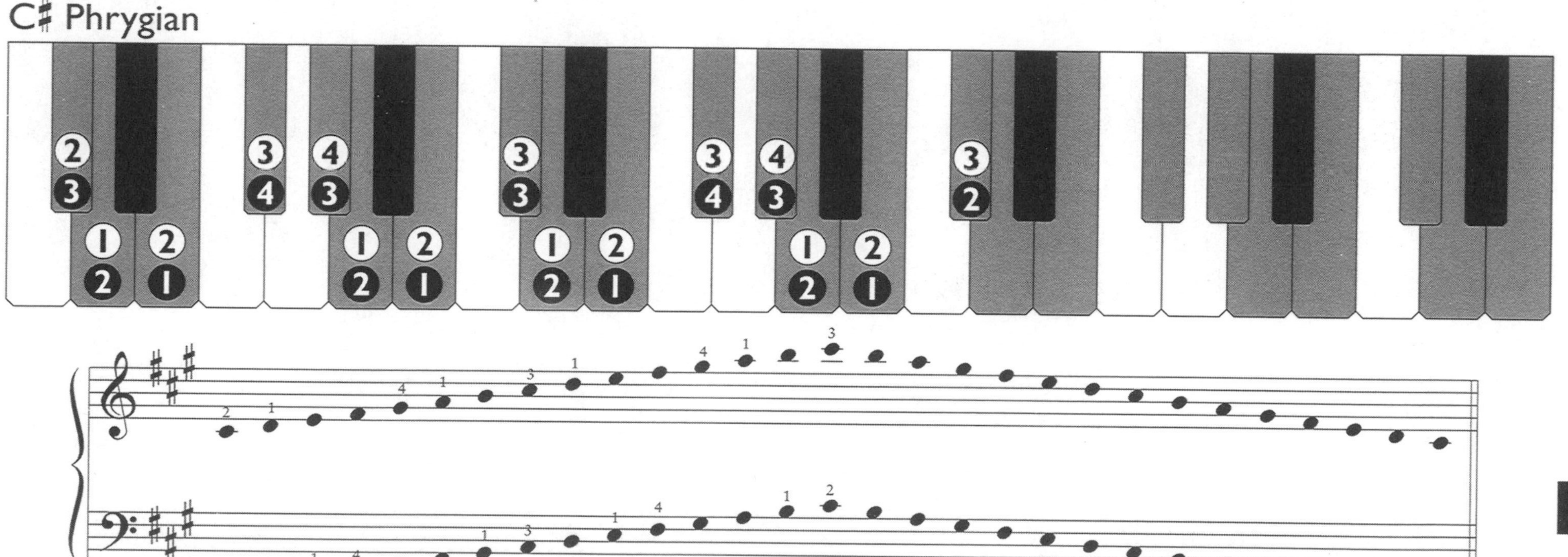

G♯ Phrygian

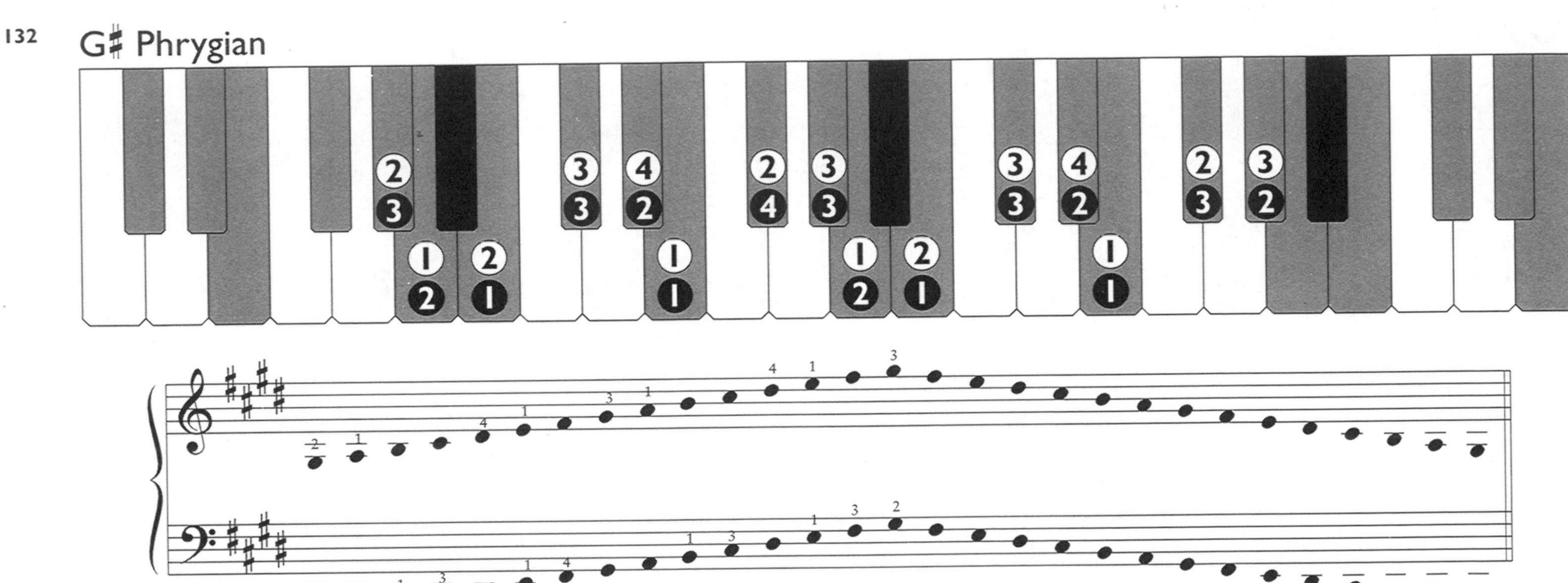

D♯ Phrygian

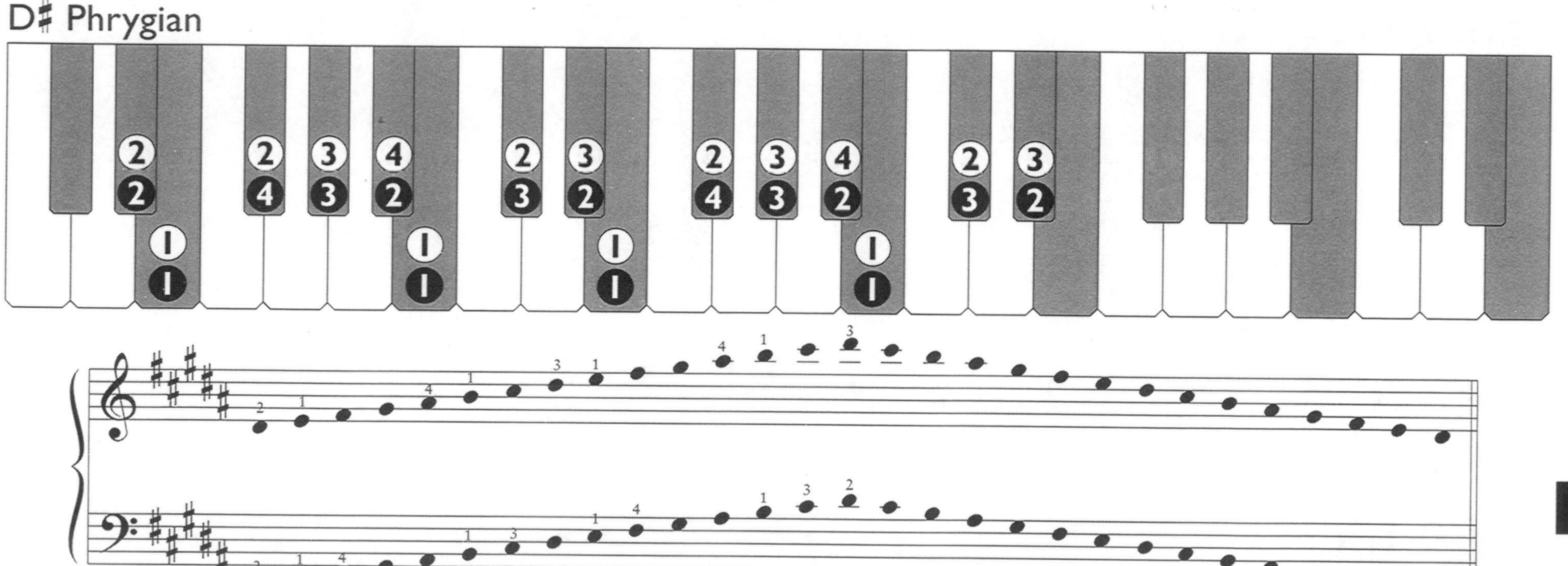

A♯ Phrygian

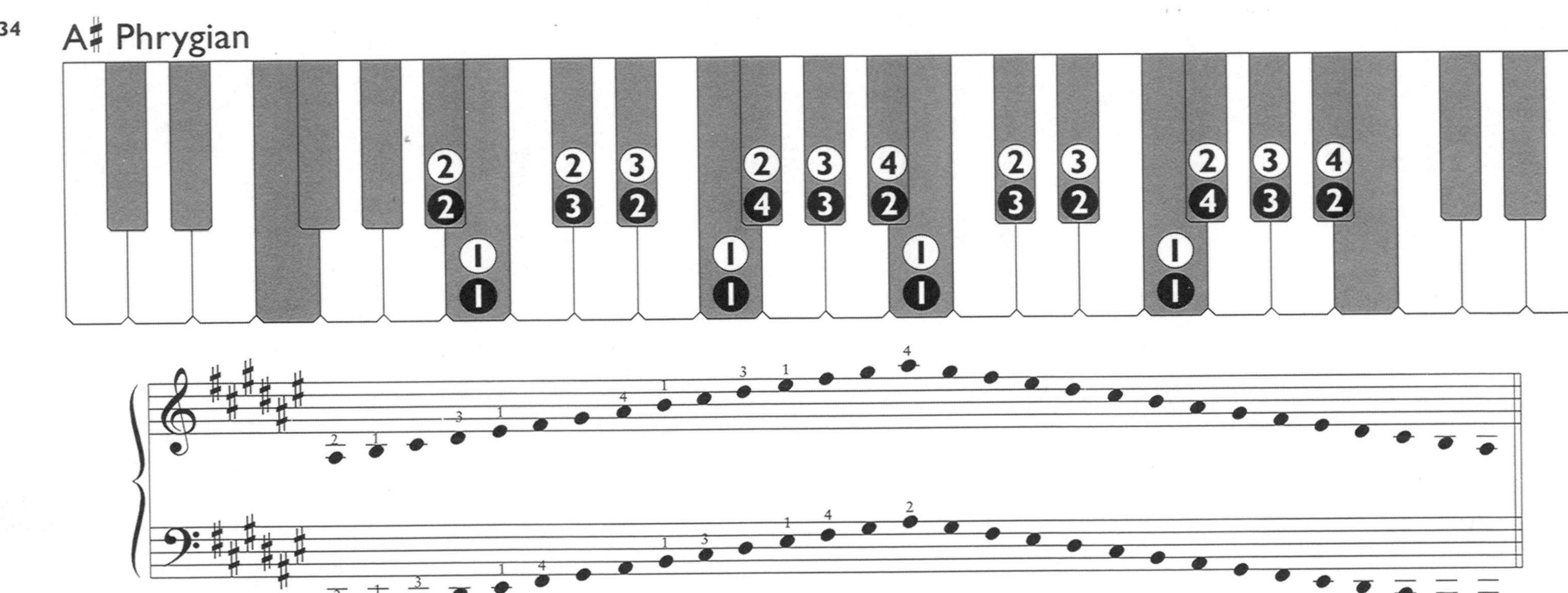

E♯ Phrygian

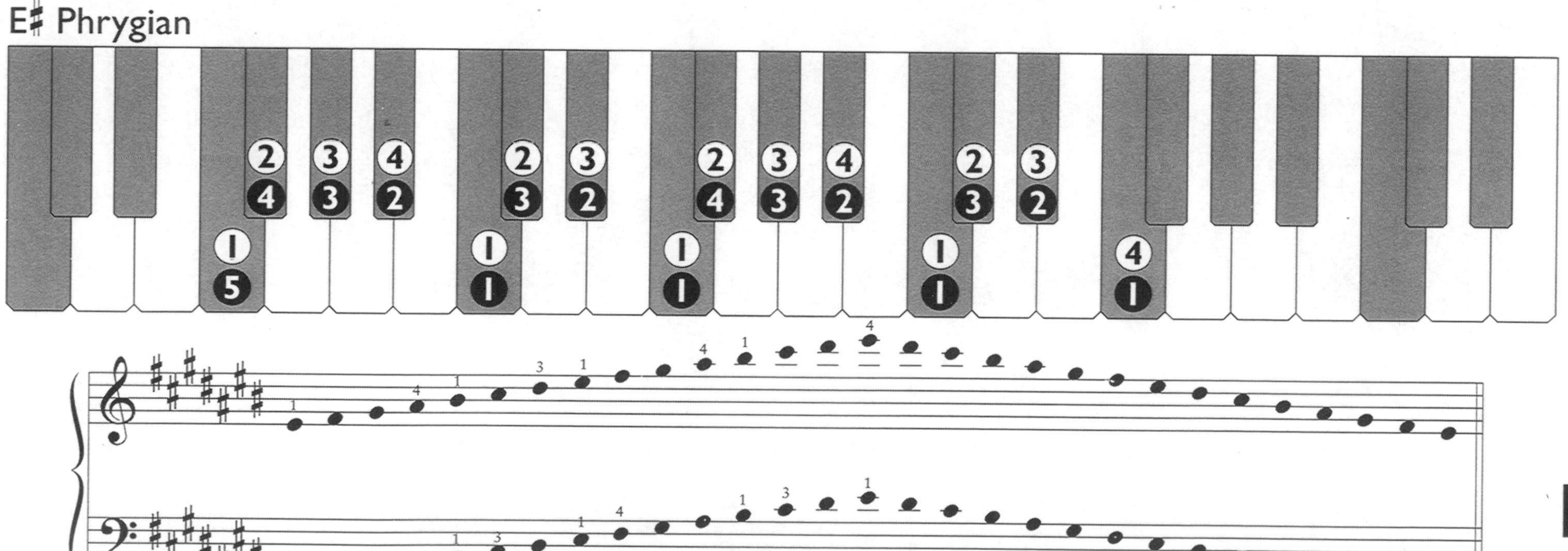

A Phrygian

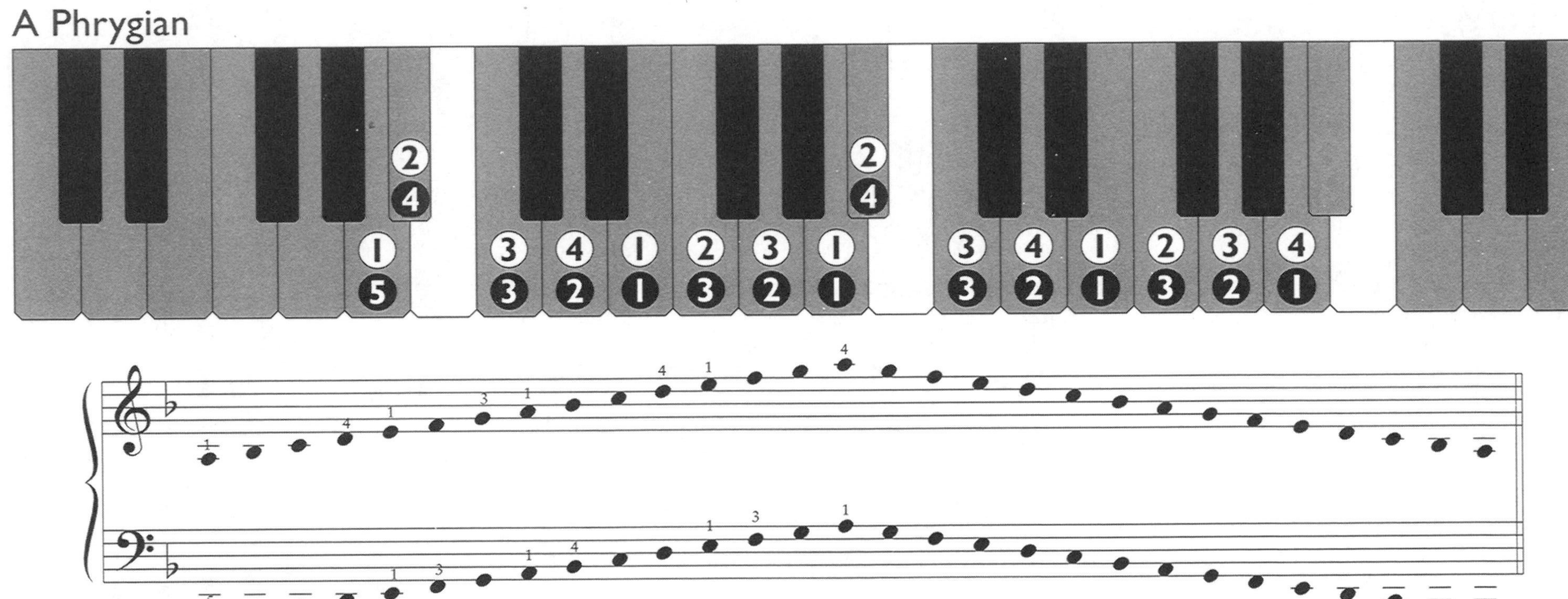

D Phrygian

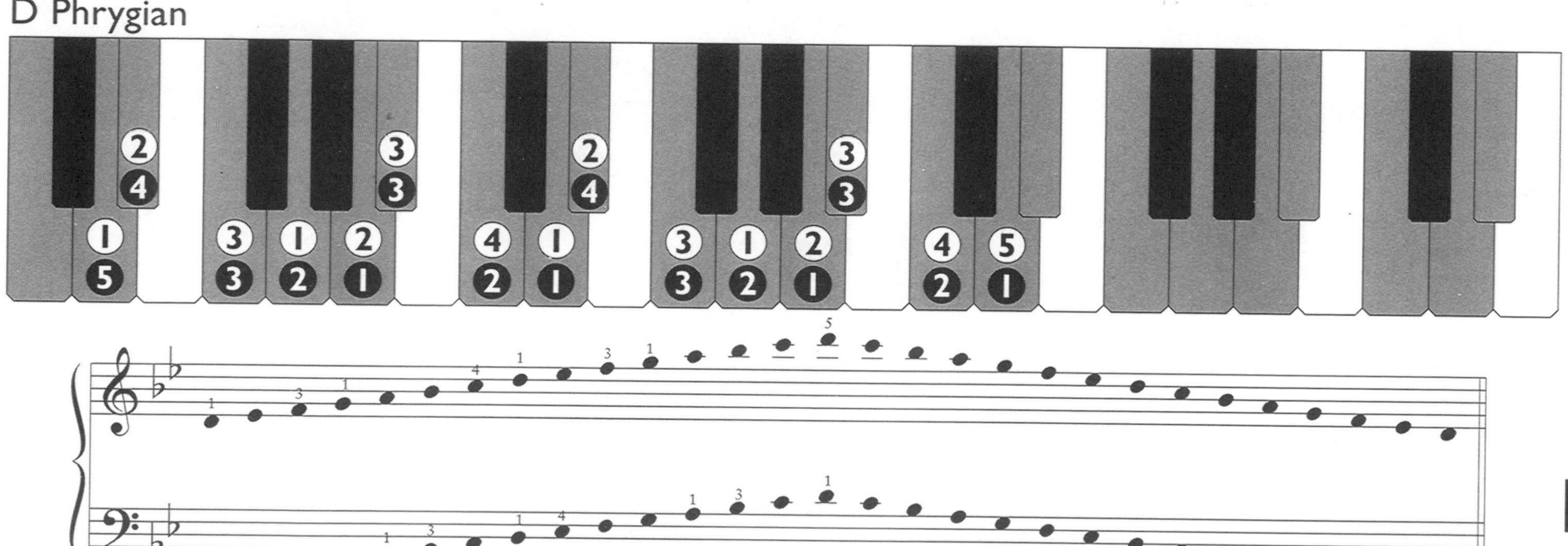

G Phrygian

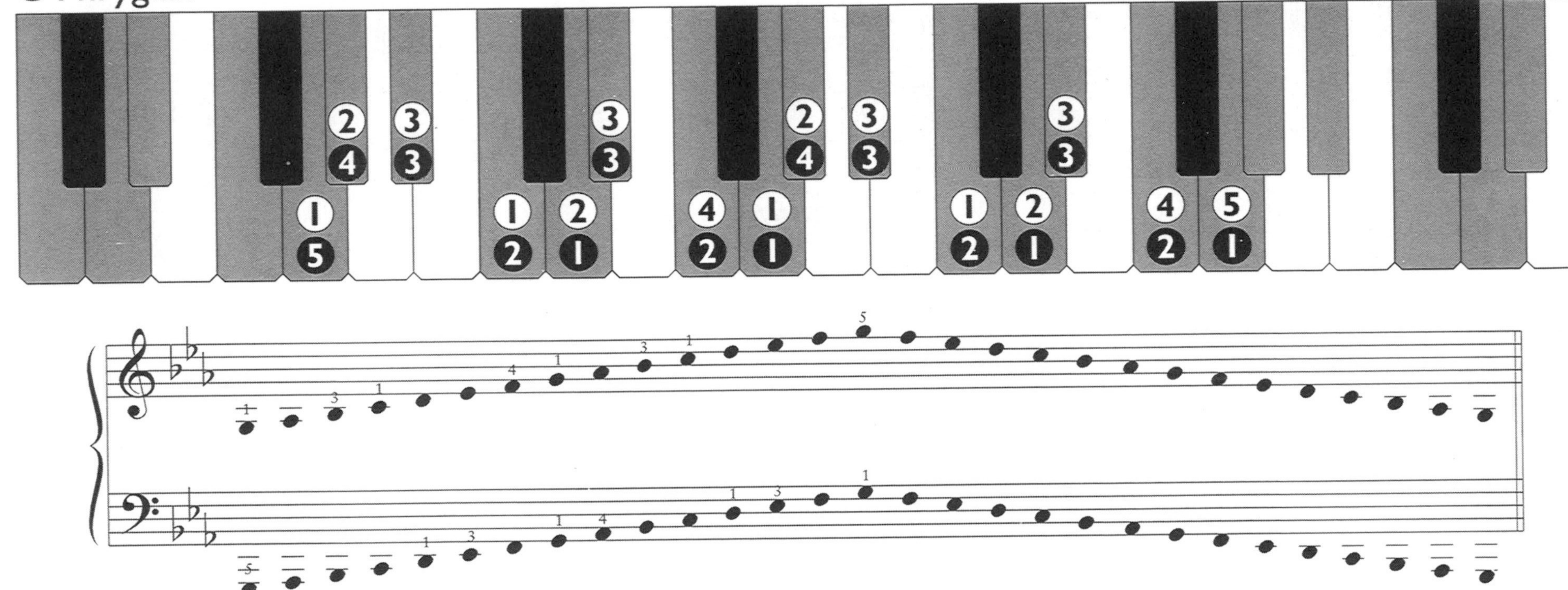

C Phrygian

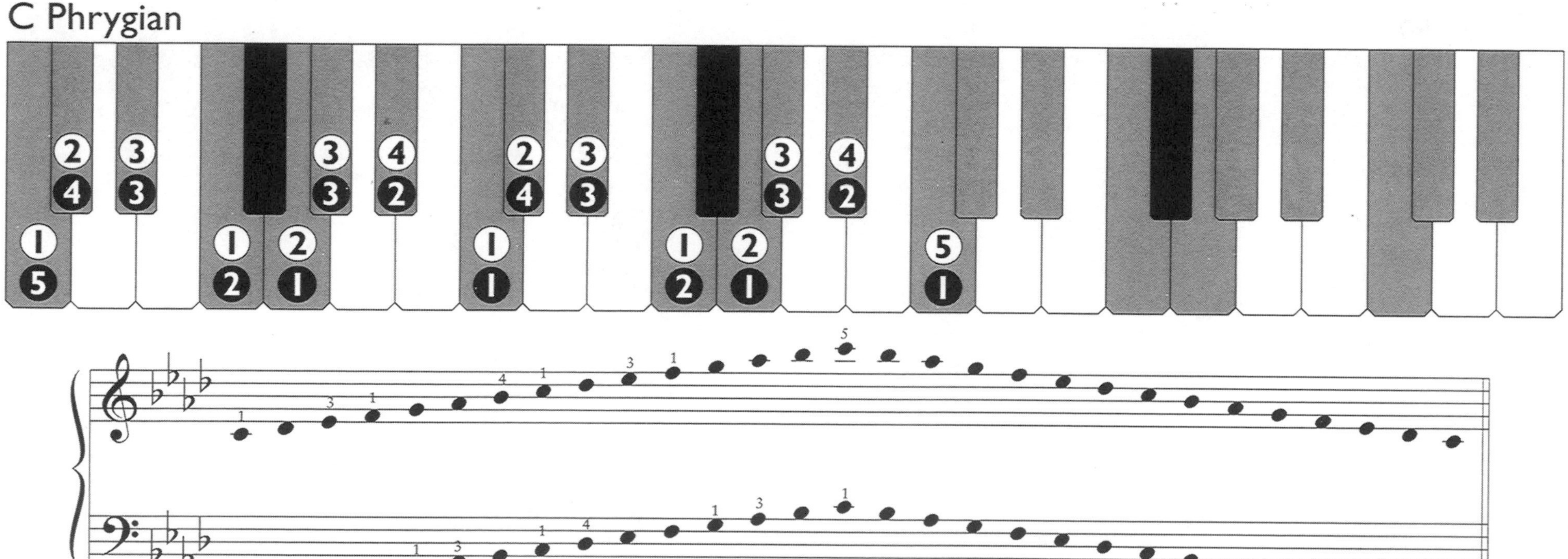

F Phrygian

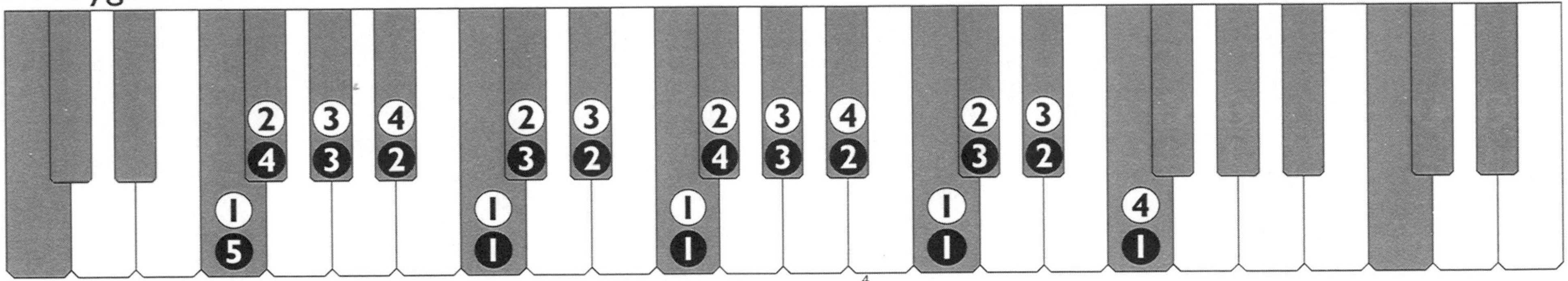

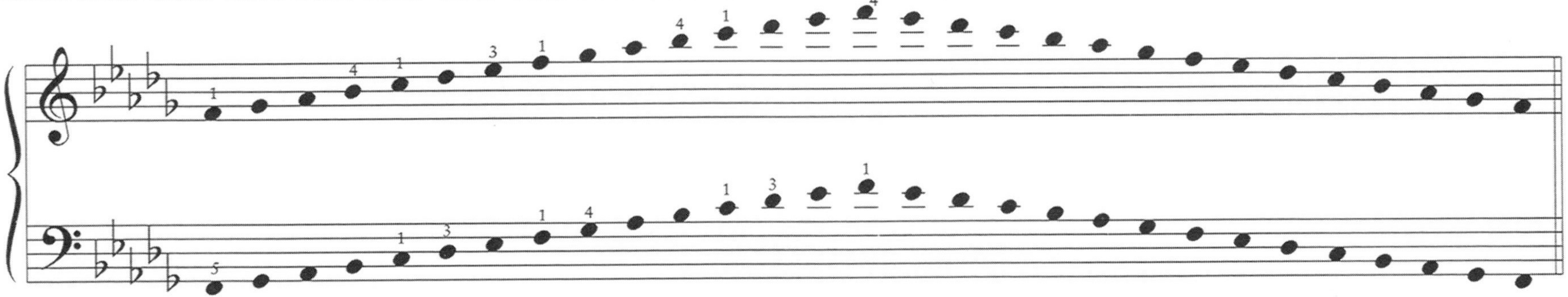

B♭ Phrygian

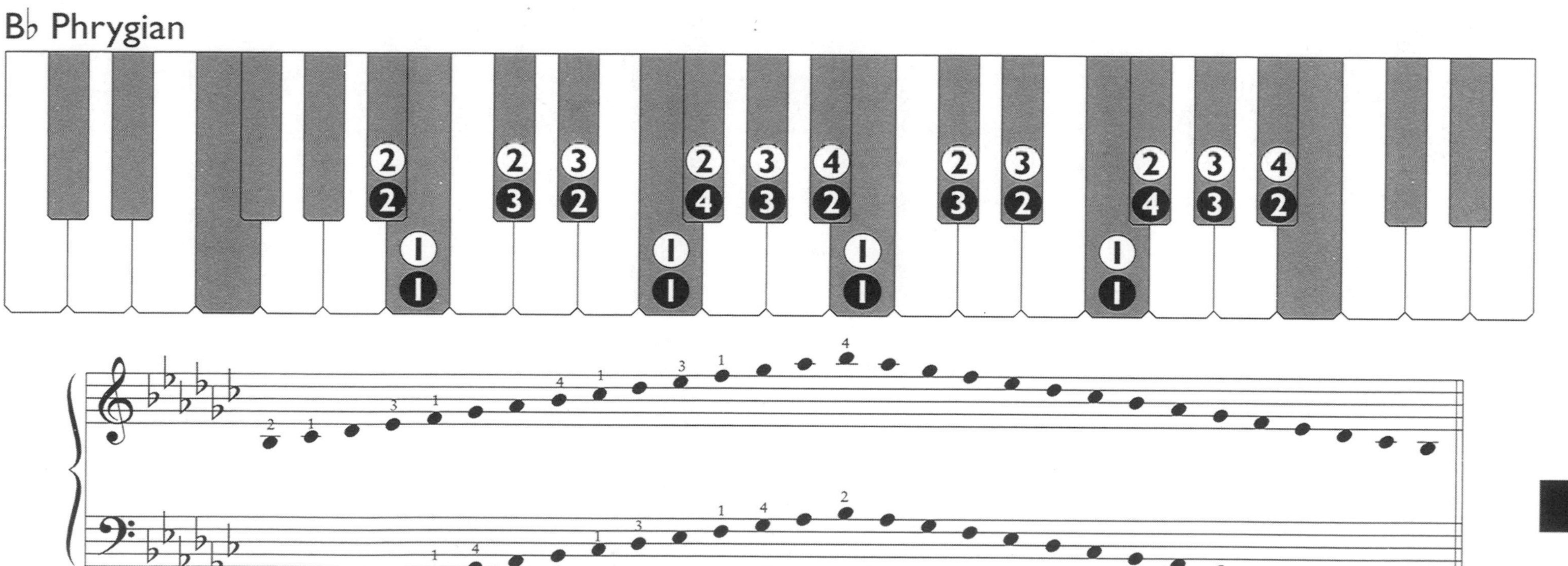

E♭ Phrygian

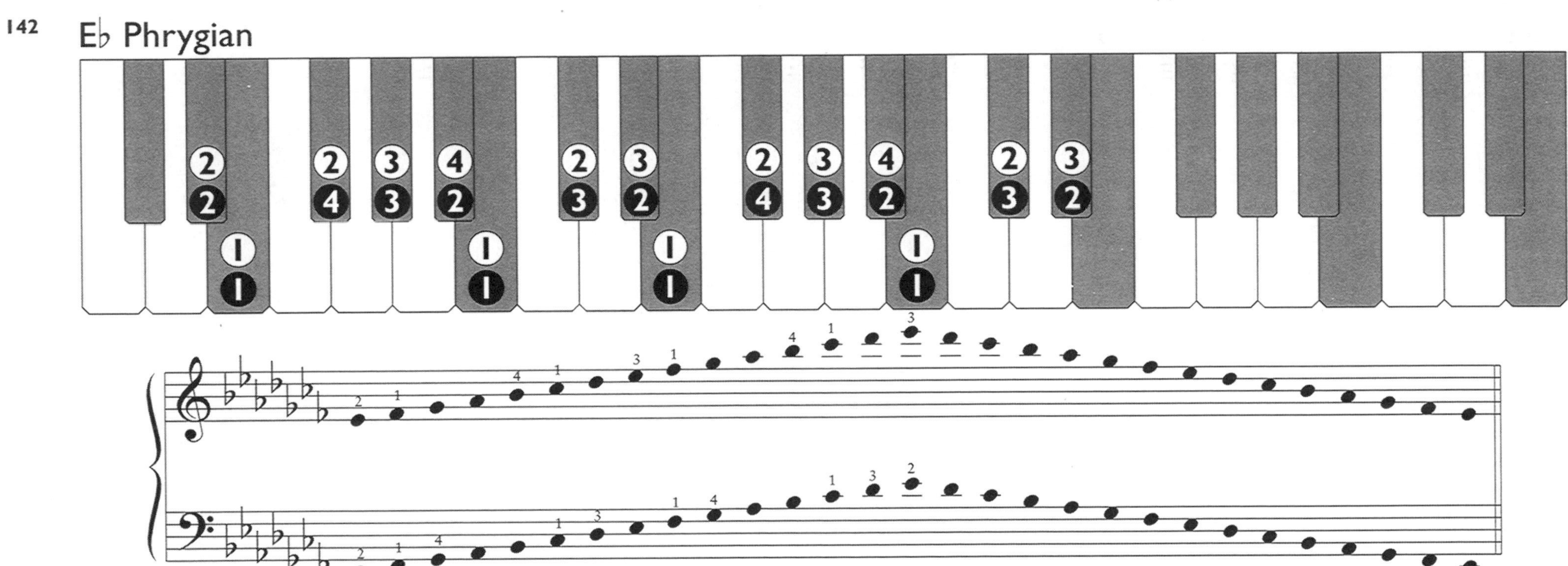

F Lydian

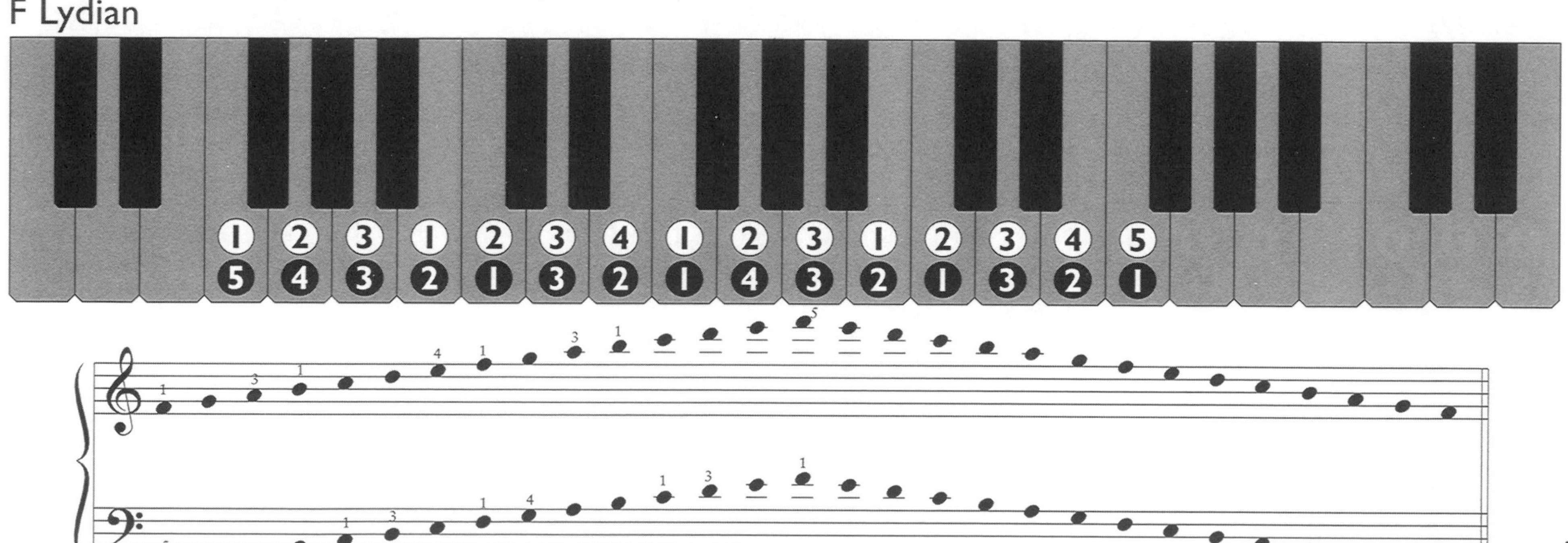

C Lydian

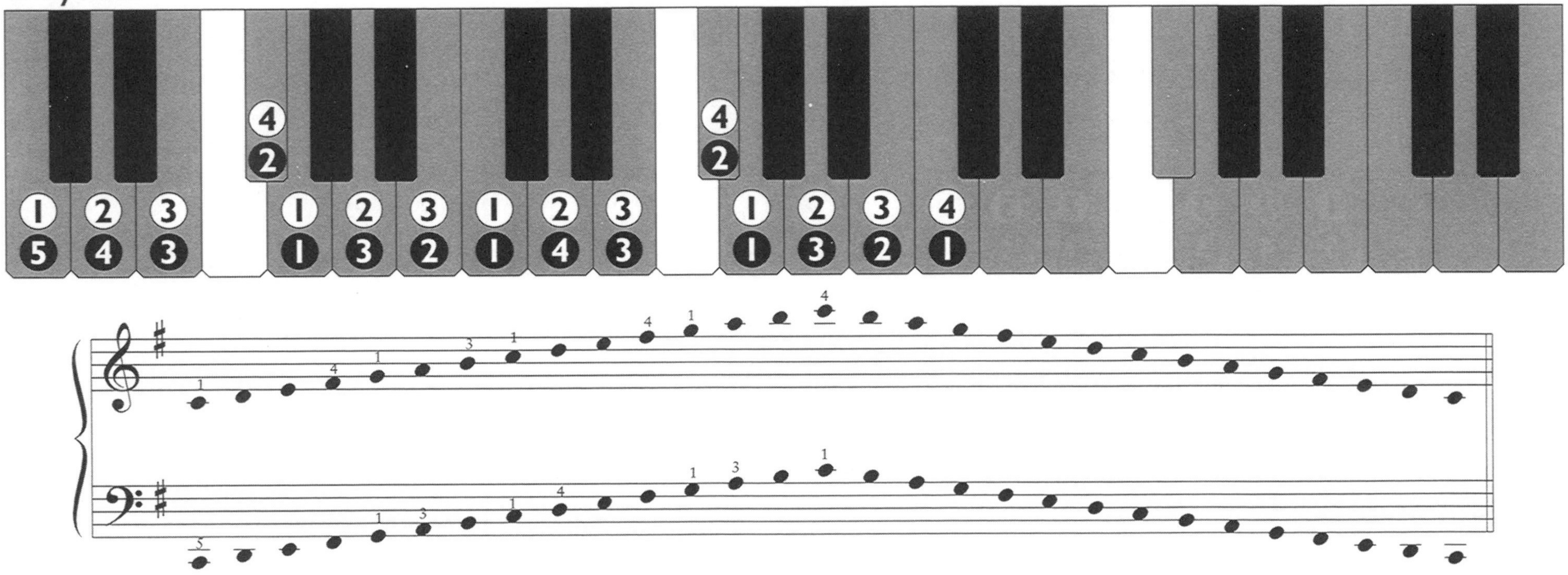

G Lydian

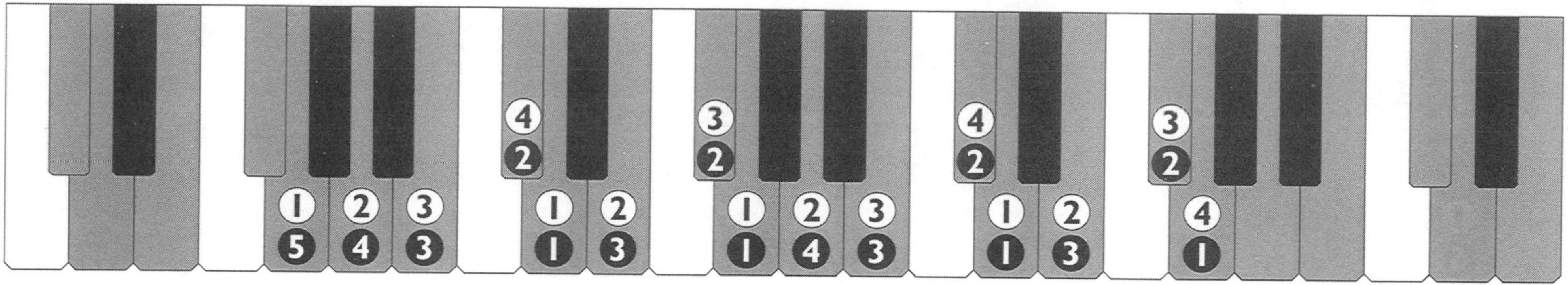

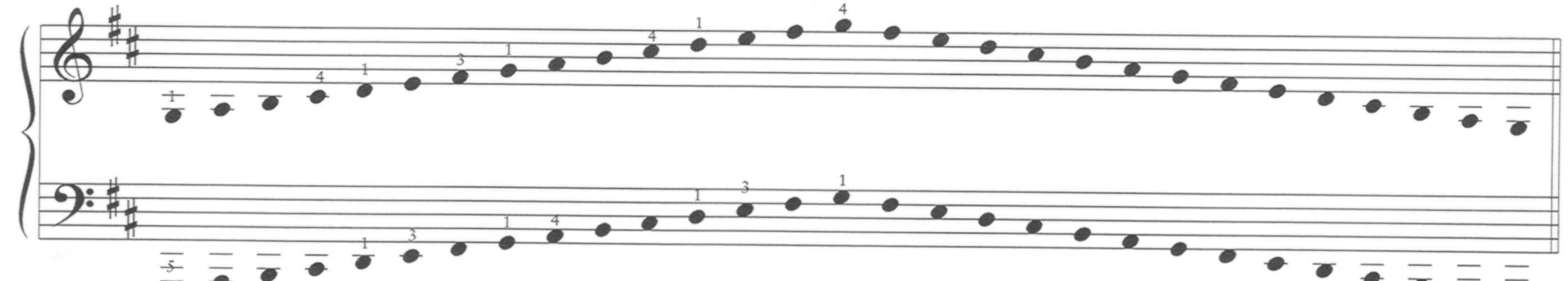

D Lydian

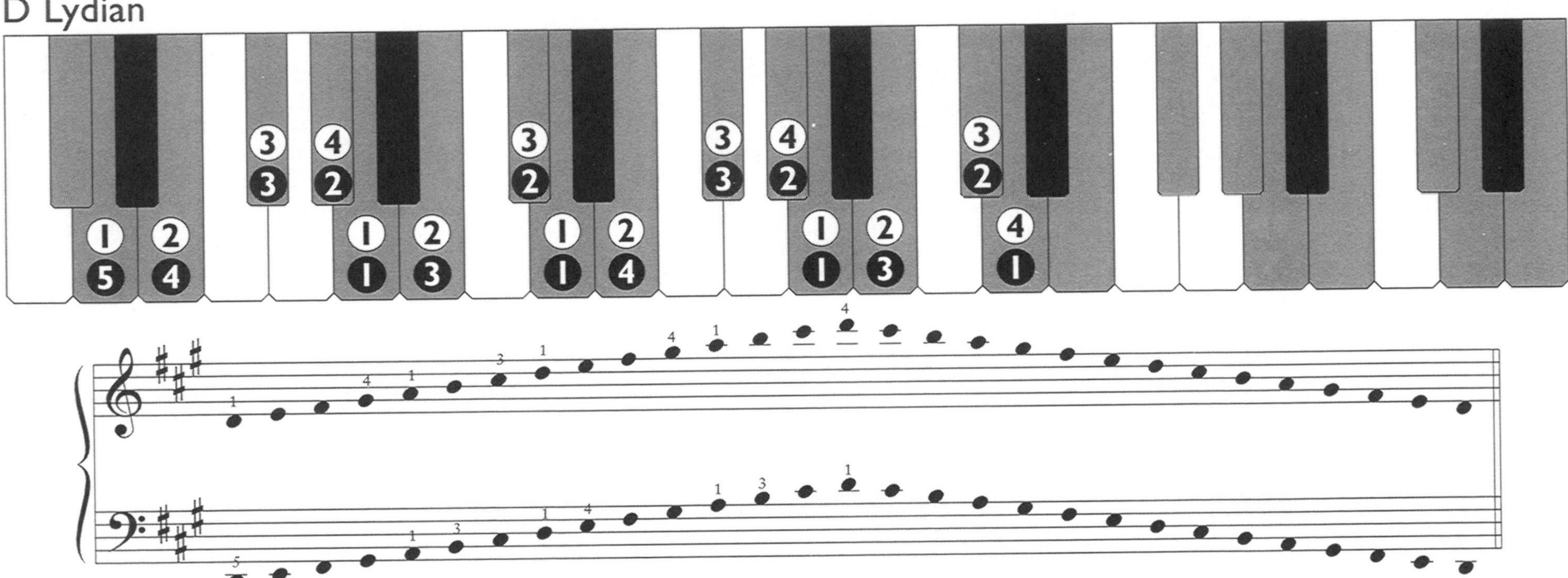

A Lydian

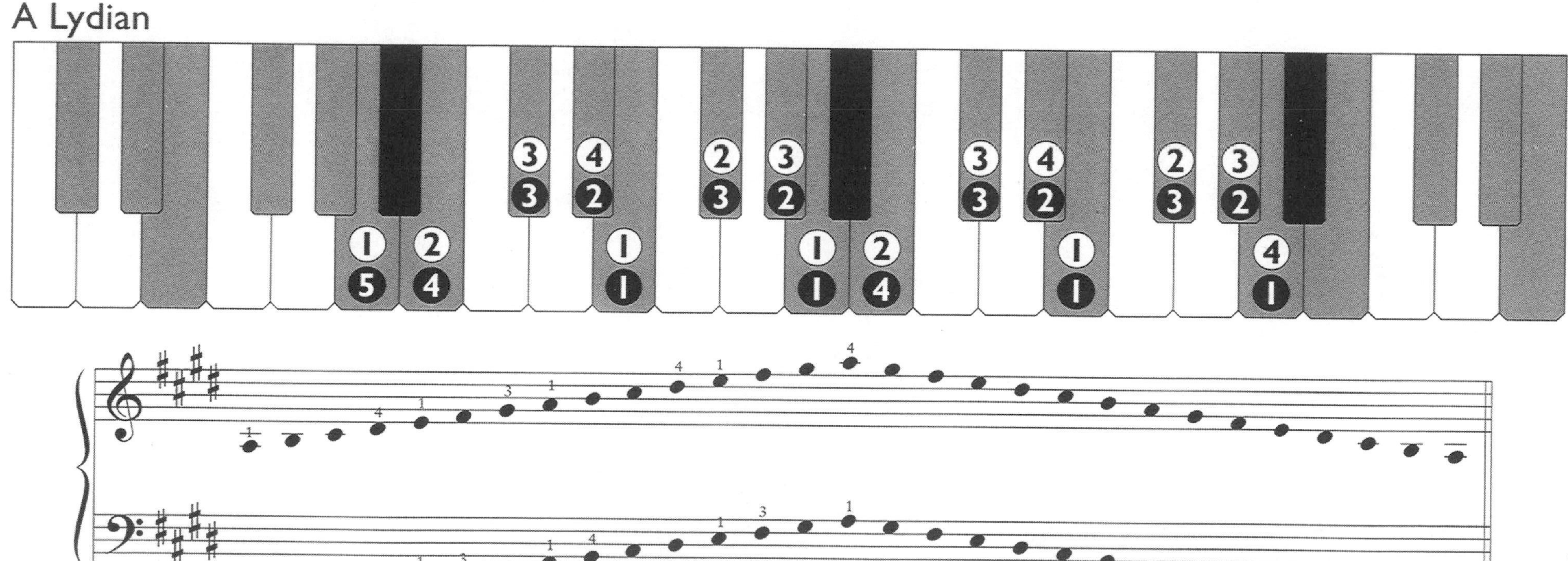

E Lydian

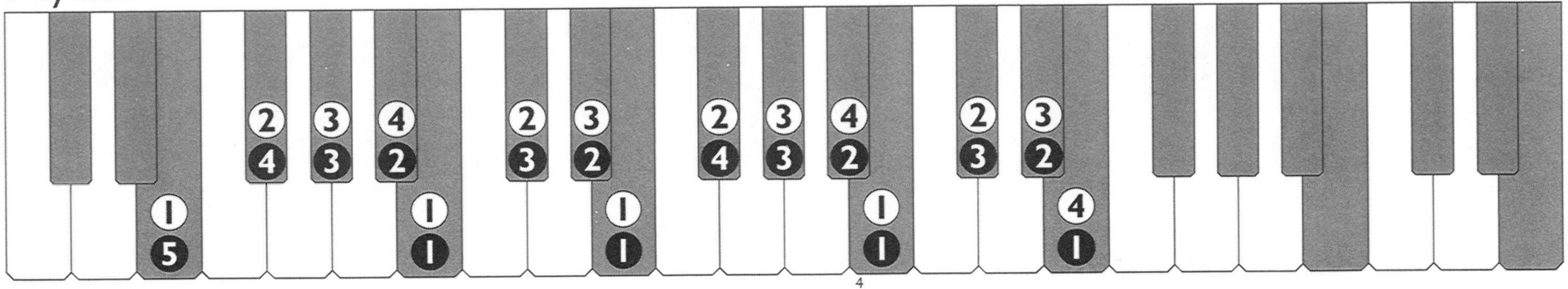

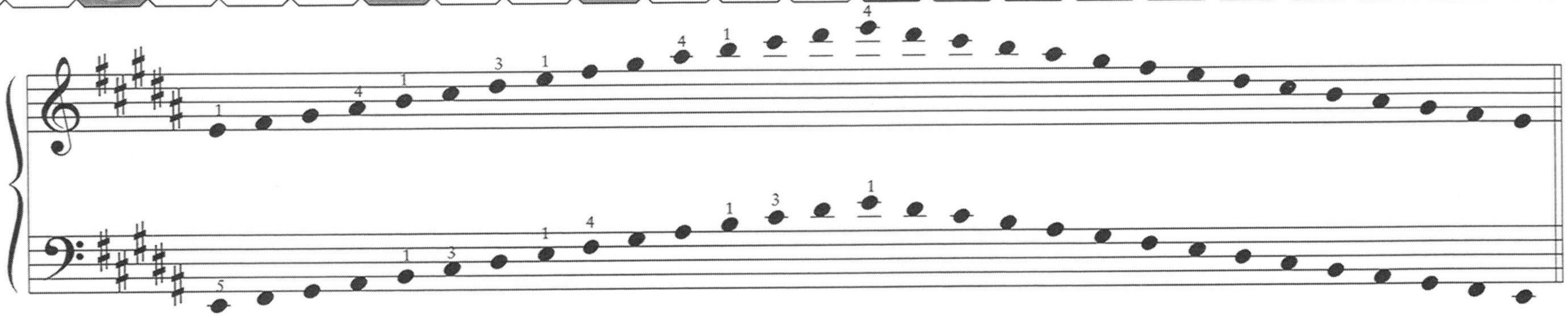

B Lydian

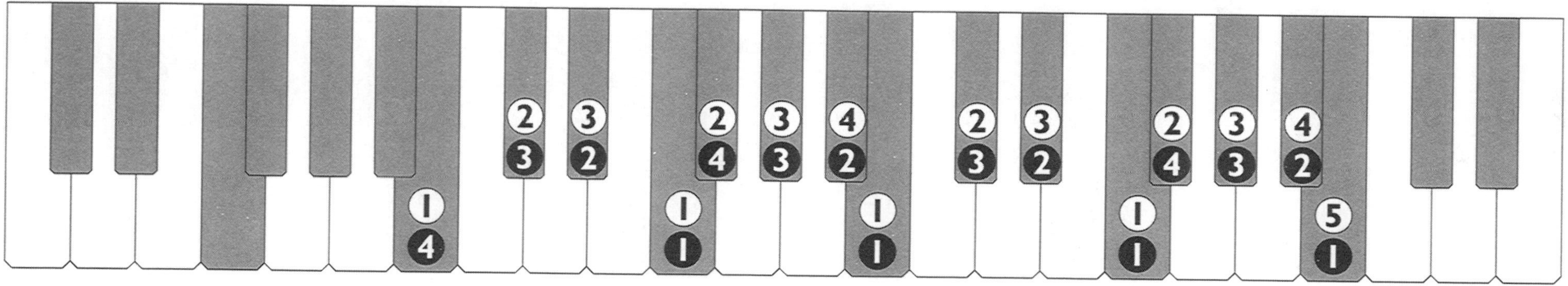

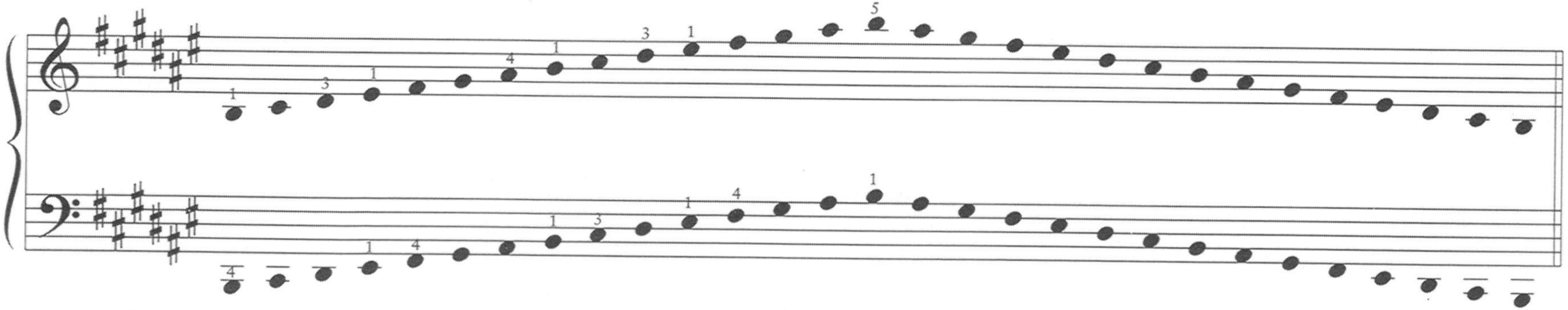

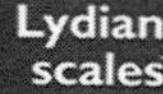

F♯ Lydian

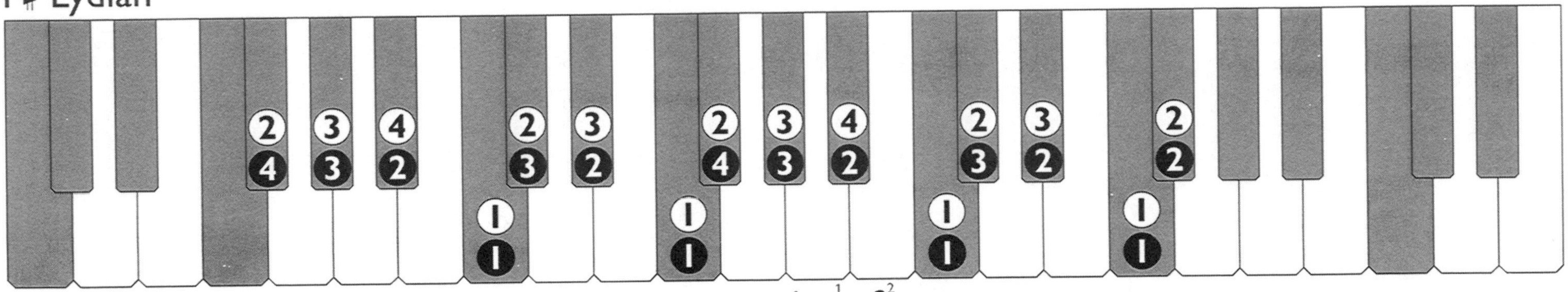

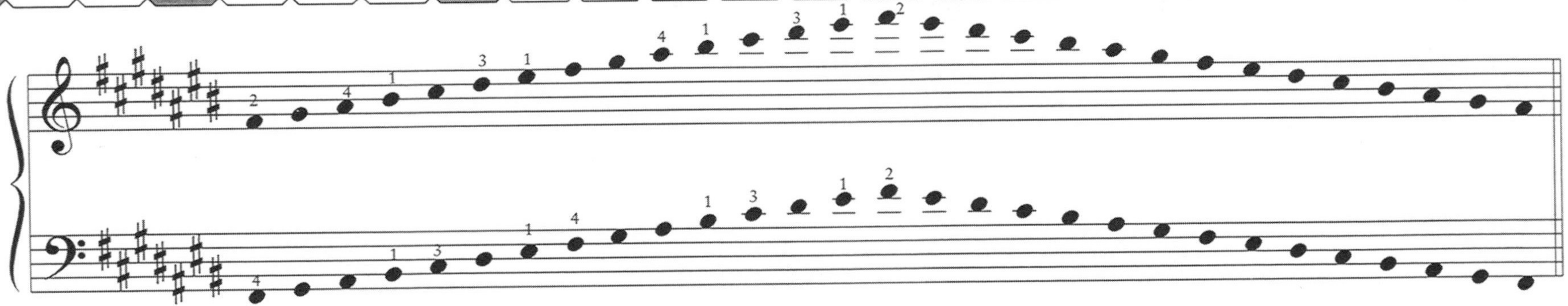

B♭ Lydian

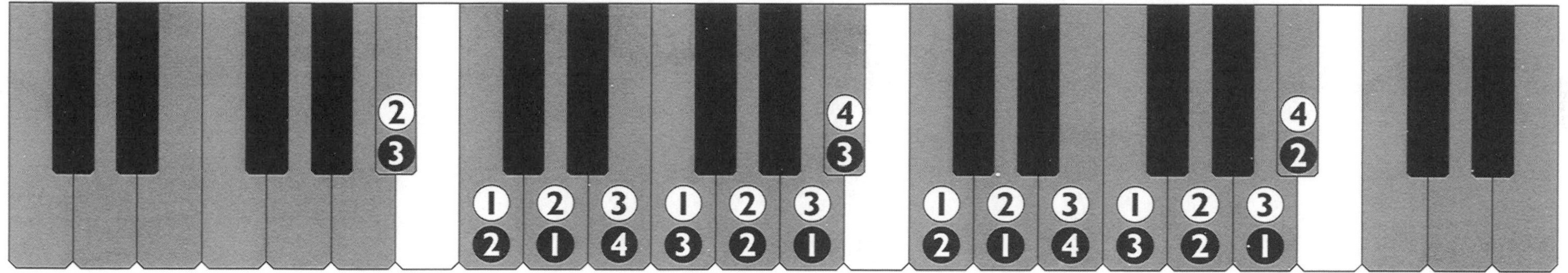

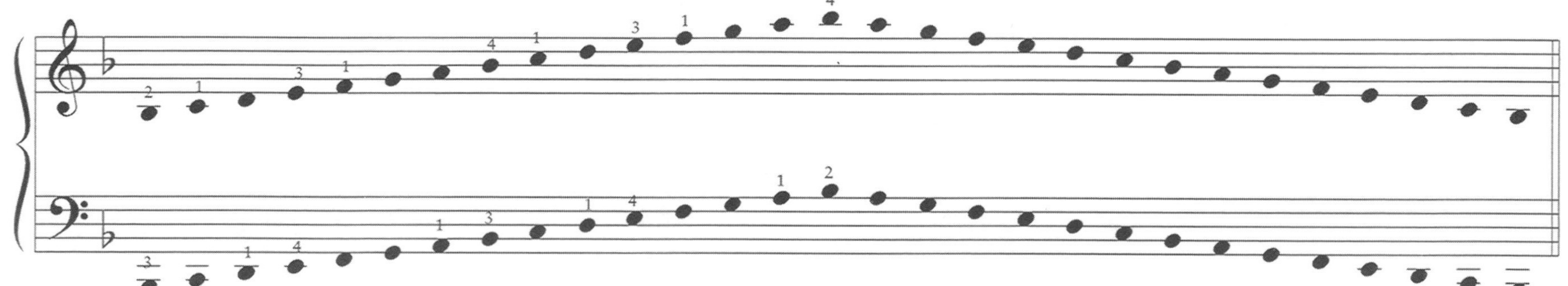

E♭ Lydian

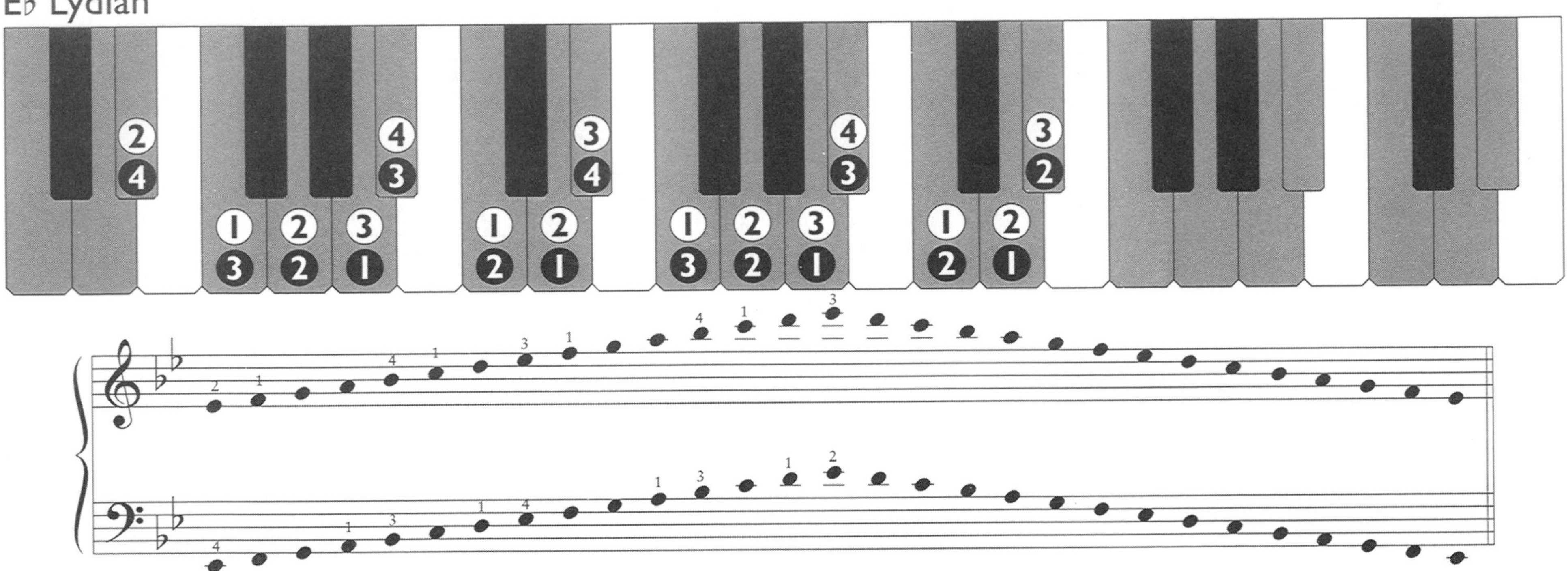

A♭ Lydian

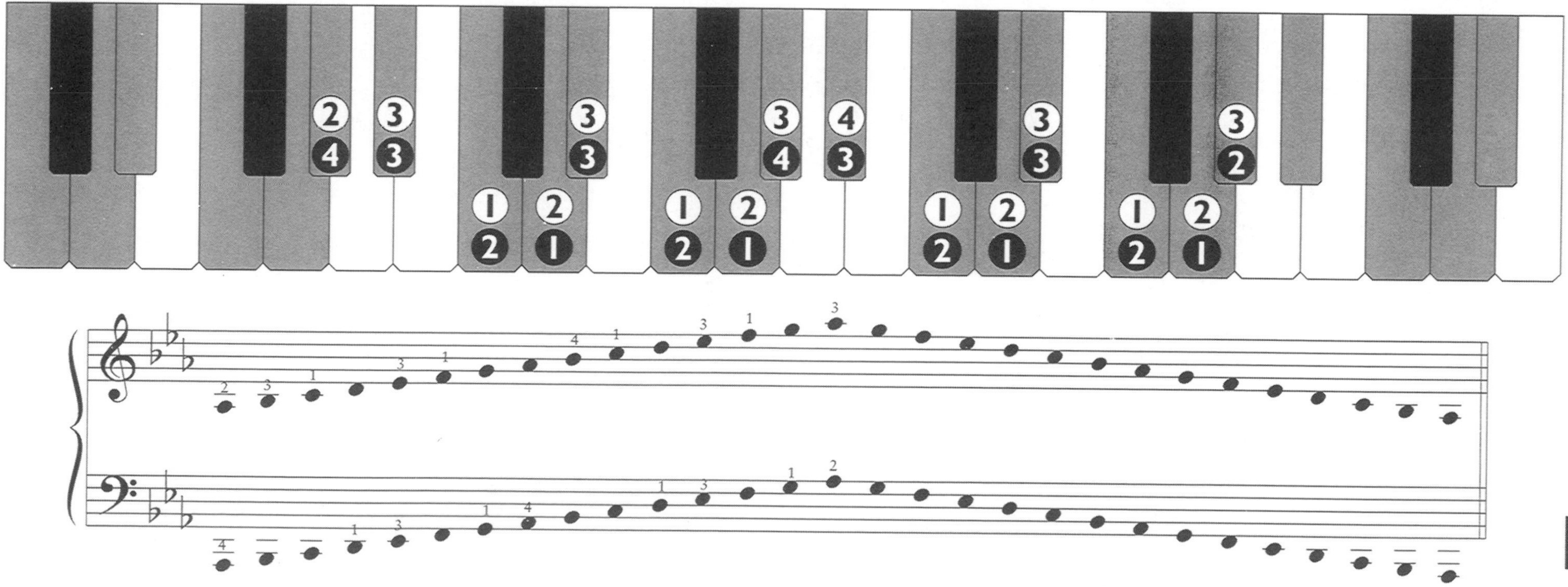

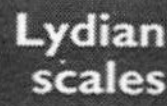

D♭ Lydian

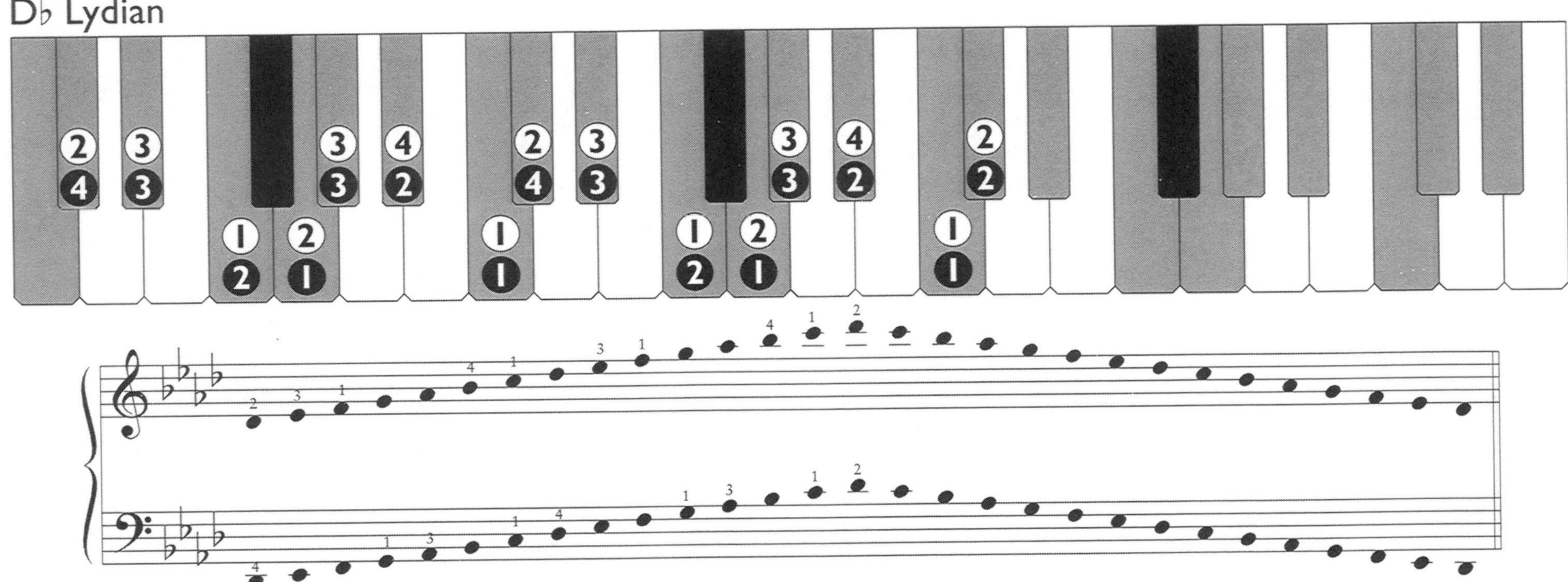

G♭ Lydian

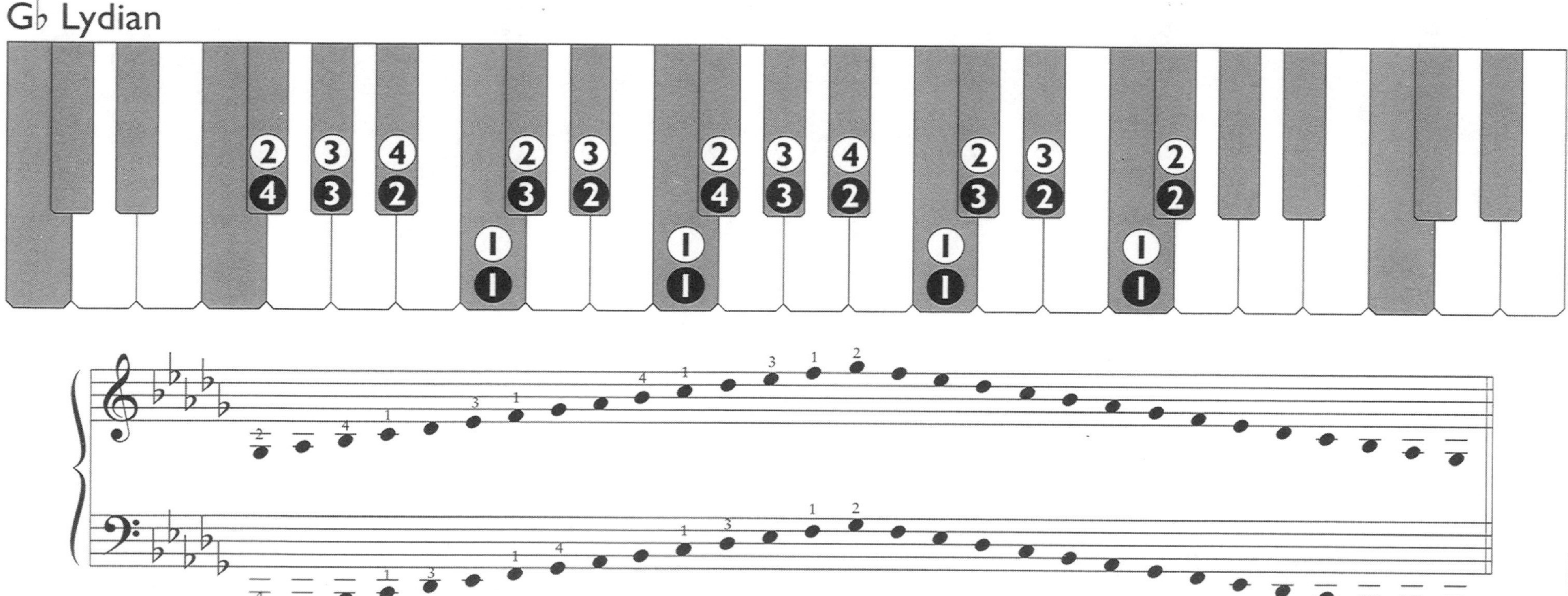

C♭ Lydian

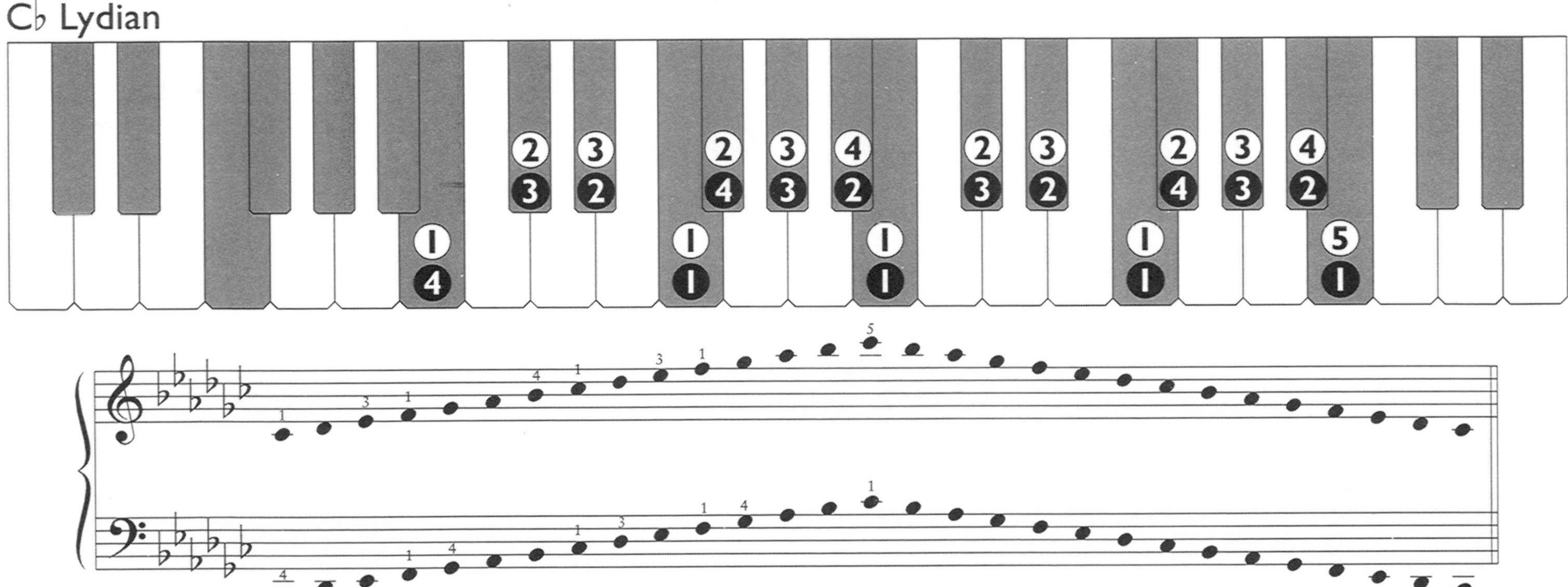

F♭ Lydian

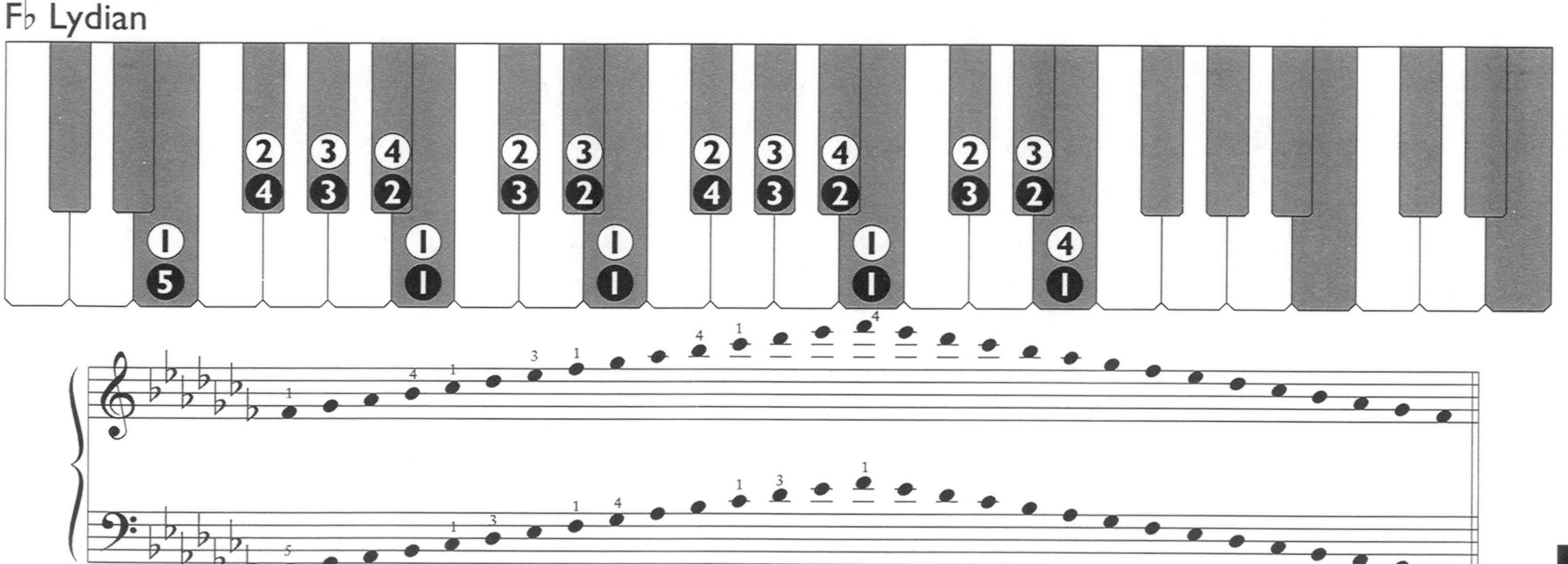

F Lydian flat-seven

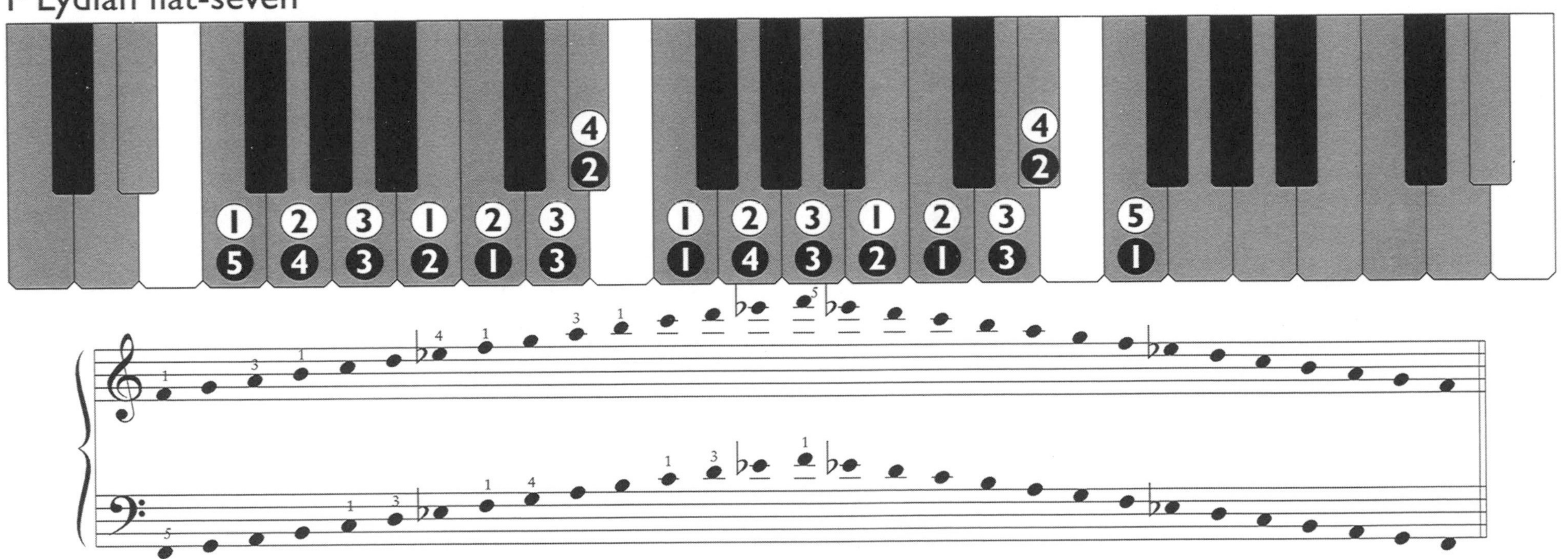

C Lydian flat-seven

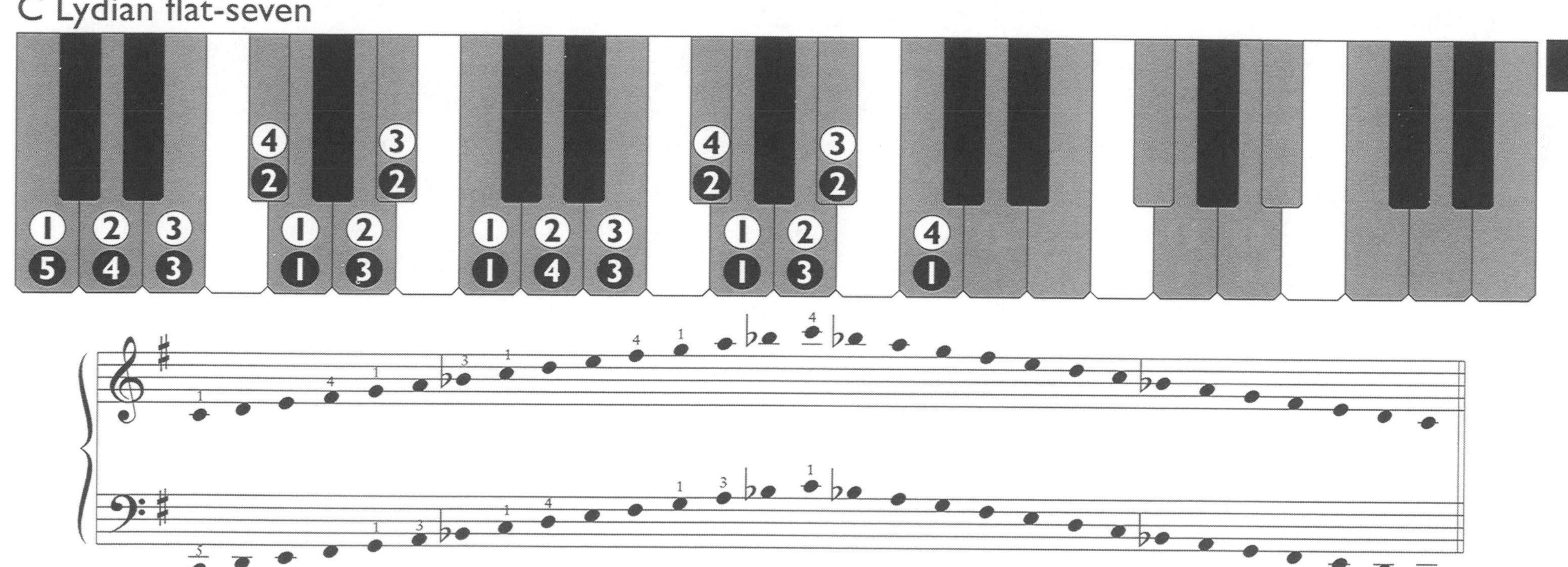

G Lydian flat-seven

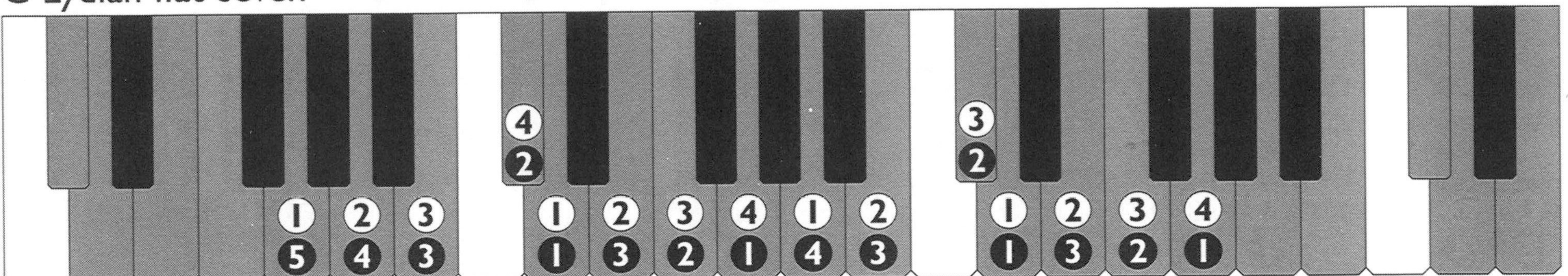

D Lydian flat-seven

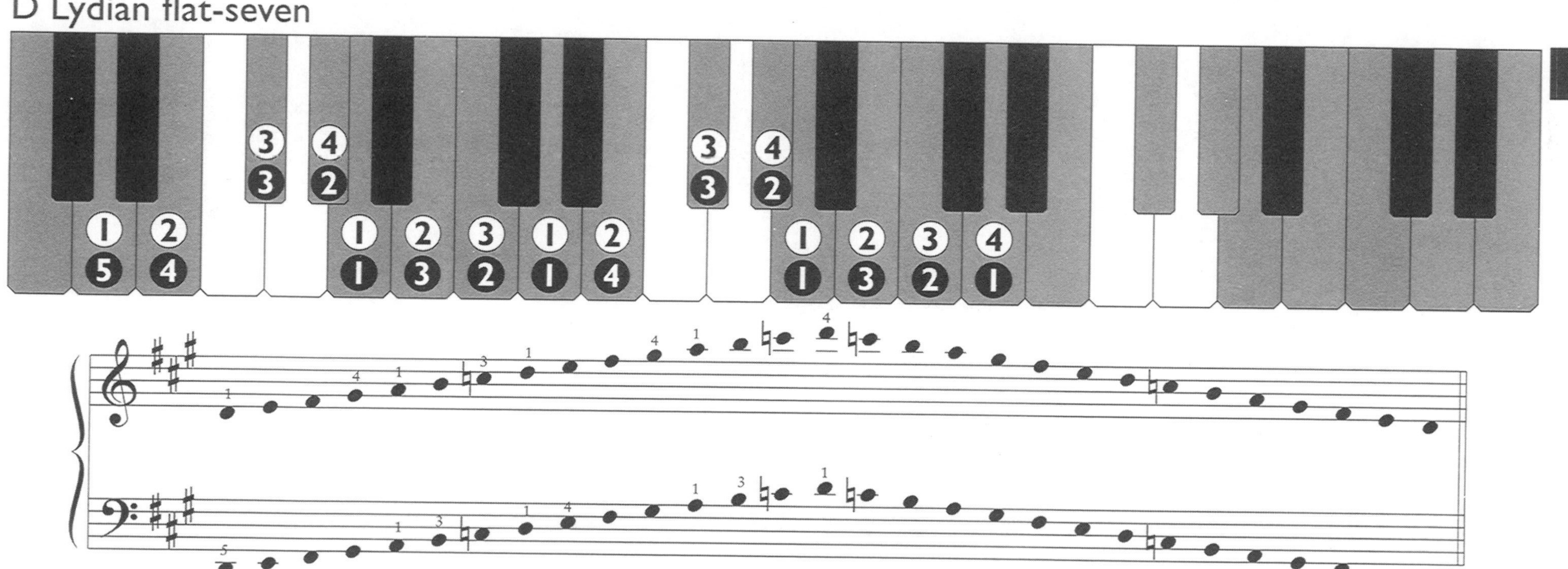

A Lydian flat-seven

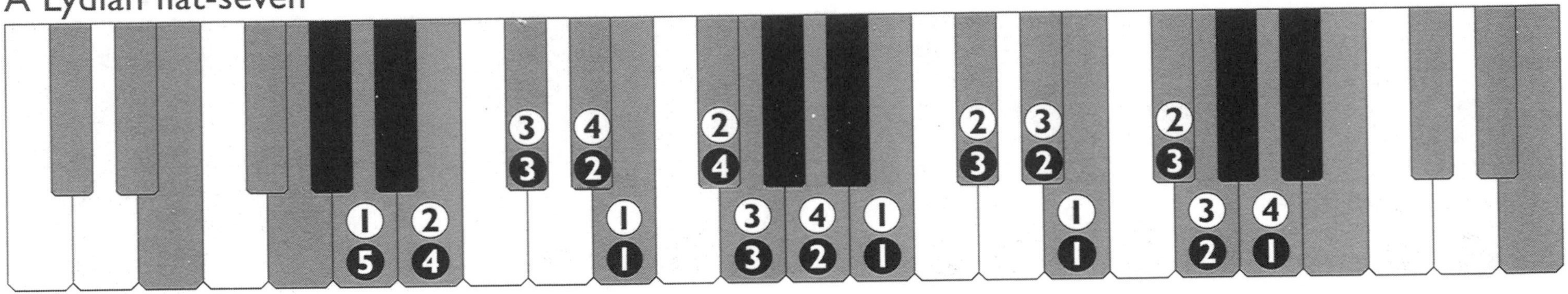

E Lydian flat-seven

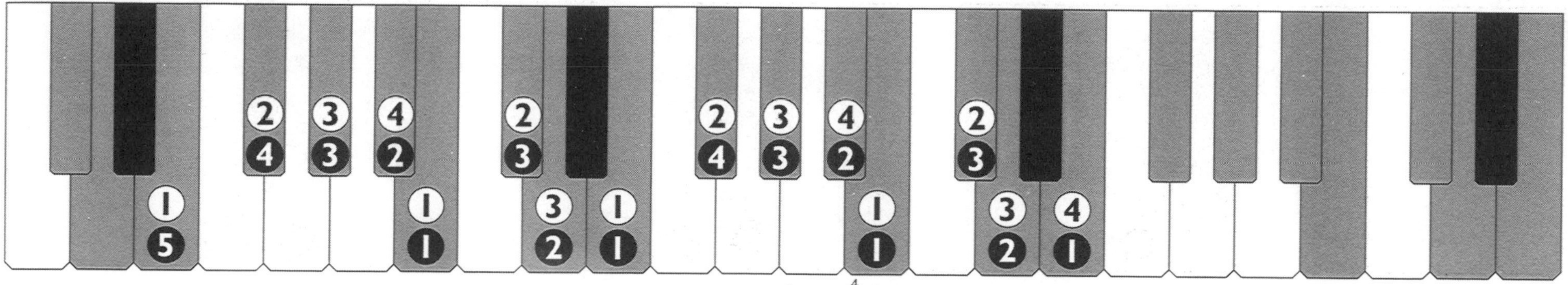

B Lydian flat-seven

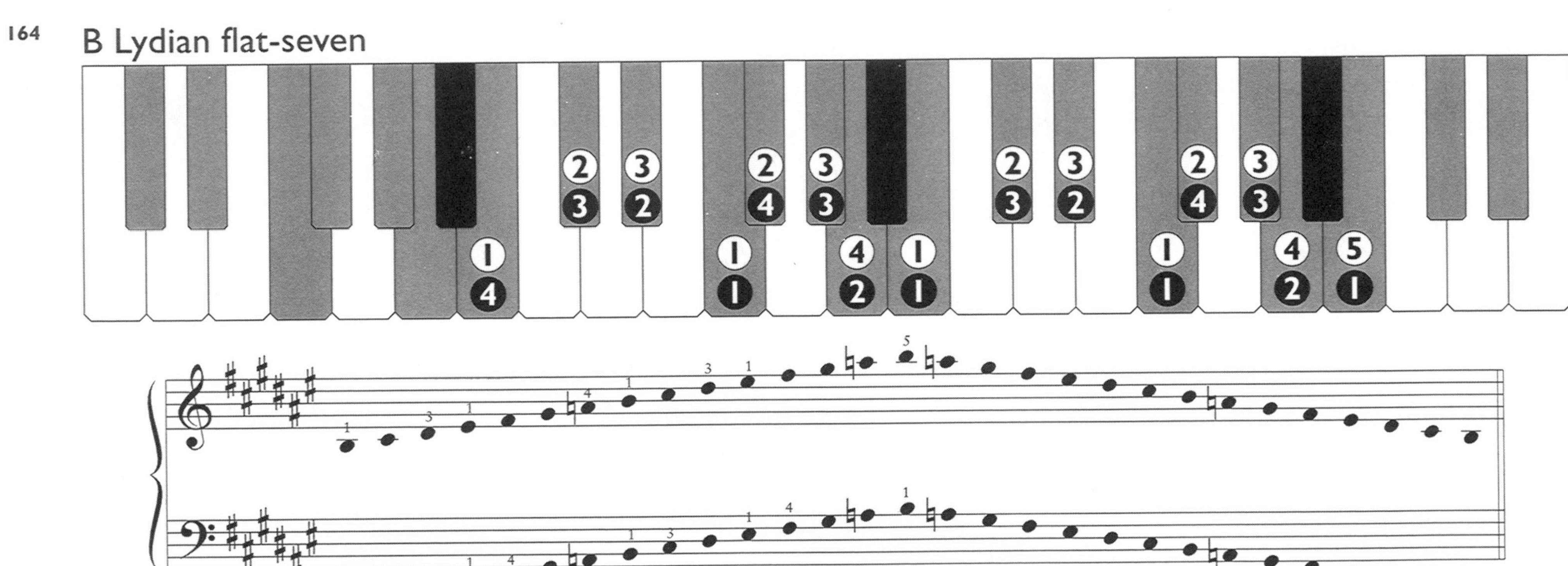

F♯ Lydian flat-seven

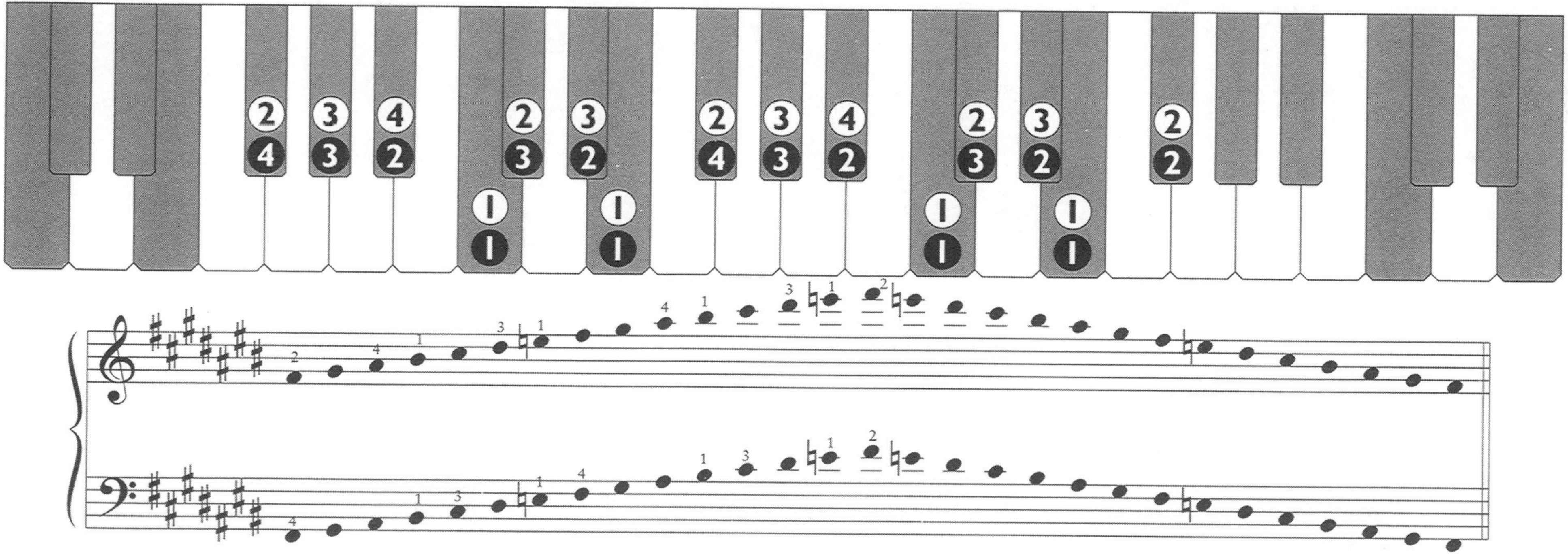

B♭ Lydian flat-seven

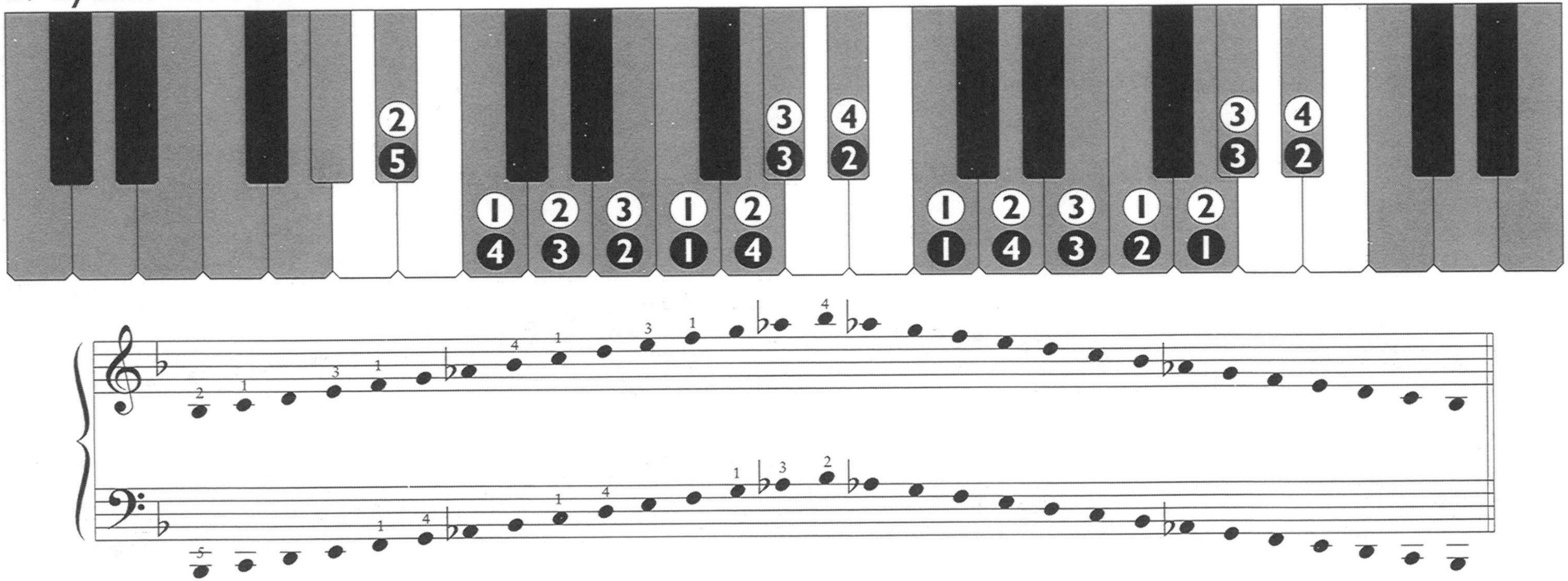

E♭ Lydian flat-seven

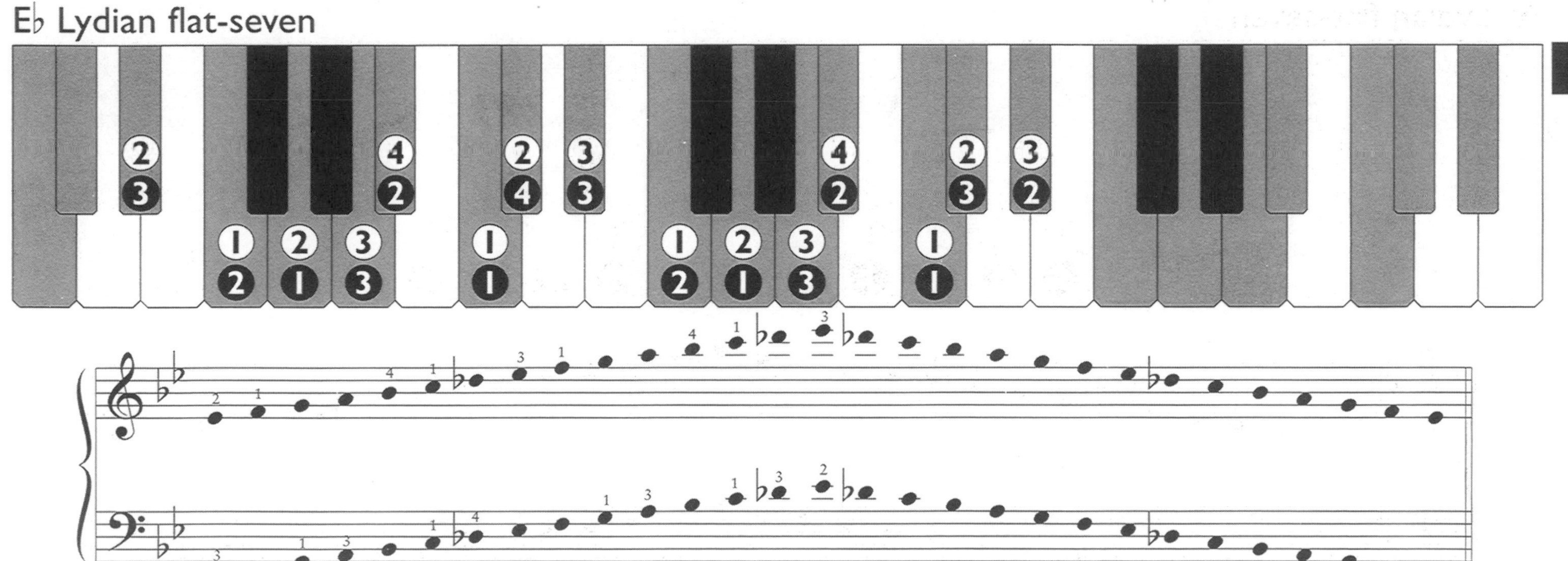

A♭ Lydian flat-seven

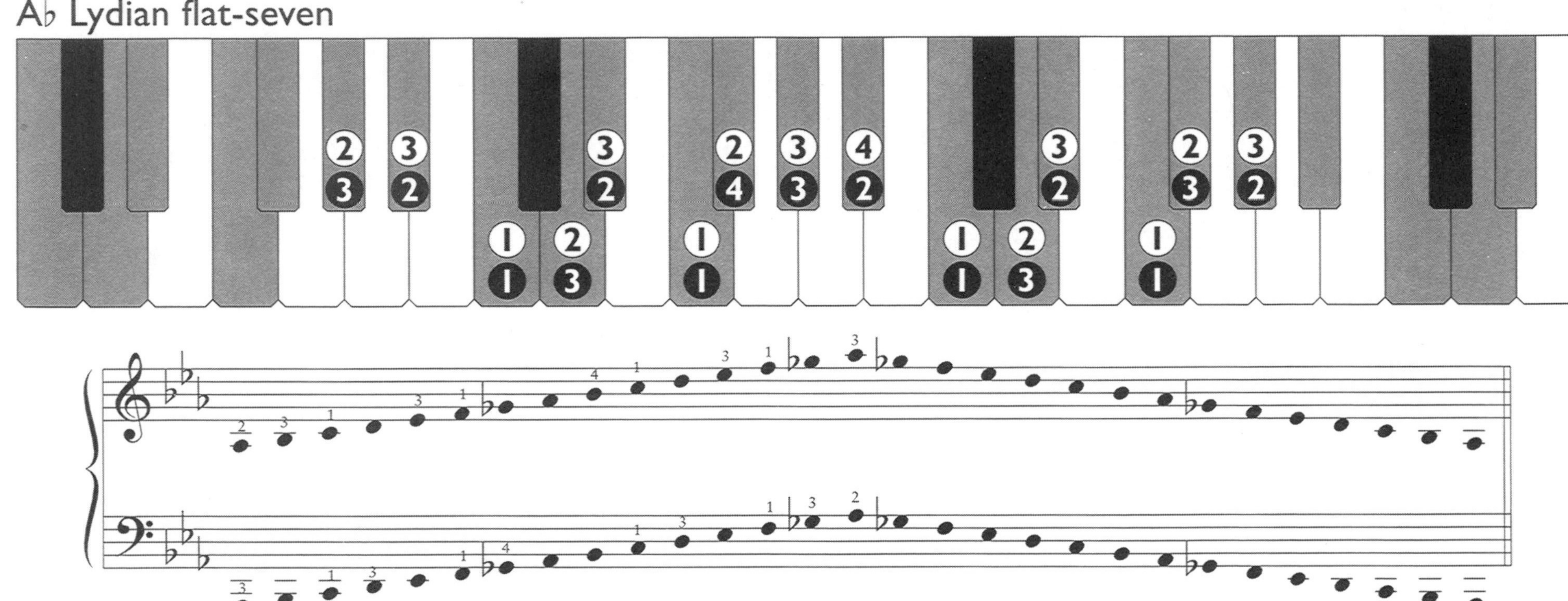

D♭ Lydian flat-seven

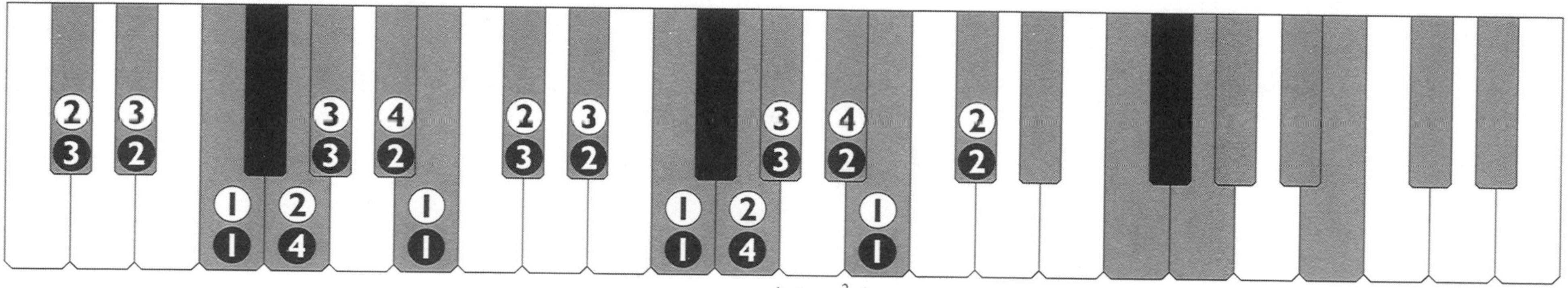

G♭ Lydian flat-seven

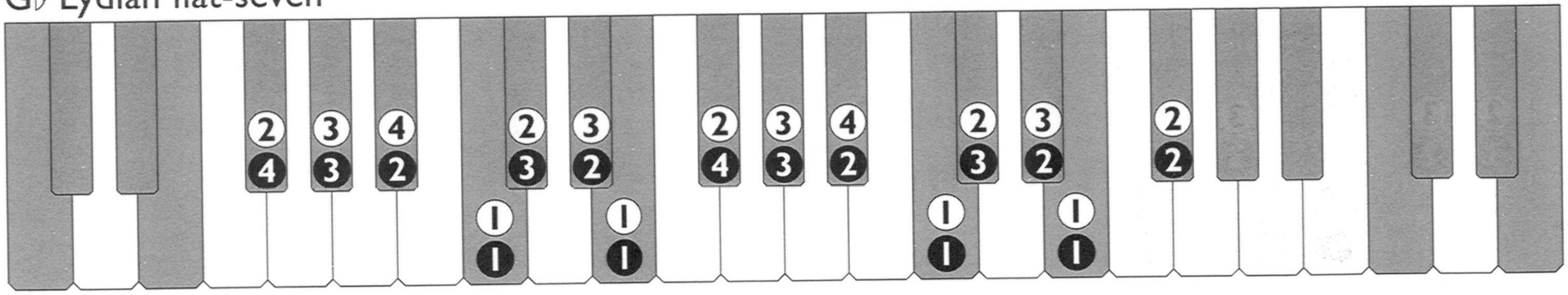

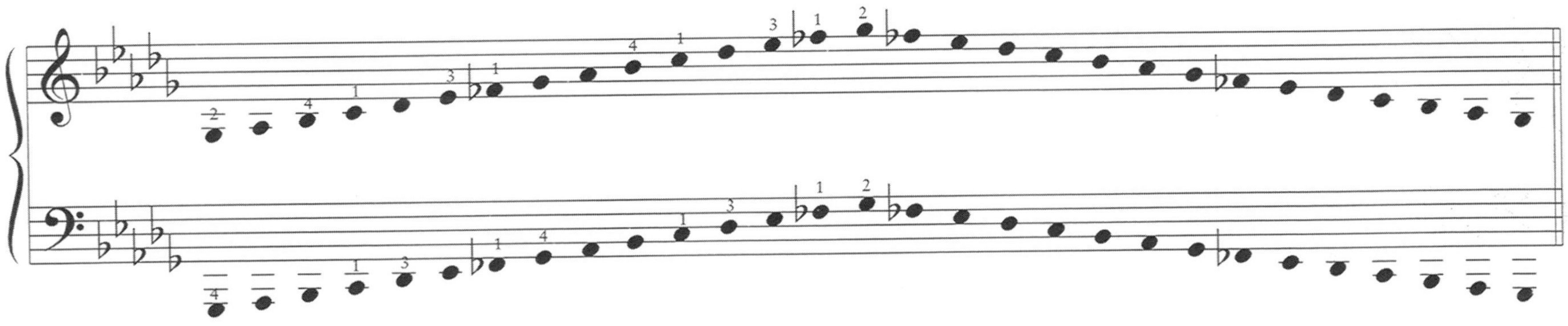

C♭ Lydian flat-seven

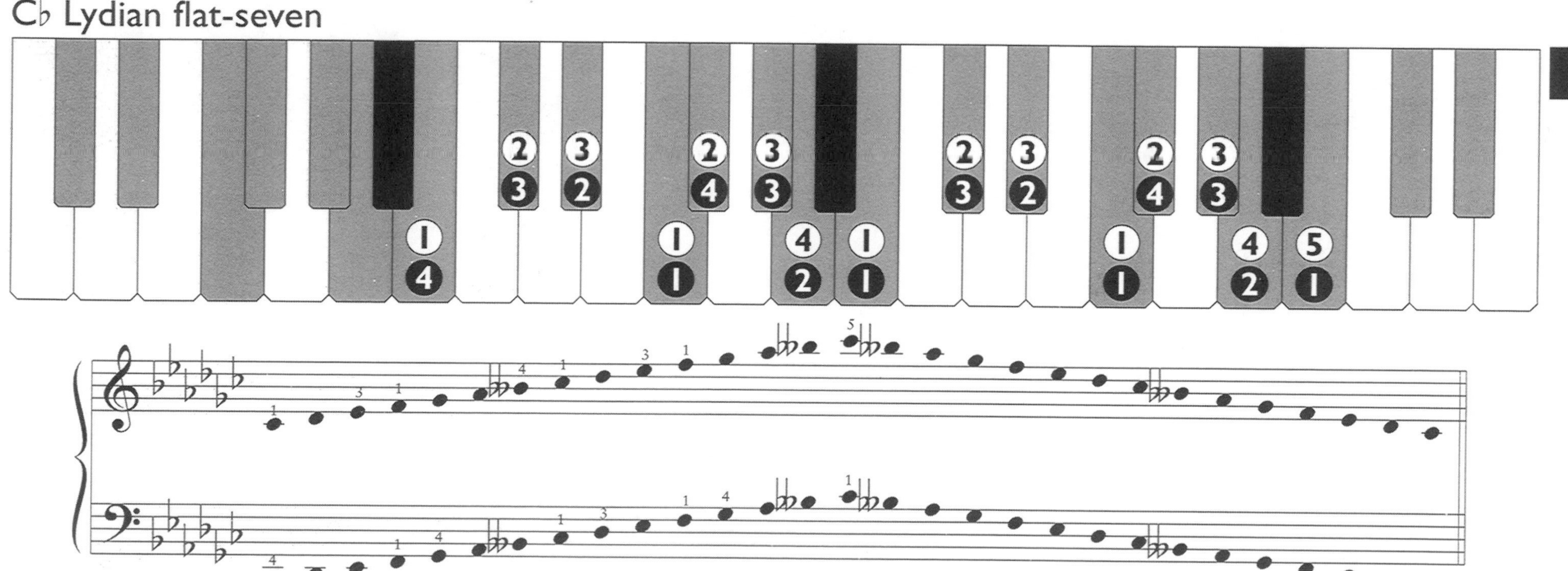

F♭ Lydian flat-seven

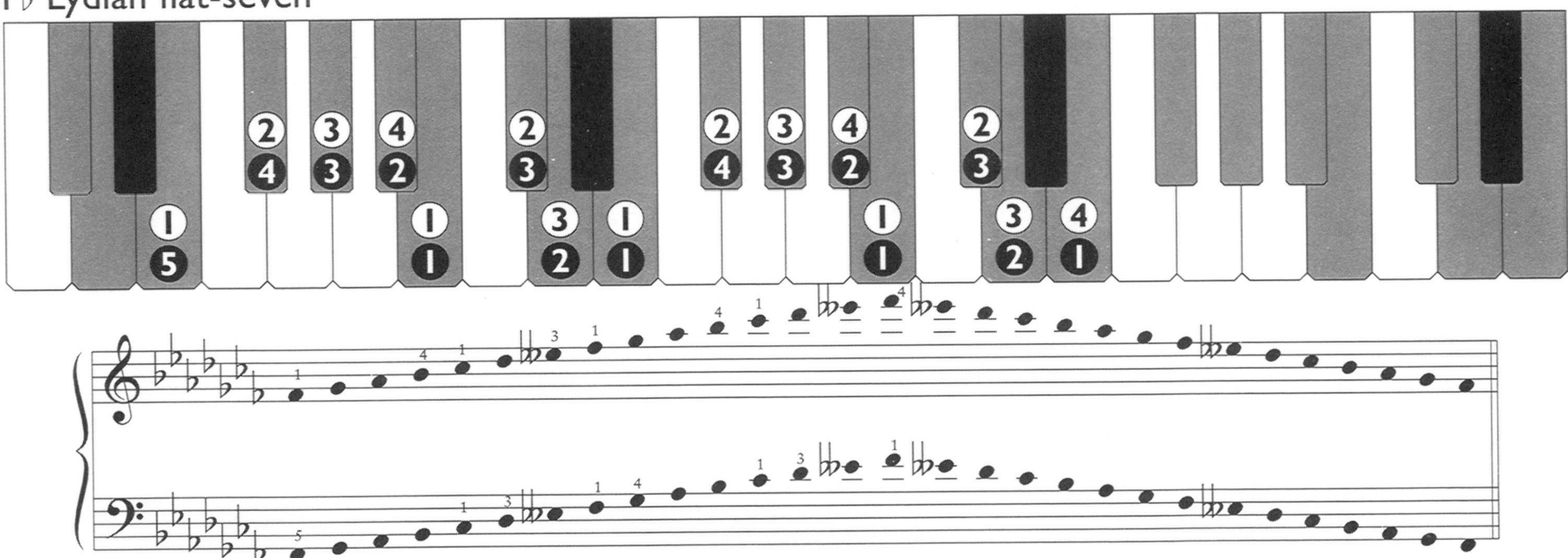

G Mixolydian

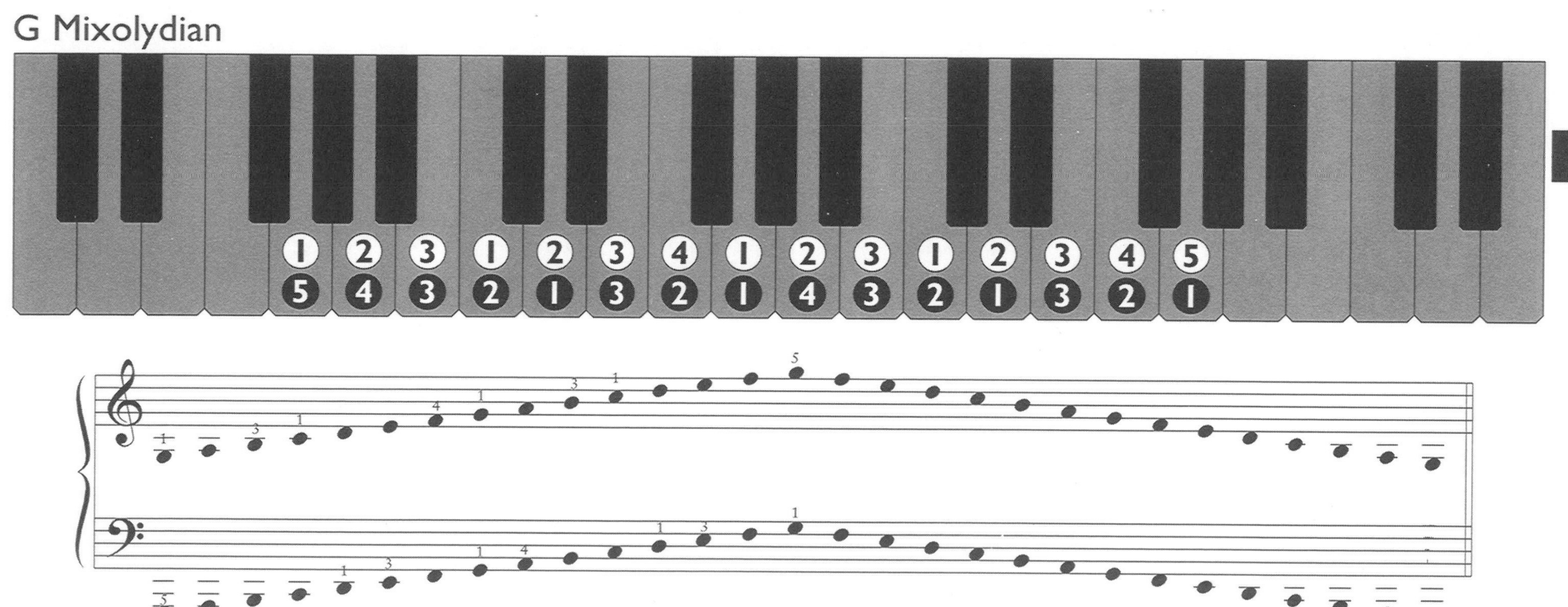

D Mixolydian

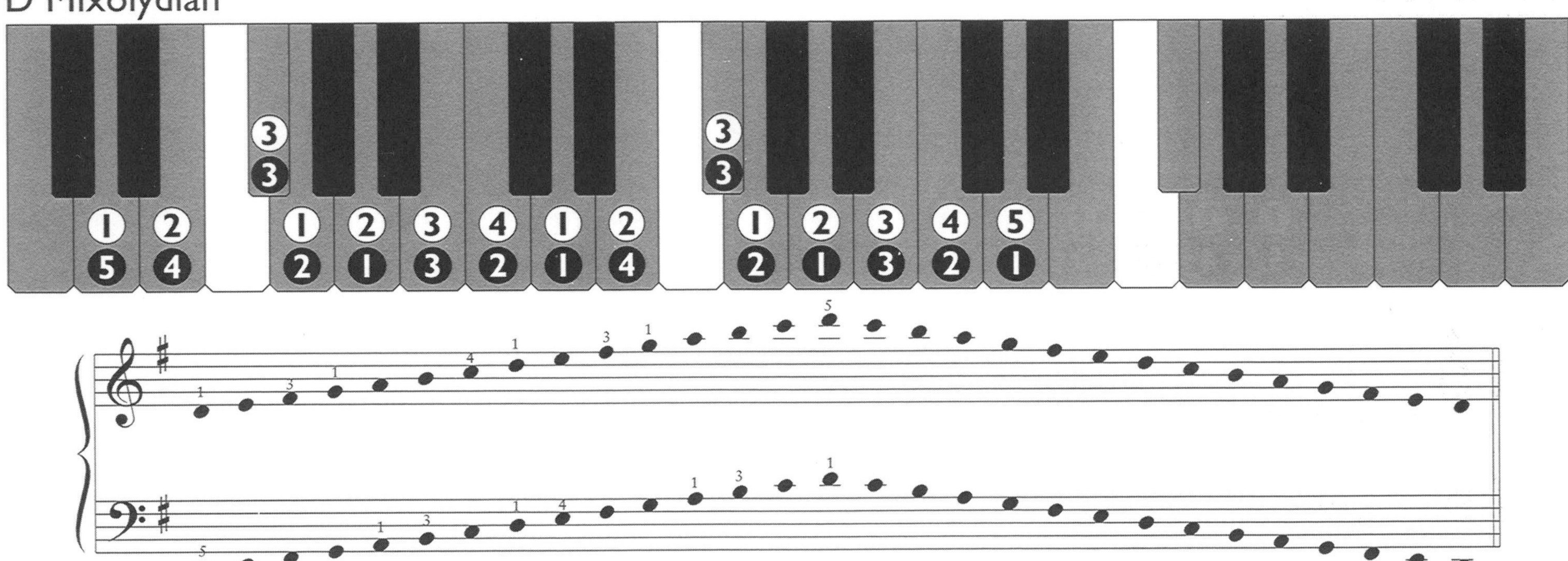

A Mixolydian

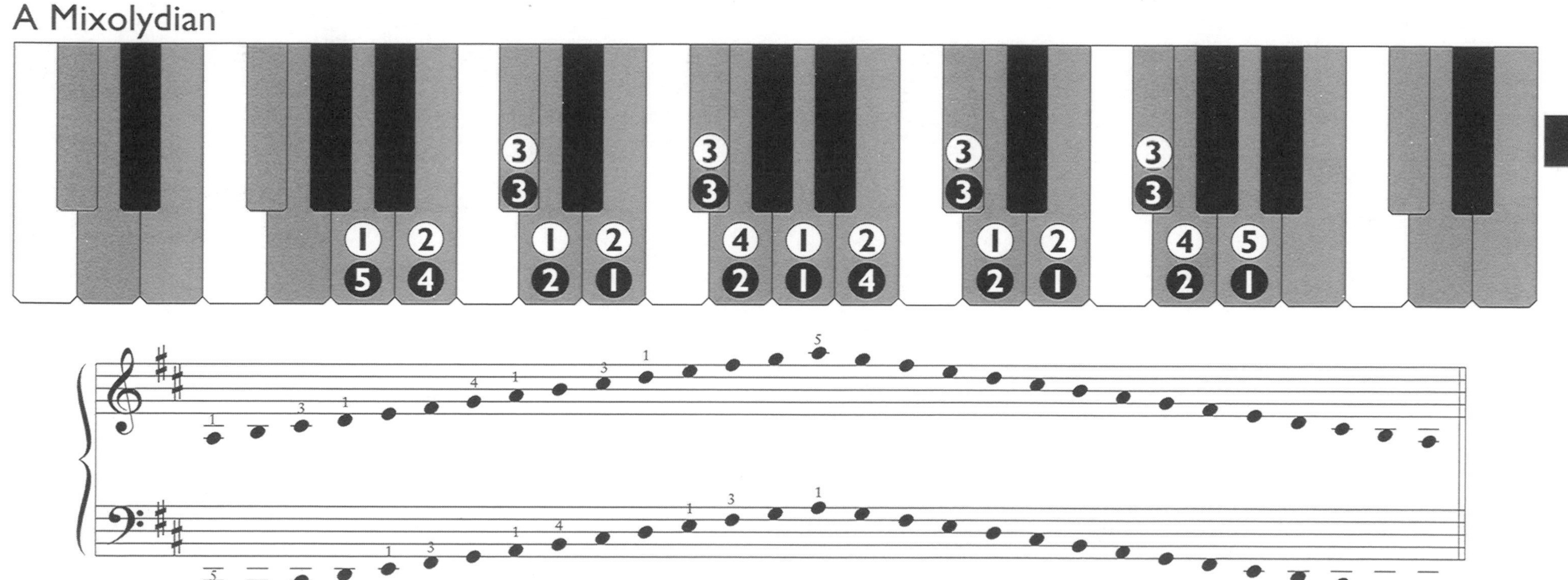

E Mixolydian

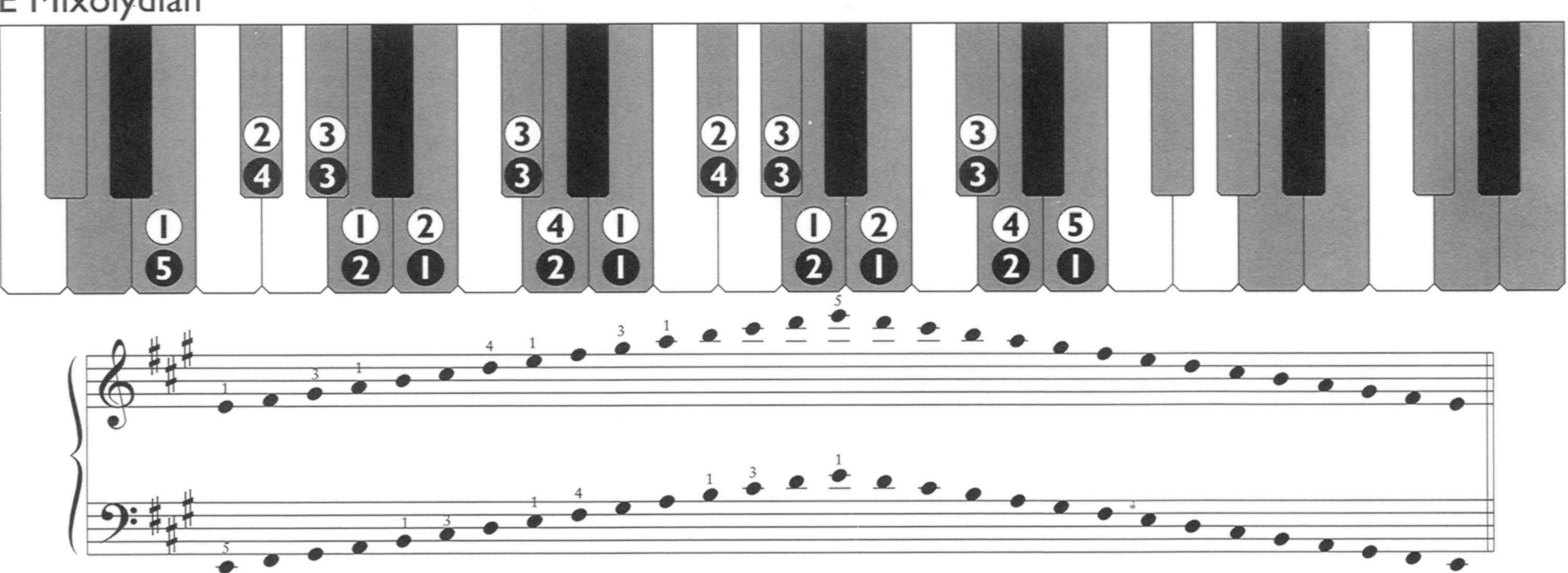

B Mixolydian

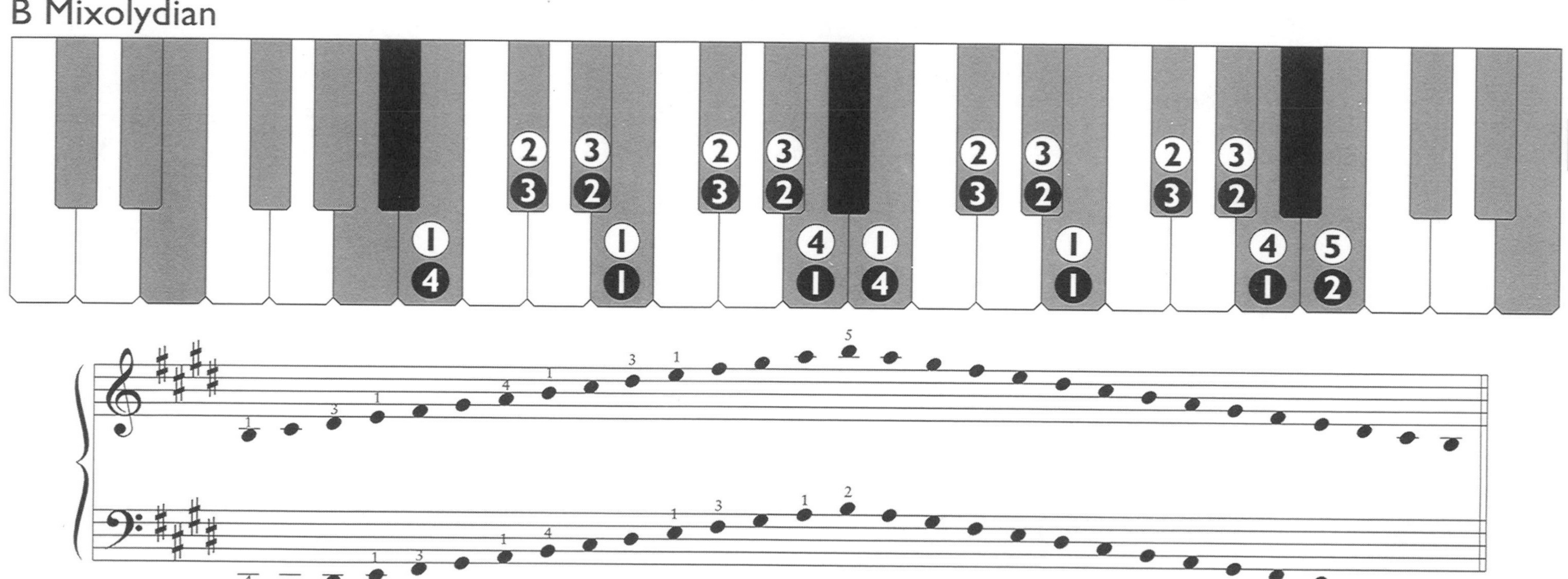

F♯ Mixolydian

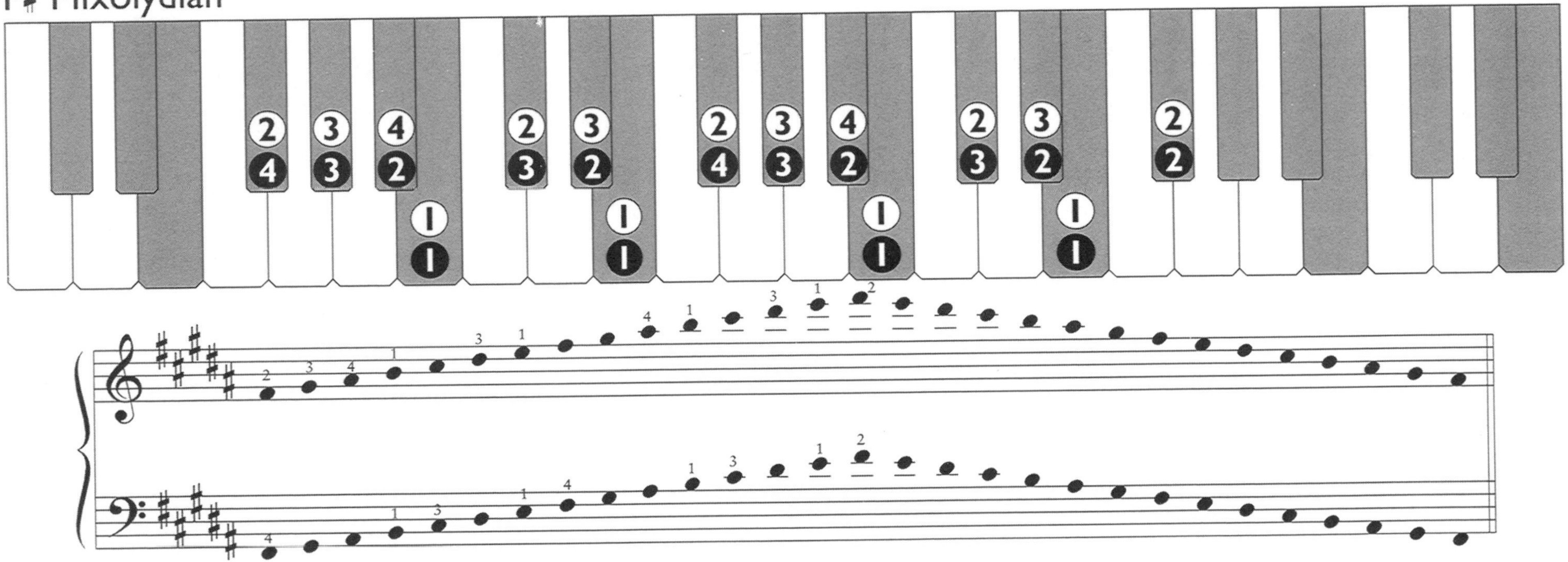

C♯ Mixolydian

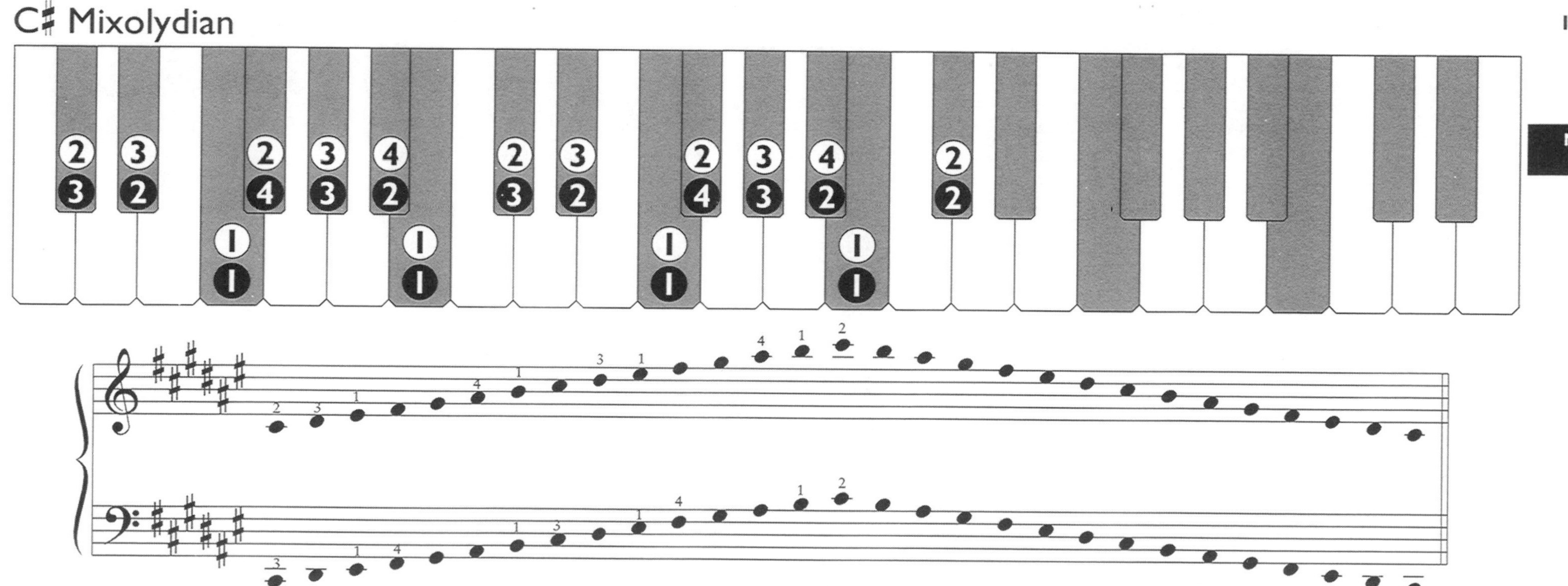

G♯ Mixolydian

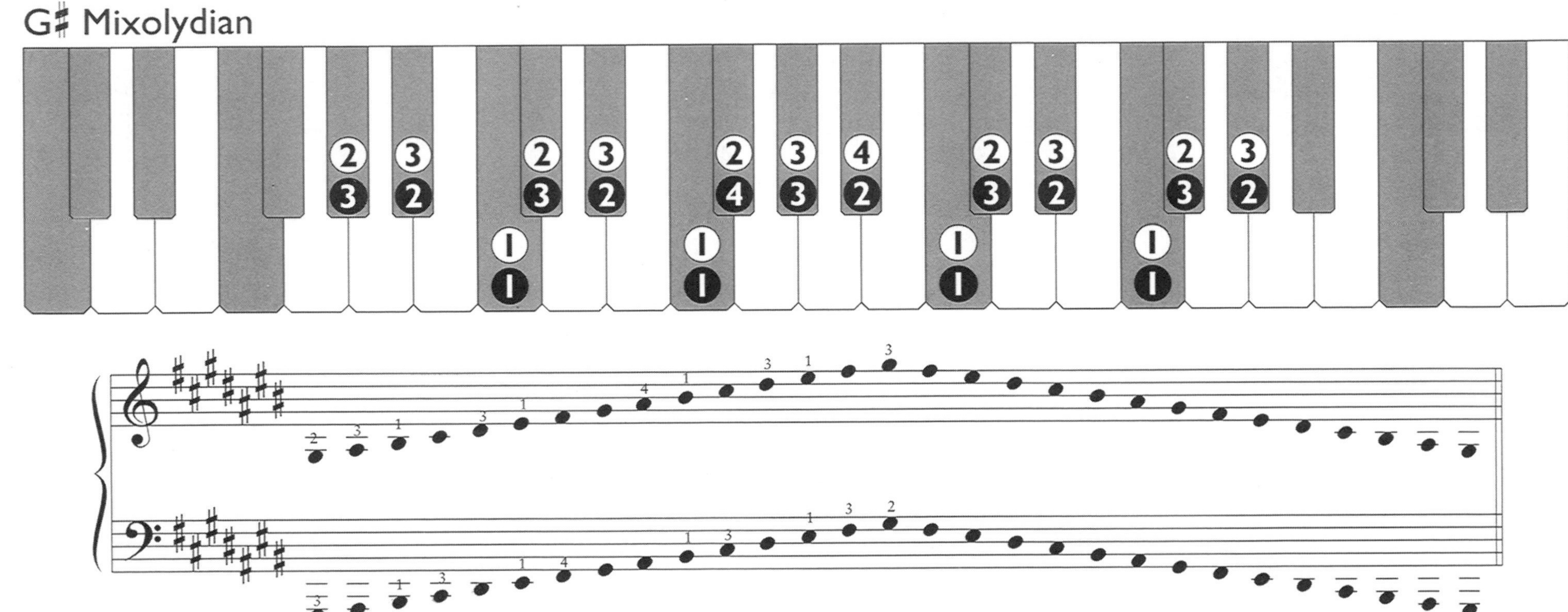

C Mixolydian

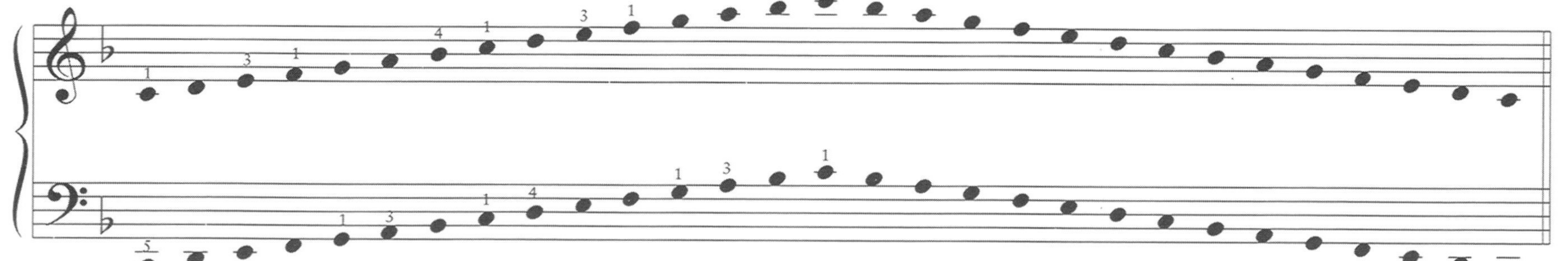

F Mixolydian

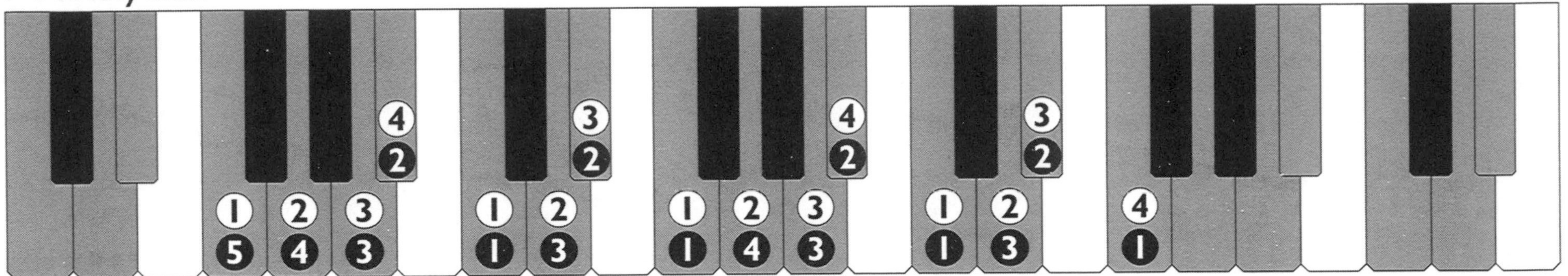

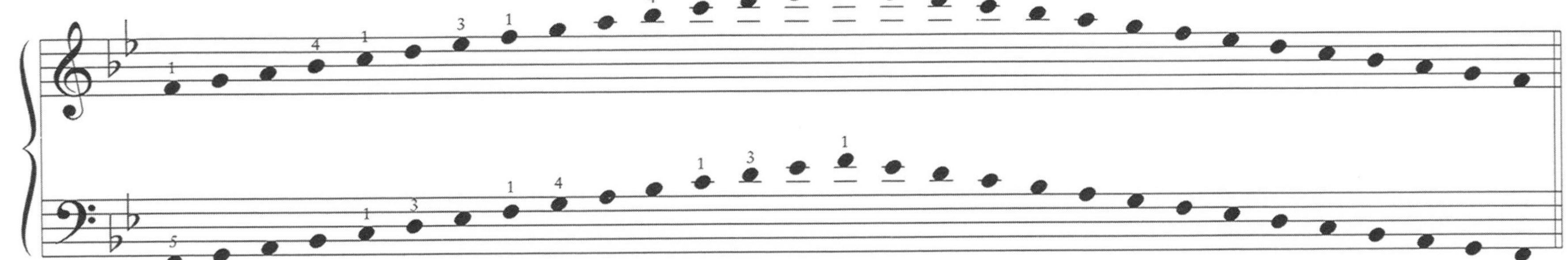

B♭ Mixolydian

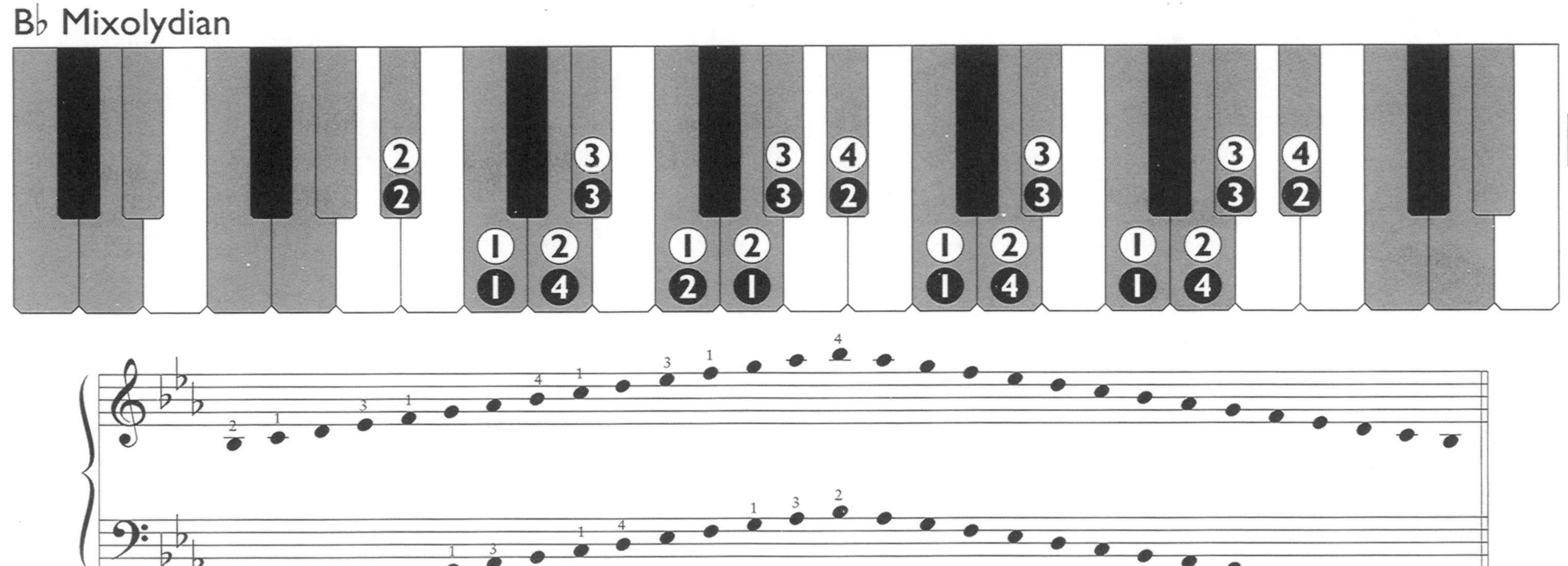

E♭ Mixolydian

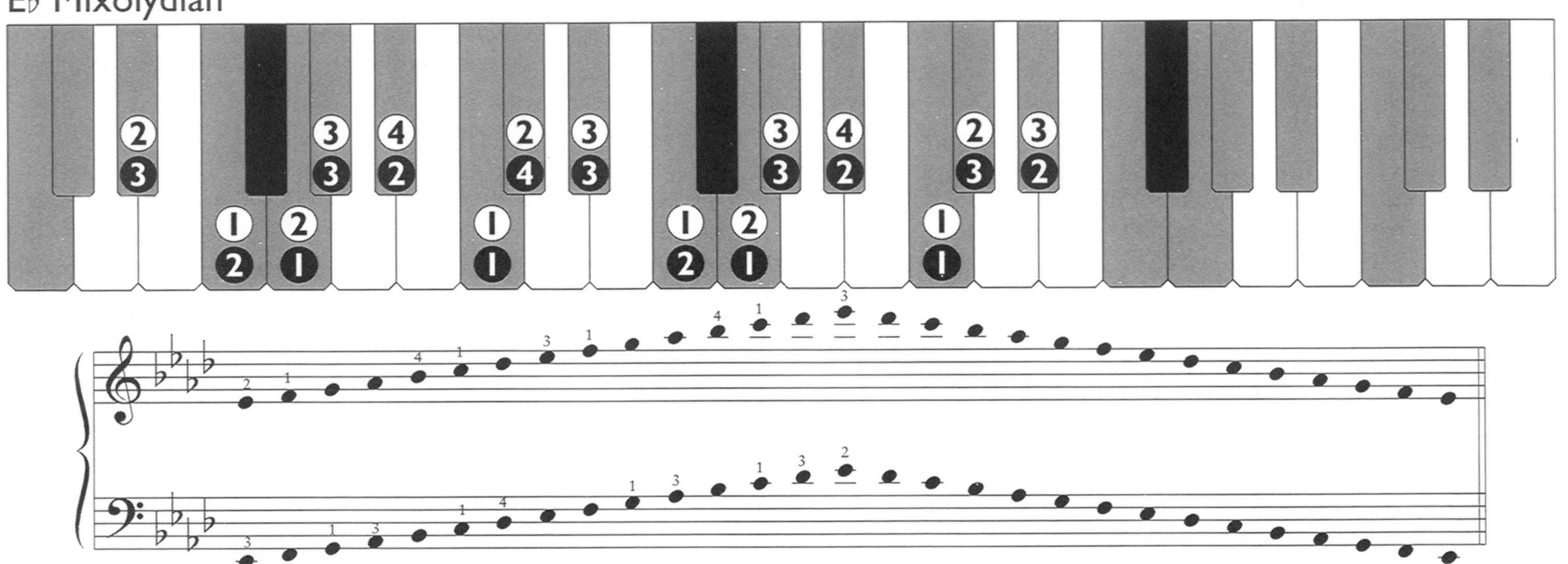

A♭ Mixolydian

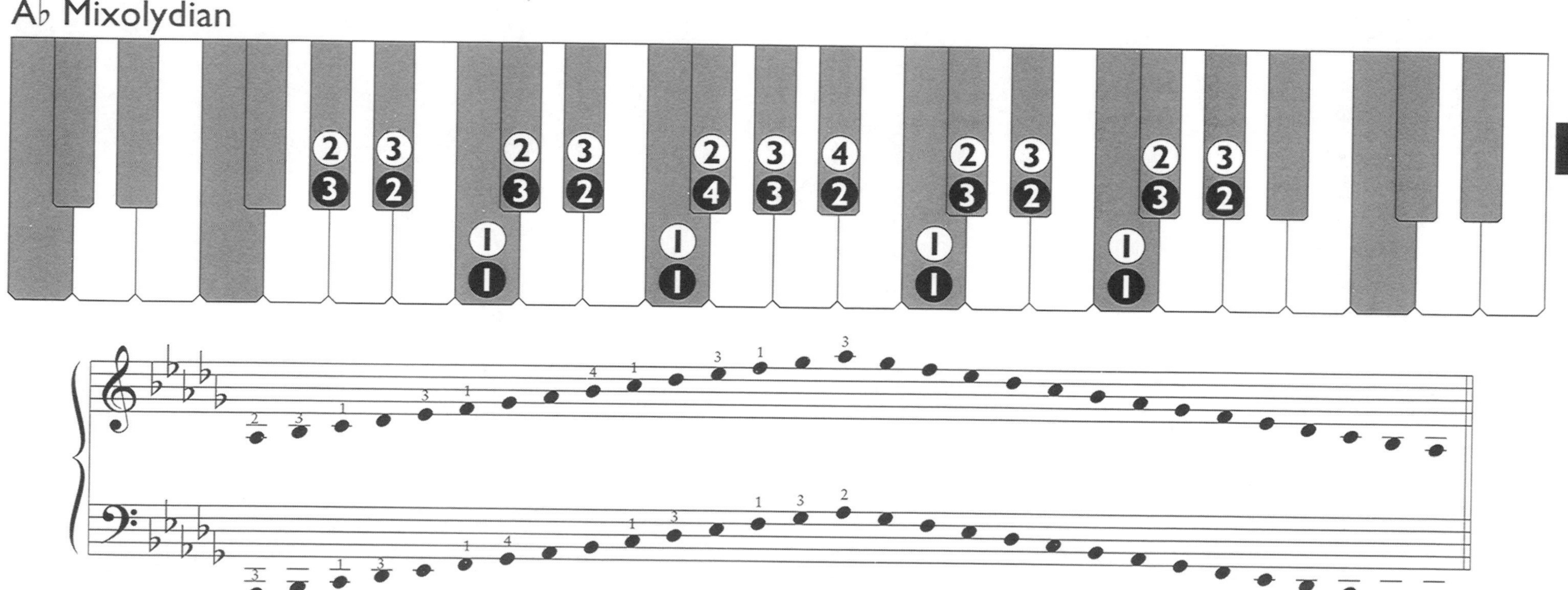

D♭ Mixolydian

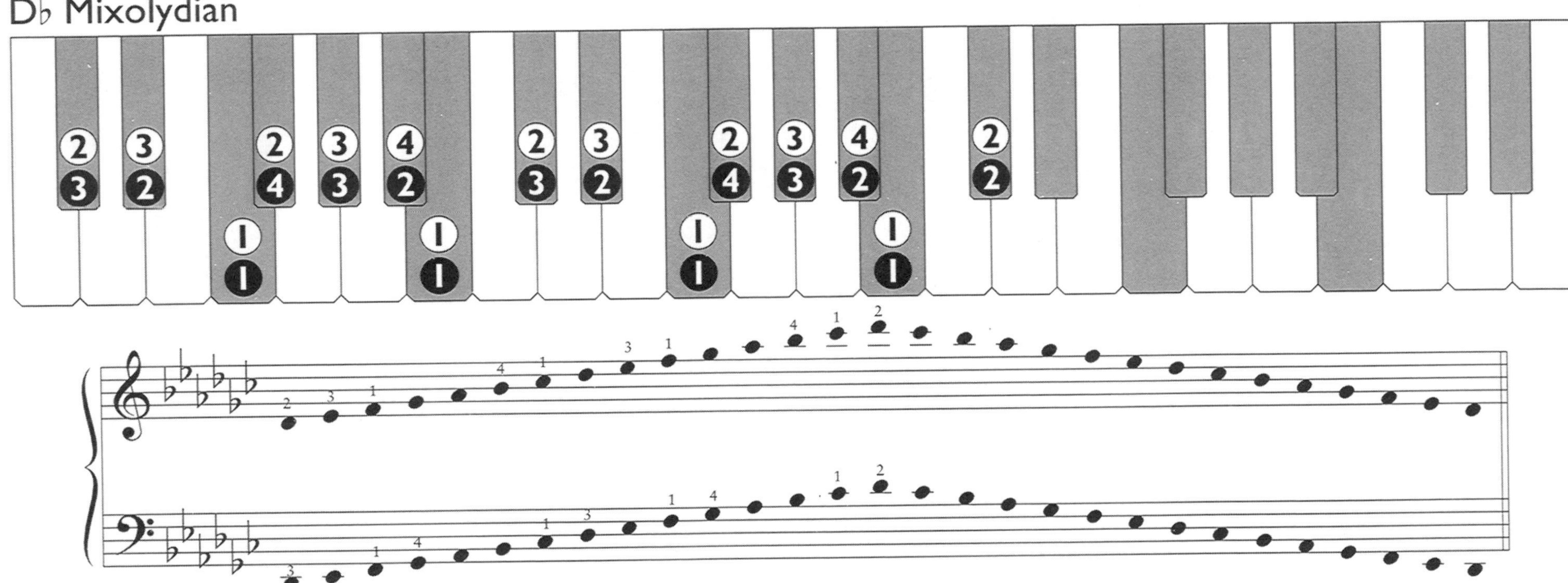

G♭ Mixolydian

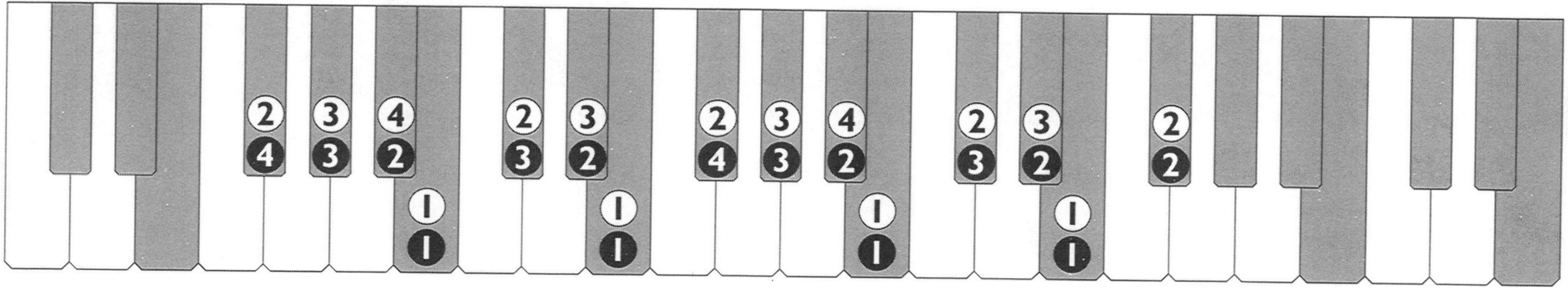

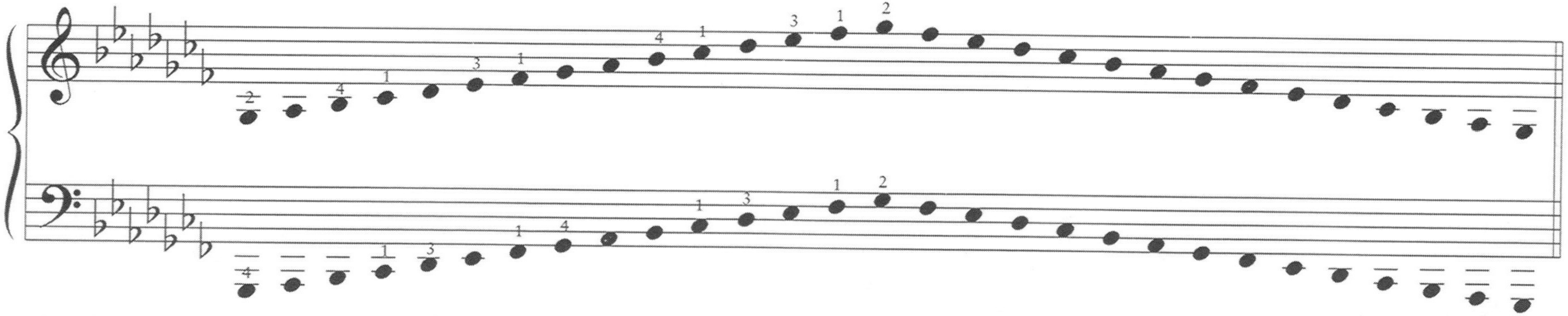

B Locrian

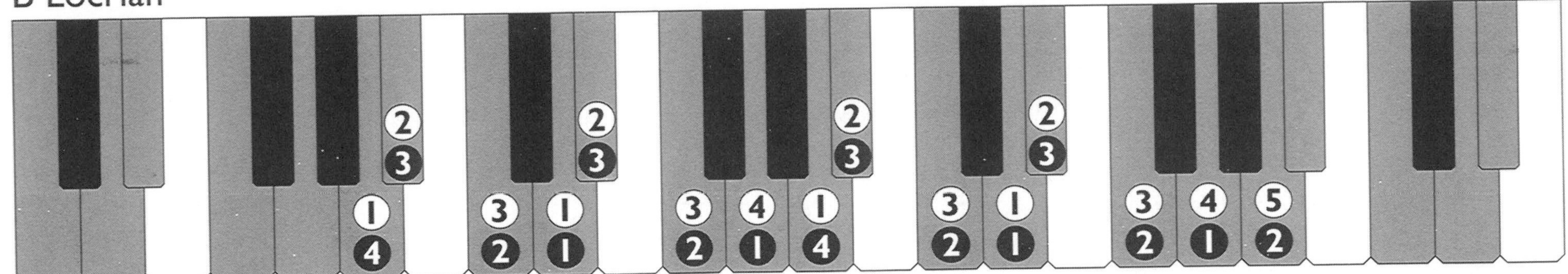

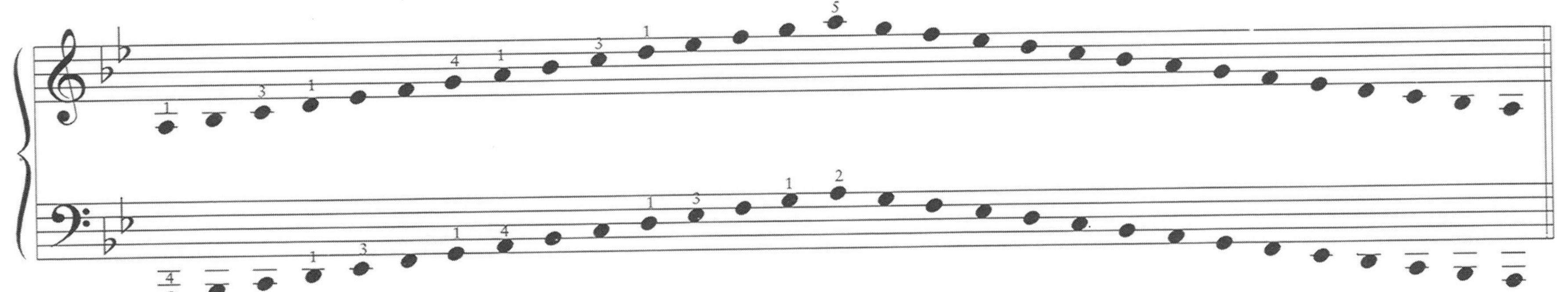

F♯ Locrian

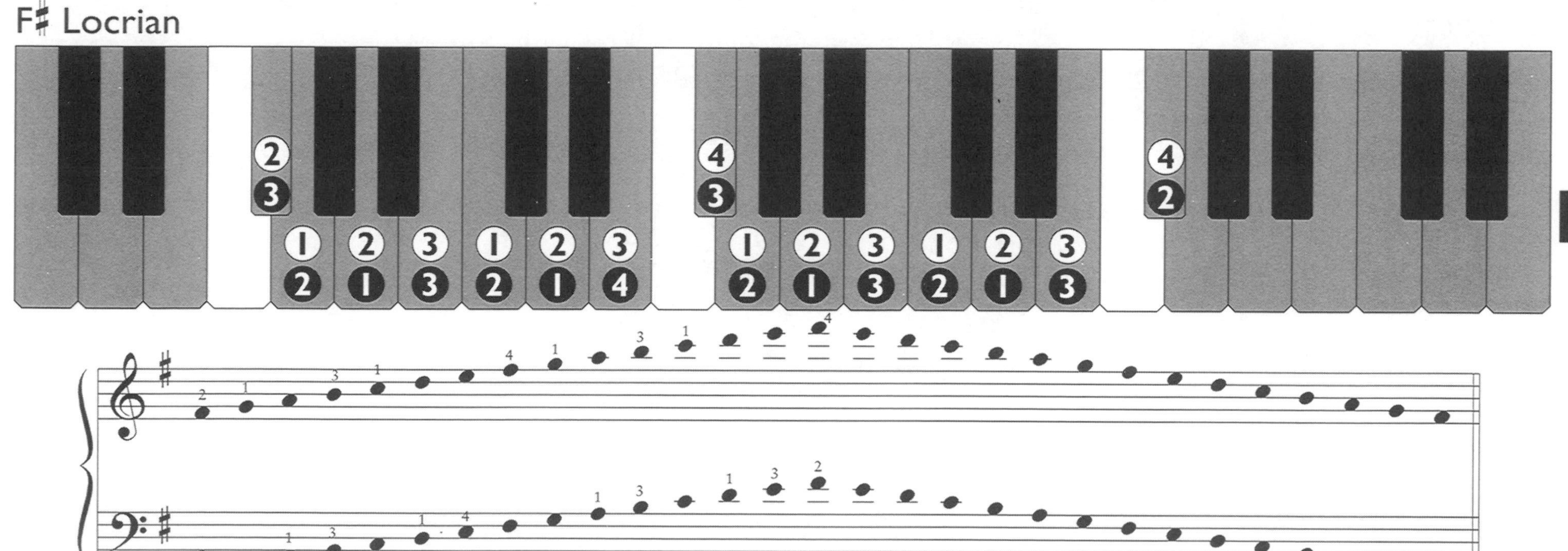

C♯ Locrian

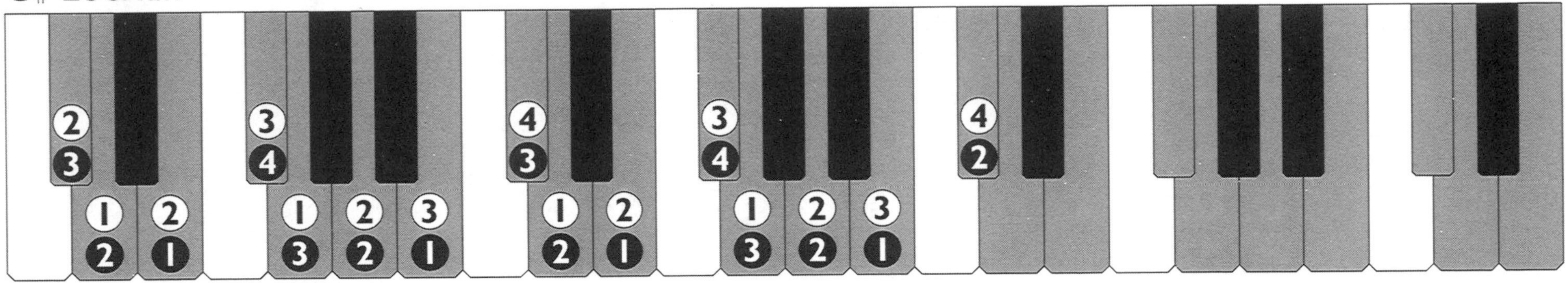

G♯ Locrian

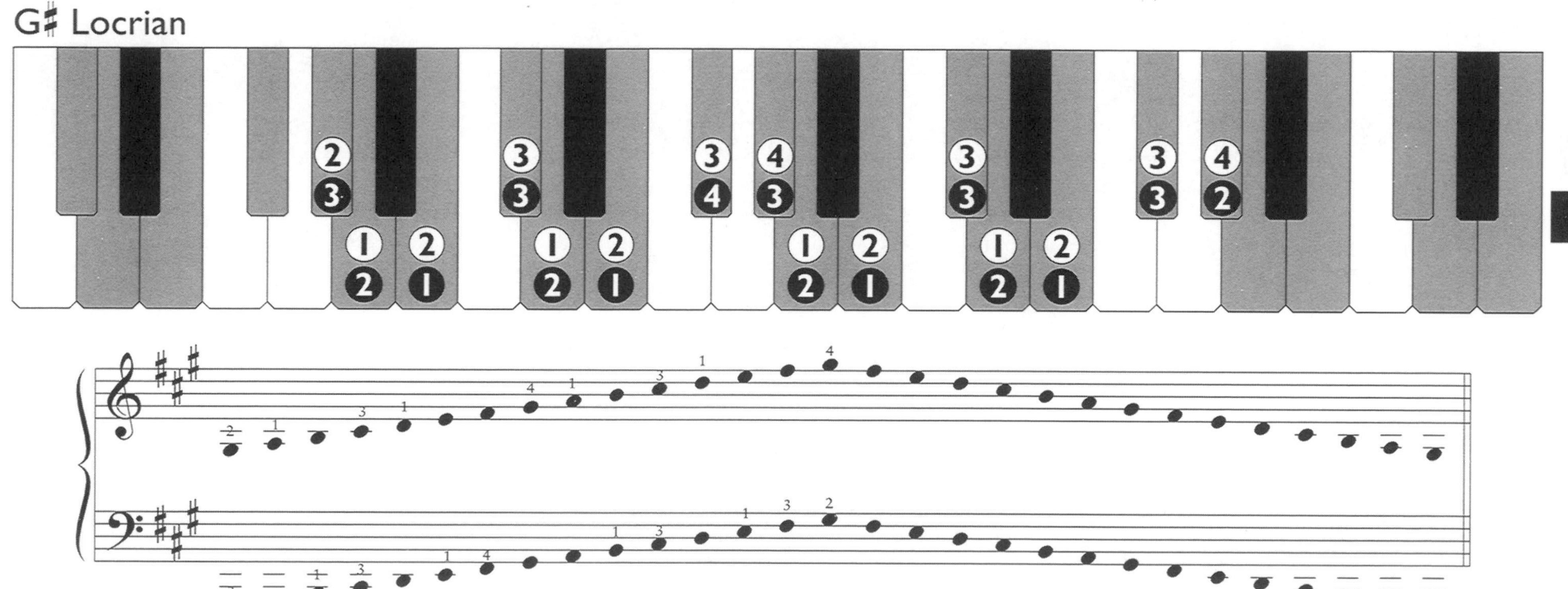

D♯ Locrian

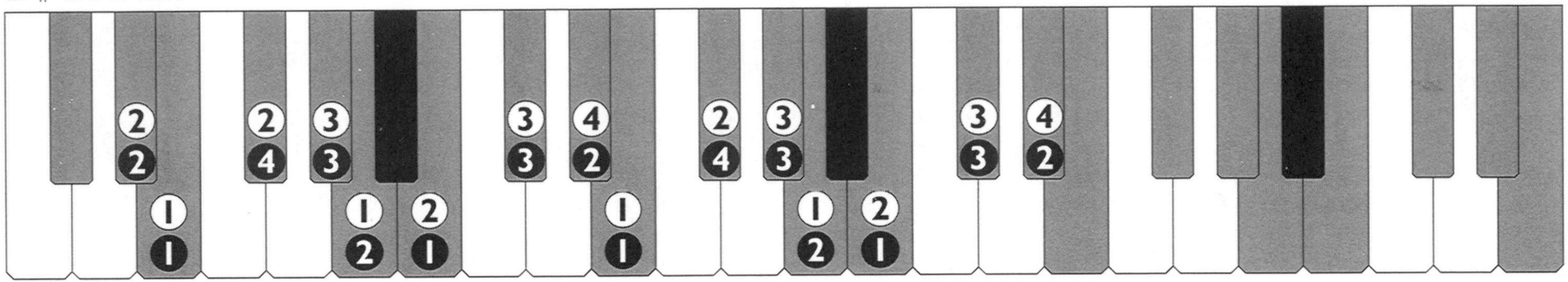

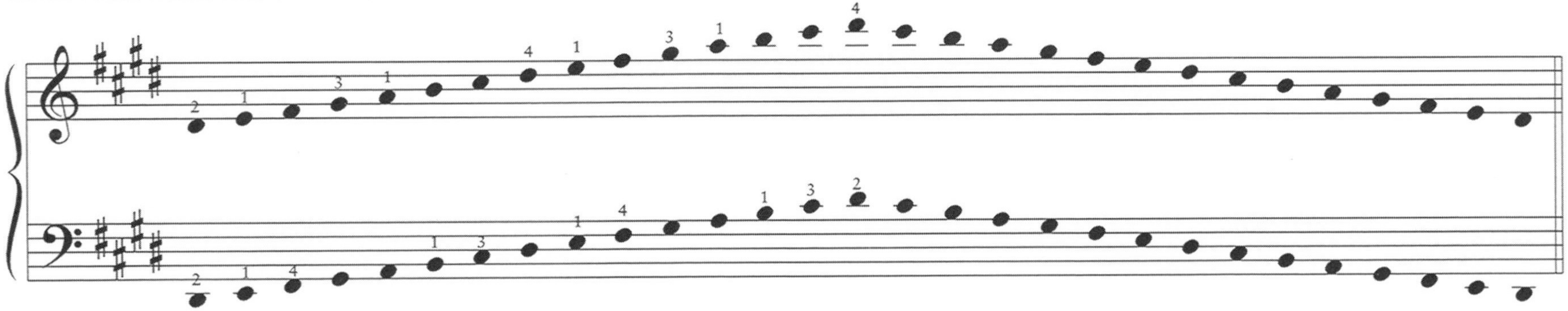

A♯ Locrian

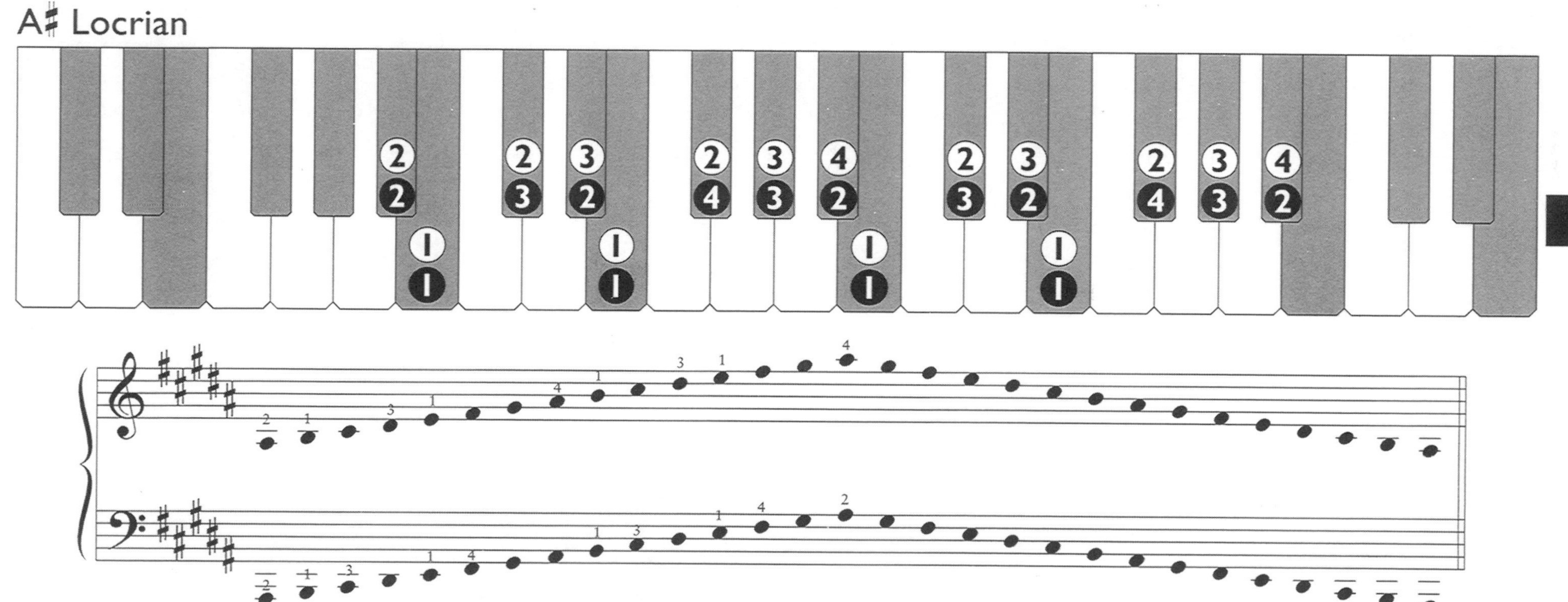

E♯ Locrian

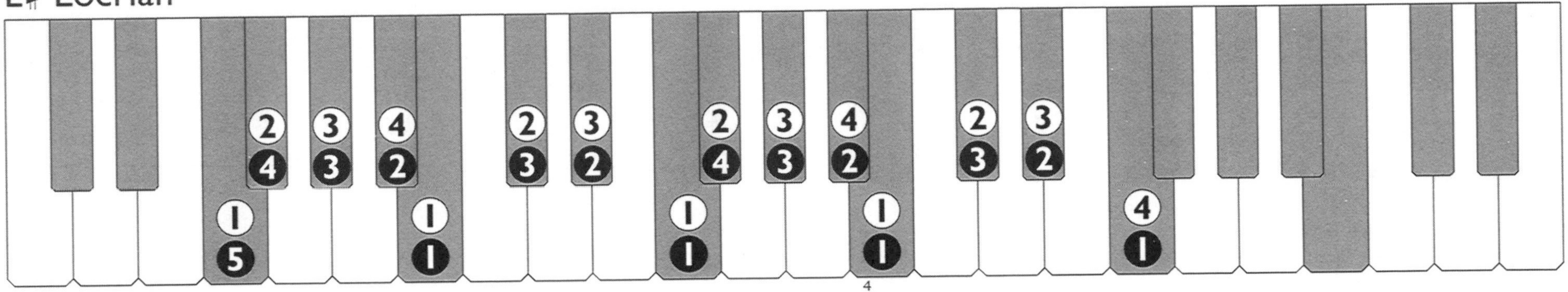

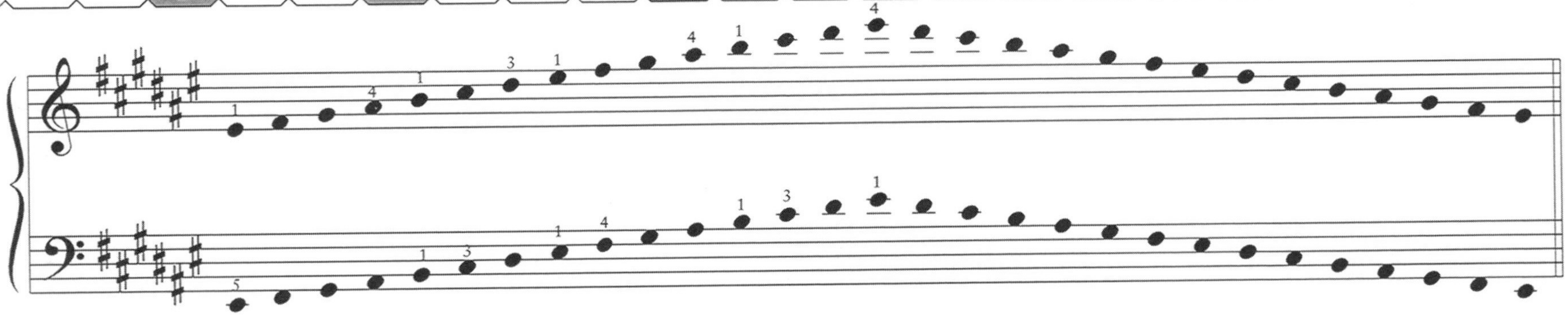

B♯ Locrian

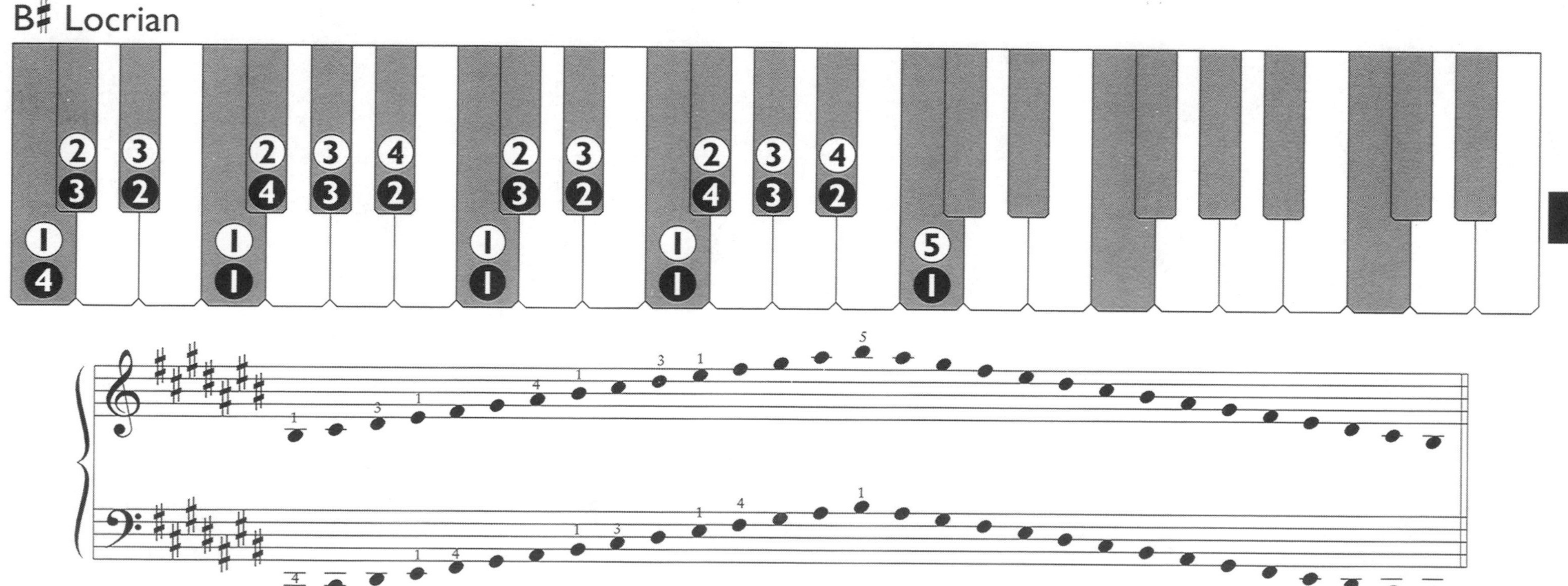

E Locrian

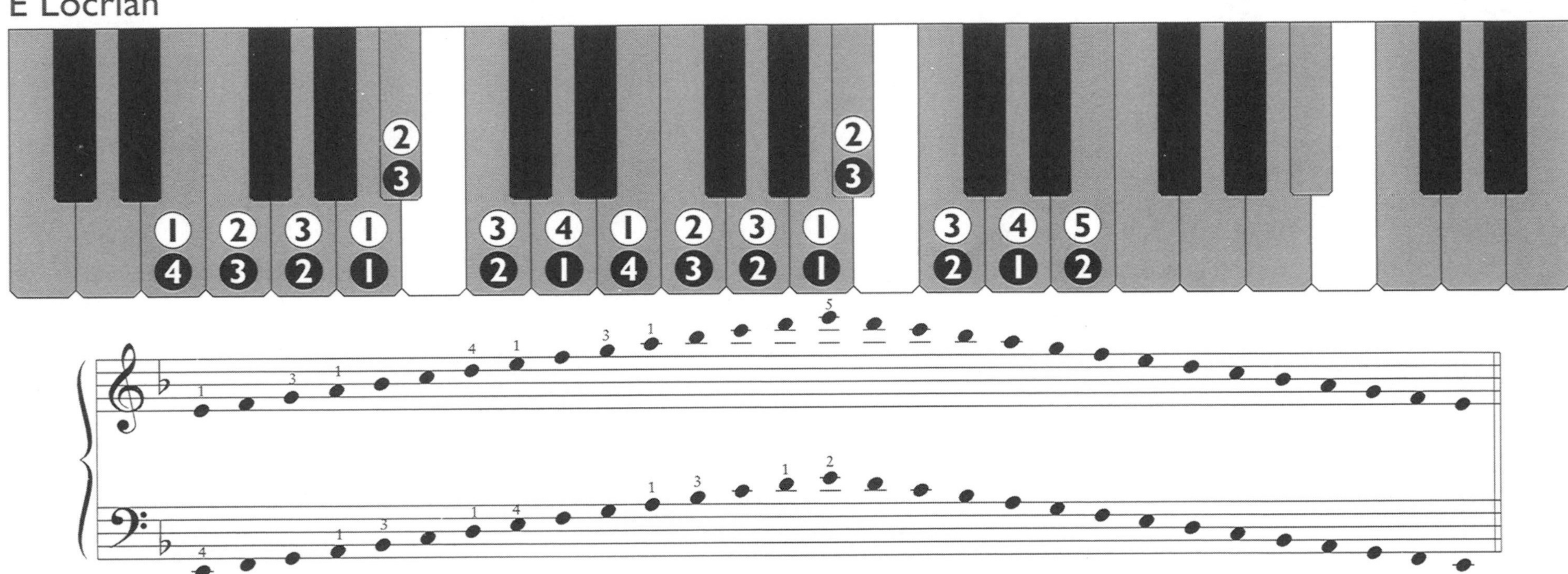

A Locrian

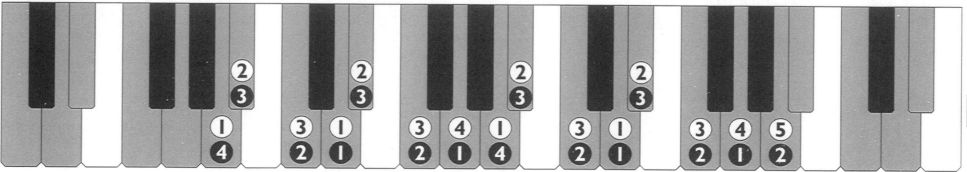

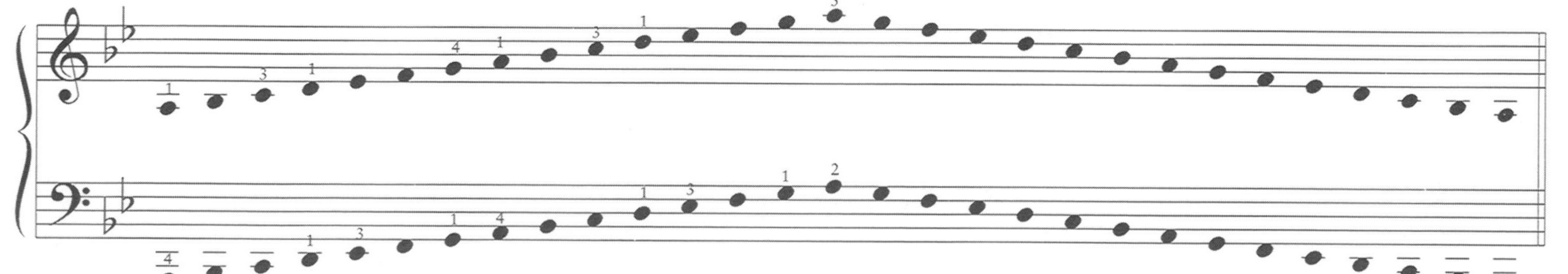

D Locrian

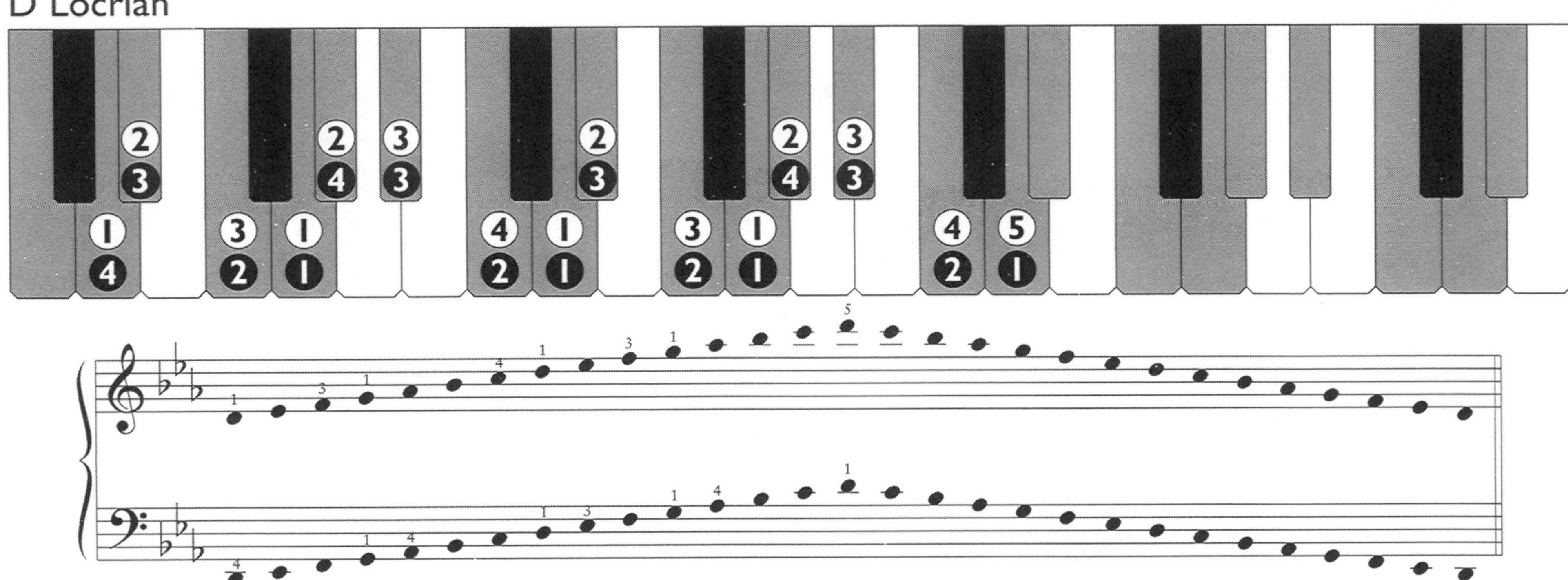

G Locrian

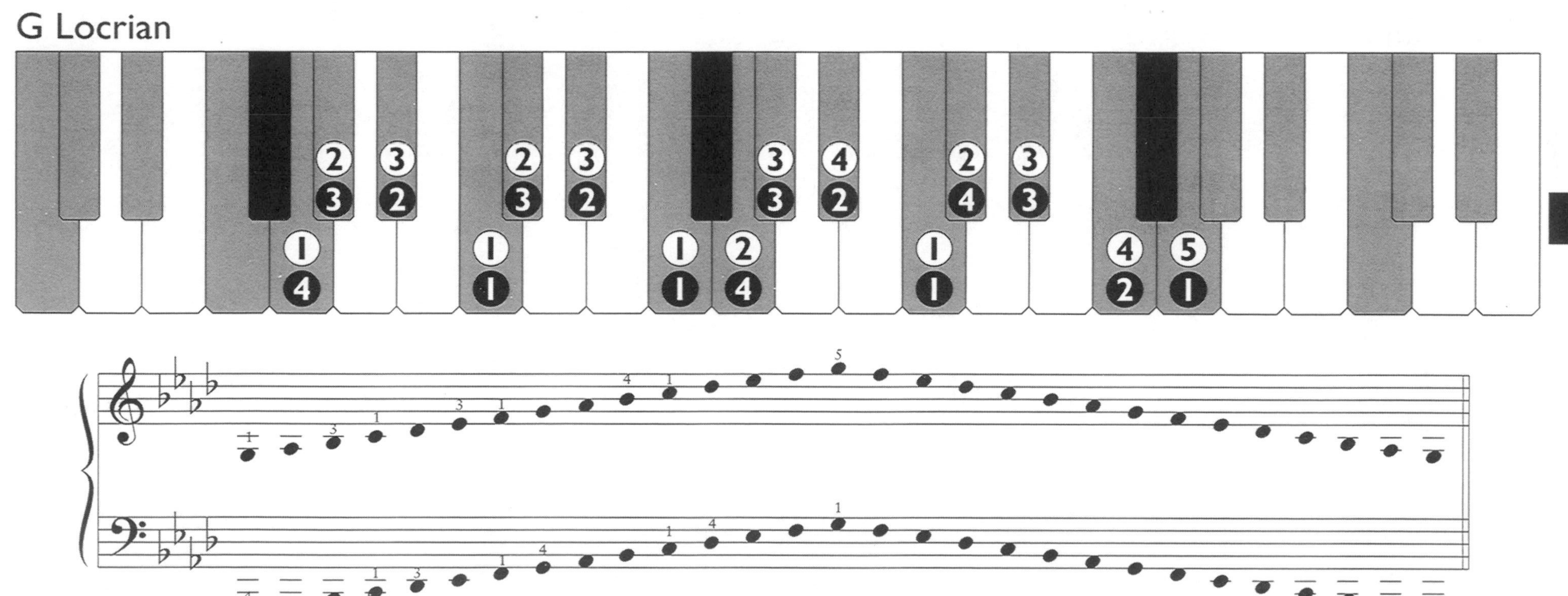

C Locrian

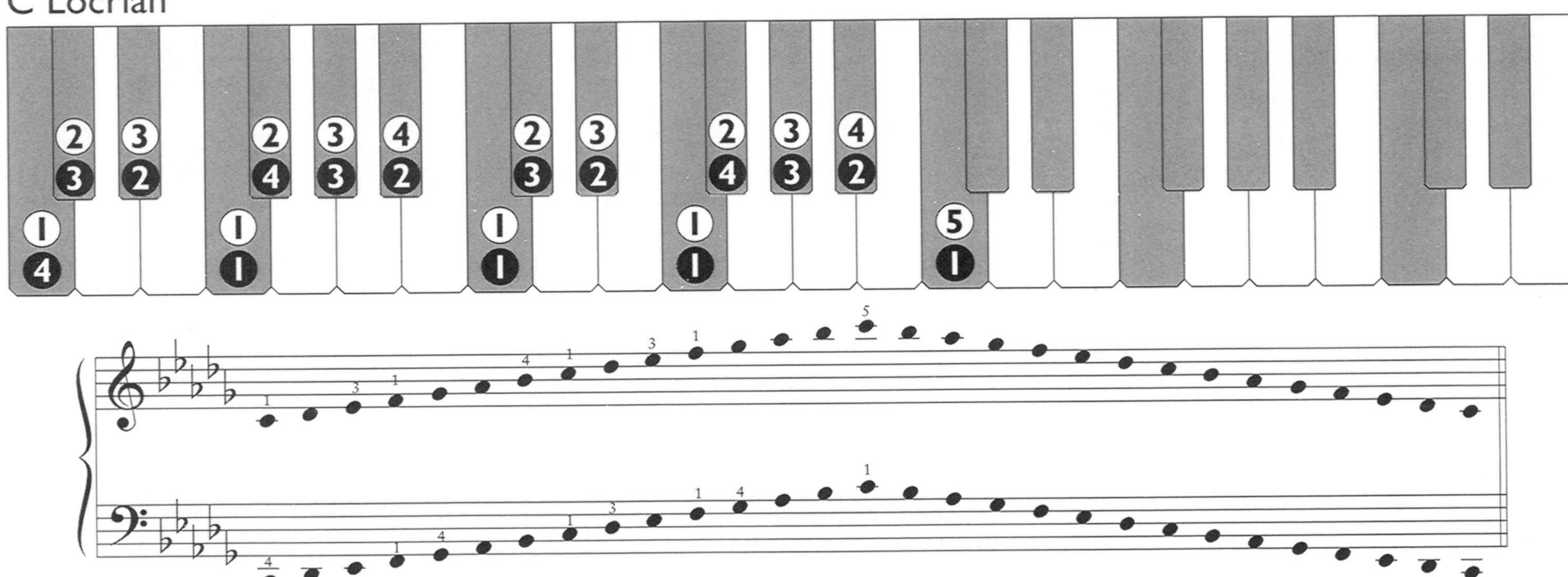

F Locrian

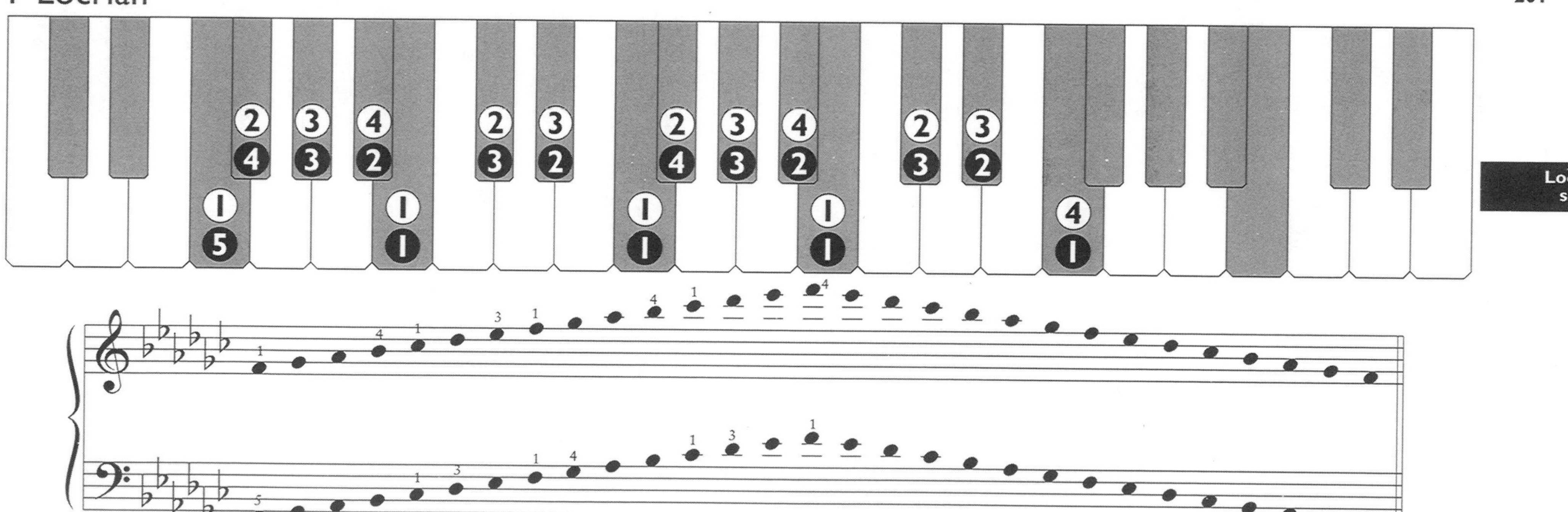

B♭ Locrian

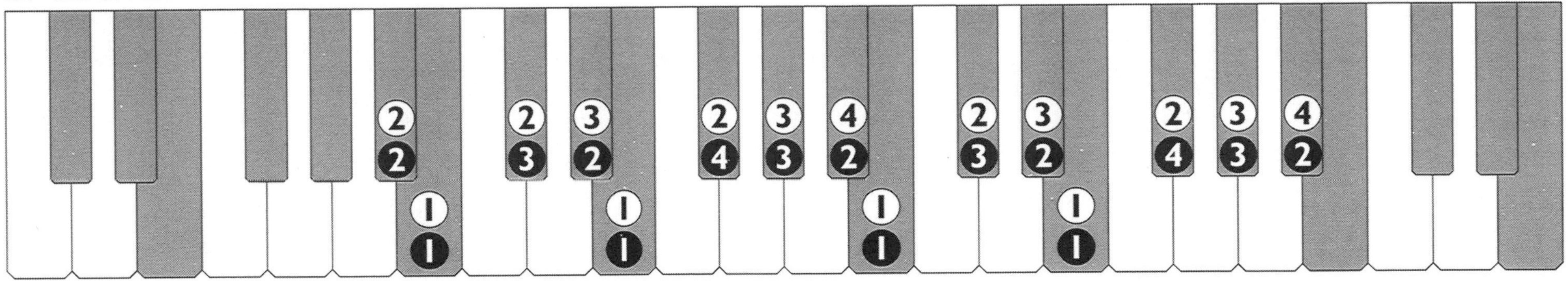

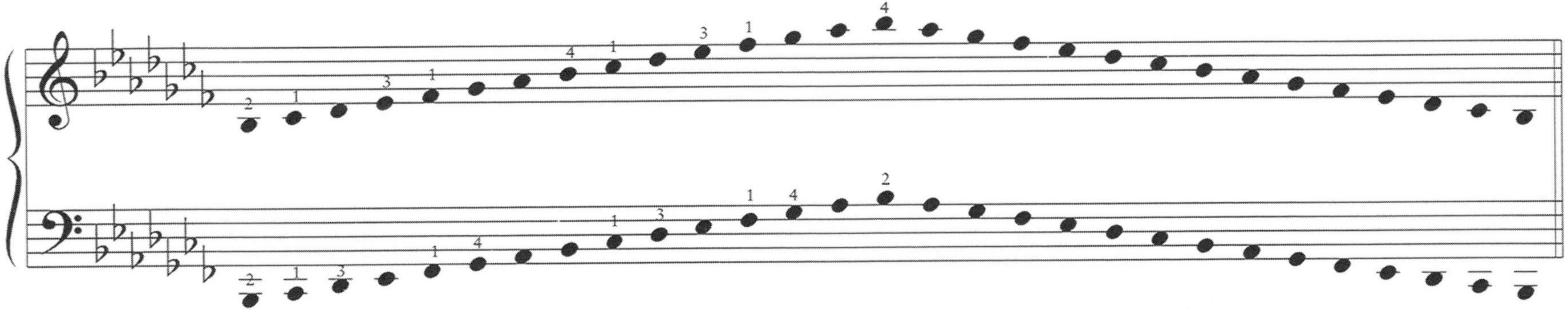

C pentatonic

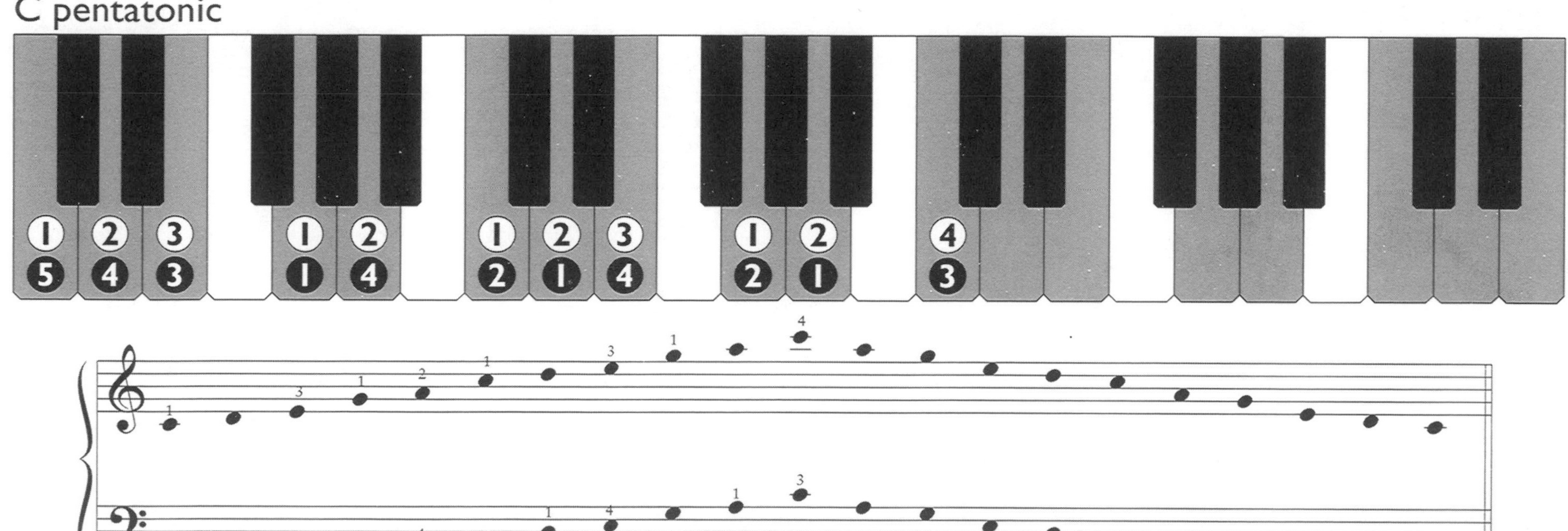

G pentatonic

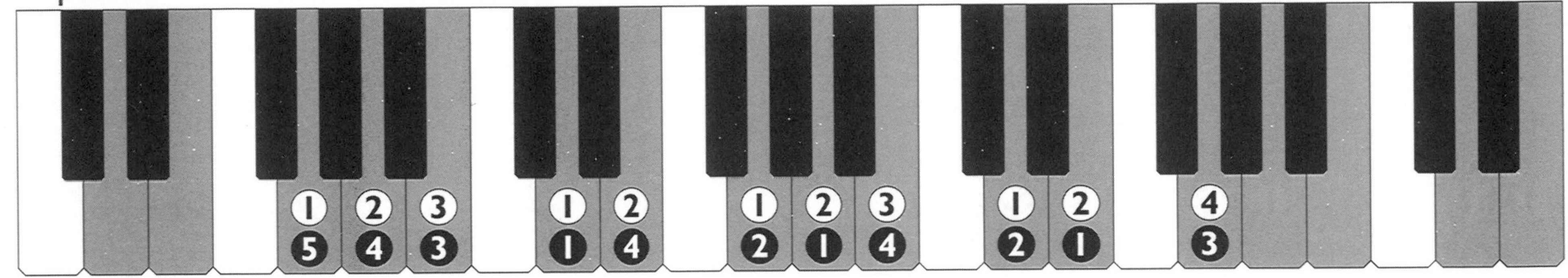

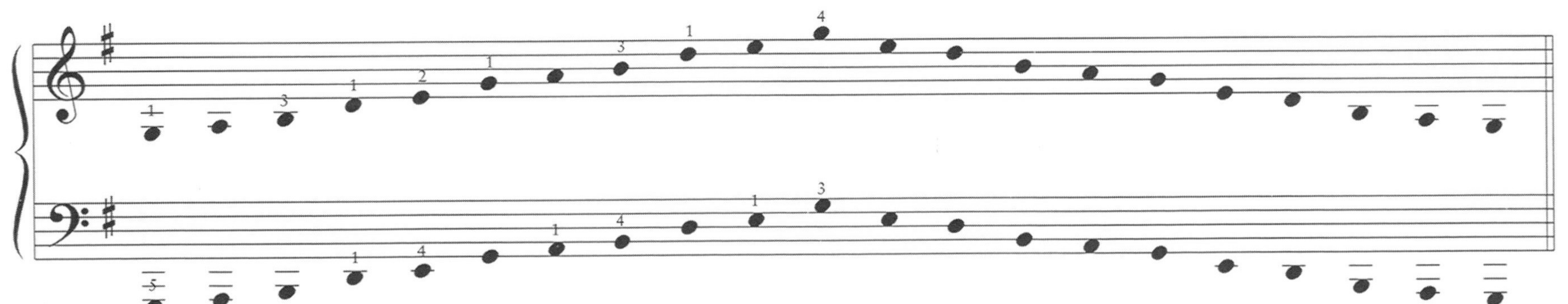

D pentatonic

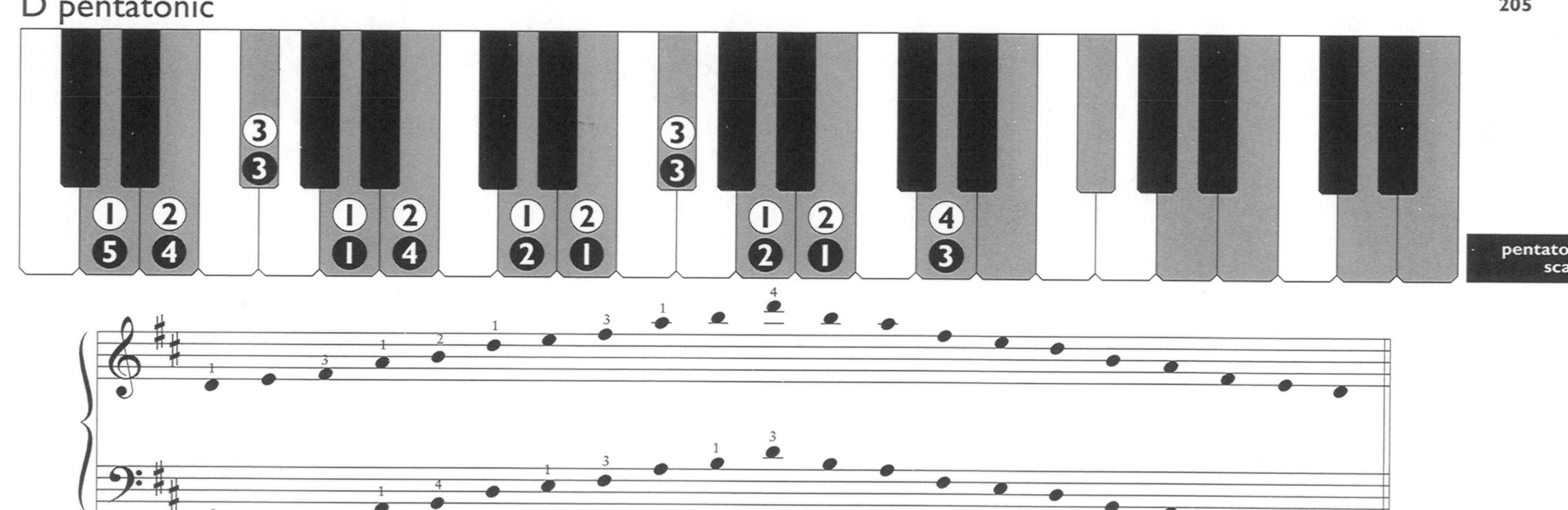

A pentatonic

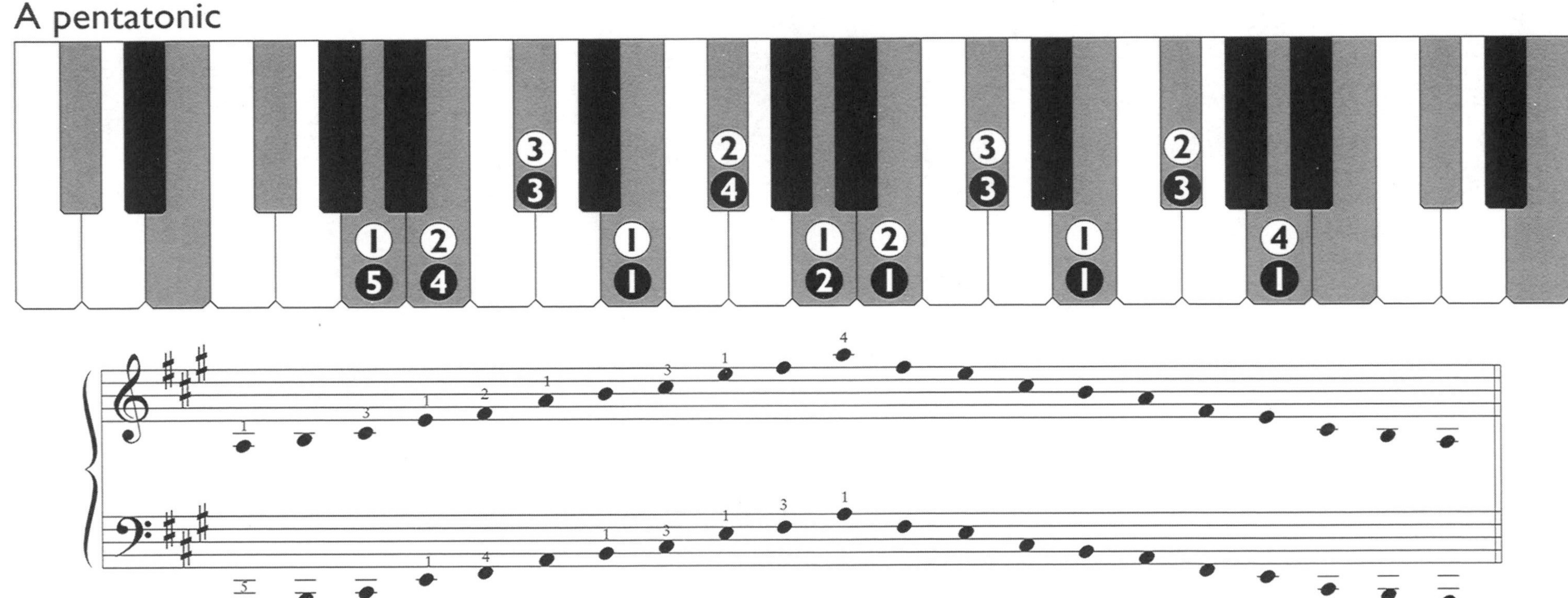

E pentatonic

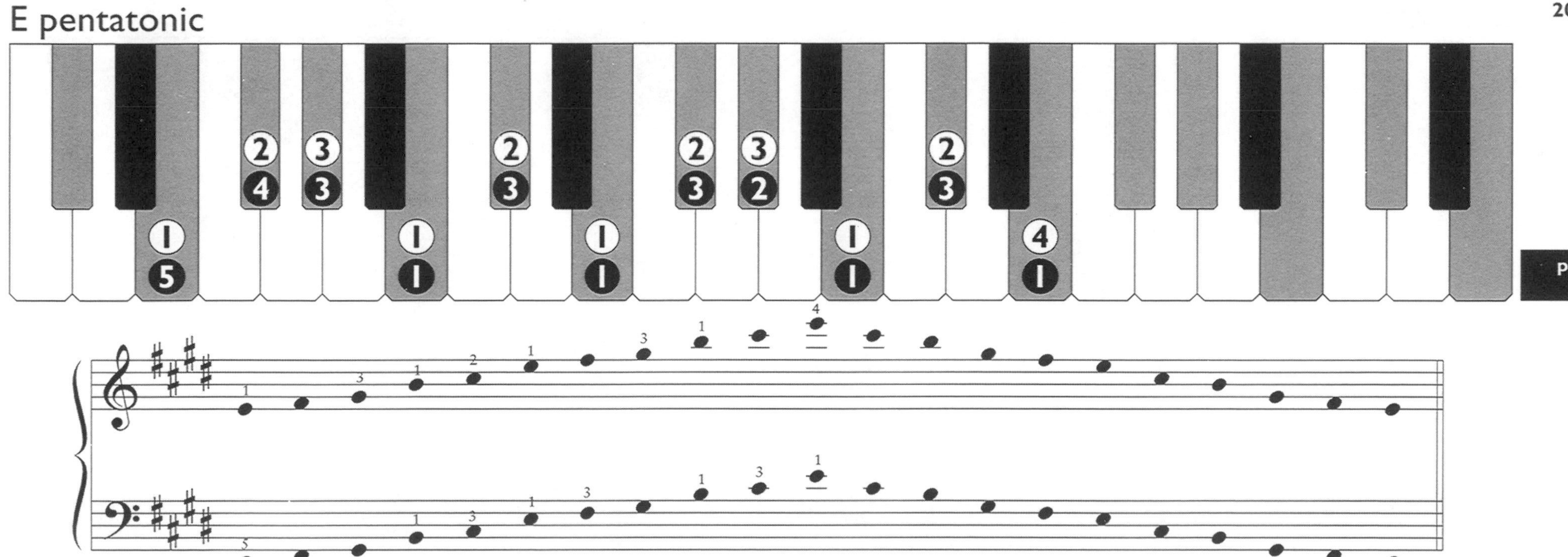

B pentatonic

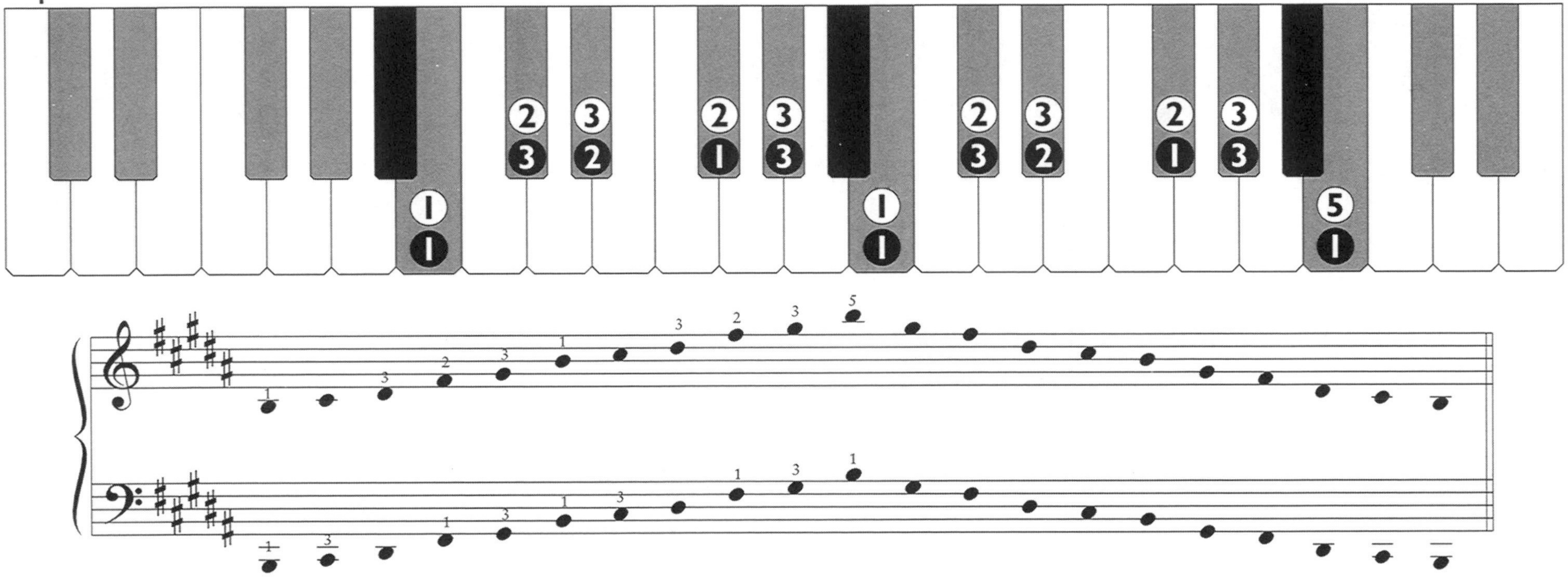

F♯ pentatonic

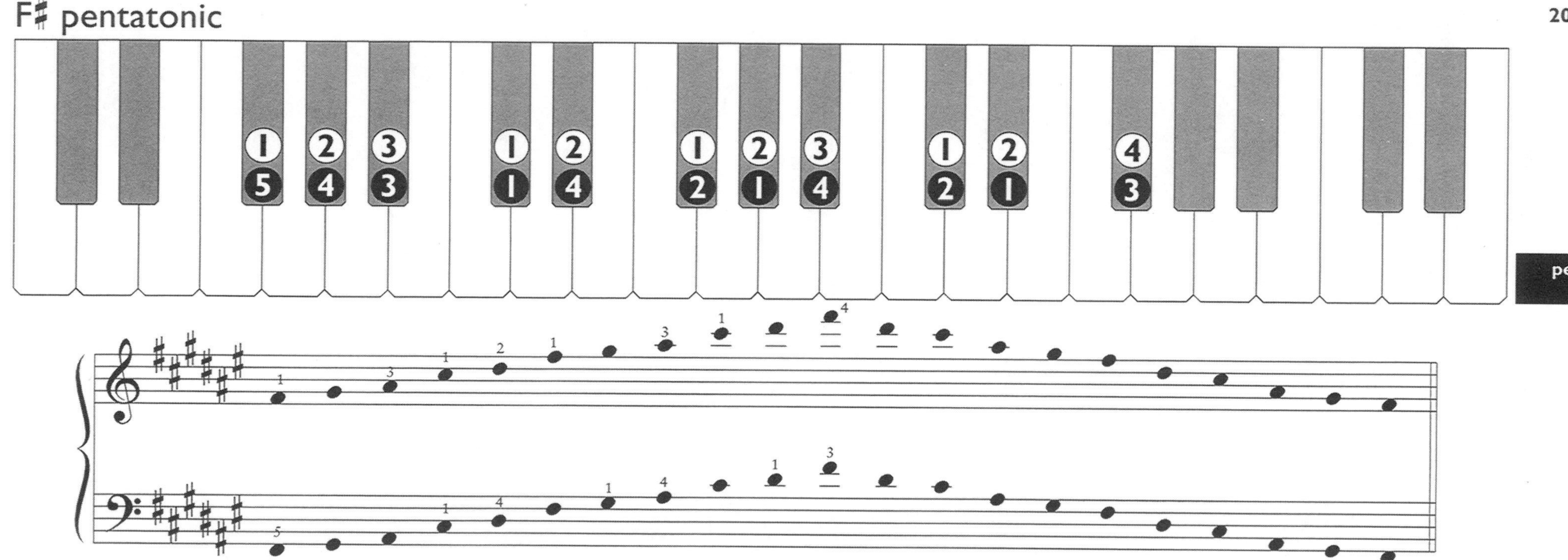

C♯ pentatonic

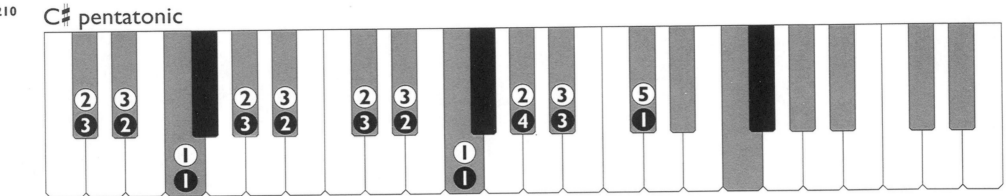

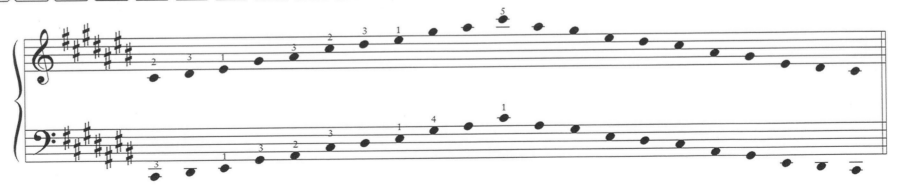

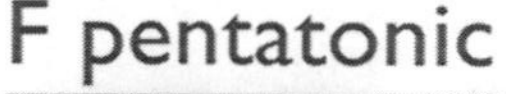

F pentatonic

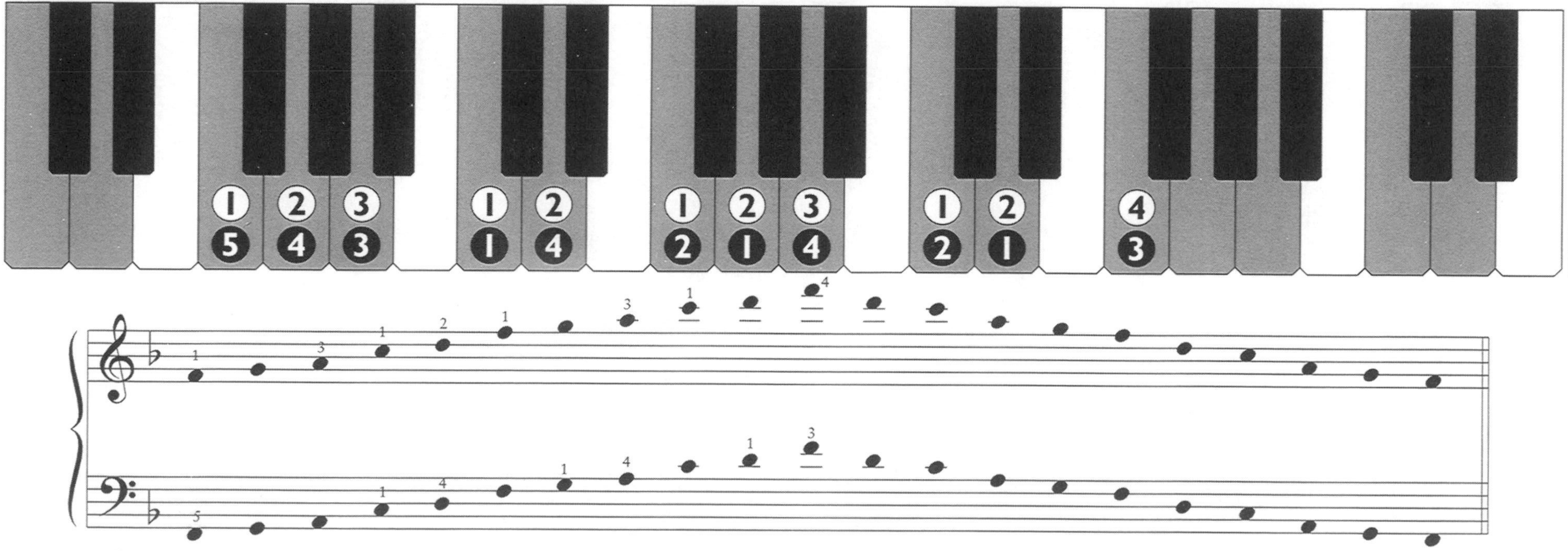

B♭ pentatonic

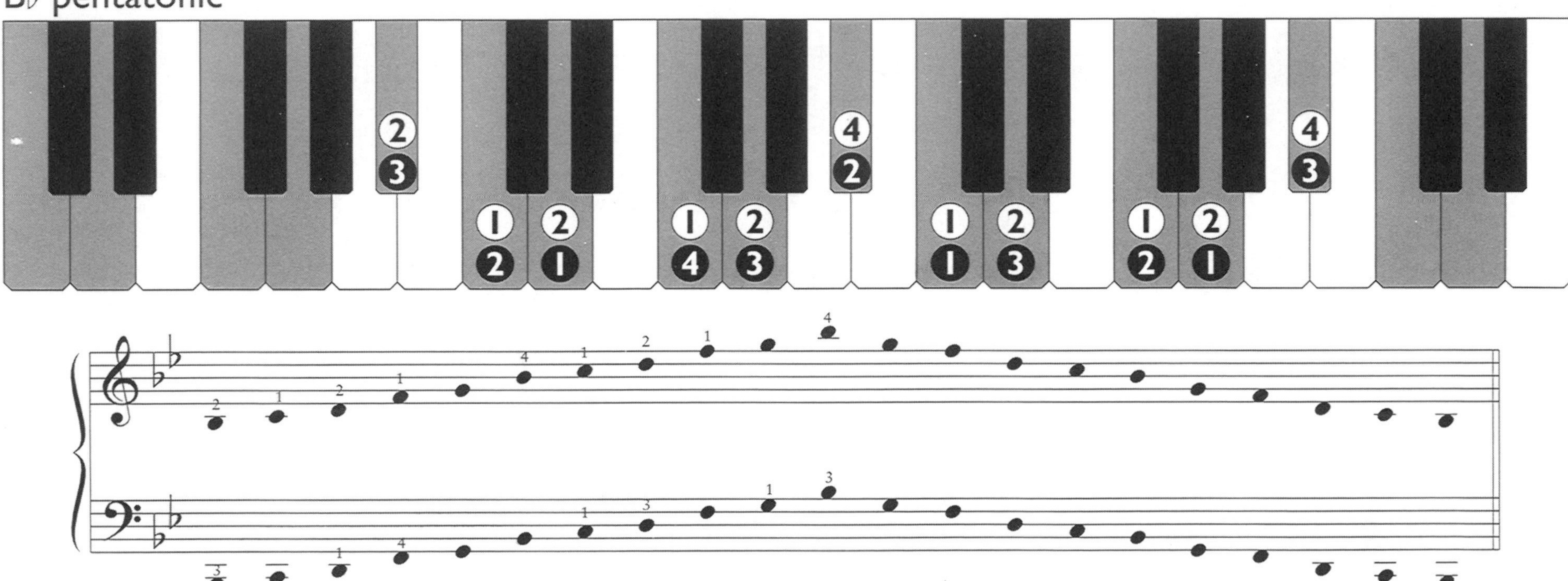

E♭ pentatonic

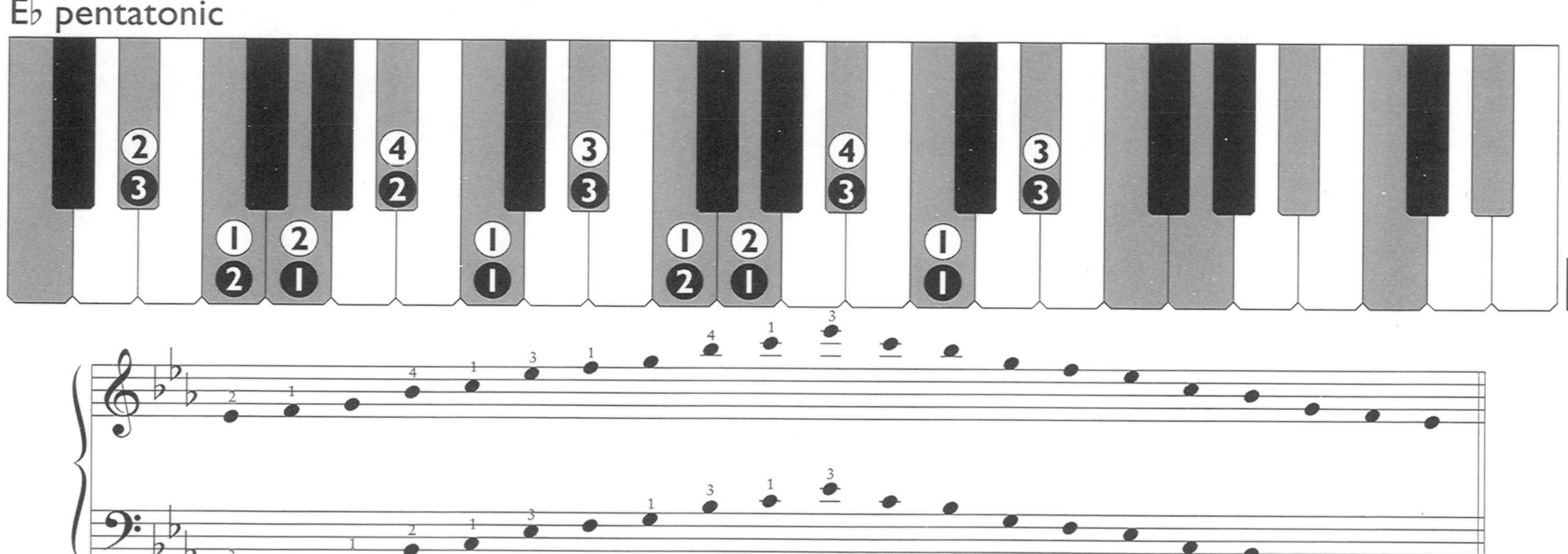

A♭ pentatonic

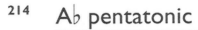

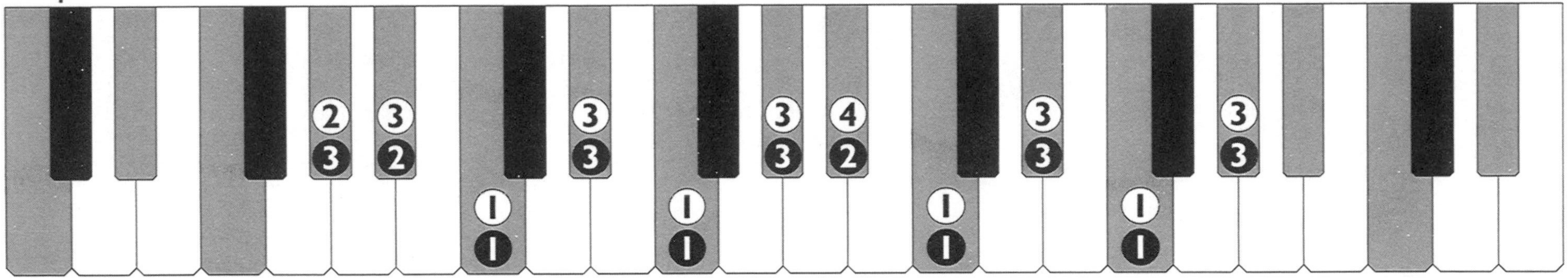

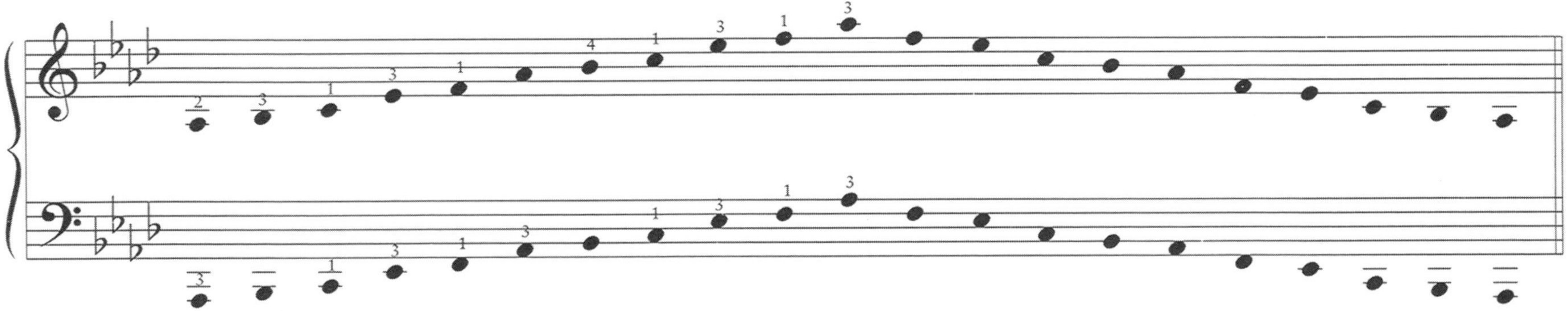

D♭ pentatonic

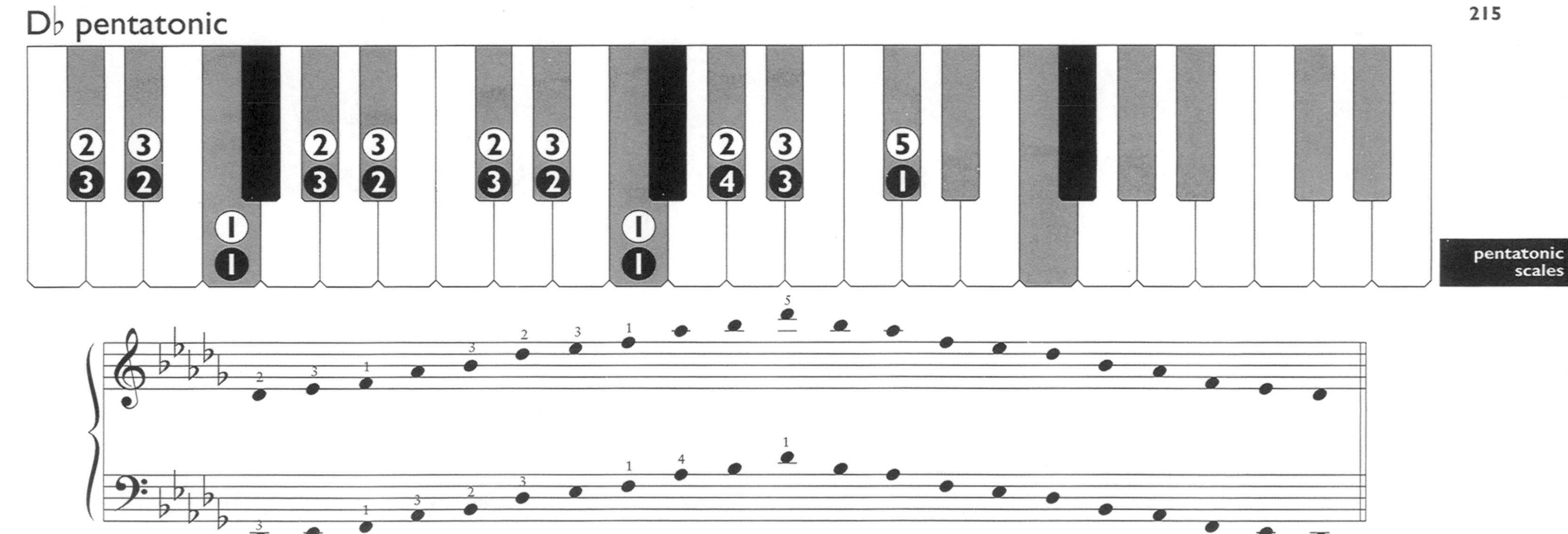

G♭ pentatonic

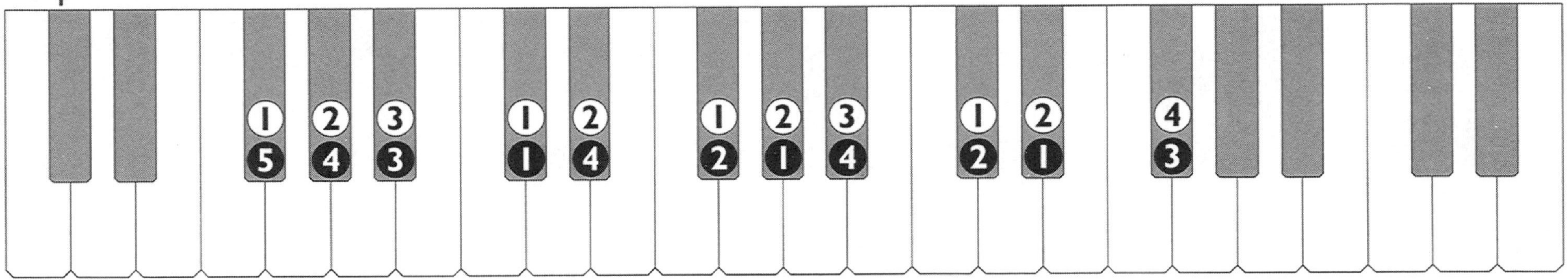

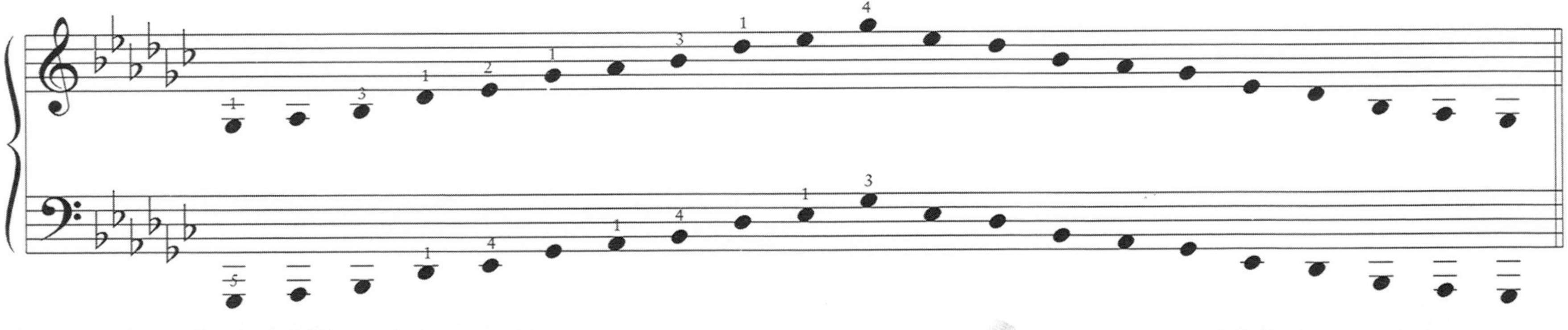

C♭ pentatonic

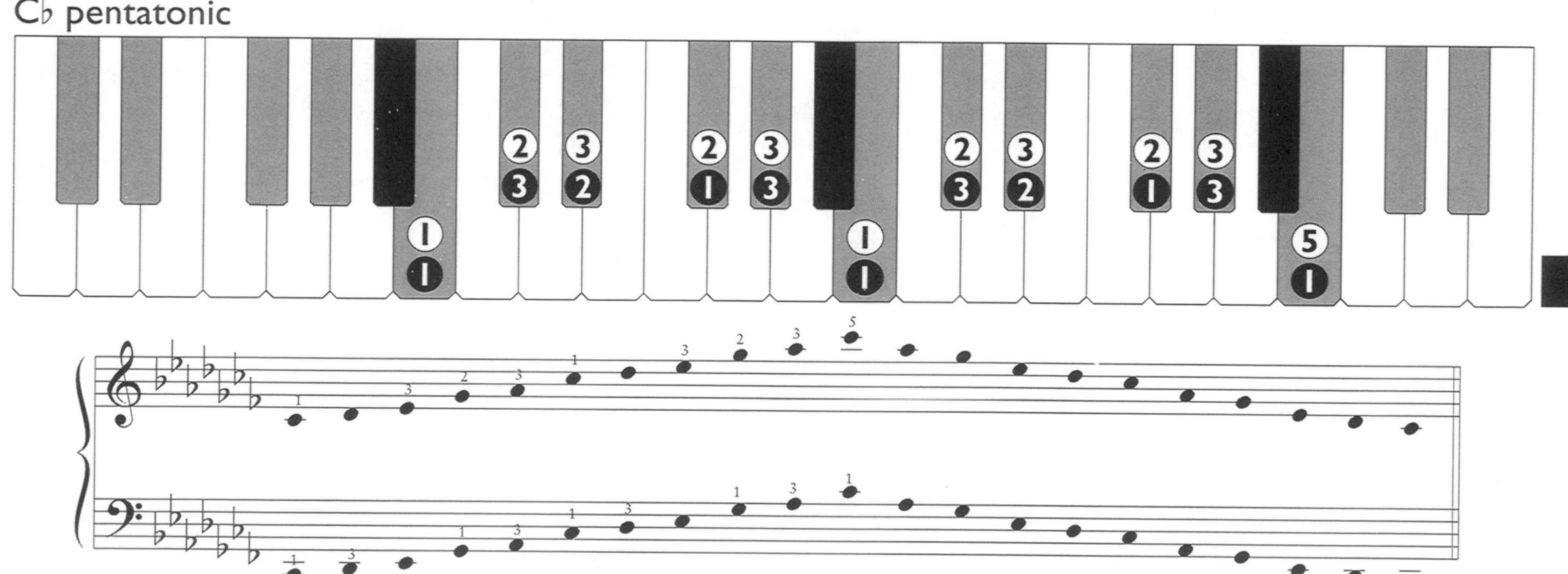

A pentatonic minor

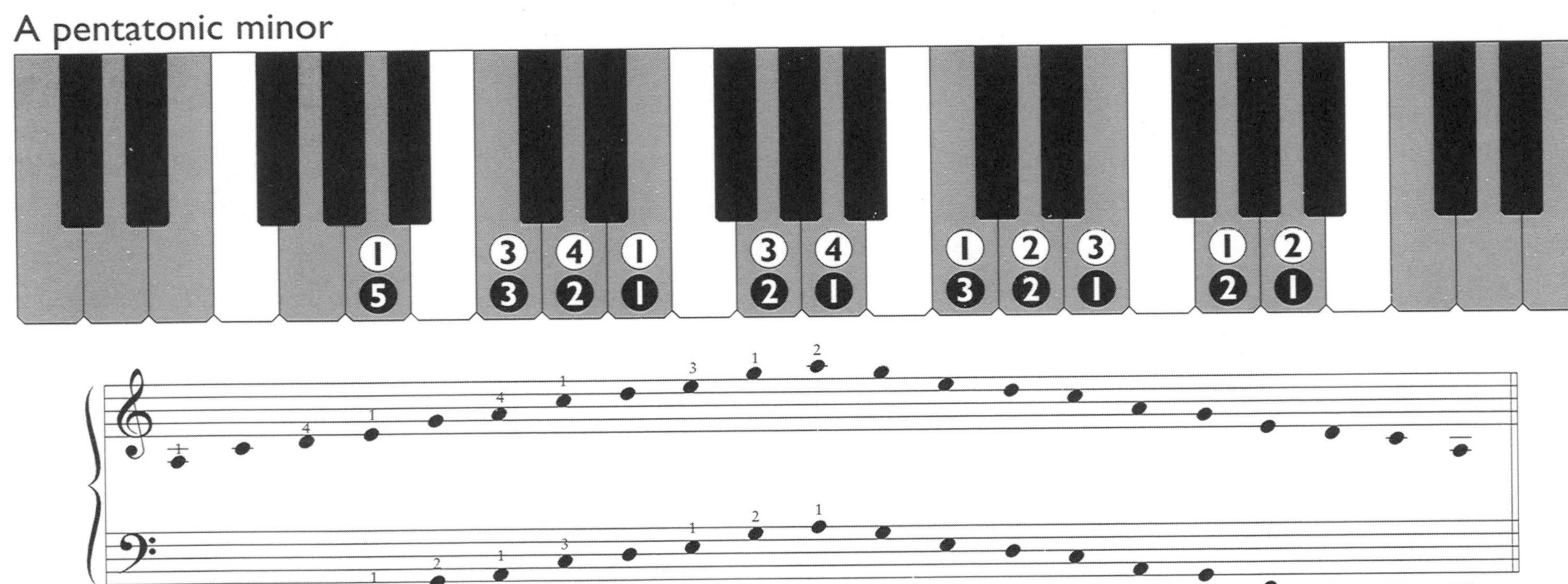

E pentatonic minor

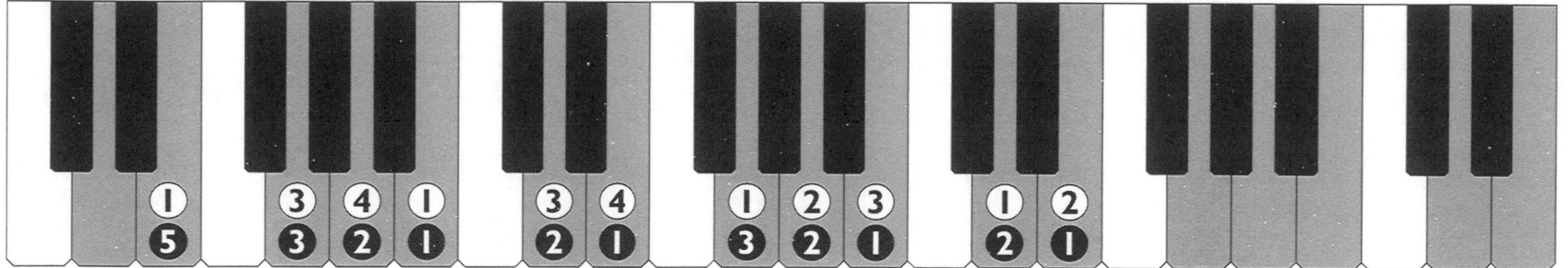

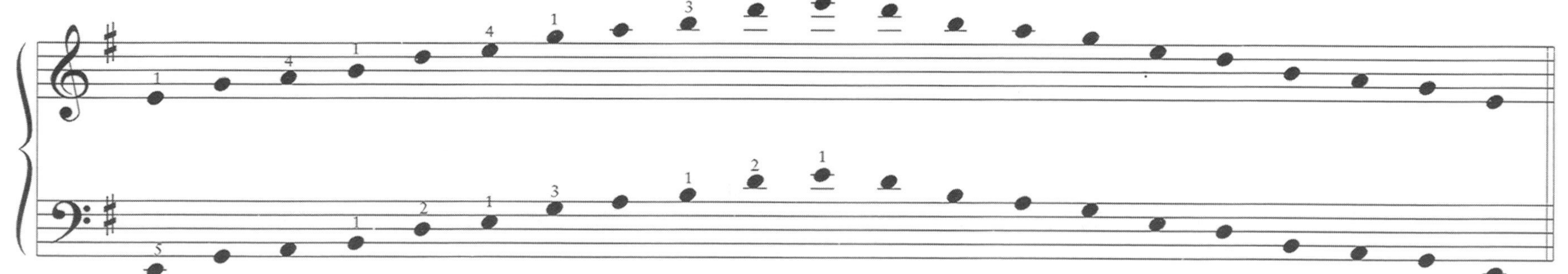

B pentatonic minor

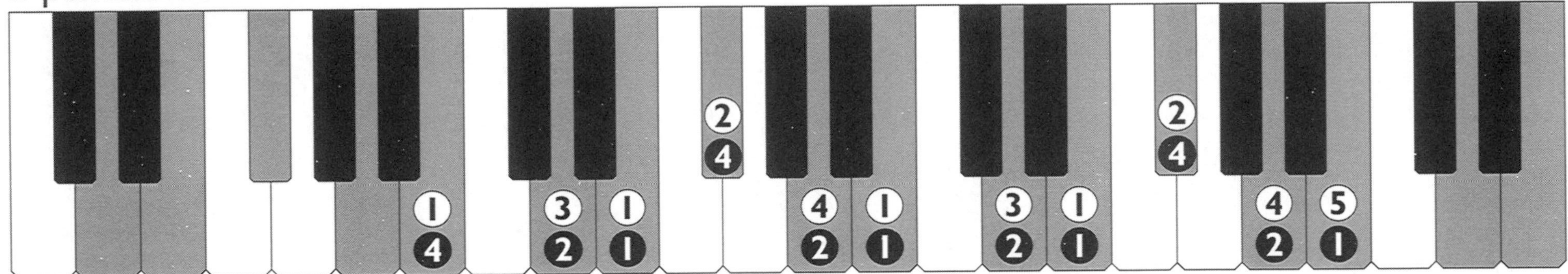

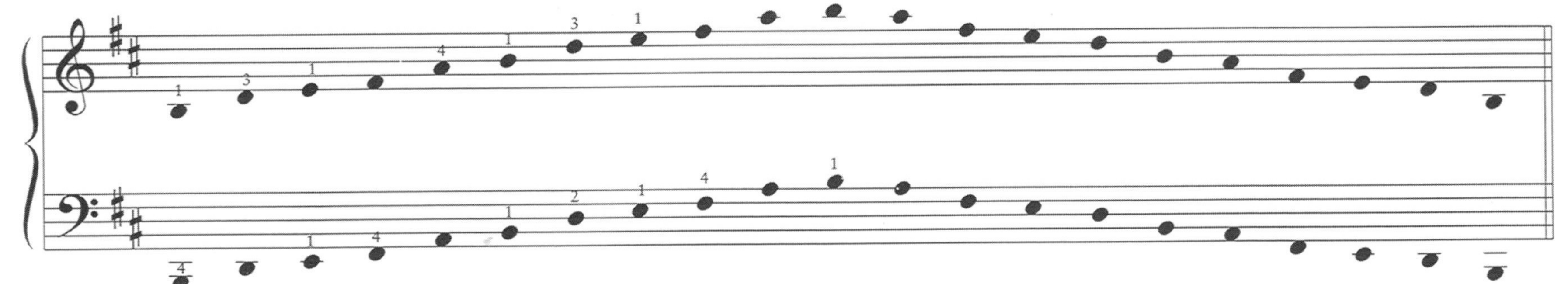

F♯ pentatonic minor

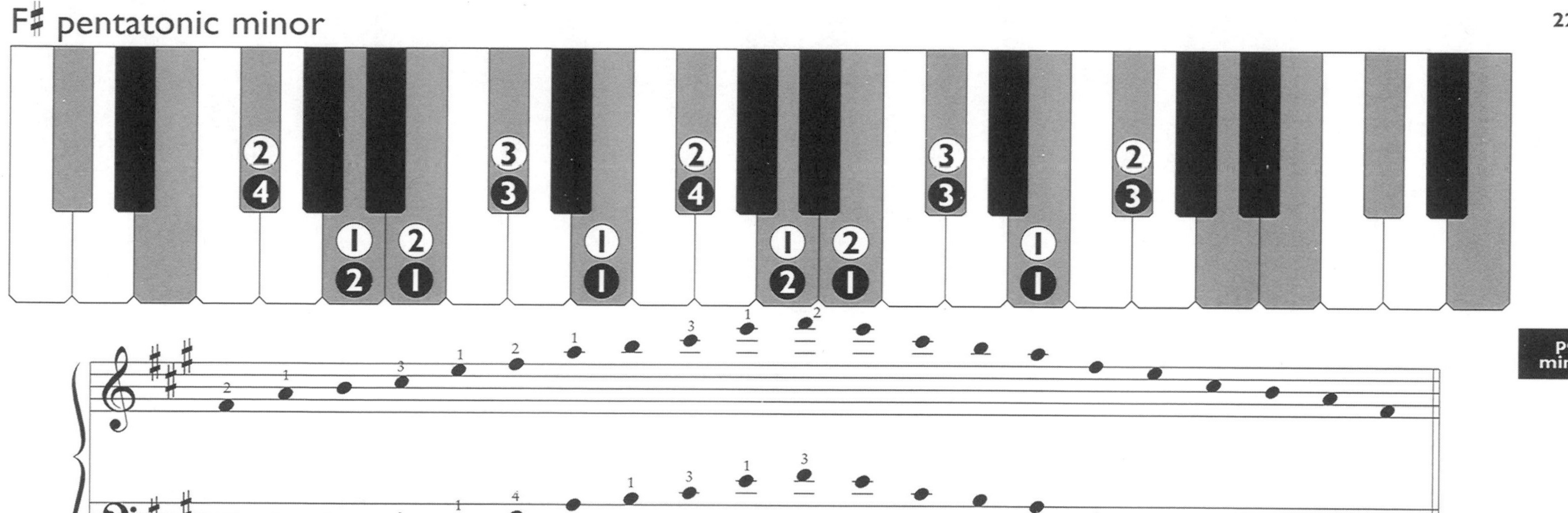

C♯ pentatonic minor

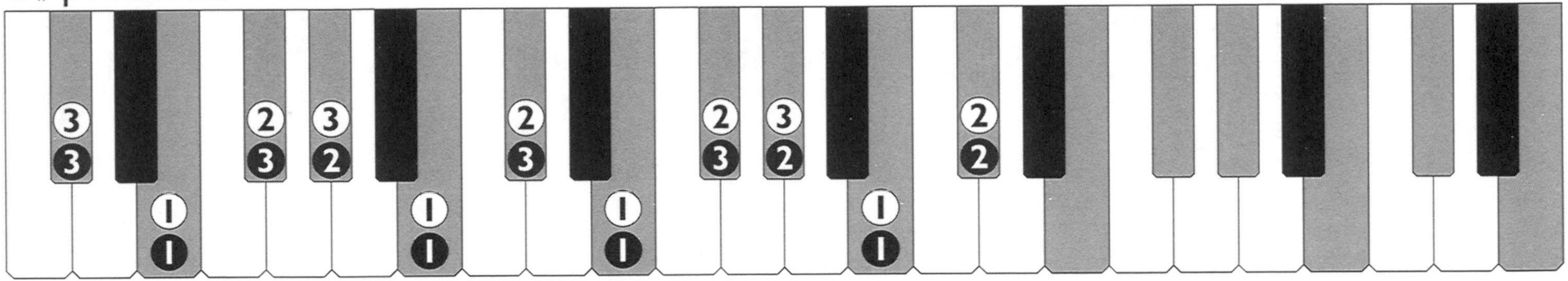

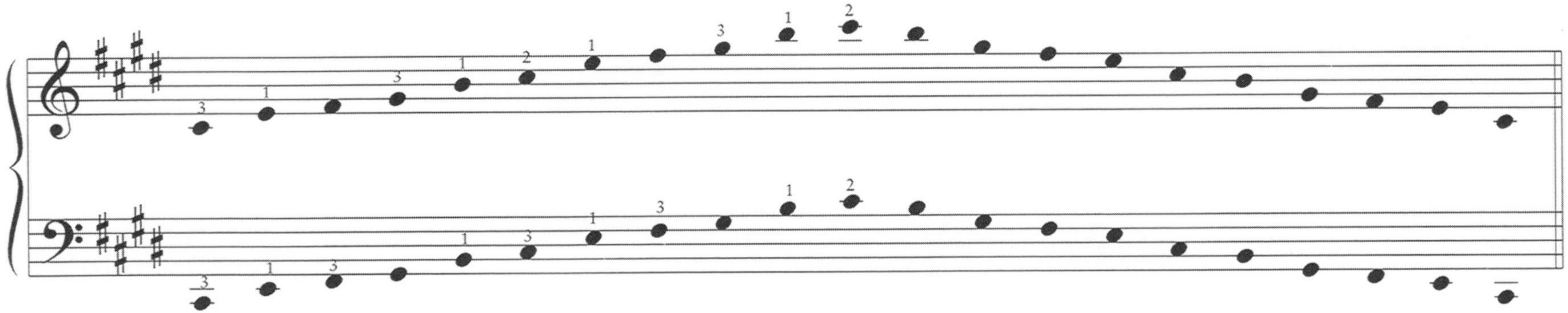

G♯ pentatonic minor

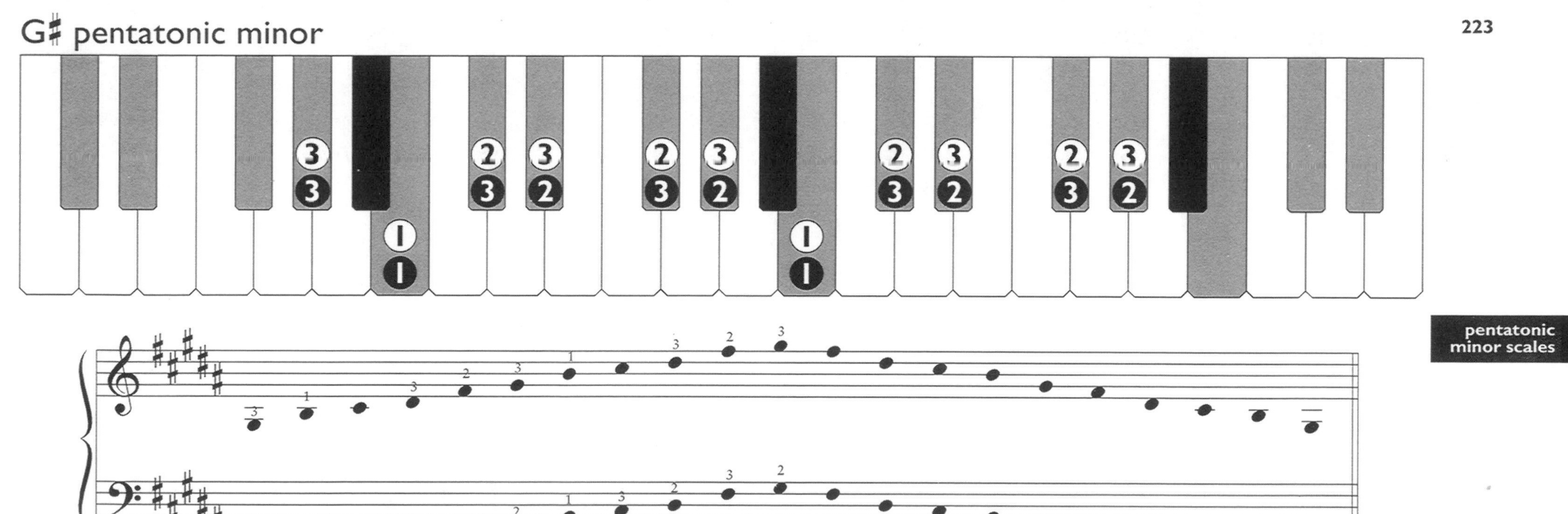

D♯ pentatonic minor

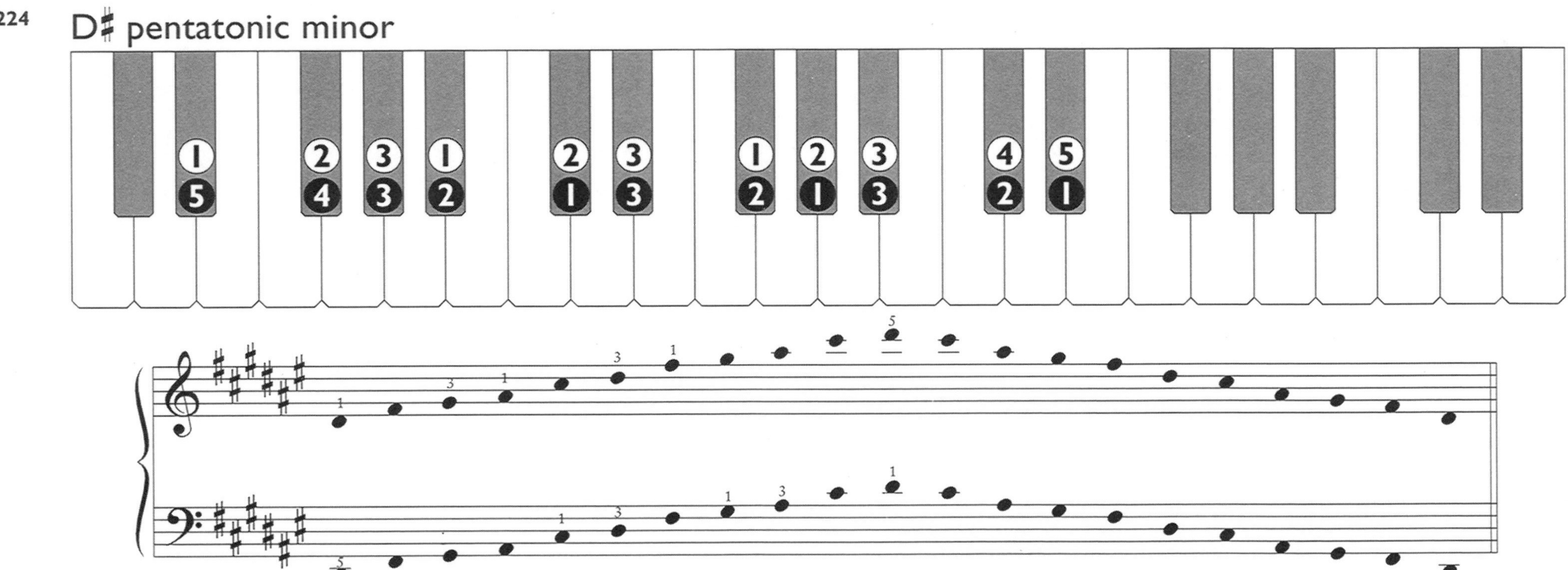

A♯ pentatonic minor

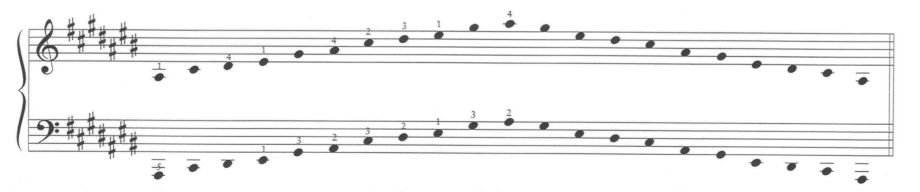

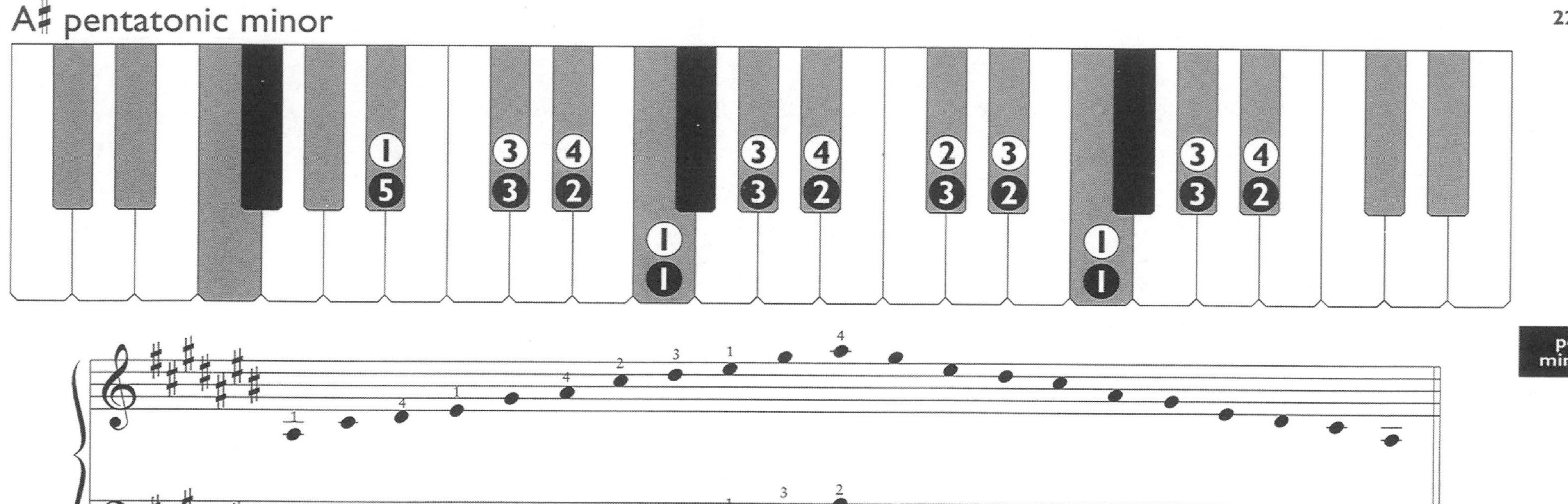

D pentatonic minor

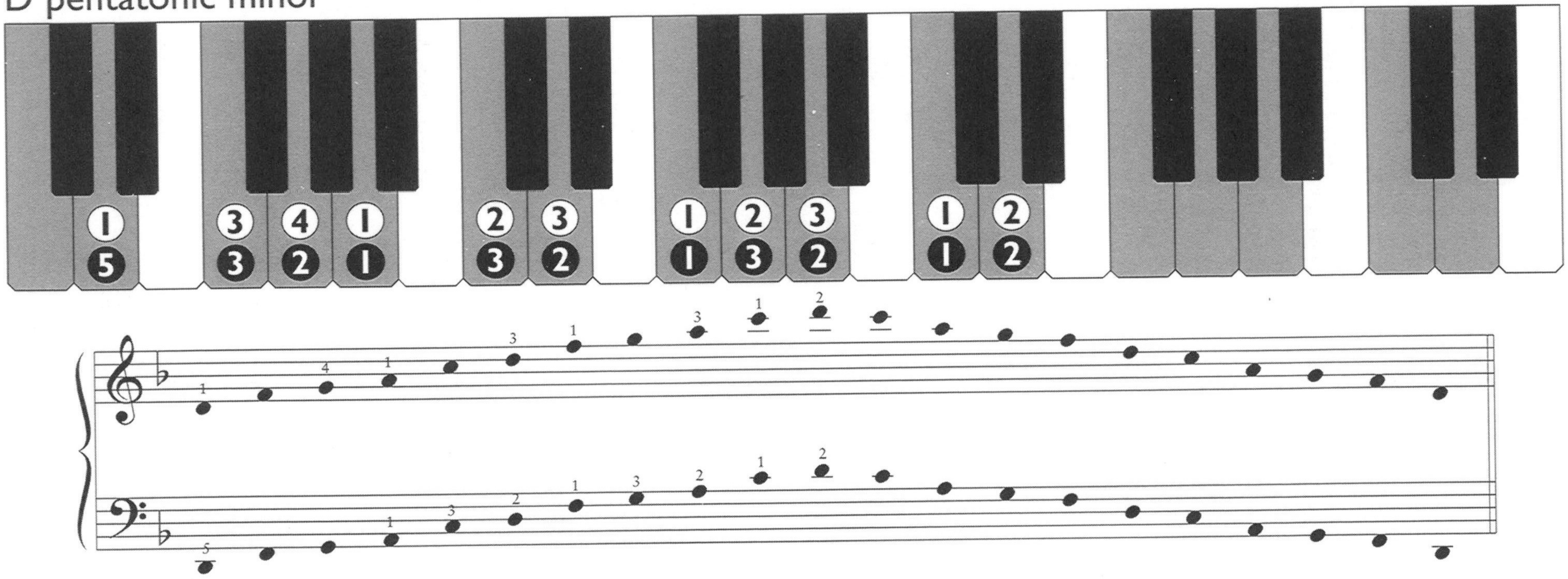

G pentatonic minor

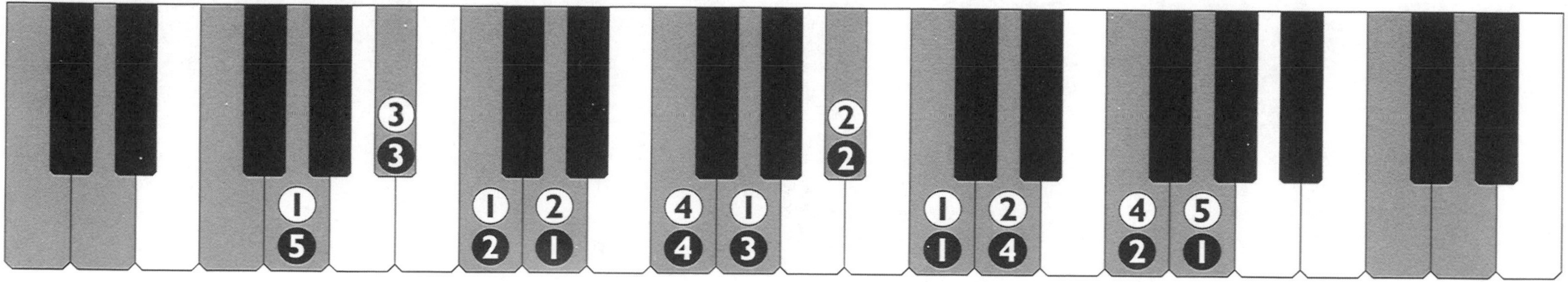

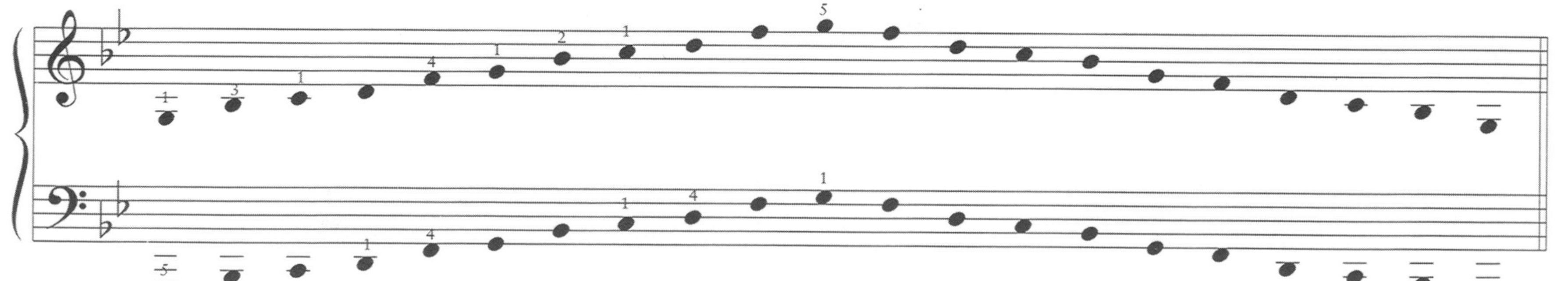

C pentatonic minor

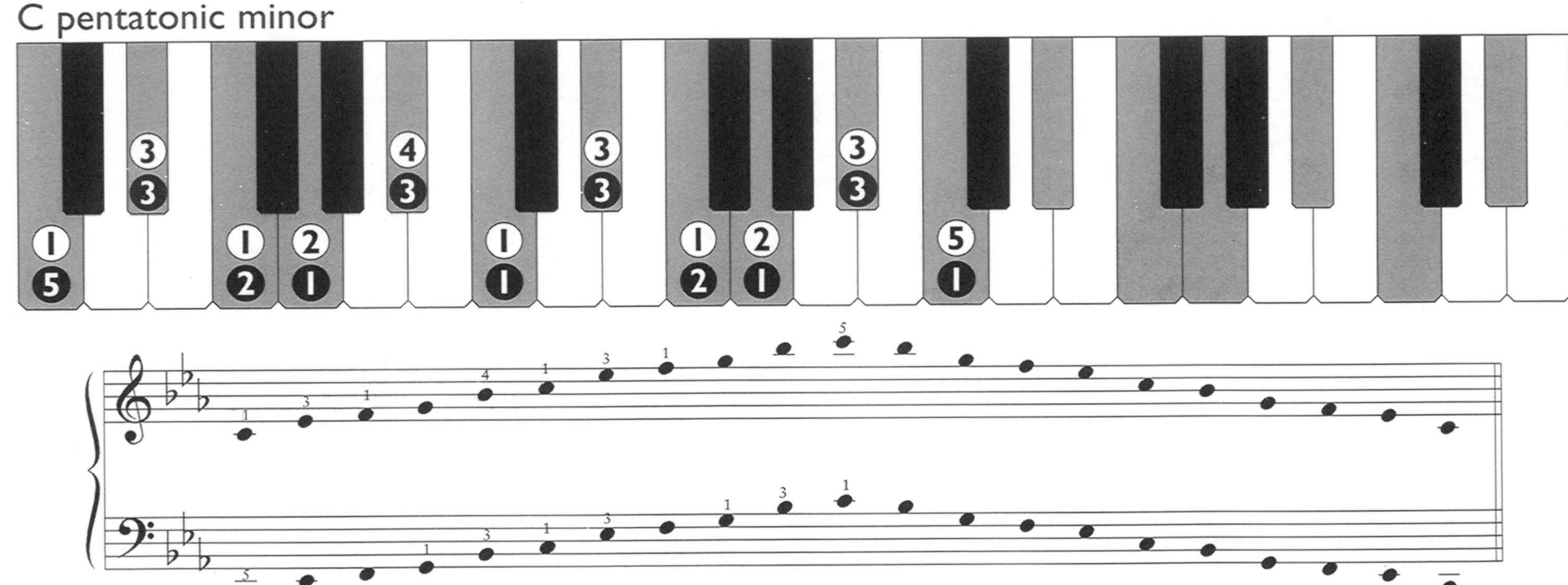

F pentatonic minor

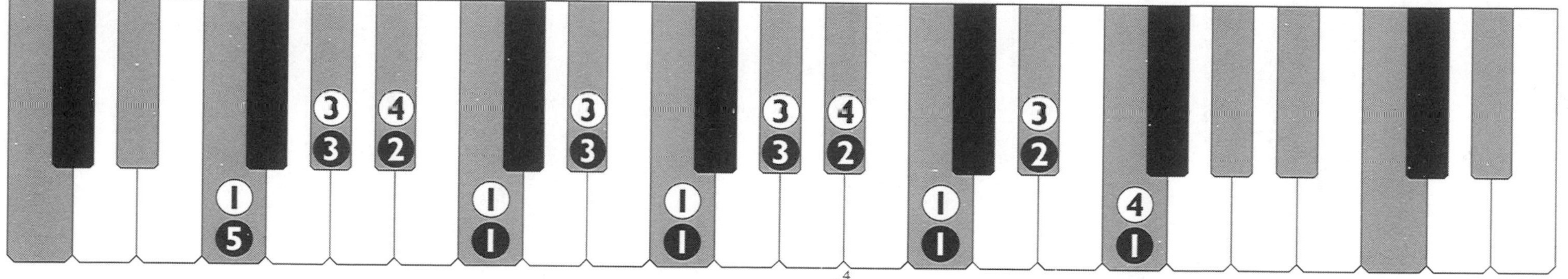

B♭ pentatonic minor

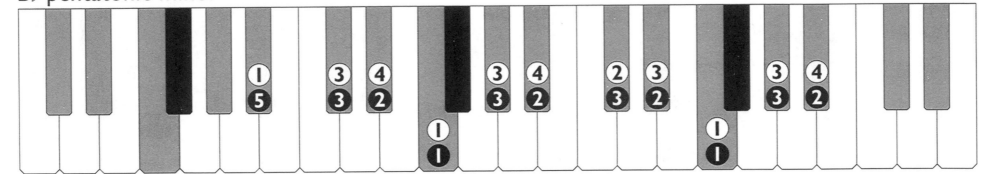

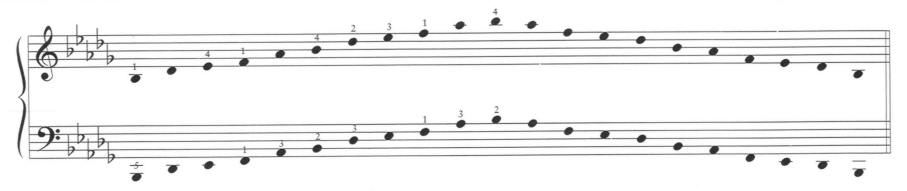

E♭ pentatonic minor

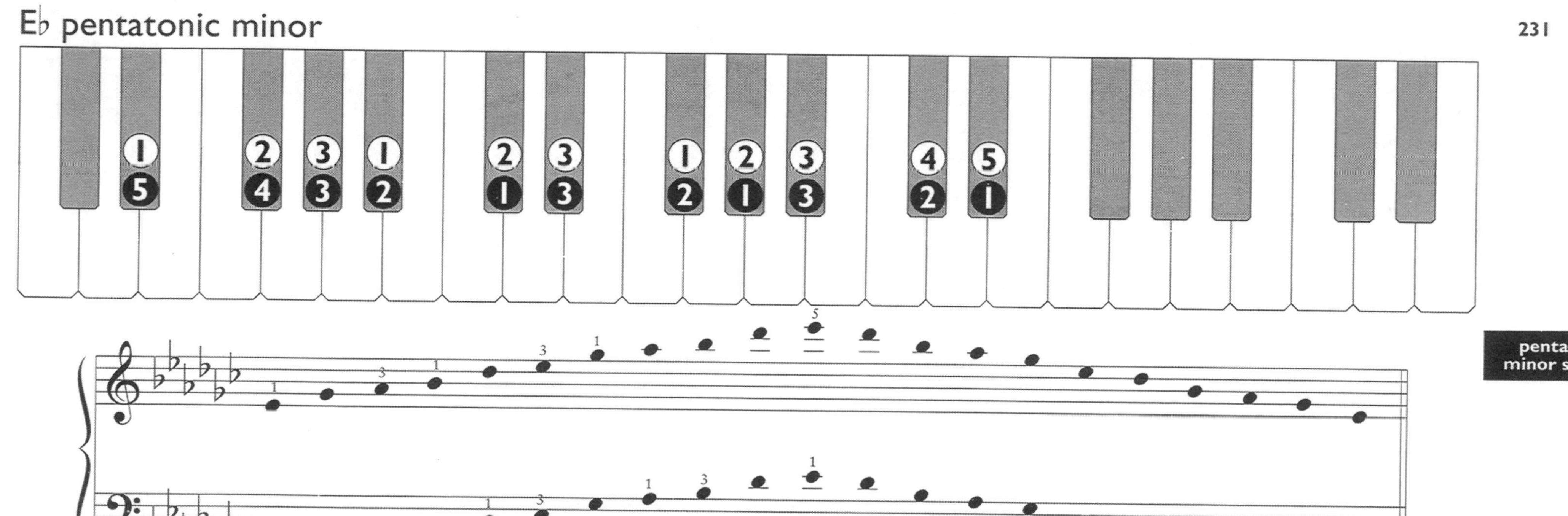

A♭ pentatonic minor

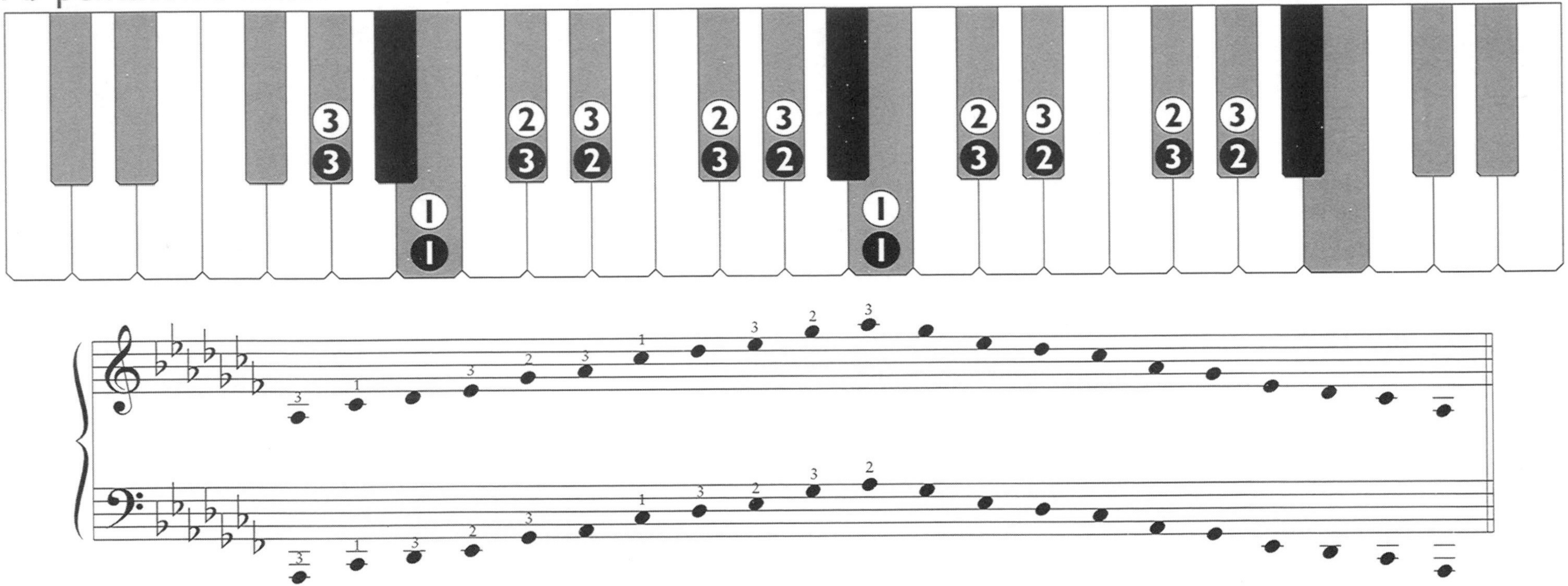

C blues

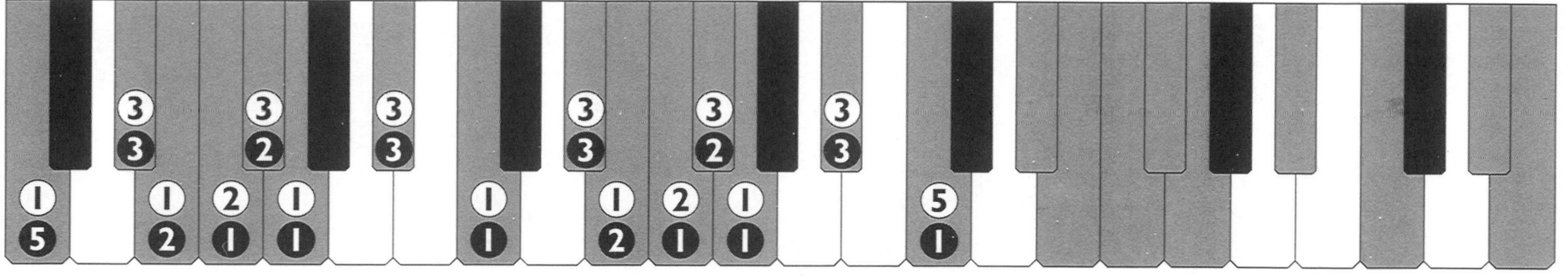

G blues

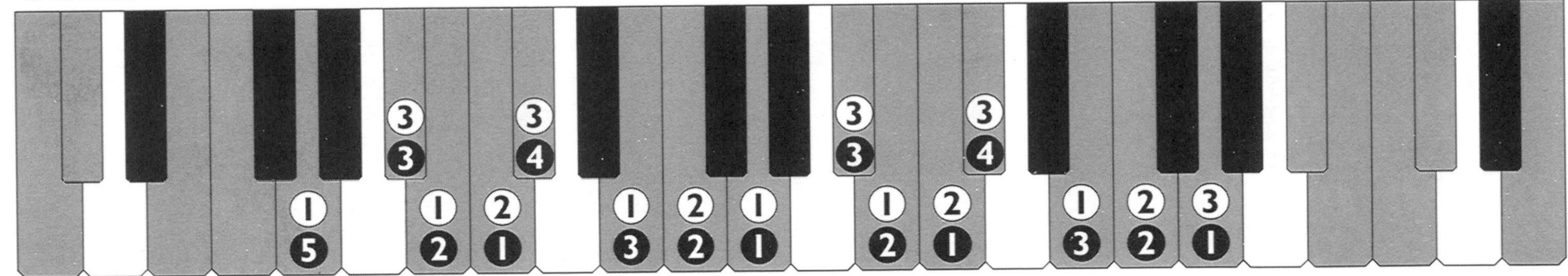

D blues

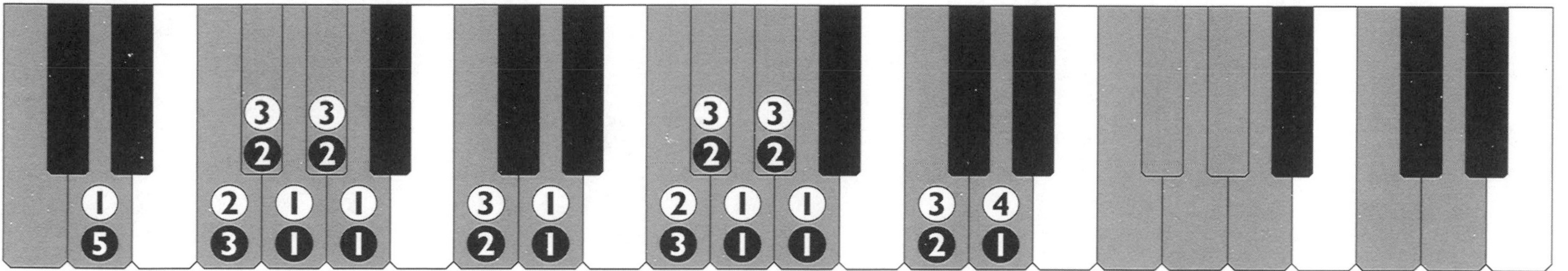

A blues

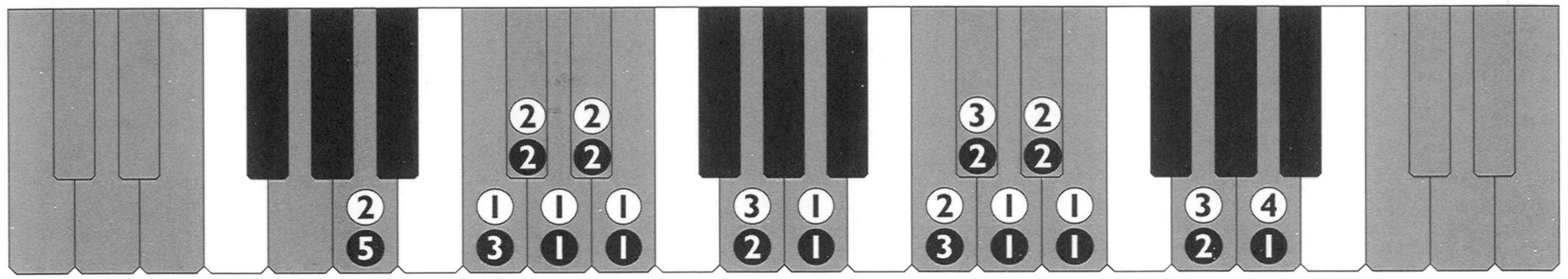

E blues

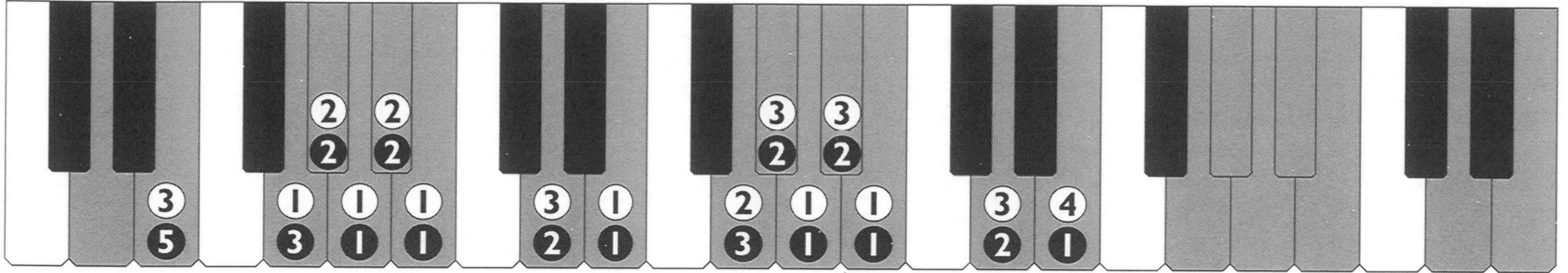

B blues

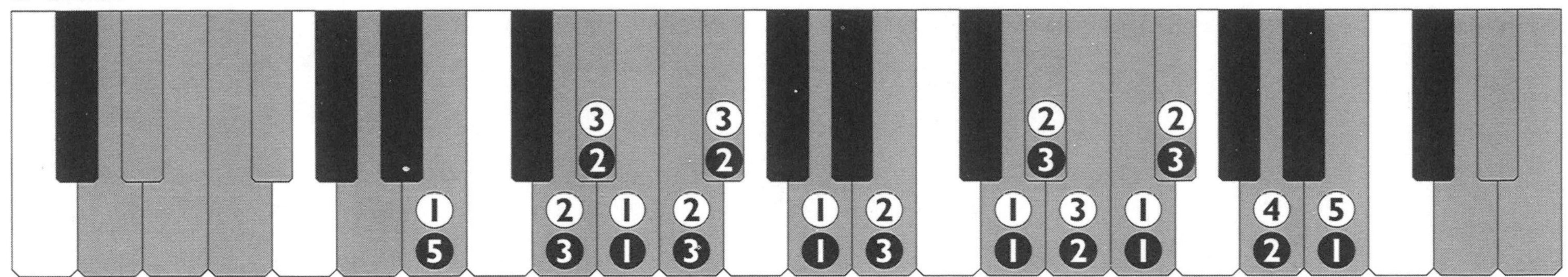

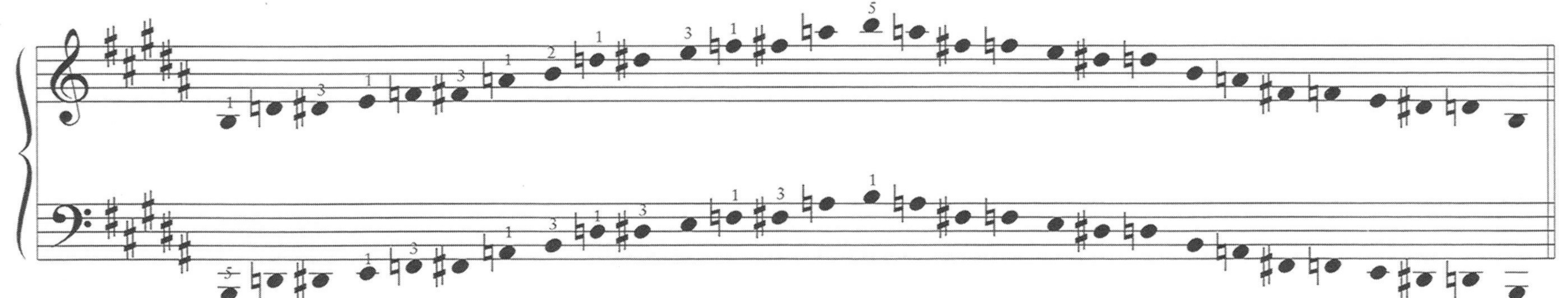

F♯ blues

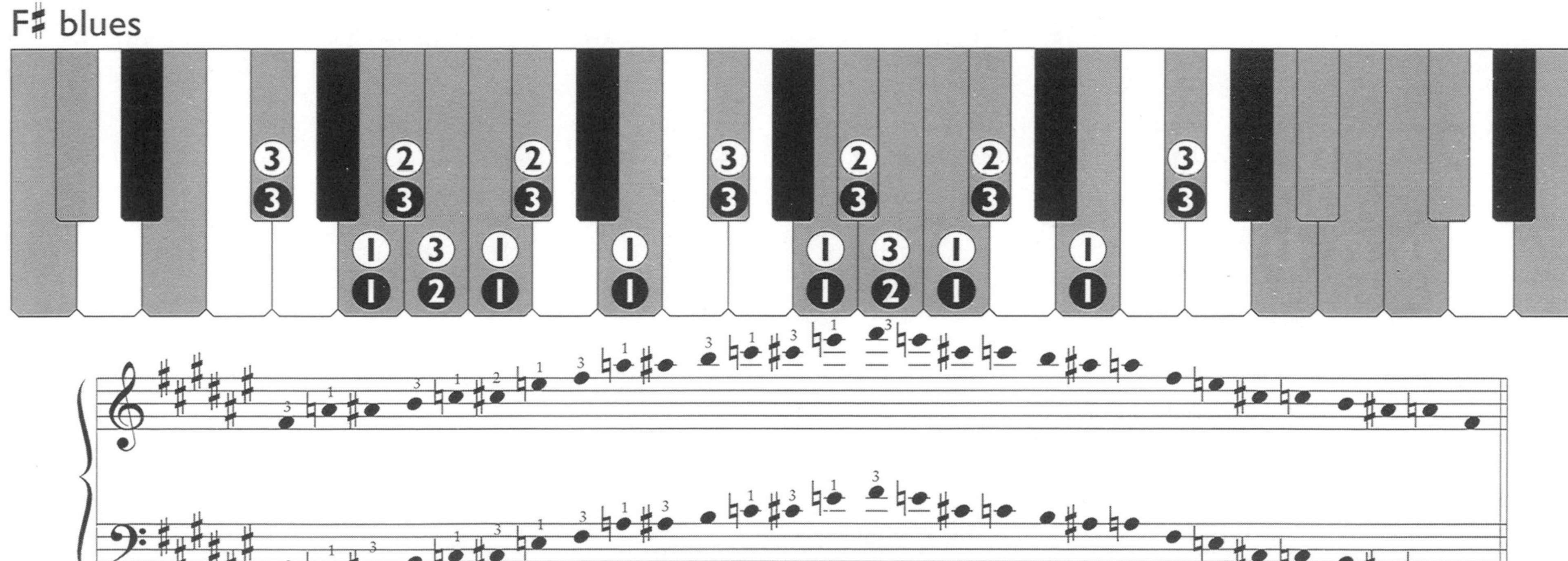

C♯ blues

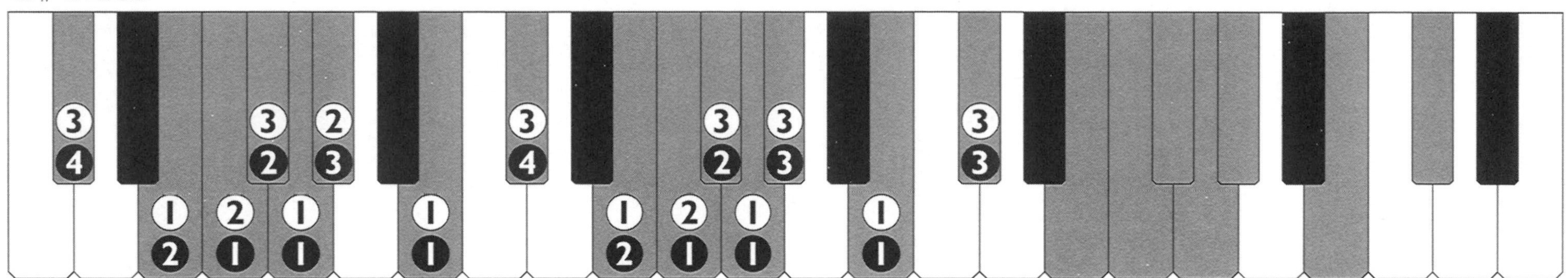
3
4
3
2
2
3
3
4
3
2
3
3
3
3
1
2
2
1
1
1
1
1
1
2
2
1
1
1
1
1

3
1
3
1
2
1
3
1
1
3
1
3
1
3
4
1
2
1
3
1
4
1
2
1
3
1
3

F blues

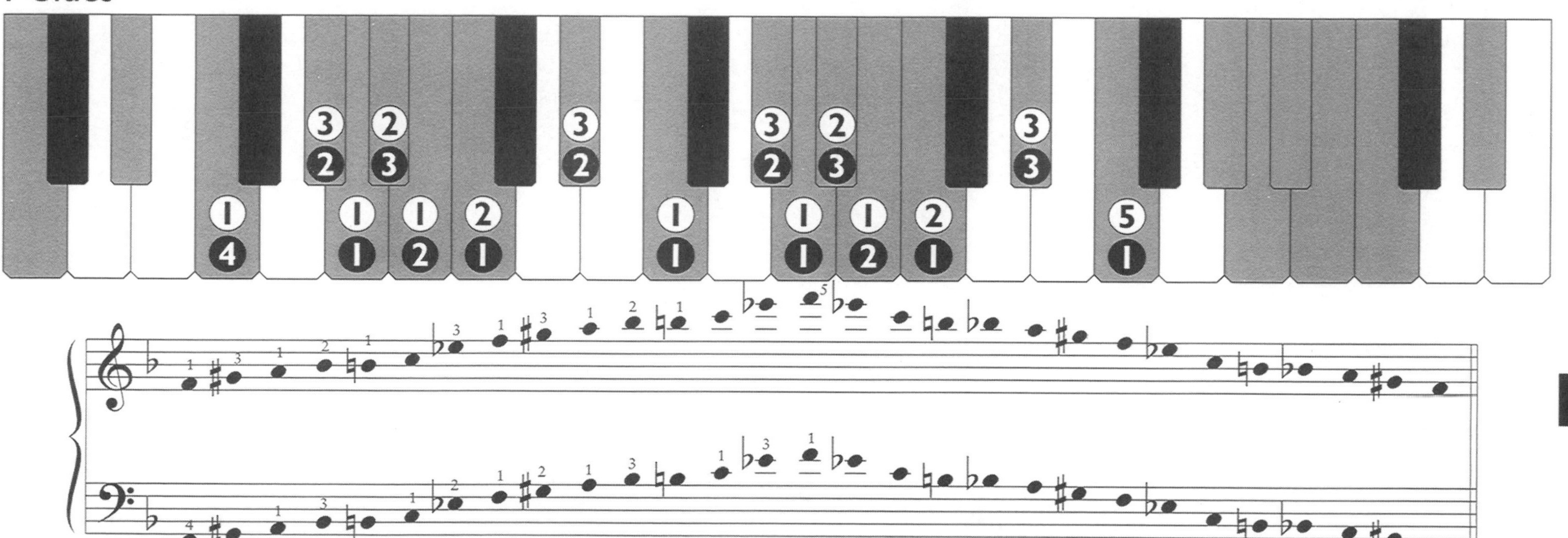

B♭ blues

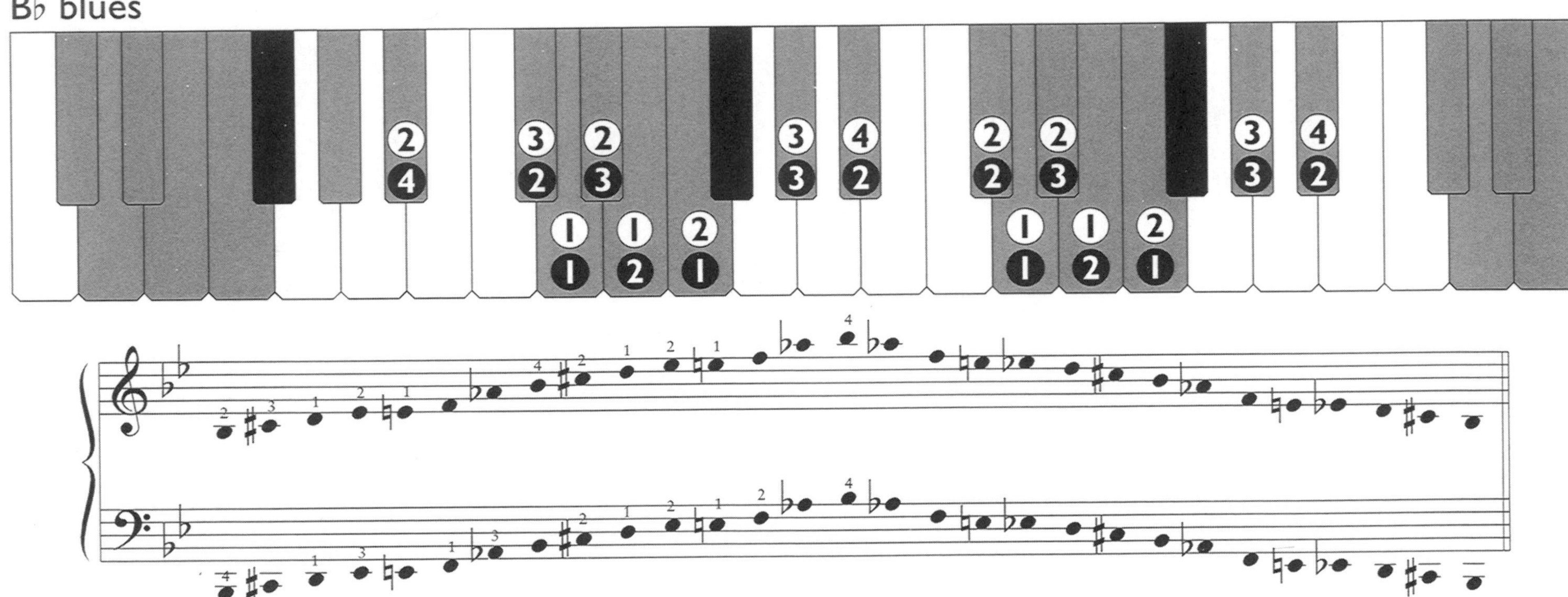

E♭ blues

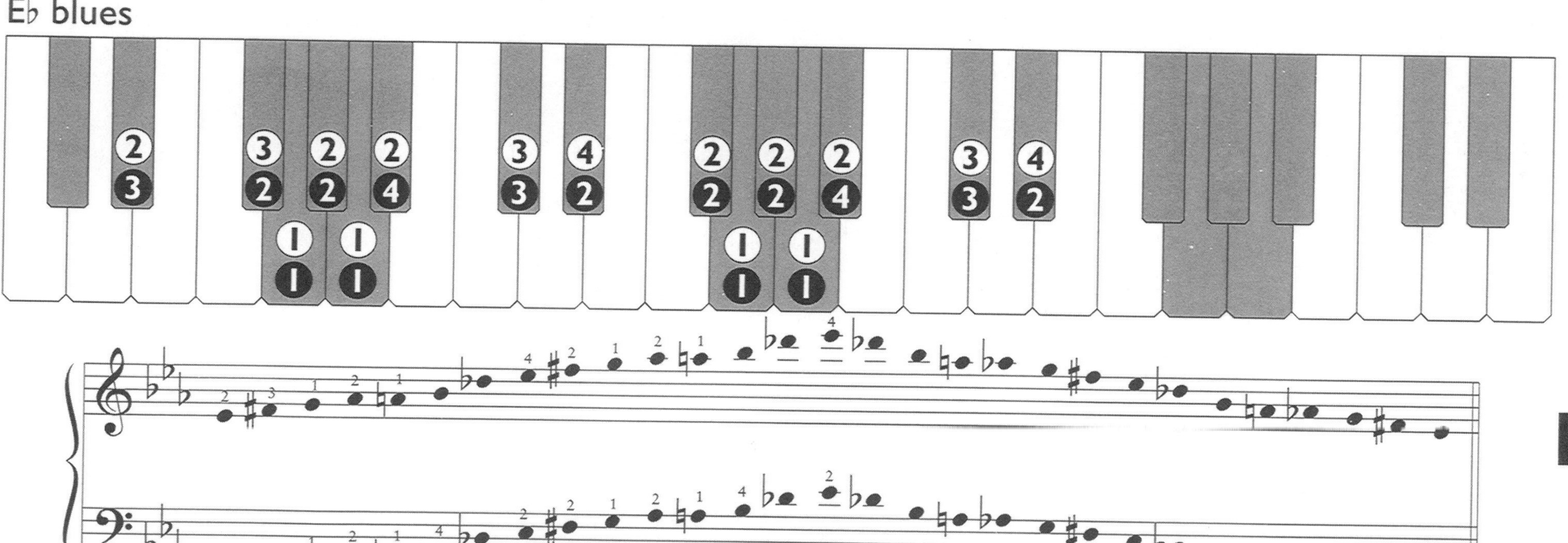

A♭ blues

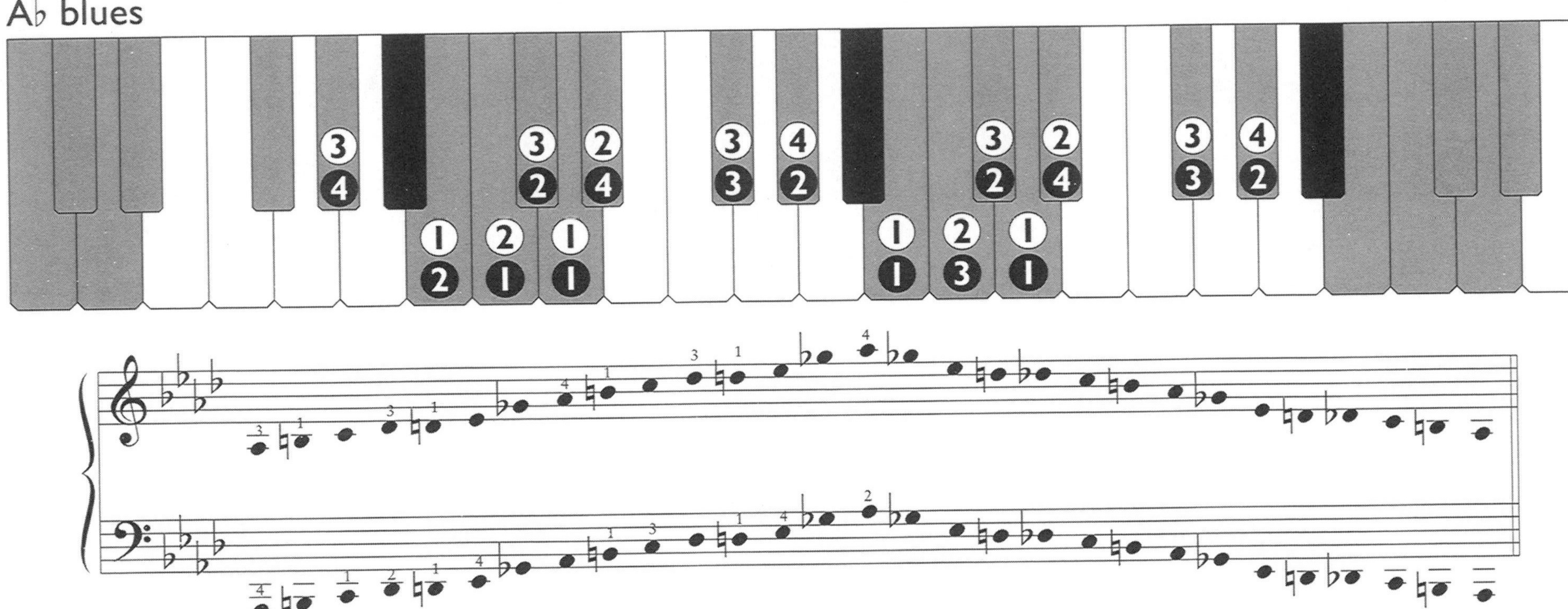

D♭ blues

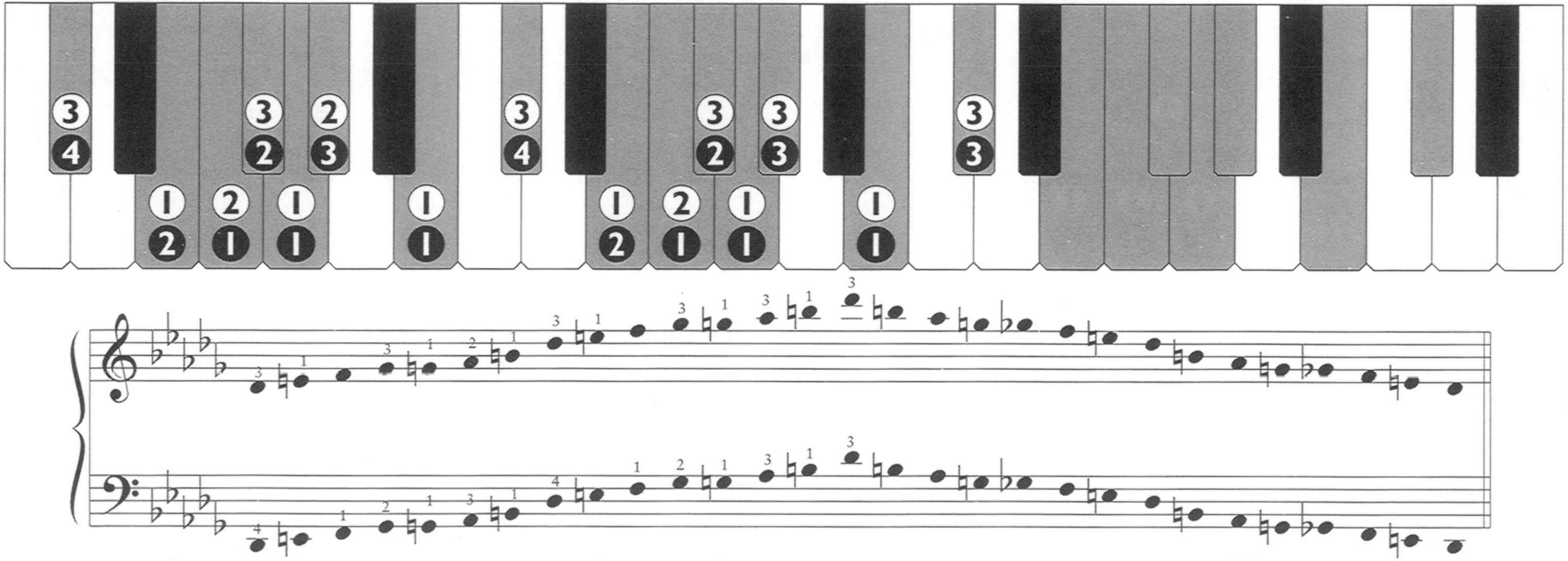

G♭ blues

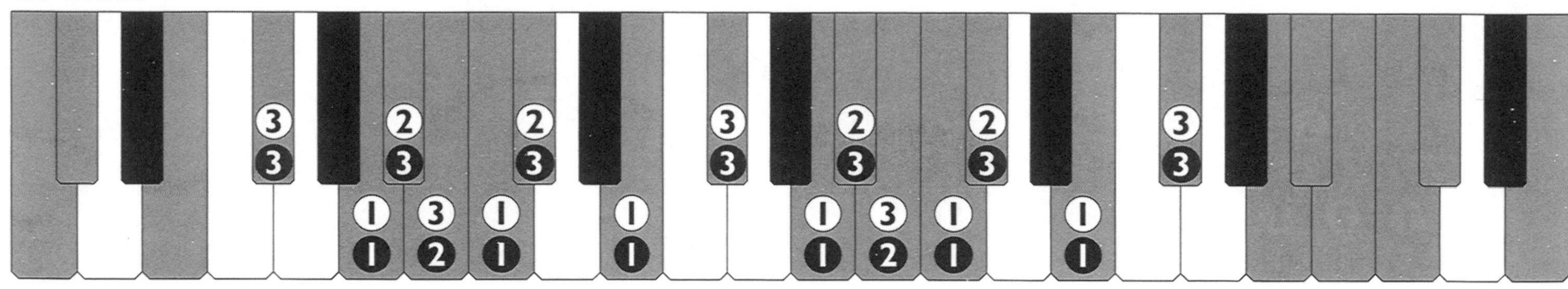

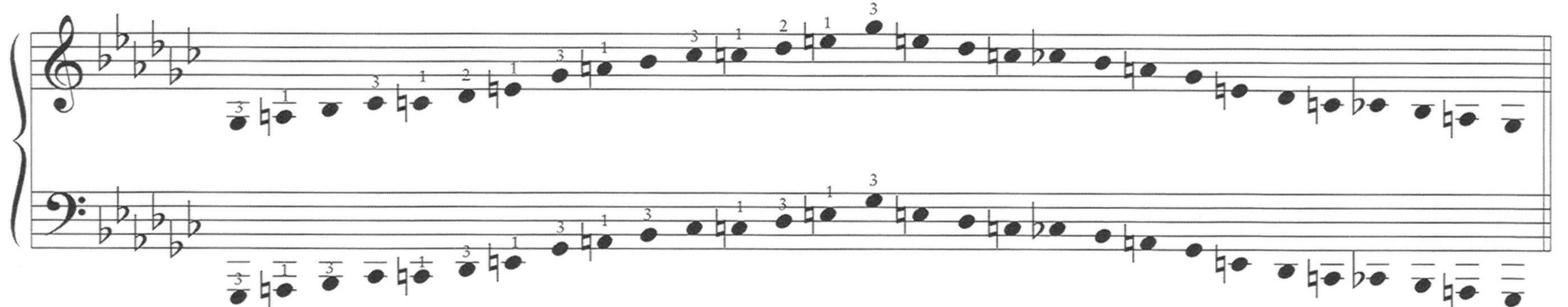

C♭ blues

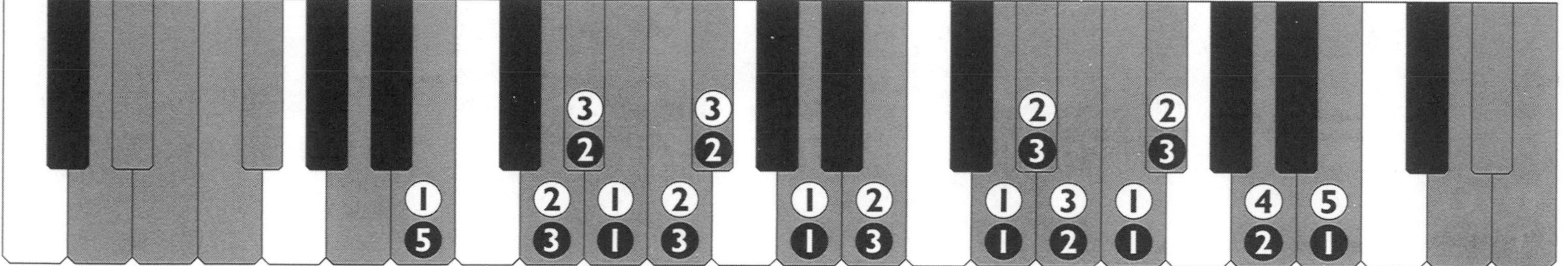

C whole tone

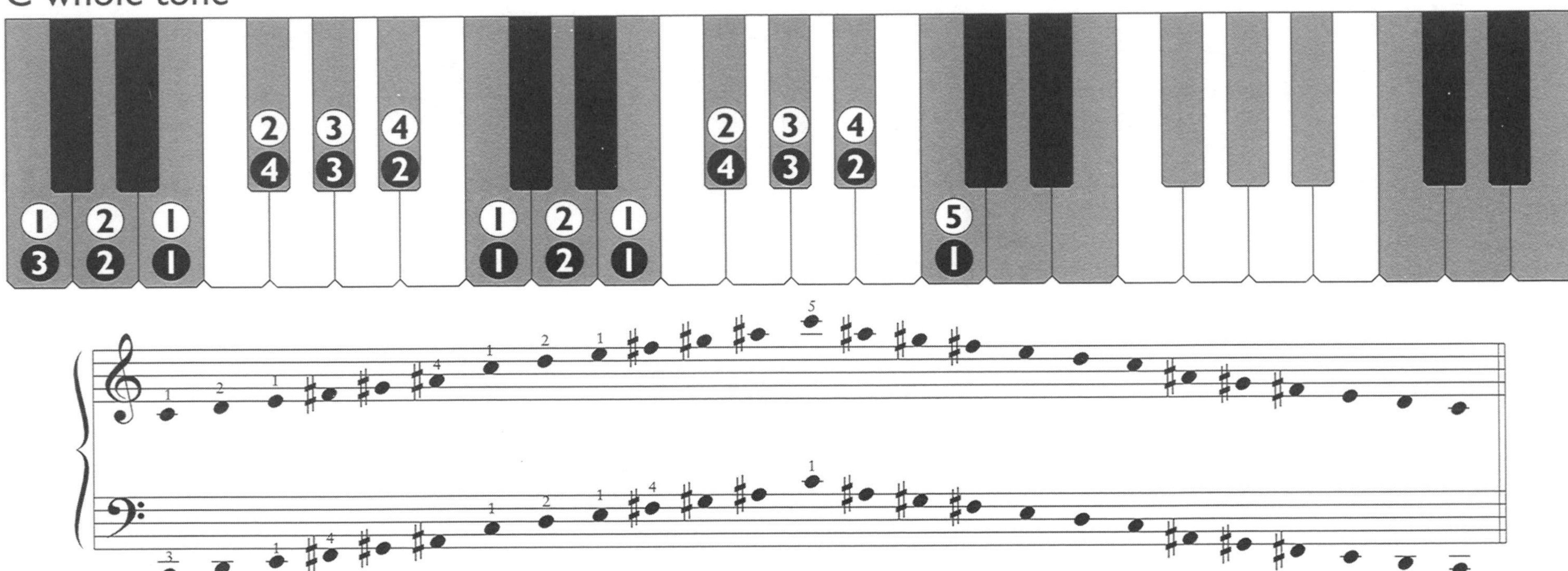

G whole tone

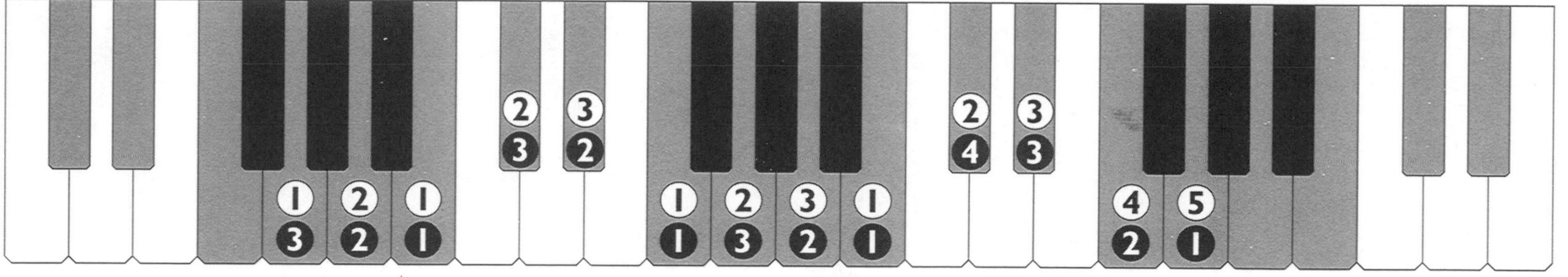

D whole tone

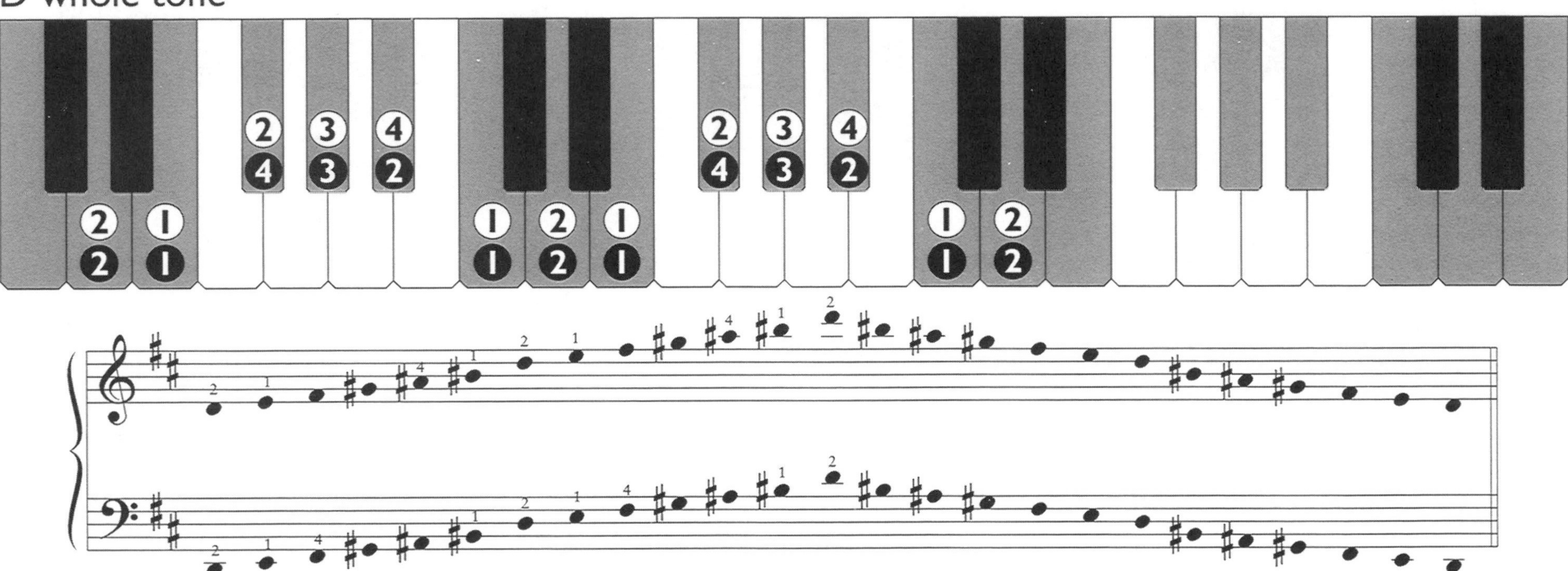

A whole tone

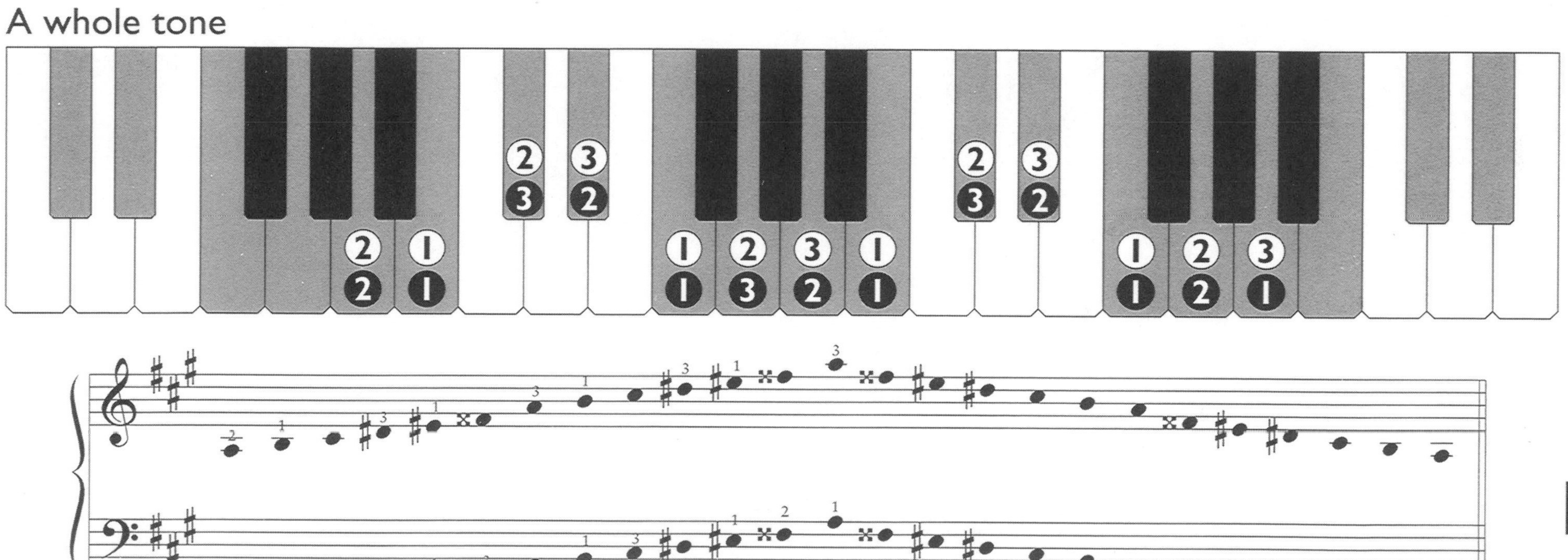

E whole tone

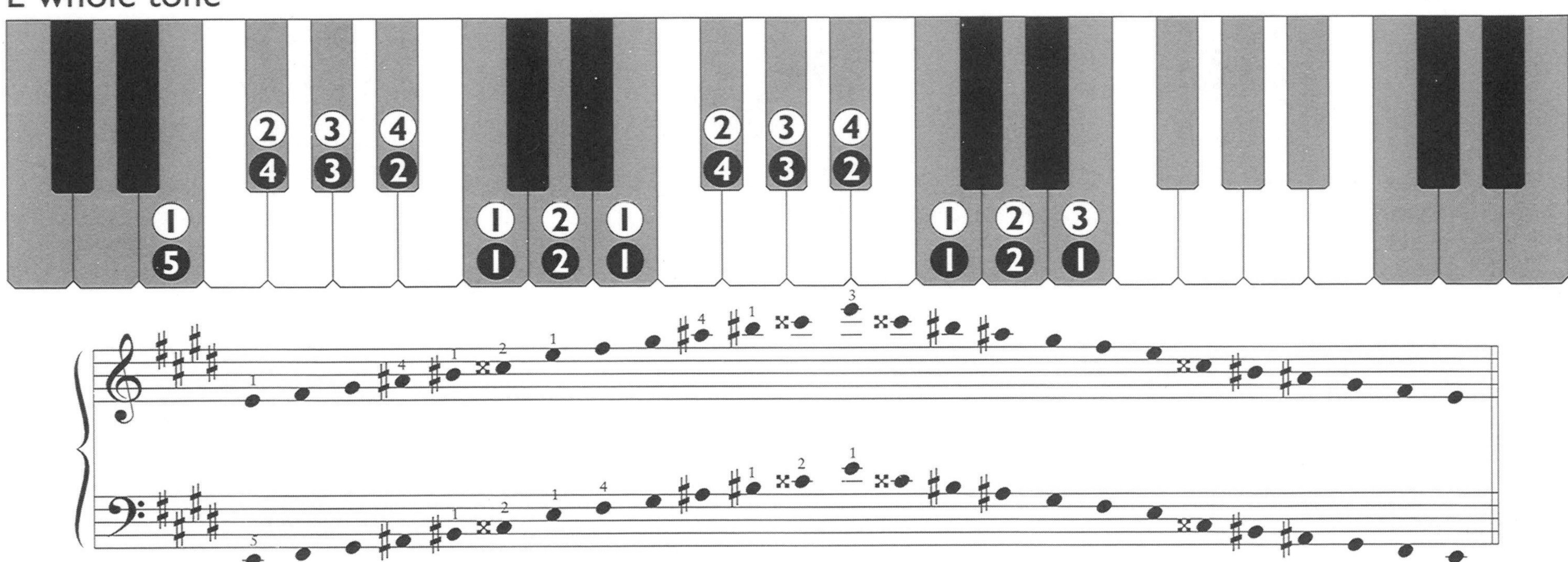

B whole tone

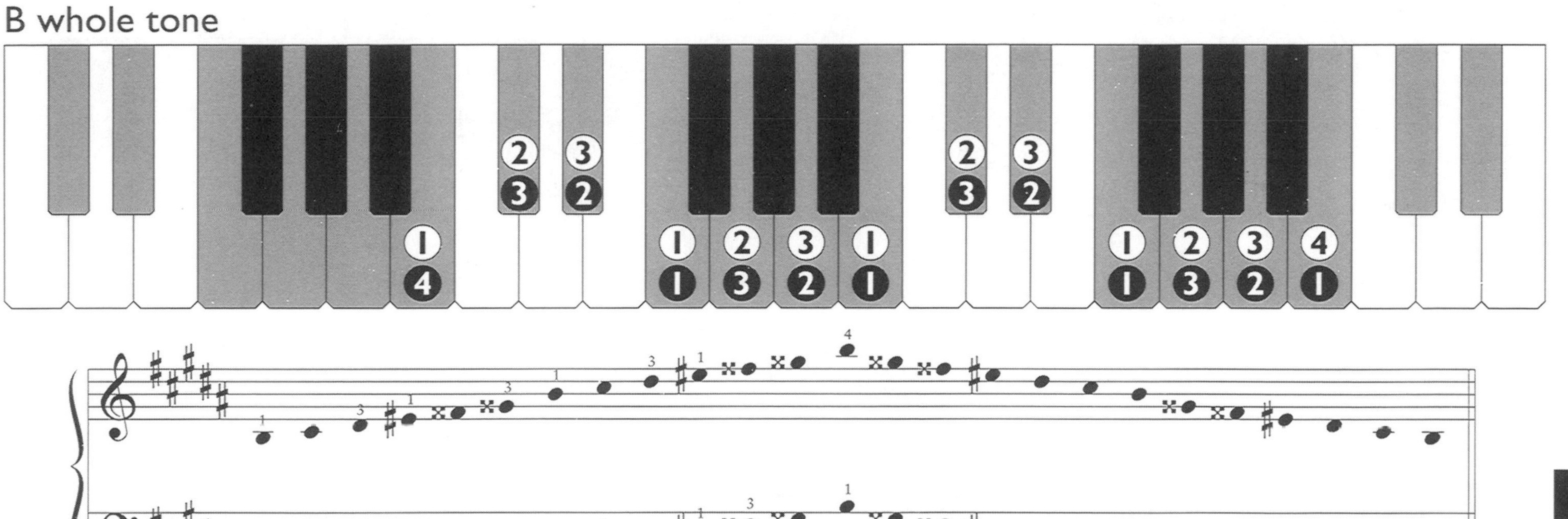

F♯ whole tone

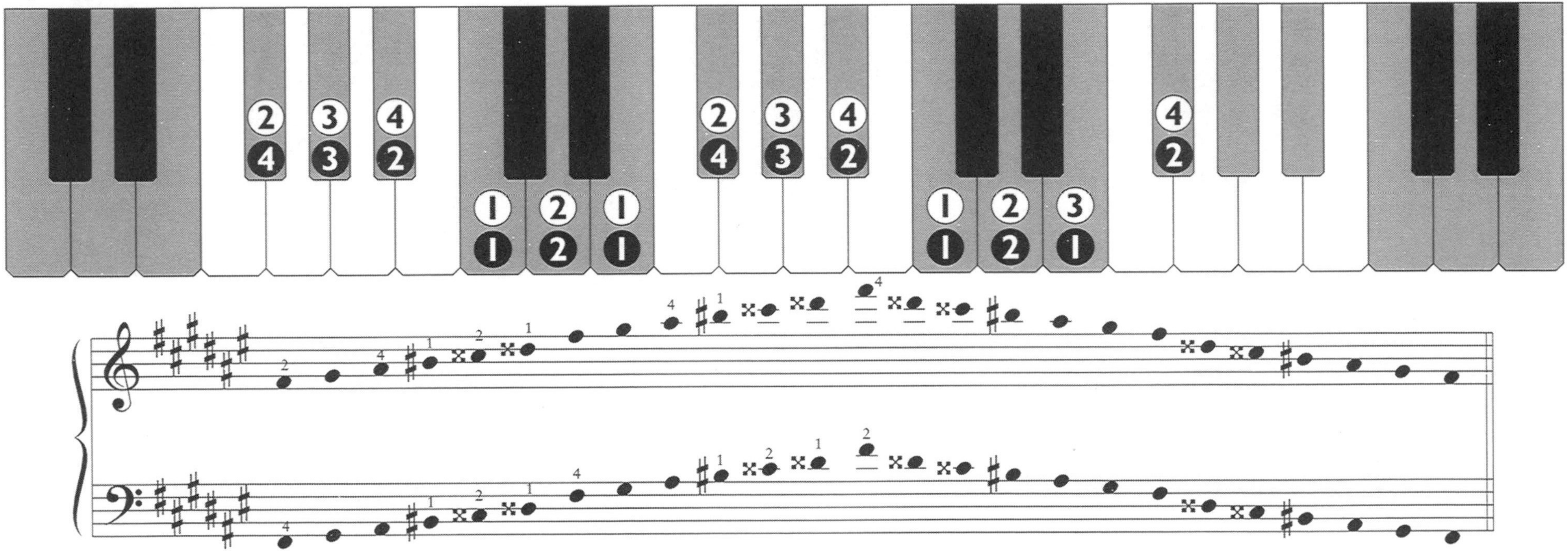

C♯ whole tone

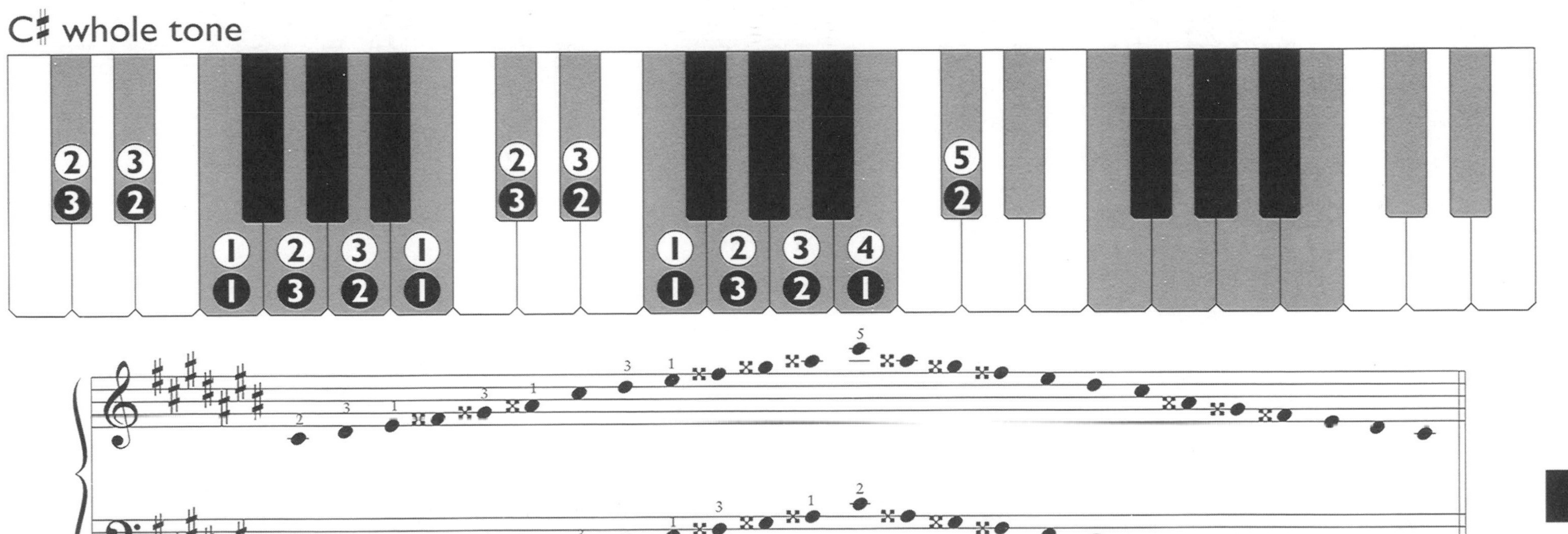

F whole tone

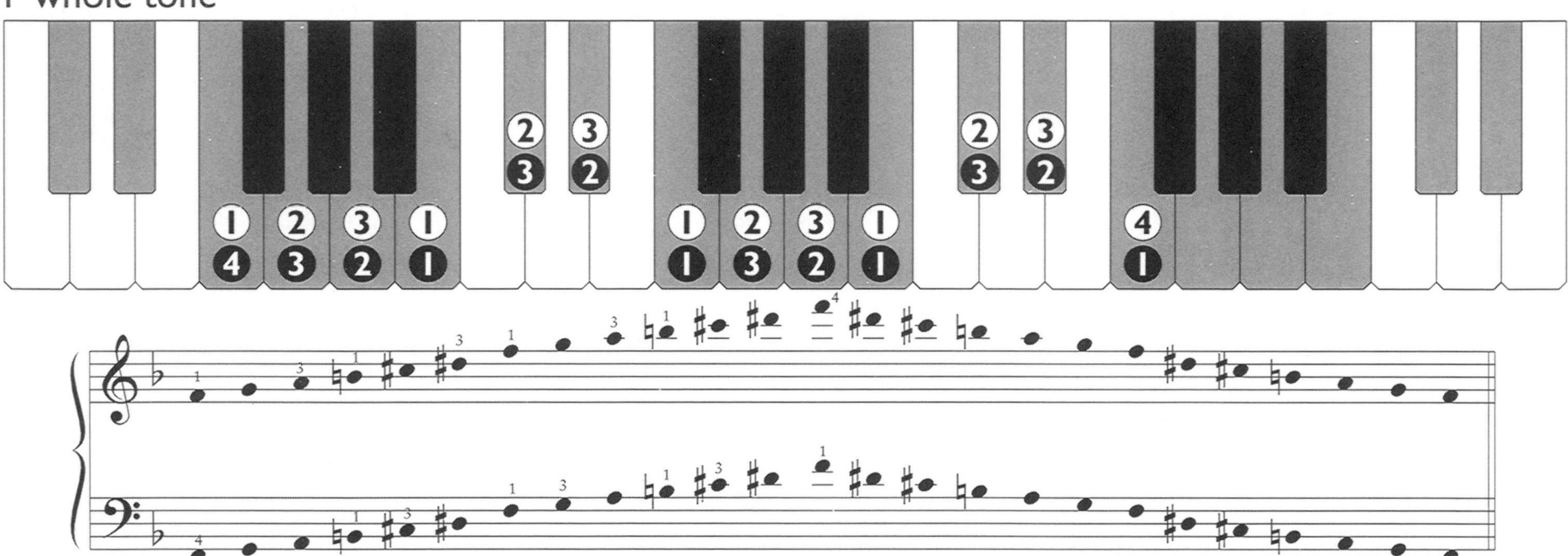

B♭ whole tone

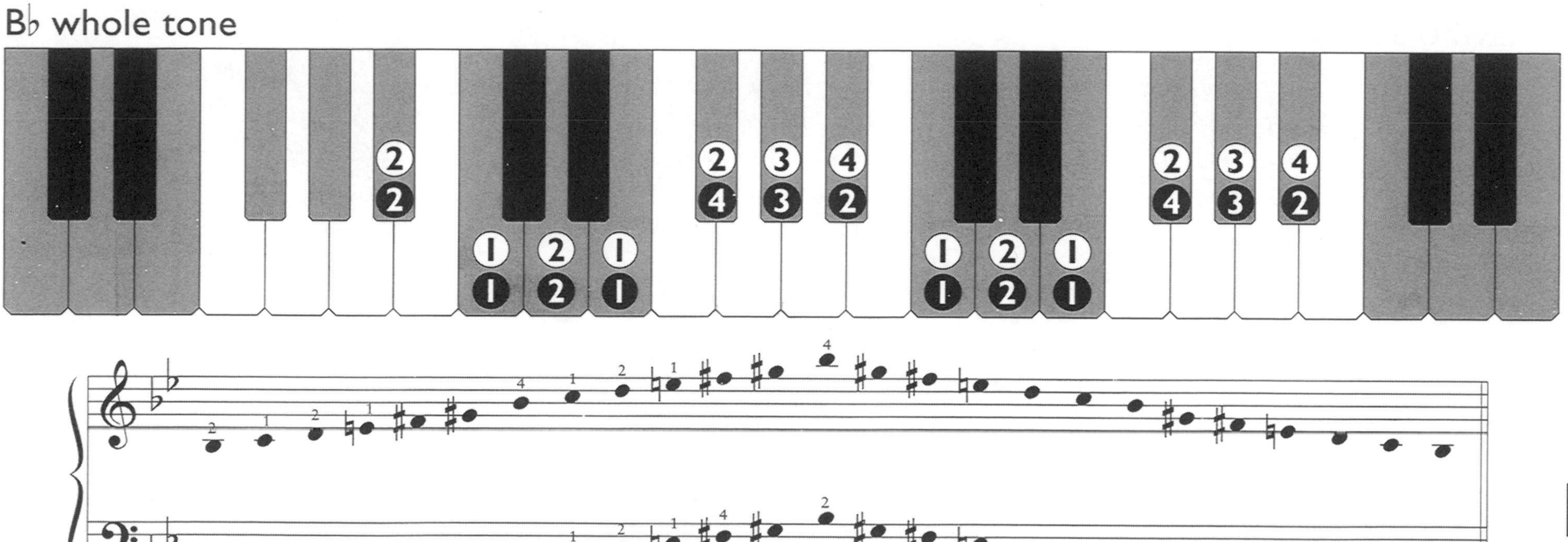

E♭ whole tone

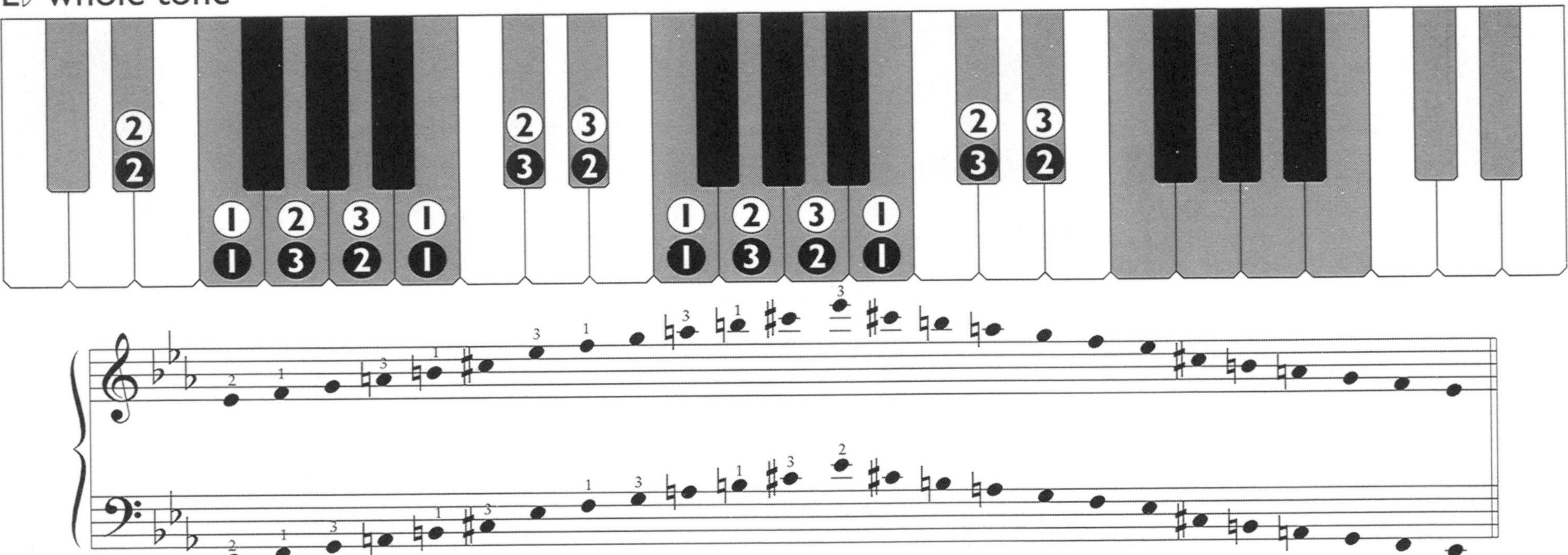

A♭ whole tone

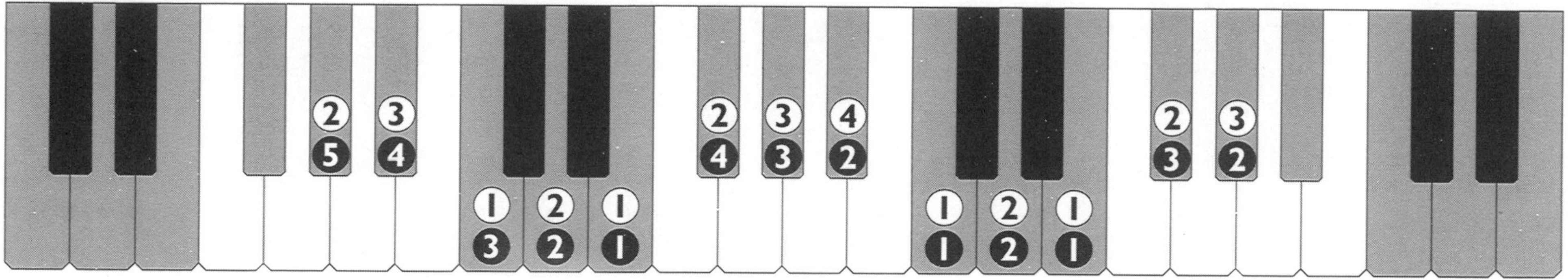

D♭ whole tone

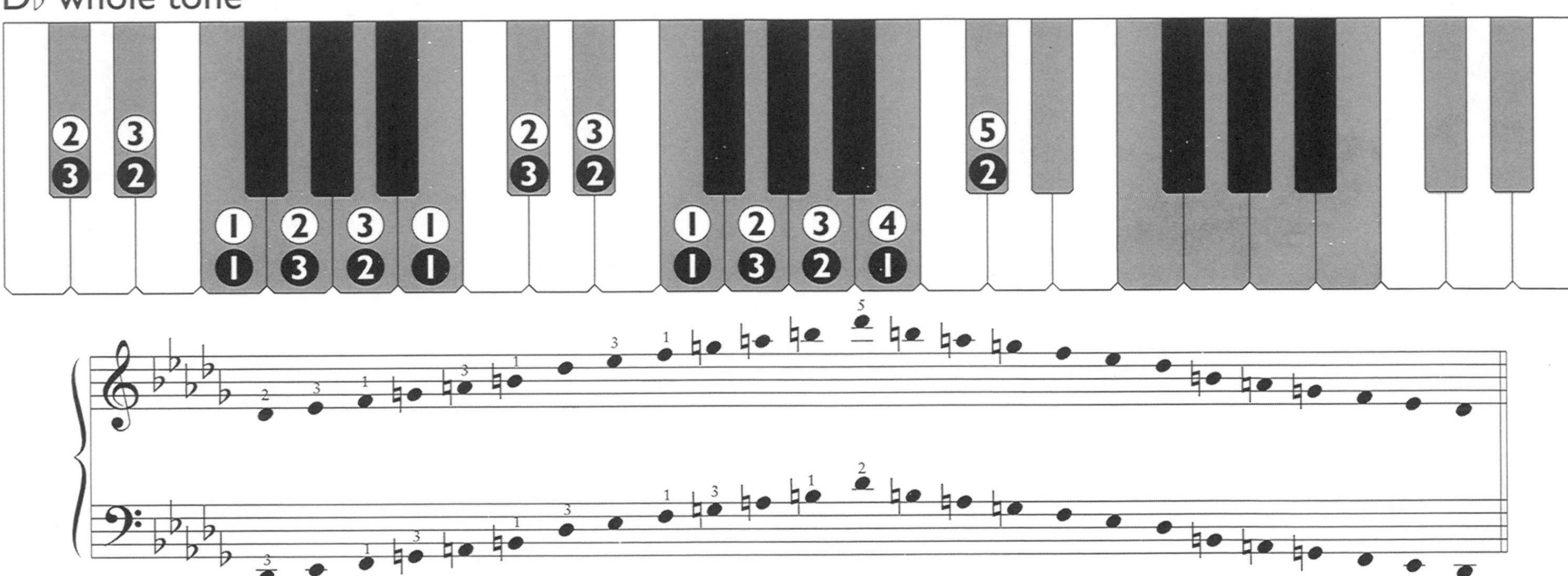

G♭ whole tone

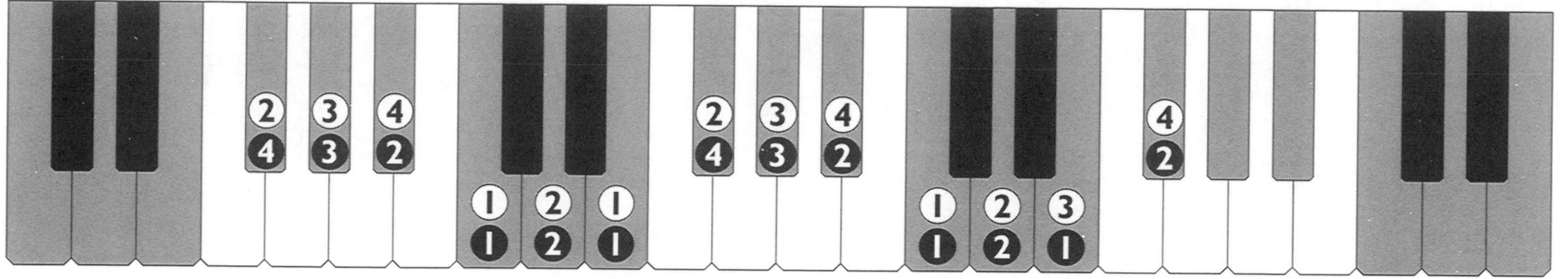

C♭ whole tone

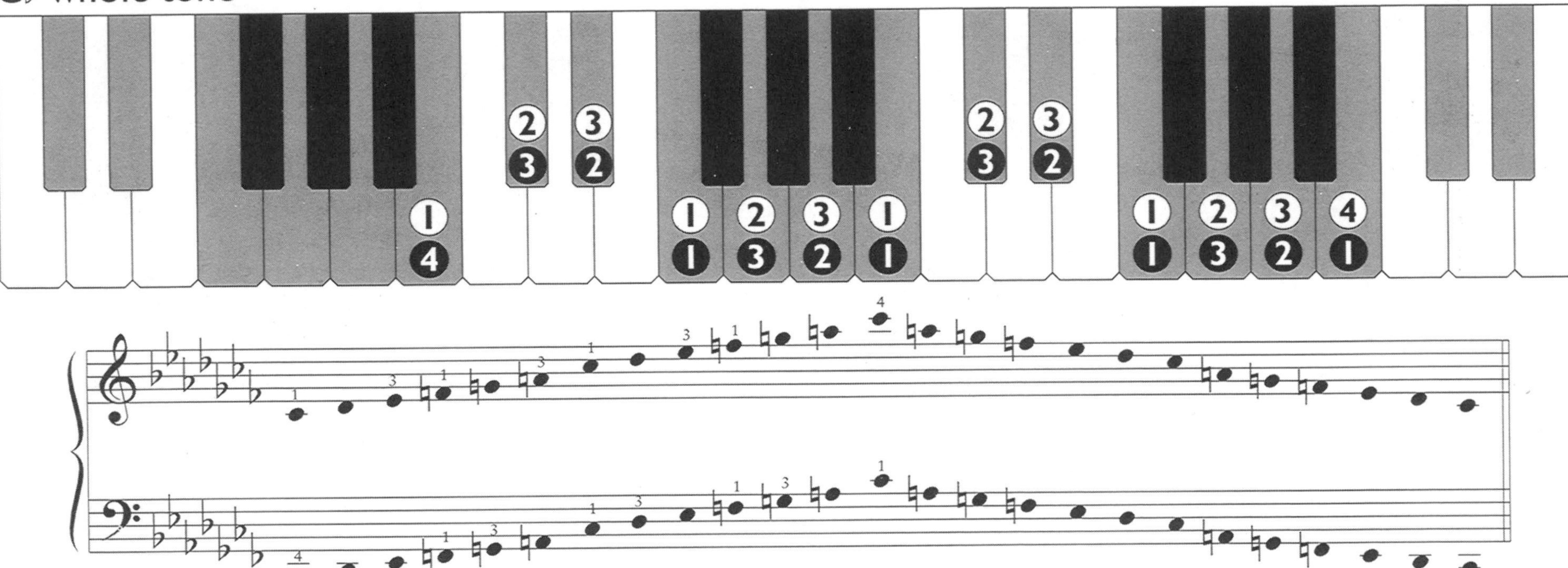